Francis Bacon 1909-1992

To Encompass the Infinite

by

P.T.Miles

Contents

Introduction.

To see a world in a grain of sand,
And a heaven in a wild flower,
Hold infinity in the palm of your hand,
And eternity in an hour.
William Blake. Auguries of Innocence. 1803.

'The creative process is cocktail of instinct,
skill, culture and a highly creative feverishness.
It is not like a drug; it is a particular state when
everything happens very quickly a mixture of
consciousness and unconsciousness of fear
and pleasure ......'
Francis Bacon (1909-92).

The meaning and significance of William Blake's poetry, (1757-1827), has been much commented upon and needs no further embellishment here. I should imagine that most readers of this text will know that Blake was also a visual artist, if not then I invite you to be delighted by his etchings and graphic works that are well-represented upon the Internet. Both Bacon and Blake belong to a stream of British personalities that have possessed unusual abilities with regard to their conscious apprehension of the World. I have no intention of exploring this theme here, but there can be no doubt that Bacon recognised in Blake a kindred spirit. Bacon produced several paintings based upon the life-mask of Blake during a short period, "Study for Portrait 1 (after the Life-mask of William Blake)", 1955, (ill. 2), "Study for Portrait 11 (after the Life-mask of William Blake)", 1955, (ill. 3), "Study for Portrait 111 (after the Life-mask of William Blake)", 1955, (ill. 4), "Study for Portrait V (after the Life-mask of William Blake)", 1956,(ill. 5). The fact that Bacon produced five works upon the same subject indicates more than a casual interest in William Blake, it seems inconceivable that Bacon would go to these lengths unless Blake's work and life had a vital appeal to him. It is my intention in this *critique* to demonstrate that Bacon himself possessed unusual perceptual abilities and that these informed and molded the path of his creative career. This study will take the reader upon a journey that some will find exhilarating, whilst others will find it utterly unacceptable, and in composing this study I am fully aware that it will be deemed, critically, as issuing from obscure and irrelevant, to the mainstream, sources.

In common with virtually everyone who views Bacon's work for any length of time one is at first completely disorientated by Bacon's powerful and emotionally charged images, one then finds oneself at a loss to be able to definitively pinpoint exactly what it is that is so significant about these images. I shall demonstrate below that Bacon was able to transcend his ordinary consciousness, through a concentrated meditative technique, to that of a 'higher consciousness' which unravelled perceptual, dimensions of the human being not available to his ordinary consciousness. This is a task that is complex and demanding in nature, and for the reader, if they are to gain anything from this text, they will have to examine their own preconceptions regarding the nature of the world they inhabit. The focus of Bacon's artistic endeavours was the Human Being. Although study of the human form has a long and distinguished history in the West, principally from the Renaissance onward, Bacon's work to some extent undermines this tradition for his painting highlight the 'inner' world of the human being rather than concentrating on the surface of the human form. Naturally Bacon could not ignore the fact that a human being has a specific form in the 'material' world, which distinguishes it from a plant or an animal, but what fascinated Bacon was how the state of the Soul and the Spirit of an individual were revealed by the manner that they transformed the 'outward' appearance of the human form. Bacon was able to perceive the formative forces inextricably moulded into the seeming static appearance of the human. Thus Bacon during his meditations perceived how the soul and spiritual condition of an individual modified the organizing and determinative principle that governs the appearance of a human being for ordinary consciousness. My task is difficult for modern science does not accept the blatantly obvious fact that all that is living has such an organizing and determinative principle, even when it is also blatantly obvious that all that we create, from an art-work to a car, has an organizing and determinative principle, commonly known as an *Idea*. This organizing and determinative principle dwells upon the invisible, to ordinary consciousness, planes of existence that are the font of ourselves and the world we inhabit. There is no suggestion here of Dualism which is an illusion of ordinary consciousness, for everything is differing conditions of everything else brought about by varying circumstances. This is not to deny that to ordinary consciousness there appears to be a separation of Mind and Body, of an Inside and an Outside, but this appears so only by viewing local conditions exclusively from the limited perspective of our present consciousness, and then extrapolating these local conditions into a world view.

Anglo-Saxon Empirical postulations concerning the Mind and the Body are interpretatively threadbare, and unconvincing, with regard to uncovering the significance of Bacon's *oeuvre*. For the purposes of this study I define as **Anglo-Saxon Empiricism** the world-view that espouses that the only true foundation of the Universe is matter, that all else arises from a material substratum, and although it has been adopted world-wide its roots are in the English language of America and Britain (Anglo-Saxon). This is frequently referred to as **Materialism**, and philosophically speaking is a *monistic* world-view. By highlighting the flaws of **Anglo-Saxon Empiricism** I will demonstrate that this mode of thinking is in fact a false **Monism.** The **Anglo-Saxon Empirical** approach to the riddles of existence arose as a response to **Naïve Realism,** which simplistically could be defined as a belief that the world is the same as we first apprehend it as a raw perceptual fact, which it patently is not for the world is in constant metamorphosis, and thanks to the gift of memory we are able to understand that a rose we perceive today is not the same phenomenon several weeks later, under any circumstances. Raising the question of memory logically leads to enquiring what role **Mental Representation** plays with respect to our knowing the world, and this issue will be addressed later. Clearly **Anglo-Saxon Empirical** thinkers cannot accept the *earthly* as it first appears due to the flaws of a Naïve Realistic approach and instead seek to comprehend the inner constitution of all that may be said to comprise the material fabric of the Universe. In doing this it is proposed that their exists a metaphysical world apart from the world we ordinarily inhabit, composed of atoms etc, and that the workings of this invisible realm gives rise to the world we are familiar with. It is postulated that this metaphysical world underpins all that is perceptible, but is itself utterly imperceptible, and as such is *invisible*, and is in this respect no different from the metaphysical speculations of various religions. However, such postulations could never be accepted as epistemologically true unless there was some proof to validate such an assertion. In consequence there has evolved the methodology of *experimentation,* and a reliance upon the use of technical instruments such as the microscope and telescope which have reached unparalleled levels of sophistication. These instruments are now depended upon to authenticate **Anglo-Saxon Empirical** postulations concerning the nature of matter, meaning that we have moved from the human to the non-human in a search for *truth*. I have no intention of justifying these statements presently, nevertheless, as this *critique* unfolds it will become abundantly why I have made such statements. In the interim I will make the following comments.

With Anglo-Saxon Empirical postulations concerning the Mind, both its healthy functioning and malfunctioning, there is a tendency to regard mental conditions in the same manner as phenomena of the material world, such as a stone etc. This thinking extracts a mental state from the totality of a person's being so that it may be studied as being analogous to material objects, thus a mental condition is conceived of as being essentially of the same nature as any phenomenon of the natural world. The central characteristic of this approach is that of linearity, there is an attempt to identify points of genesis from which there is an identifiable progression to an end-point. Whilst, initially, I have no disagreement with such an approach, by remaining within the context of this analytical approach there is a tendency to 'freeze', or solidify, mental processes to some psychological incident, or moment in time. I find this is inadequate because the Mind is not linear and mechanical, rather it behaves in the fashion of a 'non-linear dynamic complex system'. Such a system cannot be equated with the linearity of our ordinary powers of logical reasoning that are based upon abstract, intellectual assumptions related to the mechanical. Our ordinary, abstract, intellectual consciousness reveals a world that in its material construction has varying states of stasis from rocks to roaring winds, within this are found all that is living, which again reveal various states of stasis from plants to animals. Plants are rooted to the ground and although we cannot escape noticing that they go through a process of germination that leads to the formation of flowers and seeds so that the cycle can repeat itself, we are never able to perceive this process of growth at any single moment. Consequently because we can hold in our minds the concepts of seed, leaf and flower there is assumed to be a linear development from one to the other, because this is how it appears to the episodic nature of our consciousness - I plant a seed in the ground in spring, I go away and several days later I see the first shoot, some period after this I see leaves etc to the production of fruit as the year progresses. Even if I could sit down and watch this whole process whilst wide-awake for the period of its maturation I would only see the expansion and contraction of changing forms I would not see that which promotes these changes, i.e. my ordinary consciousness is focussed upon outer appearances. I shall return to this below. This mechanical apprehension of not only all that is living, but the material basis of the universe as well, is gradually being undermined as scientific community attempts to unravel the mysteries and characteristics of, let us say Quantum Mechanics, many of which defy the assumptions we ordinarily make of the surrounding world. Clearly the notion of a 'non-linear dynamic complex system' applies to the human being, and is critically relevant to Bacon's Figures which, aesthetically, display all the characteristics of a 'non-linear dynamic complex system'.

My concerns regarding the interpretative paucity of Anglo-Saxon Empirical hypotheses first surfaced whilst I was researching my M.A. (Critical Studies), and it was at this time that I began an intensive study of Continental theorists, as will become clear as this *critique* unfolds. In comparison the books commenting upon Bacon's work by Gilles Deleuze ("Francis Bacon: The logic of Sensation") and Ernst van Alphen ("Francis Bacon and the Loss of Self") had a textual richness and openness lacking in British authors. Although I have found that John Russell's book "Francis Bacon" contained useful insights, and information unavailable elsewhere, there is, nevertheless, a parochial strand to the text that on occasion veers towards local interests rather than remaining centred in Bacon's work, and this applies to other English authors. Although Russell, in common with Deleuze and Van Alphen, emphasises the fact that the profundity and impact of Bacon's images derives from Bacon's all-consuming focus upon what may be loosely termed the Human Condition, this is the point where a noticeable contrast appears. One reason why Continental theorists differ so greatly, and have a richer content, than Anglo-Saxon Empirical theorists is that upon the Continent Academia has shown a greater willingness to absorb indispensable and crucial aspects of Esotericism, mainly through Freemasonry, and other associated organisations, into its intellectual life. Even in those parts of Europe where such establishments were suppressed, because of their revolutionary aspirations, this did not necessarily mean that the knowledge-content of such organisations was rejected by the Universities of such areas, rather it was shorn of its rebellious dimensions before being absorbed. This subject is far too vast and complex to be examined in any depth here, however it directly impinges upon my *critique* because Bacon's *oeuvre* invokes vital ontological questions concerning exactly what is a Human Being if one rejects Anglo-Saxon Empirical assumptions.

My dissatisfaction with English authors reviewing Bacon's work, with their unacknowledged Anglo-Saxon Empirical assumptions, created an interpretative *impasse*. It was impossible to found any analysis of Bacon's images upon them, and it was also clear that chasing down the esoteric roots of both Deleuze and Van Alphen works would be a sterile and time-wasting endeavour with respect to my goal. As Anglo-Saxon Empiricism has conducted a root and branch exercise to expunge it's own esoteric roots, in contrast to the Continent, I decided upon a radical approach. I would deploy Geometry as the backbone of my *critique* of Bacon's *oeuvre*, as this would unearth the positive aspects of Anglo-Saxon Empiricism whilst enveloping the thrust of Continental theorists, hence the quote from Blake at the beginning of this Introduction. Blake had an acute awareness of the importance of Geometry in any consideration of the world surrounding us, this being the case it is a particular branch of geometry, Projective Geometry, that I shall employ as this has the advantage of introducing one of the major theorists deployed in this *critique*: Rudolf Steiner.

Projective Geometry.

Geometry which is essentially concerned with Form, and as such transcends number, for number, as it is commonly understood, is only an aspect of Form. Form combines number and shape within itself, as with a square, triangle, tetrahedron or any of the other Platonic Forms. Mathematics is concerned with numbers, but predominately the quantitative aspect of Number not its qualitative aspect. The Qualitative aspect of number largely lost to the mists of time, only survives now in such specialist subjects as Sacred Geometry. Sacred Geometry, minus its symbolic dimension, is more commonly known through Euclid's Geometric theorems. This Geometry is concerned with Forms and their inter-relationships on a plane, and thus represents first attempts to cognise the plane of the Earth through an abstract, intellectual consciousness, and interestingly coincides with the appearance of abstract logical thinking as developed by the philosophers of Classical Greece.

The quest to understand the plane of the Earth upon which we dwell, which subsequently led to present materialistic postulations as to the constitution of the Universe, is tied to the phenomenal development of the quantitative, through Logarithms, Integration and Differentiation etc, side of Mathematics, and there has been a remarkable proliferation of this aspect of mathematical reasoning   since the Renaissance. The outcome of this is that it has facilitated a cognition of the phenomena of the Universe from their most basic aspect of number, weight and measure, a vision that is now commonplace knowledge. There is, however, a quality that is common to both Geometrical and Mathematical thinking, and that is they are both examples of 'Pure Thinking', and by this I mean that they are internally coherent systems of thought that require no reference to, and are not derivative of, the outside world, even if they assist in understanding the outside world, meaning that they are from this perspective sense-free. Something that was attempted within the Arts through Abstraction, a movement that has faltered due to its falling prey to the very abstract, intellectual thinking it set out to transform.

Geometrical and Mathematical thinking thus transcends gender, race, emotions, opinions, attitudes and everything else as a universally accepted language of communication, and at this fundamental level of thinking forms the bedrock of our consciousness. Both Geometrical and Mathematical thinking are abstract, intellectual systems of symbols that have to be learnt, however, Mathematics is marked by the fact that it does not immediately address the Imagination, which is not the case with Geometrical thinking. Projective Geometry received its primary formalisation through the theorems of Pappos, and less well-known is that there occurred alongside the flowering of Mathematical thinking during the Renaissance (see Rene Descartes, (1596-1650), a similar blossoming of Geometrical thinking within the field of Projective Geometry through the brilliant insights of Girard Desargues, (1593-1662). A distinguishing feature of Geometry is that it demonstrates the intimate relationship between number and form. Although this is made explicit in Sacred Geometry it can be readily understood through Euclidean Geometry with the proof that the square of the length of the hypotenuse is equal to the sum of the square of the length of the other two sides of a right-angled triangle.

All that is living expresses itself through Number and Form, and irrespective of one's beliefs as to the nature of the universe it cannot be denied that there is a creative font and force responsible for all the phenomena to be perceived within nature. However it becomes a question of how this creative force makes itself manifest before the final appearance of phenomena upon the earthly plane. We are all to aware through our senses of the world of nature but not how this world came into being. Both the current scientific and religious explanations are examples of dogma that cannot withstand rational examination. At present the shortcomings of the scientific, materialistic explanation of the universe are overshadowed by the dazzling technological advances of Western civilisation, which has now become world-wide subsuming all cultures. Due to the limitations of Anglo Saxon Empirical postulations only a partial view of the 'material' world is known resulting in a stilted understanding of natural forces. Traditionally phenomena were conceived as issuing from the plane of Chaos, which was understood not as is presently interpreted as the 'jumbled-up' and chaotic, but rather as an ordered plane where incipient and embryonic creative Forces and Forms resided awaiting manifestation upon the earthly plane.

It cannot be ignored that all that is living also expresses itself through manifold qualities, and some explanation is due here, if one takes the element Chlorine it is possible to describe Chlorine through the abstract, intellectual paradigm of atomic theory, but this will provide no insight into the essential, qualitative nature of Chlorine as a gas, for this other aspects of human knowing have to be deployed. So as to understand this essence of Chlorine one has to develop an empathy with Chlorine and thereby merge with its essential nature, a meditative technique completely at odds with present scientific methodologies that rely exclusively upon objective abstract, intellectual reasoning. To be sure we can use our other senses and say that it has a particular taste and smell, however these do not reveal its inner essence as a gas. Significantly the qualitative aspects of phenomena have been excluded from Anglo-Saxon Empirical postulations, and this has been a deliberate policy with qualities be relegated to a secondary position in comparison to the valorisation of quantitative factors. Initially, and by itself, Projective Geometry provides no insight into the qualitative nature of phenomena, but it does perform something of vital importance, which I will come to shortly.

Euclidean and Sacred Geometry are essentially static and planar and are not equipped to shed light upon the absolute and constant metamorphosis continually being enacted within the world of the living. Notwithstanding they have been extremely helpful in other areas. There exists a wealth of publications investigating how the tenets of Sacred Geometry are applicable as an interpretative tool for an understanding of the manner by which an artist has constructed his picture-space. In this respect it is now well-known that the tenets of Sacred geometry provide an insight into the organisation of elements within the picture-space of particular Renaissance paintings, and, as I will demonstrate, it is the case that the Laws and Theorems of Projective Geometry provide the same service for an understanding of the appearance of Bacon's work. An early proponent of Sacred Geometry as an investigative tool was Jay Hambidge, an art historian at Yale University during the 1920s, he demonstrated, via the creation of a logarithmic spiral by the "whirling rectangle" method, that the spirals of an ancient Greek temples Ionic column capitals were identical to his logarithmic spiral, however it can be seen that this is essentially static, and movement is implied rather than witnessed. Sacred Geometry has consequently proved to be an invaluable tool for unravelling the mysteries of both the construction and the iconography Renaissance paintings, thus demonstrating the validity of Geometry as an interpretative methodology. As stated I shall deploy Projective Geometry as part of my *critique* of Bacon's *oeuvre*, and Projective Geometry is particularly useful because it is primarily concerned with the metamorphosis of forms that are inherent to the process of Growth, subsequently there is a mobility to the operative modes of Projective Geometry that is entirely lacking in the Euclidean Geometries. Projective Geometry has this inherent mobility because it furnishes a mathematically precise rendition of how one form is transformed into another, and is, as such, concerned primarily with metamorphosis, and this is actually perceived as one goes through the various stages of any transformation, albeit in a linear, episodic fashion where the totality of which, from beginning to end, has to be imaginatively recreated. Limiting as this is, it is now possible to view simulations of such transformations upon the Internet, thereby gaining an impression of the manner by which Projective Geometry describes processes in the real world.

By integrating the methodologies of Euclidean Geometry, especially as Sacred Geometry, and Projective Geometry one gains an overview of the cycle of a plant's life from its germination at the beginning to maturity and seed formation at the end. Keith Critchlow's book "the Hidden Geometry of Flowers: Living Rhythms, Form and Number" presents a basic exposition upon how it is possible through ordinary observation to perceive that there is an inherent geometrical construction to flowers, and is especially good at mapping out the planar nature of a flower's geometry. This brings to mind all those postulations that suggest that the Creator created from a primordial geometric fundament, however it has to be remembered in this context that Geometry is an abstract human thought system that seeks to make sense of what is perceived, and is not that actual creative process in itself. Critchlow's acknowledgment of Rhythm brings a lively and sensual quality to what can seem at first to be dry and arid postulations. Beautiful and exhilarating as Critchlow's work is, anyone who becomes aware of the geometric patterns underlying the phenomena of the natural world, will logically wonder how such an arrangement came about. Following from suggestions by Rudolf Steiner to the Anthroposophical Society that Projective Geometry was an excellent tool for comprehending how the forces of growth function George Adams and Olive Whicher in their book "The Plant between Heaven and Earth" go some way in answering this question. In distinction to the planar exposition of the plant kingdom in Critchlow's book they depict the spatial stages by which the creative force of the cosmos eventually leads to the panorama of phenomena we perceive before us. Adams and Whicher perform this task by utilising the principles of Projective Geometry, and by considering Critchlow's work alongside that of Adams and Whicher we gain a wonderful insight into the nature's creative dynamism, but again it has to remembered that this is an abstract, intellectual insight and not the actual process itself, for an actual witnessing of how the created world comes-into-being, which is possible, other methods have to be employed. Crichlow's work describes how the natural phenomena of the world are distributed upon the plane of experience of our ordinary consciousness, whereas Adams and Whicher describe the workings of the life-force that produces this tableau. Projective Geometry is able to do this because it has qualities and principles that are inherent to the life-force itself, for instance a fundamental principle of Projective Geometry is that of Polarity (point and plane) and Polarity is absolutely essential to not only Growth, and all that is living, but to the fabric of the Universe itself.

Projective Geometry is the gateway for the intellectual aspect of the Mind to formally understand, or encompass, the **Invisible** forces of the Cosmos, and the reason for this is that Projective Geometry mathematically explains, through its tenets, theorems and principles the *modus operandi* of all the invisible forces described in this *critique*. So as to give a context for my proposal to make use of Projective Geometry interpretatively I will refer to the artist Kazimir Malevich (1879-1935) who was influenced by the ideas of the Russian mystic-mathematician, philosopher P.D. Ouspensky (1878-1947), who was a disciple of Georges Gurdjieff (1866-1949). Ouspensky wrote of "a fourth dimension" or a Fourth Way which he conceived as an enhancement of the three dimensions given by our ordinary senses. Around the turn of 19th and 20th centuries, until W.W.1, there was much speculation about such a possibility and it is noteworthy that Steiner in lectures, published as "The Fourth Dimension", contributed to the debate. Also during the 19th century differing mathematicians developed several non-Euclidean geometries, and Malevich made plain the influence of non-Euclidean geometry upon his production through the titles he gave to several works, such as the work "Two Dimensional Painted Masses in the State of Movement". The complexity and ramifications of the Fourth Dimension, aesthetically, prevent further exploration at this point, instead I will return to Projective Geometry and informally discuss it's applicability to ordinary sensory perception. Before proceeding further it is as well to state that my deployment of Projective Geometry interpretatively can only be descriptive at this point, there is no possibility at this stage of any precise, numerical investigation of Bacon's work. This may weaken the 'truth value' of my argument for some, but I would counter this by stating that since Steiner demonstrated how Projective Geometry was explanatory of invisible forces there has been much precise, numerical analysis within the Anthroposophical Society of plant growth, and this is freely available to anyone irrespective as to whether or not they are members of the Anthroposophical Movement. The fact that I will demonstrate that the basic tenets of Projective Geometry are descriptive of Bacon's work is indicative of the fact that Bacon was aware of the *modus operandi* of invisible forces, and was thus able to perceive something more beyond the immediate appearance of a person, and, further to this, Bacon through his paintings demonstrated that this something more was inextricably woven into immediate appearances.

Polarity is a basic principle of Projective Geometry just as it is of our sensory experience of the Cosmos, and the universal agreement that bi-polarity lies at the heart of our ordinary sensory perception of the world finds expression through the ancient symbol of the Ying-Yang. For instance an example of a fundamental Polarity is that of Expansion and Contraction, and it will be easily appreciated that all phenomena exist in a state somewhere between absolute expansion and absolute contraction. Consequently when considering my assertion that Projective Geometry is descriptive of Bacon's work it is important to uncover evidence that supports this assertion, and this is supplied by Deleuze's identification that expansion and contraction is an important critical element that aids a deciphering of the import of Bacon's work. As such Deleuze's text is instrumental in validating Projective Geometry as an interpretative tool. I have already given indications of Bacon's empirical approach to his subject-matter - the human being viewed from multiple angles - and this facet of his personality I first discovered through John Russell in his book "Francis Bacon":

"Francis Bacon's clean-shaven face, at once chubby and tormented, and as roseate as that of some eighteenth century English empirical philosopher discoursing over his brandy or his sherry, seems to reflect wide-eyed astonishment, as well as intellectual stubbornness and - allied to an hidden fury - the sensitive distress of a man who has not forgotten that he was once a child whom almost anything could move to wonder". (Russell, 1997: 169-172).

As will be seen further on this astute observation is important for an understanding as to why Bacon painted as he did, although Russell's comments are only anecdotal I will, nevertheless, bring other evidence to substantiate the value of Russell's remarks.

Clearly my approach to a critique of Bacon's *oeuvre* challenges common assumptions as to the nature of reality. This is no easy task for it immediately plunges the enquirer into the maelstrom of heated debate that surrounds the question as to what is the precise nature of the world we inhabit. Whilst I have no problem accepting scientific discoveries I do have, as already indicated, a problem with the intellectual and imaginative thinking deployed to explain the nature of these discoveries. For instance, I have no problem with the existence of atoms but I do have a problem with their present characterisation, which appears, to me, to be an inadequate description of their constitution and properties. If I were to proffer an opinion then I would state that it is an understanding of the elusive and mysterious nature of Infinity that will move the debate along. Infinity, although *real*, is utterly invisible to ordinary consciousness, yet Blake professed to be able to hold it in the palm of his hand. During the course of this text I will discuss various imaginative, mental exercises by which one can familiarise oneself with some of the properties of Infinity, the effect of which is to enliven the imaginative pole of consciousness. This presents a major obstacle, for, as with Goethe's methodology, to be discussed below, this requires an individual effort be undertaken, and for such an undertaking to be initiated then the individual has to believe that there is 'something more' to be found in the first place. Bacon I believe, as will be argued below, had by birth, along with Blake, a natural, nascent ability to perceive this 'something more', and in subsequent years continued to develop this ability through heightened and intense observation of the human being.

Johan Wolfgang von Goethe.

So as to not leave the statement in the previous section-'other methods have to be employed'-hanging in the air I will now introduce a famous personality who developed such a method for actually witnessing the processes of Growth, and this is Johan Wolfgang von Goethe (1749-1832). In order to fully understand the extent of Goethe's achievement a diversion is necessary that has a vital role to play in comprehending the ramifications of Bacon's work, and this concerns the role, and value, of artistic cognition for Epistemology. Firstly it is rarely appreciated that an artist is just as much an empiricist as a scientist (in fact we are all empiricists by default, and this applies not only to sight but all the senses), and by mentioning empiricism in relation to artistic activity, which in the Anglo-Saxon world is almost purely associated with scientific methodologies, I may be accused of capriciousness but as far as I am concerned this is certainly not the case. It is only with Immanuel Kant (1724-1804) postulations (whose ideas still today form the backbone of specific modes of Anglo-Saxon Epistemology) that artistic cognition was deemed to be inferior to that of so-called scientific, abstract intellectual reasoning. Indeed, it could be argued that the entrenching of Kant's ideas upon the epistemological value of artistic comprehension during the 19th century has led to a contemporary impoverishment of Public Art. Regardless of my opinion there must be some *rationale* behind the relegation, and downgrading, of the epistemological importance of artistic cognition with regard to understanding the Universe we inhabit. Even if one produces evidence of the social benefits of creative work, all this pales to insignificance compared with the 'truth value' that is accorded to current scientific theories, concerning the nature of the Universe. One reason for this is the stunted image of the human being, already referred to, promulgated by Anglo-Saxon Empiricism, but far more telling is the epistemological reliance upon only a partial use of our powers of reasoning.

The fact that particular essential aspects of human cognition have had to be downgraded so as to privilege abstract thought has had a number of unsavoury consequences. Specifically qualitative and emotional responses to phenomena, together with our imaginative faculties, have been rendered impotent epistemologically so as to facilitate a purely abstract, intellectual interpretation of the Universe . Epistemology has become so wedded to the abstract intellectual dimension of our being, and consequently entrenched institutionally, that it is difficult for anyone developing within a Western educational environment to think any differently. So wedded are we to thinking of mathematics purely in terms of number for calculation we have lost sight of the fact that mathematical thinking is a logical mode of thought that is more than mere number, and that this logical mode of thought is equally pertinent to the Imagination. It is now known, through studies of the brain, upon which our thinking is focussed, that our consciousness operates through two specific modes that are related to the two hemispheres of the brain: the Intellectual and the Imagination. The implication of this knowledge is that for Empiricism - the bringing together of a concept (an idea) and a percept (an observation) - to be a truly fruitful endeavour, then all aspects of our being have to be utilised. This, also, implies a thorough understanding and use of all our sensory capacities and not a limited privileging of Sight married to Intellectualism alone. The Arts, in *toto*, are such a utilisation of all the senses to understand the world and, importantly, do this through a combination of the Intellect and the Imagination. The deleterious effects of our present bias in education is highlighted by Betty Edwards in her book

"But the emphasis of our culture is so strongly slanted toward rewarding left-brain skills that we are surely losing a very large proportion of the potential ability of the other halves of our children's brains. Scientist Jerre Levy has said … That American scientific training through graduate school may entirely *destroy* the right hemisphere. We certainly are aware of the effects of inadequate training in verbal, computational skills. The verbal left hemisphere never seems to recover fully, and the effects may handicap students for life. What happens, then, to the right hemisphere which is hardly trained at all?" (Edwards, 1979: 37).

A good question, which this text attempts to answer, and it comes as no surprise that despite the intensification of a concentration upon left-hemisphere skills, for utilitarian purposes, the effect of this is a diminution of children's ability to learn those very skills, as is being constantly highlighted as one of the basic failings of our current educational system, and, furthermore, is a failing that is still to be addressed.

Blake's verse at the beginning of this Introduction indicates that Blake had a unique manner of perceiving the world, and that this was based upon an empirical approach that only received its formal validation as a methodology with Goethe. Goethe is the first public, historical figure who developed a methodology for the transformation of his consciousness so that his Intellect and Imagination resonated with each other to unfold a 'higher' order of empiricism. 'Higher' in the sense that Goethe's empirical methodology utilises Sight in harmony with both the Imagination and the Intellect, rather than just Sight and the Intellect alone. In this context it is apposite to make a distinction between the imaginative powers of a child before puberty, definable as fantasy, and how fantasy is transformed, ideally, into Imagination as a road to knowledge in the adult. At present this is not the case and the Imagination functions, feverishly, as unbridled fantasy that pays little regard to reason. So, although Goethe is an individual world-renowned for his literary works, it is generally very little appreciated that during his lifetime Goethe had a considerable reputation as a Natural Scientist, and undertook research in many diverse fields (see Henri Bortoft's book "The Wholeness of Nature: Goethe's Way of Science). Goethe was not content with a one-sided intellectual interpretation of natural phenomena (Isaac Newton's 'Theory of Colour' for instance), but strove to combine his intellectual conclusions with his imaginative capacities. This *modus operandi* is unambiguously demonstrated by his efforts to cognise the plant realm. Goethe did not simply take a plant and divide it into its constituent parts (Linnaeus) and then formulate generalised overall connections, naturally he was aware of the parts of a plant, instead Goethe went out into nature and observed how these abstractly derived parts altered according to the environment in which they grew. Later he would imaginatively recreate his observations and by doing this Goethe honed his empirical observations, thereby broadening his range of abstract concepts, with the result that he had, intellectually, a more complete 'picture' from which to theorise. Alongside this intellectual and practical activity Goethe carried within his imagination images of all the different stages of plant growth, and tried to envision how, imaginatively, they were able to transform into each other. This process carried out over many years finally yielded what he named the Archetype (the governing Principle) of the whole of the plant realm. That is he had a *living picture* in his consciousness that was not merely an intellectual and abstract idea of a plant comprised of a summation of the parts of a plant, and nor was it of the same order as a *mental representation,* which may be described as a memory-picture of something previously perceived. Goethe was able to *perceive* how this *living picture* regulates the growth forces of a plant so that it is able to develop from seed to flower. Goethe named this methodology Exact Sensorial Fantasy (ESF), and was able to apply his methodology to the inorganic as well as the organic world. Although it cannot be discussed further here there is evidence that Goethe was associated with the Freemason movement of the 18th century, even to the extent of being initiated himself into the Amalia Lodge in Weimar in 1780.

In summation, Goethe demonstrated how the polarity of our Intellectual and Imaginative abilities could be harmonised and enlivened so that he experienced a new vision of nature, a methodology accessible to everyone. In all his scientific endeavours this is how Goethe proceeded, by firstly observing nature, thus with his Theory of Colour Goethe went out into nature and contemplated both the sunrise and sunset until he realised that through the polarity of yellow and blue, at these times, there occurred an Intensification (another basic operative mode of Projective Geometry) which was responsible for the appearance of red. Goethe then realised that Intensification was not only the basis of the manifestation of colour, but a primary process for all that occurs within the Cosmos, and I will explain, below, how the principle of Intensification is a crucial characteristics of Bacon's Figures. The Intensification of the Polarity between Light and Dark 'squeezed out', so to speak, colour from the fabric of the Universe where it lay dormant otherwise. It was only after Goethe had spent long periods contemplating the environment so as to absorbed into himself a lived experience of the effect of the natural world upon his soul and spirit that he then Goethe continued to confirm his findings through experimentation in the confines of his laboratory.

Above when examining Geometrical and Mathematical thinking I stated that these were the only examples of a sense-free thinking commonly known at present, and further that the implication was that these were the examples of sense-free thinking based upon the Intellect alone as abstract, intellectual thinking. The achievement of Goethe is that his methodology leads to a *sense-free thinking that is a harmonisation of both the Intellect and the Imagination,* that is the conceptual mode of the Intellect is fructified by the picture mode of the Imagination. It will be realised that this is sense-free because the physical organ plays only a preliminary part in gathering the information from the outer world, and that the beholding of the Archetype, as a living picture, takes place through the auspices of the *mind's eye*. Goethe's prolonged efforts transformed the formative forces of his body so that a new organ was within his Mind. This is what occurs as the end result in all Initiation, and is not the only type of organ that can be created by this method, however the concern here is with Bacon. Everyone has these organs lying dormant within themselves awaiting activation, except that there are individuals who are born with these organs already in a highly developed condition in comparison to the general population, and both Bacon and Blake are two individuals that fall into this category. A further implication of Goethe's methodology is that it brings Initiation to the public world stage, something furthered by Steiner's life-work, and it is now possible for any individual to walk the **Path of Self-Initiation** (at its lower grades, although Steiner did provide exercises for achieving higher levels of Initiation) if they are prepared to suffer the trials and difficulty associated with such an act, and it is simply missing the point to sit down and read of Goethe's achievements and think that he did not undergo much tribulation as he struggled with his own constitution and the prejudices concerning the outer world. Bacon as I will show was careful to protect himself from public opinion and so on, so as to fulfil his life mission. Goethe's methodology is a response to the problematic nature of adopting a naïve realistic stance with regard to the perceived world, and is a response that has demonstrated that there is no need initially to have any preconceptions as to the nature of reality, such as a metaphysical realm of atoms and so on, but only a correct integration of the faculty of memory into our ability to think, which is not the case with **Anglo-Saxon Empiricism**.

Rudolf Steiner.

Goethe was no Philosopher, or Mathematician, and so was unable to formulate his empirical methodology into a Theory of Knowledge, this was a task undertaken by Rudolf Steiner (1861-1925). Given the complexity and wide-ranging nature of Steiner's work I can do no better than quote the thumbnail sketch provided of Rudolf Steiner upon the back-page of many books published by the Rudolf Steiner Press, this will furnish a brief introduction for those unfamiliar with Steiner and his work.

"During the last two decades of the nineteenth century the Austrian born Rudolf Steiner (1861-1925) became a respected and well-published scientific, literary, and philosophical scholar, particularly well-known for work on Goethe's scientific writings. After the turn of the century he began to develop his earlier philosophical principles into an approach to methodological research of psychological and spiritual phenomena. His multi-faceted genius has led to innovative and holistic approaches in medicine, science, education (Waldorf schools), special education, philosophy, religion, economics, agriculture (Bio-dynamic method), architecture, drama, the new art of eurhythmy, and other fields. In 1924 he founded the General Anthroposophical Society, which today has branches throughout the world".

For me Rudolf Steiner is critically significant for three achievements with respect to this *critique* of Bacon's *oeuvre*. Firstly, in a somewhat jocular manner, his overall work constitutes an 'A Beginner's Guide to the Esoteric', and what I mean by this is that he demonstrates the connections between an ancient mode of consciousness, and its wisdom, to a modern, intellectually based consciousness. In the process he elucidates the meaning of many esoteric documents, for example the Kabbalah, the Old and New Testaments and Alchemical tracts for present-day intellectual epistemology. Secondly through his research he proposed a radical, revised and new understanding of the human being and our sensory capacities that, although it does not eschew the findings of modern research, has scarcely been broached or understood. Thirdly he demonstrated the necessity for thinking, in any mode, to be appraised as the absolute centre of the Mind, with respect to our present evolutionary stage.

Steiner defined the human being as follows

Spirit - here considered to be our self consciousness ability to Think
Soul - sometimes called the Astral Body, the realm of all emotional responses.
Body - our corporeal being.

The Plane of Etheric, or Formative, Forces.

Controversially, for some, he proposed that a realm of Etheric forces existed, sometimes called the Body of Formative forces, that is responsible for the *growth and well-being* of not just our physical body but is in effect the primary basis of all that is living, below I will present arguments that it is more important that the corporeal body, and which also acts as a link between the higher members of our being, the Spirit and the Soul, and our corporeality. This realm of forces, under diverse names, has been known to every culture since the beginning of time, and have no connection to the postulations of an Ether during the 18th and 19th centuries. As stated Steiner clarified such ancient knowledge as this for a modern, intellectually-based consciousness, and as has already been referred to he resurrected Goethe's Empirical Methodology, which had been over-shadowed by the avowedly materialistic bias of mid 19th century epistemology, as an example of the manner by which a modern mind could become familiar with these forces. It is appropriate at this point to state that Projective Geometry is the primary means that the *modus operandi* of the invisible forces referred to here may be evaluated. The controversy surrounding the concept of Formative Forces is compounded by Steiner's statement that there is a force that is opposite to, but just as powerful as, **Gravity** which he called **Levity**. Both **Gravity and Levity** are the same *force* of attraction except one is acting towards **Absolute Darkness** whilst the other is acting towards **Absolute Light**, where **Absolute Darkness** is utter **Density** whereas **Absolute Light** is limitless **Expansion,** both of these concepts have a vital role to play in this *critique* of Bacon's work, and will be returned to below.

Returning to the Etheric, or Formative Forces, it is apparent that this raises the thorny issue of the role and relevance of the **Invisible** in our lived lives. The Invisible is to this day bedevilled by, firstly, religious dogma, which may or may not contain some useful thoughts upon the subject of the Invisible, and, secondly, the ill-digested thought-patterns, from the perspective of modern consciousness, that have persisted unreconstructed from ancient times when the world was perceived in a different manner. This as stated above was an absolutely vital achievement of Steiner's to bring clarity to this subject, and it is true that whatever one believes, whether one is a hardened materialist or a starry-eyed dreamer, it cannot be denied that the Invisible plays an instrumental role in our lives upon every level. Goethe, even though he has been side-lined, is the only person in the modern era, outside of the world of Initiates of various Occult Schools, to demonstrate how an ordinary person, albeit through the stint of hard-work and dedication, can become aware of the Invisible forces vital to our own continued being: in this instance the forces of Growth (Etheric or Formative Forces). Just imagine for one second what wonders could have emerged if the concentrated effort of human research had travelled in Goethe's direction, for, and this is only one example, the power and dynamism of the forces of Growth far outstrip those of material origin, as is shown by the ability of insects and plants to lift huge (in comparison to themselves) lumps of matter whilst foraging or growing, an example being the deterioration of driveways covered in tarmac and asphalt by the up-thrust of growing plants over time. As outlined above this is an epistemological conundrum, for there are literally thousands of concepts that do not have a percept, and our civilisation simply could function if not for the utilisation of the invisible forces of Electricity and Magnetism. Electricity and Magnetism are examples of how the Invisible hovers upon the edge of our ordinary sensory abilities, its presence being easily detected, to start with, by arranging matter in particular configurations, and, in this context, its presence was detected thousands of years ago by very basic technical apparatuses. How these forces of Electricity and Magnetism come into being cannot be investigated here, except to say that they are a densification and compacting of higher forces under the force of gravity, and it is this densification and compacting that makes them amenable to detection within our everyday lives, however there is a plane of Electricity/ Magnetism, with its attendant characteristics just as there other planes identified here.

There is a point, and in Projective Geometry this is named the cross-over point of Lemniscatory Space, when through particular circumstances something becomes visible that was previously **Invisible**, and this is because what is called the material world is not fixed but exists in a kind of flux, and this is demonstrated, artificially, by boiling a concentrated saline solution whereby after a while salt will crystallise out of the solution due to the reduced water content being unable to contain the amount of salt present. This is known in Chemistry as a reversible reaction, and although it has other more complex applications, nevertheless the example of salt-solution is illustrative of operations occurring around Infinity, which may be considered as the centre of Lemniscatory Space, I will define Lemniscatory Space and present further explanations later in this text. The flux of the material world is dramatically established by contemplating the ebb and flow of all that is living especially with geographical meteorological changes. This contemplation reveals the fact that not only is matter being constantly reconfigured through the forces of growth, but a similar process is enacted simultaneously through the forces of decay, or destruction. These two mutual forces are completely invisible to the naked eye, but nevertheless are responsible for all that we behold.

Steiner's other vital contribution to an understanding of the human being, which is critically relevant to this text, are his postulations concerning how our senses are integrated into the totality of our being, and rather than five senses Steiner proposed that we do in fact have twelve senses comprising of three groups of four.

Sense of Life
Sense of Balance
Sense of Movement
Sense of Touch

Sense of Sight
Sense of Taste
Sense of Smell
Sense of Warmth

Sense of Language
Sense of Ideas/ Thought
Sense of Ego
Sense of Hearing.

I do not propose to argue prolonged explanations for the validation and justification of Steiner's postulations, but will, as the opportunities arise, demonstrate their explanatory potential for making sense of Bacon's work, and this also applies to various other theorists deployed in this text. Due to both Goethe's and Steiner's efforts, with regard to Initiation and Esotericism, there is a greatly reduced threat of harm to public figures for revealing any secrets of Initiation and Esotericism, as was the case with Mozart and his opera "The Magic Flute", and the reason for this is that such secrets are now widely disseminated, in the public arena, through the Anthroposophical Movement, although such threats have not completely disappeared. As stated one could say that through the example of Goethe and Steiner's work there has now been created the circumstances whereby any individual can bring about their own initiation, that is, henceforward, individuals are able to effect a *self-initiation*, without recourse to secret societies etc. This is an important step forward for the evolution of humanities' consciousness, and I will show that, although, Bacon was born with the propensity for developing an 'higher' consciousness he achieved this by dint of his own concentrated and focussed efforts.

Self and the World.

The World.

I would be very surprised if anyone reading this text had not heard of the Atomic Theory of Matter that is the bedrock of the Anglo-Saxon, Empirical World View, given that it is so widely disseminated within schools and the media etc. I also have no doubt that many readers will be vaguely aware that the Ancient Greeks, amongst others, did not view the Cosmos in this manner but rather as the interaction of four states of energy, or forces, those of Fire, Air, Water and Earth. It was believed that these four states generated the fabric of the Cosmos, and whose interaction in turn gave rise to the four qualities of Cold, Moist, Dry and Warm. In its hubris the modern-day proponents of their Atomic Theory have a patronising and mistaken attitude to those who supported this World View, regarding them as quasi-primitive thinkers in comparison to the assumed sophistication of modern, abstract, intellectual theorisations. This attitude is somewhat destabilised by the fact that the very culture that propagated such a theory as the interaction of Fire, Air, Water and Earth as the basis of the Cosmos is the very culture that laid the foundations for our ability to think logically. How could such a culture espouse such mistaken ideas? But in essence both world views are not so far apart, with much of the misunderstanding arising from the assumption that the citizens of Classical Greece had the same mode of consciousness as ourselves only less developed. This is not the case and will be further examined below.

Anyone familiar with the Atomic Theory will be aware that through the propositions of the String Theory it is now assumed that the ultimate basis of what may be termed 'reality' consists of particular, and specific, patterns of energy, and that these patterns of energy under distinctive conditions give rise to all the proposed particles of the atom that have so far been discovered, that is they have an *exclusive* forms from each other, just as the form of a cat is exclusive from that of a dog. There is with the methodology of modern science a journey undertaken from the immediacy of lived experience to that which is regarded as fundamental, and as such is an attempt to pierce the illusion of appearance through the Intellect alone. But as inferred a consciousness predicated upon the intellect alone can only cognise the surface of phenomena not their inner essence, due to the fact that an abstract, intellectual consciousness can only 'objectify' phenomena. Fire, Air, Water and Earth are states, or fields of 'energy', that are unknowable in themselves (cannot be objectified), their existence only becoming known when a particular phenomenon arises from their interaction, thus a flame comes into being only when there is a specific interaction of Fire, Air, Water and Earth, and will fail to materialise if any of the proportions do not satisfy the conditions for its appearance. At present only a narrow spectrum of the available 'energies' enfolded into the Cosmos are known, and these other 'energies' comprise of orders that are utterly different from the commonly known energies such as electricity and magnetism, and even with these we are nowhere near knowing their full potential and operative modes. This may seem fantastic but as more mysteries of the Quantum World are uncovered it will rapidly become apparent that our present manner of considering this world will have to change, especially when trying to understand how the Quantum World relates to Einstein's General Theory of Relativity, that is how the microcosm and the macrocosm interact to form the world of our ordinary experience.

The current on-looker mode of consciousness that relies upon the interpretation of data gathered by technical instruments, such as the electron microscope, to verify empirical postulations regarding what constitutes the Universe, has its origins with the invention of the microscope during the 17th century. Since that time scientists have relied upon the telescope and the microscope to investigate the macro- and micro- worlds of our experience, however with the refinement of both the telescope and microscope to register 'energy signatures' (that are invisible to ordinary sight and consciousness) Anglo-Saxon Empiricism has now moved out of the ambit of the human being to that of machines. The reading of these invisible 'energy signatures' is now predicated upon theorisations as to what form they possess, that is the data obtained from an instrument, let us say the electron microscope, is taken to confirm that which was only a postulation in the first place. In effect nothing has been proved for instruments are only technical constructs, and can only be said to produce 'objective truths' when we turn a blind-eye to the fact that the meaning of all data obtained by such methods has to be construed by a human being. What I mean by this is that instruments have to calibrated in a particular manner in harmony with what is already known of the phenomena being assessed by the instrument in the first place so as to have any meaningful results. This is only a quantitative assessment and furnishes no new knowledge, furthermore information recorded from such an instrument as a cyclotron would have no meaning unless it was interpreted within a pre-existing intellectual paradigm. No-one sits down and says just a minute does what we have obtained through this instrument really have this meaning, because no-one questions the veracity of the pre-existing intellectual paradigm. This is a self-fulfilling fantasy as everything is based upon speculation, and reminds me of the story of the Emperor's New Clothes. In effect there has been no departure from human observation.

Historically it is Robert Hooke's experiments with a microscope that are the template for the above empirical, observational procedures, and which are illustrative of the epistemological debilitation that occurs when artistic cognition and sensibilities are side-lined, or ignored. Robert Hooke's experiments with a microscope led him to conjecture that human thought does not reproduce, or reflect, the real content of the world, that is he claimed that what he perceived through the microscope was proof of the non-reality of human concepts. Hooke's mode of reasoning epitomises the abstract, intellectual thinking that denotes an observer style of consciousness. Thus he considered the 'ideal' concepts of a point and a straight line in relation to his examination of a needle and a razor under a microscope, and concluded from this examination, which revealed that both the razor's edge and the needle were not straight or pointed but jagged, that therefore human concepts bore little connection to how things were in the real world. Hooke's methodology is curious because he is allowing artificially created sense-perceptions, which have no correlation to his lived life, to dictate his reasoning. Hooke looked at the magnification of a razor's edge without realising that in making any conclusions that he himself had remained the same, and that there was thus a disjuncture between his state of being and what he artificially observed. To state it in a nutshell observations through a microscope are of a different perceptual order and not identical to observation without the instrument. This disjuncture could only be adjusted if he was in the same state of magnification as the razor, but then of course the razor's edge would appear perfectly straight. Hooke's artificially induced disruption of his 'state of perceptual being' provides no evidence that human thinking, *per see*, is flawed. If Hooke had been so minded as to not ignore his imaginative powers and stood on a cliff edge, on a clear day, then he would have observed the manifestation of straight line in the natural world with relation to the horizon. There is no doubt that simple observation of the horizon on a clear day with no obstructions reveals to all intents and purposes a straight line, and this does not alter with the magnification of a telescope or binoculars, provided there is no impedance. The observation of constructed objects (needle and razor) by artificial means is completely different from observing natural phenomenon with our bodily senses. This faulty reasoning which led to an existential crisis in philosophical circles precipitated by David Hume's famous declarations "All our distinct perceptions are distinct existences" and "The Mind never perceives any real connections between distinct existences". The implication of which is that all that we know through our senses have no connection to each other, and that any connections theorised are illusions and false, an attitude that persists to this time, and has only been partially ameliorated by Kant.

Nevertheless it is possible to delve further into how the Mind functions, and if we do this we discover that 'Sharpness' and a 'Straight Line' are ideal concepts that, because of their nature, can never find absolute manifestation by any process of manufacture, and as such have only a process of 'coming-into-being' that is infinite. They are as such concepts that have no beginning or end. This means that we have concepts which we perceive with the mind that, following on from the way in which the physical world is constituted, can never have an absolute manifestation, but which are, nonetheless, perceived to be regulatory of the physical world we inhabit, as is demonstrated by the instance of the horizon. This means that with 'sharpness' and a 'straight line' we are aware of concepts which to the abstract, intellectual consciousness we possess at the moment have no definitive percept. It follows that Hooke's experiments possess a functional, utilitarian value because if we have tools consonant with the degree of magnification we can achieve degrees of 'sharpness' and a 'straight line' impossible to achieve without them. Hooke's experimentation with the microscope upon plants, and his discovery of the cell as being fundamental to organic structures, is on much firmer epistemological ground, because here he perceived a *form* that is inherent to the plant, albeit from the aspect of an abstract, intellectual observer-consciousness. It is on firmer ground in that the concept 'form' can be perceived to have an actual knowable percept with the observation of a 'cell', even if this is not ordinarily perceptible, and begs the question as to whether human beings have other cognitive modes as yet undiscovered that would obviate the need for recourse to technical instruments.

Hooke's microscopic observations of a needle and a razor do however indicate an important fact, and this only becomes apparent when imaginative powers are combined with intellectual powers, and that is that there is no absolute separation between the phenomena we observe. It might appear that a sharp razor and a pointed needle have through their being honed an absolute separation from other phenomena and although they have an internal cohesiveness that is unique to their form, this is not the case. Certainly by sharpening and honing the razor and the needle we have induced a purer expression of 'sharpness' and a 'straight line' than before they were sharpened and honed, but Hooke's experiments demonstrate that this is only relative. When observed through the microscope a razor and a needle are seen to be jagged, that it is shown that their separation from the surrounding world is not as absolute as it appears without magnification. There always exists a boundary where on one side of a phenomenon one thing takes place whilst on the other side something else takes place, and this boundary is permeable, to a greater and lesser extent, and depending upon whether circumstances shift one way or the other. With living organisms things are very different - I observe a plant and perceive its form, I then subject it to microscopic examination and perceive another form, the cell, the cell, however is interlinked with all other cells even if I am able to see that it has a definite shape, and this becomes clearer at higher magnification for then the boundary between the cells becomes fuzzier, but other interlinked forms then appear up to limits of magnification. There is at this point another boundary that is the unknowable to human senses allied to an abstract, intellectual consciousness and the nature of that which lies on the other side of this boundary can only be subject to conjecture at present. From the above it will be readily appreciated as to why the qualities of phenomena are problematic for Anglo-Saxon Empiricism, especially when mistaken assumptions are compounded by further mistaken assumptions as with David Hume's famous dictums. The final icing on the cake of this edifice of mistaken thinking was provided by Kant with his postulations concerning the limits of human knowledge, postulations that were vigorously rebutted by Goethe.

It may be a mystery to current Anglo-Saxon Empirical thinking as to how phenomena can arise from nothingness, but it certainly wasn't to William Blake who encapsulated his actual perception of such an occurrence in the verse that opened this Introduction. Because he had attuned his consciousness to the invisible planes that give rise to phenomena in the world as they issue from the point of infinity that is at the centre of Leminiscatory space, he was able to

> To see a world in a grain of sand,
> And a heaven in a wild flower,
> Hold infinity in the palm of your hand,
> And eternity in an hour.

The Soul and The Self.

Before entering into a close examination of the Soul and the Self it will be as well to say a few words about the dramatic change of consciousness we all experience as we grow out of the first 3 yrs of life, and embark upon the journey into adulthood. The event that denotes this tremendous change is the learning of a mother tongue. I say denote because the consciousness of a neonate up to the learning of a language is utterly unknown to modern science and psychology, and the baby can only be looked after and cared for in response to the instinctive sounds it makes with regards to the demands of it's immature corporeality. In adulthood there is no memory of what was perceived and known during this approximate three years of life, there are however individuals who have had extraordinary powers of memory and have been able to communicate to their peers their experiences during this time, and notable amongst these are the poets William Wordsworth, (1770-1850), ("Ode: Intimations of Immortality from Recollections of Early Childhood") and Thomas Traherne (1636-1674). I believe that Bacon possessed this remarkable ability, and will during the course of this critique furnish evidence that substantiates this claim, in consequence I will henceforth refer to this period as the 'forgotten self'. Above I characterised the World as being composed of the interaction of four states : Fire, Air, Water and Earth. It is as well to say here that a more accurate description is to portray them as planes of existence, or being, that are internally coherent and distinct, and which as far as our present consciousness, and for the foreseeable future, cannot be perceived in themselves. What we ordinarily perceive is the end-product of creative processes, perception of the conditions leading up to these end-products can only be achieved with an enhanced consciousness, as with Goethe. Although loath to use such terms as 'energy' and 'wavelengths', as commonly understand with respect to 'grosser and coarser states' such as electricity and magnetism, these planes of existence, or being do nevertheless possess emanations, and qualities, which despite the fact that they are utterly different from the 'grosser and coarser states' known to our abstract, intellectual consciousness they are detectable, and perceptible to a consciousness refined through meditative exercises. By refining their consciousness an individual is able to weaken our exclusive focus upon the plane of the Earth that is the hallmark of our predominantly abstract, intellectual consciousness of everyday life, so that an individual may peruse the circumstances within which this plane is situated. An analogy for how our present consciousness cognises the world would be if we were to behold a piece of fruit, and would only be able to perceive the seeds and not the flesh of the fruit which has a more refined materiality in comparison to the seed.

So in addition to the states, or planes, already depicted when considering all that is living a further three planes have to be added: the astral plane (emotional), plane of formative forces and the plane of the mind. The plane of formative forces permits a living entity to exist and then develop, whilst the astral plane bestows the gift of sentience which, with the inclusion of the ego, promotes self-sentience. The plane of the mind bestows upon us the ability to think, without which we would only have a vegetative, or animal, state of being. It is necessary to understand that for each of these planes to be operative in our being there has to be a 'vehicle', or configuration, within that plane from which we can work, and exist. Consequently there are constructions, or organisations of forces, for all of the planes so far mentioned, and these are related to and part of, our corporeality. The 'vehicle' within the astral plane that is responsible for our sentience is named the **Soul**, and is a 'vehicle' that has undergone many transformations in the course of our evolution.   24

The Soul.

At birth we merely have the basic construction of a soul body, and are this stage within the sway of, and under the influence of, the Soul of the Mother. It takes a prolonged period of development for an individual to develop their own self-consciousness with regard to the soul they possess, an event that is only initiated with the onset of adolescence. The difficulties of adolescence are commonly known, and everyone has suffered from the emotional vicissitudes that are typical of this period of life. There is thus nothing mysterious or unknowable about the astral plane, we are constantly part of it whilst alive, however given the irrational opprobrium attached to words like 'astral' etc, I propose on occasion to refer to the astral plane as the Emotional Plane, and it is noteworthy that presently more attention is being given to this plane in relation to our health and general state of well-being, as is instanced by Daniel Goleman's book "Emotional Intelligence".

The soul is not an homogeneous entity for during our evolutionary path we have developed and matured various aspects of it during differing stages of our life. Within Anthroposophy these varying aspects are known as

The Sentient Soul, (the world of emotions and passions)
The Intellectual (or Mind) Soul (the world of thinking and ideas)
The Consciousness Soul,

each of which once mastered is capable of developing further to profound levels, reflections of which sometimes intuitively enter our consciousness. At approximately 21 years of age the Ego descends more fully into our corporeality, but this appearance of the Ego into our being is by no means its full potential we are only at the very beginning of realising the depth and profundity of this member of our being. With the onset of the Ego we start to work upon the Sentient Soul which in effect means that we initiate a process of purifying the passions and desires that are inherent to our character and personality. At approximately 28 years of age we become more directly aware of our Intellectual (or Mind) Soul thereby becoming more acquainted with our ability to think, in all its shades. The Consciousness Soul comes to the forefront of our awareness at around 35 years of age, a time which coincides with, what may be described as, the highpoint of our corporeal development. Consequently the Consciousness Soul may be described as an *objective self-awareness*, meaning that we become more fully cognisant of who we are and what we have achieved in our lives so far. Given this deepened introspection this is a time when many individuals feel the urge to change the direction of their lives. However this time is very little understood and this lack of cognition leads to what is commonly termed a 'mid-life crisis', and can occur at any time after, and around, 35 years of age depending upon an individual's circumstances. Because the Soul is a unity, if not homogeneous, these phases are not separate from each in zones, or the such like, rather as our corporeality matures they emerge from the depths of the Soul to the forefront of our attention for a period of time. It will be shown in what follows that each of these phases has a varying pertinence for construing the significance of Bacon's *oeuvre*, however it will be demonstrated that of the three it is the Sentient Soul that is most important in this respect. It is even, although this will not be examined in this volume, possible to demonstrate that there is a consonance between Bacon's own development through the phases described and his subsequent output.

A consideration of the Soul and the astral plane would be weak and anaemic without a commentary upon Qualities. Paramount to understanding the Soul and the Astral Plane is Polarity, where the most fundamental polarity is that of Love and Hate, a polarity that colours all our responses to the world. When this is taken into account the subtlety of the Ancient Greek model of the Cosmos becomes apparent, for the qualities of Cold, Moist, Dry and Warm demonstrate that the Ancient Greeks comprehended how the astral plane is intimately entwined into the four states of Fire, Air, Water and Earth that comprise the fabric of the Cosmos.

The Self.

Just as we need a vehicle, or body, known as the Soul to have sentience so we need a vehicle, or body, that can act as an instrument for our consciousness, personality and character thereby bestowing upon us an **identity** and sense of individuality. The Self due to its nature is a blossoming of the Soul and this virtually indistinguishable conjunction is the very essence of our being without which we would not only be inhuman, but we would have no **identity**, and would instead be the **not-me.** This may seem a peculiar way of phrasing things, but it is crucial when considering questions related to the **Other**, a subject amusingly explored by Umberto Eco in his book "The Prague Cemetery". The subject of the **Other**, as will be shown, has a decisive role to play in deciphering the meaning of Bacon's images. Our sense of Self is forged within the presence of the **Other** in its many guises, and everything which is the *non-I* is from this perspective the **Other.** Our sense of Self is thus founded upon a polarity Self/ Other, or I/ non-I, and primary to this polarity is our gendered condition as Male and Female. For us to know who we are it is necessary that there are distinct demarcations between Self and the Other, and when these boundaries become porous and indistinct an individual's sense of self becomes indeterminate. This leads to an individual inhabiting a mental landscape that is blurred and hazy with no firm landmarks, and consequently the individual is prone to anxiety, and other mental conditions, but by far the most common effect is that of lassitude resulting from a paralysis of the will. It is quite obvious that we live in a time when the boundaries between Self and the Other are being deliberately deconstructed, a tendency that has gathered pace since the Second World War. As I will demonstrate this theme is critically instrumental in understanding Bacon's work, and central to this theme is Bacon's handling of the polarity of male and female.

There is an additional factor to the Self that is vitally important to this *critique* which I will describe as the **Unconscious Self**. The **Unconscious Self** has had many designations throughout the ages, for example the Doppelgänger, the Lower Self and the Double. As we emerge from the **'Forgotten Self'** of infancy we become subject to all the influences, good and bad, that comprise our environment and these are all internalised and live, unconsciously, within our emerging personality. Depending upon the nature of these internalised experiences, and their intensity, they exert a lesser or greater influence upon our behaviour and our conscious mind. They have the propensity to strengthen aspects of our personality and negate others, and at present psychological and psychoanalytical theorisations are aware of only a restricted portion of the **Unconscious Self,** and deny that this internalised world of experiences can come together as an entity that has a will and volition of its own. Depending upon the individual the **Unconscious Self** assumes a virulent, deleterious (to the individual) power and strongly defined life-form that is difficult to cope with under normal everyday circumstances, whilst with others it remains only at a nascent state. This is common knowledge within esoteric circles, however Bacon was perfectly aware of its existence and power as I will demonstrate in my analysis of Bacon's series of portraits of George Dyer. In fact one may say that Bacon made understanding how the **Unconscious Self** affected the well-being of individuals his life work. Dimensions of the **Unconscious Self** will be further explicated below, especially with considerations of the Other, a theme already touched upon.

Before leaving the subject of the Self there is one issue that has a crucial determinative role to play in everything that we are conscious of, and this is the **Plane of Time**. There is nothing that is not subject to this mysterious and little understood facet of the reality that we live within, despite the fact that we have such an intimate familiarity with it corporeally. An intimate familiarity that is reflected in the relationship between the Mind and Thinking. There is gradually a movement away from considering time purely as a linear phenomenon (something which is only true for the mechanical and the formlessness of gross materiality) to the non-linear, and in this respect attempts to depict the non-linearity of the **Now** are certainly to found in Bacon's images. Changes in our collective thinking about time are being prompted by the growing realisation that all that is living cannot be mechanically explained, but that dynamic, non-linear, complex models have to be deployed of which, we presently, only have a embryonic level of comprehension. All the planes spoken of here operate with time-modes utterly different from that of our common awareness of time, and it is not possible to talk of these planes in terms of linearity or non-linearity, or any other intellectual category, these planes are both *beyond time and time in its fullness* simultaneously. Traditionally these states have been referred to as the Eternal, the Everlasting, the Oneness and so on, although I shall use such terms occasionally they are in the last resort unhelpful due to the connotations loaded upon them. A prime example of an incursion of modern thinking into these realms is with the world of Quantum Mechanics which presents many conundrums for our abstract, intellectual thought processes. It is with a delving into the enigmatic qualities of the **Now** that progress can be made for this is a condition we are constantly within even if our consciousness is distracted from its presence through a bias towards intellectuality. The human being, in all its facets, is a dynamic, non-linear, complex system of forces, the wisdom of which is way beyond current conceptualisations. Meditative exercises of the type undertaken by Bacon, which can lead to Initiation, attune the Mind to the planes referred to above by enhancing our receptivity to the presence of the **Now**

The Mind and Thinking.

One way of cognising the presence of the **Now** with our ordinary consciousness is through an examination of our ability to think. Before doing this, however, it is necessary to expand a little upon the 'Forgotten Self' and what developments take place subsequent to learning to speak. To facilitate this I will quote from Henri Bortoft's book "The Wholeness of Nature: Goethe's Way of Science" where Bortoft draws attention to discoveries made in Developmental Psychology concerning how there are changes in modes of consciousness as we grow out of infancy into adulthood;

"Psychologists have discovered that there are two modes of organization for a human being: the action mode and the receptive mode. In the early infant state, we are in a receptive mode, but this is gradually dominated by the development of the action mode of organization that is formed in us by our interaction with the physical environment…The result is an analytical mode of consciousness attuned to our experience with physical bodies. This kind of consciousness is institutionalised by the structure of our language, which favours the active mode of organization. " (Bortoft, 2004: 15-16).

Since the late 19th century there has been a mushrooming of interest and speculation concerning the importance of our early years of development as a precursor for our adult consciousness, in all its characteristics. Regardless as to the question of the quality and validity of this investigation it is the case that virtually no understanding of the first three years of life, up until the acquisition of language by the infant, has been brought to light. There is a very simple reason for this and that is, and this is true for every human being, with the learning of a language the previous mode of consciousness is subsumed by the brilliance of our Intellect. At the pain of some repetition there is no way of communicating with a new-born child, all that can be done is to see to its needs in order to ensure its survival. Notwithstanding this this period is of vital importance because during this time we have an utterly different, as stated, cognition of the world than our adult consciousness, except that during the first years of life we have no means of formally retaining these early experiences because we have no I consciousness. Bacon, along with Goethe, again as stated, are certainly not the only individuals to realise the importance of what I have named as the 'forgotten self' of childhood, it has in fact been common knowledge within esoteric orders since time immemorial, even if it has been characterised differently and obfuscated so as to prevent misuse, but as I will demonstrate it has now become an urgent necessity that humanity starts to grasp the true nature of their being, and Bacon, through his example, is instrumental in this process.

To explicate some more of the implications of this 'forgotten self' of childhood, which are inexhaustible, I will first state that during this period we have an Intelligence (that never leaves us, even if it retreats to the background of consciousness) which is a largely unconscious (it can be nothing else during our first years of existence) higher mode of knowing, in that it never loses its awareness of the absolute inter-connectedness of everything, from which our abstract, intellectualism devolves as we grow into adulthood. The consciousness of an infant before the acquisition of language (approx. three years of age) is one that lives in the Imaginative, picture realm, and this is so simply because the physical basis, within the brain, for Intellectualism has not developed and is in an embryonic state. To believe that the Imagination possess no critical Intelligence for an understanding of the world, as does modern epistemology, is a mistake. The period of infancy and childhood with its immersion in play is the engine of our sensory understanding of the Cosmos, and without which all the postulations of an abstract, intellectual empirical methodology, with respect to the world, would be without basis, drifting like phantasms through the Mind without any means of anchoring our consciousness to our living existence. Why is this so? Our Imaginative Intelligence is an unconscious faculty that unbeknownst to us in our early years orders, and rationalises, our sensory experiences into a meaningful body of knowledge of which we are unaware as we continue to mature. Our sensory organs are graded with respect to their interaction with the world at large, for instance the eye only allows extremely rarefied matter to enter the body through the light it receives, whereas our sense of taste permits the passage of the dense matter of food that enters the mouth. One might characterise this by saying that we have through our sensory organs an extruded interaction with the world, with the eye remaining aloof in distinction to the sense of taste which 'sucks' us deeply into the world. Clearly we have very complex sensory experiences which if they were not ordered in a meaningful way would precipitate chaos in the corporeal body.

Rudolf Steiner drew attention to the fact that we are aware of three dominant spheres to our consciousness, those of Thinking, Feeling and Willing. Of the three it is thinking that is the most transparent to our consciousness, whereas our cognisance of feeling is much more clouded, and we simply cannot move within the feeling realm with the same ease as we do with that of thinking. For the majority of people the feeling realm is a mystery unto itself where it is not easy to divine how it functions, whereas thinkings *modus operandi* is much clearer due to our understanding of logic and reason etc. The realm of willing, which is closely associated with our metabolism, is the realm that we know least about, and of which we are absolutely unconscious of its actions in sustaining our corporeality through our digestive processes, and how, particularly, a conscious act of will becomes translated into the movement of our limbs. Our digestive processes upon which our consciousness depends take place automatically below the level of our consciousness, and would in fact be harmed if we were conscious of them through our abstract intellectuality.

It is the autonomic nervous system, which is part of the peripheral nervous system, that acts as a control system for our visceral functions, that is all our bodily functions from respiration, heart beat to swallowing, and this aspect of our physiognomy is located within the medulla oblongata in the lower brain stem. The autonomic nervous system is divided into three sub-systems, the parasympathetic, the sympathetic and the enteric nervous systems all of which can act independently of each other or interact with one another, and it is awe-inspiring to me that there is a primeval ancient *intelligence,* full of wisdom, that regulates the astounding complexity of our corporeality of which, normally, I am entirely unconscious. This indicates that at present our abstract, intellectual thinking is only the tip of the iceberg of the vast potential of the ability to think, and that we are only at the beginning of the adventure to explore this enigmatic realm. To return to my comments regarding the Imagination, we can characterise our abstract, intellectual thinking that we use to cognise the world as a thinking process that has been shorn of its pictorial content. I would argue that in order to understand the world in a fuller more comprehensive manner that we now need to integrate a picture content into our ability to conceptualise, where concepts are derived from contemplating phenomena without preconceptions. and this was precisely Goethe's achievement.

Other meanings of the word visceral are: proceeding from instinct rather than reasoned thinking and showing basic emotions. Both these meanings highlight the evolutionary status of the medulla oblongata as one of the oldest parts of the brain. This part of the brain is now considered to have evolved some 500 million years ago with primordial reptiles, and it is pertinent to my arguments concerning the Imagination that all living multi-cellular creatures, with a few exceptions, are bilateral. The implications of this are obvious and Rudolf Steiner when characterising the evolution of consciousness stated that the consciousness of the Ancient Greeks was one that was based upon the metabolic system. This may seem incredulous to some, but if we consider that all that is living is consciousness, to some degree, and that this consciousness is related to a corporeal base, in some manner, then it follows to enquire what was the nature of this consciousness since there is general agreement that the brain, which has undergone a prolonged development was utterly different in the ancient past than now. It may be argued that the ancients had a similar consciousness to our own but that it was less developed in comparison to the one we now possess, this was not Steiner's opinion and it certainly isn't mine for a number of reasons. Steiner contended that the consciousness of the ancients was fundamentally a *picture* consciousness, and when looking at the world the ancients perceived *living pictures* of the phenomena surrounding them, and that they did not reason with an abstract, conceptual intellectuality, rather they reasoned by following the logic of Images, or pictures, an ability largely lost to modern humanity. This makes sense what we take into account the so-called mythologies of ancient peoples and races, and that we know for a fact that the reasoning we now deploy had its genesis in Classical Greece through the philosophers of that time. It makes sense also because when bear in mind the commentary on the 'forgotten self' of childhood above, where it was pointed out that the brain was only in the first stages of development in comparison to the metabolic and limb system, and so consequently the neonate is unable to conceptualise as an adult does, but where we know that the infant is responding to something, apart from physical needs, in its consciousness, this can only be pictures. What else is there apart from images and concepts, the twin pillars of consciousness?

The clear implication of this is that the neonate recapitulates past stages of consciousness during the journey from infant to adult, just as the embryo recapitulates stages of the evolution of the species before birth. Steiner also made the point that there has been a rapid increase in the size of the brain's frontal lobes from around the time of the Renaissance to the present, and studies in brain development confirm there have been significant increases to the overall size of the brain from the Neolithic era onwards. Difficult as Steiner's statement is to prove there are other historical and cultural factors that indicate that there is some substance to it. For instance, there can be little doubt that since the Renaissance humanity has collectively honed its intellectual powers to a remarkable degree, with this intensification of intellectual thinking consequently celebrated as the Age of Enlightenment, which is a historical period that fostered the continuing belief that abstract, intellectual thinking in itself, free of religious dogma and superstition, was capable of solving all of humanities mysteries and problems. This trend towards abstract thinking was enhanced through Johannes Gutenberg (1400?-1468) invention of the printing press. The invention of the printing press initiated a dichotomy between the written word and the spoken word, for when a language is written down this can only be achieved by symbols, and since symbols are in themselves abstract, the consequence is that abstraction lies at the heart of the written word in opposition to the immediacy of the spoken word, and this process of abstraction has intensified since Gutenberg's time up to our own. The immediacy of the spoken word devolves from the *actual* emotional input from the speaker, regardless as to whether they are dissembling in any manner or not, whereas with the written word whatever takes place between the reader and the text can only be an insular, self-absorbed affair. This process of abstraction was simply not an issue prior to the invention of printing press, purely because there was no wide-spread availability of the written word. Reading and writing were the privileges of a tiny minority of the general populace. During ancient times up until the Renaissance people were far more responsive to images due to the fact that, although in the first stages of decline, the Imaginative aspect of our being played a dominant role within consciousness. It is a well-known and generally accepted fact that it is at the time of the Renaissance that humanity began again to develop its logical and intellectual abilities through, amongst other factors, a renewed interest in the achievements of the philosophers of Classical Greece, and this burgeoning of intellectualism has hastened the progression of abstraction, via the written word, one implication of which is that we have become largely divorced from a direct inter-face with the nature from which we spring, precipitating all the problems with which we are so familiar. Artistically this blossoming of intellectuality was pictorially depicted by Raphael (1483-1520) in his work "The School of Athens". It is interesting to note that the increase in brain size since Neolithic times questions Neo-Darwinian materialistic interpretations of Darwin's original theories, for it appears that the improvement of mental processes are a powerful evolutionary force issuing as they do from the neurological impact upon the brain of creativity, not just in the form of cave painting, but the co-ordination of hand and eye in the production of tools and other artifacts.

Thinking.

The wide-spread dissemination of the written word resulting from the invention of the printing press has precipitated a rapid increase in the prevalence of a contemplative life of thinking. Prior to the Renaissance this was only available to a very small percentage of the population but has now become commonplace, and has had one significant effect and that is that humanity has an increased awareness of its ability to Think, a subject upon which Rudolf Steiner placed a particular emphasis. Steiner thought this subject so important that one of his very first books, "The Philosophy of Spiritual Activity", was devoted to examining the central role Thinking now assumes within our consciousness, and the ramifications of this for epistemology. This is not an easy subject for the Anglo-Saxon world due to the wide-spread ignorance of the thrust of German Idealism. A thorough examination of German Idealism is not necessary here but a few aspects may be highlighted here as relevant to a *critique* of Bacon's *oeuvre.* Anyone becoming acquainted with German Idealism will first be struck by the fact that the philosophers relevant to this movement struggled with the relationship between the Ego, Thinking , the Spoken word/ Written word and Ontology, some of the outcomes of which lead to diverse movements, such as Phenomenalism. Steiner having been born into this culture and who obtained his doctorate, therewith, was perfectly aware of the intellectual implications of the debates comprising the postulations of the German Idealist movement, central to which was what was a human being capable of knowing and not knowing, and was there any limit to human knowledge?

As stated above, the exclusive focus upon abstract, intellectual thinking we now display, bereft of a vital involvement of the Imagination, is only a recent phenomenon, dating from the Renaissance, a time when we witness an unparalleled mushrooming of intellectual activity. This change of consciousness, accompanied by what may be described as a coming-down-to-earth from a dreamy consciousness, is made explicit by the leading artists of this period. Taking Duccio as an example of the style prior to Cimabue and Giotto we see that with Duccio there is a pensive, far-away atmosphere in contrast to the more substantial realism espoused by Giotto and others. The hallmark of this change of consciousness, and perception, which is the onset of the Consciousness Soul, is embodied in the creation of Classical Perspective, which through its rules and vanishing points etc defined the character of the manner by which humanities' way of perceiving the surrounding world had changed. Nevertheless although we now have this ability to think for ourselves we are not even remotely fully conscious of this ability we so blithely perform, much like a fish that swims in water but is utterly unaware that it is swimming in water. Steiner made it one of his aims to change this situation and one of his radical proposals was that we set about **Thinking about Thinking**. Steiner is in the first instance referring to abstract, intellectual thinking, and the impetus of Steiner's proposal is that we become completely and consciously objective to this faculty of thinking just as we are objective to any other bodily activity, we may become briefly overwhelmed by an emotion but at the end of the day we adopt an objective stance to our emotional condition, and this is even more true of digestion and other bodily functions. Returning to the analogy of the fish this would tantamount to performing the same action as a fish stepping onto land from the ocean, and then contemplating the ocean from which it had emerged. So despite the fact that thinking, out of thinking feeling and willing, is the activity that we have clearest understanding of with regard to its functioning, it is the one out of the above three that we have the least objectivity to, and this is only one of a number of paradoxes inherent to our appreciation of thinking.

The problem with understanding the nature of thinking is that this is an activity that has to be performed by someone and this is perplexing for we are in the position of being both a subject and an object. If it was possible to become a disembodied thinker and contemplate our abstract, intellectual thinking we would immediately perceive that this thinking proceeds by making an object of everything it comes into contact with so that whatever it is can then be conceptualised, and from this can flow processes of logic and rationality. Naturally this is not possible so we unconsciously struggle with being a producer and the object of that which we produce. Alan Howard in his booklet "Thinking about Thinking" gives a basic explanation of the nub of Steiner's more complex book "The Philosophy of Spiritual Activity", and this is useful because the style of Steiner's book is that of a 19th century philosophical tract, and is not, to use a modern phrase, 'user-friendly'. Before going further into Steiner's ideas I will commence with some preliminary remarks about how we think about the *invisible.* The common factor for every human being, whether we are talking of the peoples of ancient times or those of modern times, is that we all possess what I have described as a Mind, and it is simply the case that the Mind of ancient times functioned in a very different manner from that of modern times. The central facet of the Mind and Consciousness is now that of abstract, intellectual rational Thinking, and again the manner by which we think and cognise the cosmos is very different today than it was, let us say, in Ancient Persia, when the power of thinking, as stated, was based upon images. What characterises the thinking of modern times is that it is self-conscious, abstract and intellectual, but this is only a recently acquired ability. That which grants us the ability to be self-conscious is the Ego, the I am, and at present the purpose and function of the Ego, with respect to thinking, is very poorly understood. For instance there appears to be little recognition that the Mind is fundamental to everything we know and do, and is not some merely secondary function in comparison to, for example, our muscular prowess. From this perspective the Mind is the most powerful tool that we have at our disposal and it is completely *invisible to* ordinary perception. There is no dispute that the Mind exists even if it cannot be seen, and is the first instance, if one accepts that knowledge is derived from the conjoining of concept and a percept, in this text of a concept that has no percept. Despite the existence of the Mind being undeniable,h our understanding of the Mind is very limited at present, with research into consciousness and the Mind being exclusively centred upon the materiality of the brain. The Mind and the Body are different facets of each other and not separate unrelated realms, each has a common origin in the fundamental forces and energies already described, and have evolved into seemingly, as *per* abstract thinking, irreconcilable realms so that we can be the way we are, consequently the present exclusive focus upon materiality disrupts an understanding of their relative value they have to each other.

Despite this downgrading of the *invisible* in comparison to the material it is now understood, as indicated above, that the two hemispheres of the brain perform radically different functions within our consciousness, and that these functions are related in the manner of their expression to our gendered corporeality. For me, the present assumptions concerning an understanding of the world that have an authoritative validation are very peculiar indeed, for they appear to be topsy-turvy. For instance it is assumed that our present perceptual capacities present us with all that there is to be perceived of the phenomena surrounding us in the world, but how can this be so when there are many concepts that have no specific percept, and I have already mentioned what I regard as the most important of these and that is the Mind. There is no possibility of isolating the Mind and putting it under the microscope - it is absolutely essential, but *invisible* - and this is not the only one of this type of concept. It does not take long once an individual pursues this line of enquiry to realise that there are a multitude of concepts in this category, of which 'growth' is another pertinent example, and what this indicates is that the brain as a physical organ of sight into the world of concepts is far more advanced that the physical organ of sight the eye. The eye in this respect, although it is a miracle, lags behind the rapid development of the brain in the past 400 yrs or so. There are many reasons for this imbalance, and the two I will mention in this context are the unbridled use of newly acquired powers of abstract, intellectual thought (left-hand hemisphere of the brain) to the detriment of our imaginative abilities, and the unawareness that it is the responsibility of the individual to remedy this imbalance. This is the importance of Goethe for he was fully aware of the need to correct this imbalance of our cognitive abilities. The brain-based Intellect simply cannot perceive **Life** and consequently induces a state of consciousness described as Naïve Realism: the belief that the reality of phenomena is exactly consonant to how they are perceived.

The wholeness and integrity of the world is now perceived as a multiplicity of discreet phenomena due to a shift towards the Abstract and the Intellectual devoid of an Imaginative content., a state of consciousness where the essence, and the qualitative differences, of particular phenomena are over-ruled in favour of a bias towards mere appearance and quantification, thereby inducing a bland and hollowed-out apprehension of the Cosmos. There is no difference for the Intellect upon first glance between an actual rose and an artificial one, and it is certainly the case that, through the skill of the crafter, an artificial rose is indistinguishable from a real one except by rigorous examination. The flaws associated with this one-sided cognitive mode, the Intellect conjoined with Sight, are underscored by the genre of *trompe l'oeil* paintings. Normally this technique is considered as a means of tricking the eye, giving it an almost scurrilous reputation, however in truth this not the case and is another example of how artistic cognition highlights the failure of present empirical assumptions. *Trompe l'oeil* destabilises the notion that things are as they initially appear to be, and although Anglo-Saxon Empiricism has long eschewed such Naïve Realism it has nevertheless lapsed into the mistaken quasi-Kantian belief that there exist metaphysical realms behind phenomena that cannot be directly perceived and known, and which are purported to be populated by atoms etc, in this respect it is no different from any other philosophical approach that considers the existence of such metaphysical realms irrespective of their content (God etc).

There has been no let up in this metaphysical philosophising, except now, although atoms have not been abandoned, the focus is now upon such conceptualisations as 'String Theory', the postulation that various configurations of energy are the ultimate reality of phenomena and the Universe. This has already been discussed, and given that what we perceive always has a given Form, the lack of any explanations as to how these configurations of energy become a particular phenomenon there has resulted an uneasy clinging onto outmoded conceptualisations such as atoms. The stripping of atoms of any qualitative dimension means that an abyss of explanation exists to account for how such lifeless, quality-less atoms and 'strings' can give rise to, not only, the wealth of qualities of the phenomena of which we are aware, but to their very life as well. One response to this conundrum has been Epiphenomenalism the belief that the 'mind' and all our other qualities of being have somehow arisen from atomic matter, the implication of which is to downgrade the human being and, in particular, the Mind to an abstract fantasy. Consequently it is postulated that all the qualities etc are unreal in that they are an illusory response to our sensory impressions conjured up by a Mind that is in itself an illusion as it is only a by-product of matter. The existential crisis precipitated by David Hume's famous declarations "All our distinct perceptions are distinct existences" and "The Mind never perceives any real connections between distinct existences" has only been crudely glossed over through a by-passing of actual perceptions and, instead, concentrating on such postulations as 'string' theory. Apart from the fact that this argument makes its conclusions by assuming that its unproven allegations are correct, somewhat like trying to pick one's self up by grabbing one's hair, it is curious how that which is real, the Mind, is relegated in importance to that which it creates, in this case the ideas of Atoms and Epiphenomenalism etc. Admittedly this is an extreme version of a line of reasoning that proposes that various qualities, such as let us say, 'elasticity' and 'stickiness', arise because the links between molecules/ atoms are able to stretch and have an attractive ability respectively. It is overlooked that in doing this such theorisations are in effect tautological for they ascribe the very qualities they are trying to explain to the molecules/ atoms etc that are theorised in the first place as lacking any of these qualities. No doubt the above is as 'clear as mud' for many readers, however it can be further elucidated through the analogy of driving a car, no-one would reasonably credit learning to drive a car to the car itself. Admittedly learning to drive a car has to take place in conjunction with a car, however driving is a learned ability that I have initiated so as to manipulate an inert lump of matter called a car, and which I retain whether or not the particular car I learnt to drive in remains. If individuals believe that thinking arises from the brain then there has to be an account as to how the presently theorised quality-less material constitution of the brain gives rise to the quality of thinking. It goes without saying that a rock does not 'think' as inert matter, and in all of the inorganic realm the elements that constitute this realm are to be found in the corporeality of a human being - so what has changed so that human beings are able to think. Needless to say this is because the human being has incorporated into themselves the potent *invisible* realms referred to above, such as the **Plane of Thinking**.

The thinking aspect of the Mind cannot be stressed enough for this is common to everyone, artist and scientist alike, and is at the at the centre of our knowledge of the world. However, there is a paradox intrinsic to the nature of thinking, already referred to, that is easily overlooked. As Howard points out this revolves over the status of the subject with respect to thinking, and in this context the most fundamental statement I can make about myself is that *I am here now.* This statement affirms the knowledge that I am *me* and that everything which I am not is the *non-me*, and it is at this point that the paradox is revealed. Thinking as an activity makes an object of everything that enters its sphere before the application of logic and reason by the thinker, this is the only way it can function and there has to be something thought about that can act as the object. When I am thinking then I am the subject doing the thinking, however for thinking purely in itself (the universal act of thinking common to everyone) I am an object, as this is the only way thinking functions, so that when I am thinking I am in the curious position of being both an object and a subject simultaneously. Thus Thinking is both an activity I perform and an activity that encompasses me as an object doing the thinking, and when I realise this as a lived experience it is akin to a fish stepping out of the water it swims in, for then what is taken for granted as ephemeral and ungraspable, as a phenomenon, is now known to be substantial and real. No easy matter. When thinking the *me* and the *non-me* merge into one, for both the subject (me) and the object (my thinking) are one engaged in one and the same activity and this is how things are for our ordinary, everyday consciousness. Thinking, when I think about it, comes into the category of the *non-me* (the object) for it is an activity I perform, and is something other than my ego through which I now myself as a *me*. Consequently thinking has the potential implicit to it to transcend my personal limitations, for in the process of knowing my thinking as something objective to me I then become an object to that which is exterior to myself, my thinking. That is in knowing myself as a self-conscious thinking subject there is implicit in this being known by a Universal Thinking of which my thinking is derivative. To quote Howard

"That is, I as a thinking *subject* must also be objective to a thinking that can grasp me and the world in its objective survey. That cannot be *my* thinking. I cannot say that I thought myself into being as a thinking subject - that is, that I, as a self-conscious thinking being, thought myself into self-conscious existence *before* I could be self-conscious at all - anymore than I can say that I created myself as this particular creature of flesh and blood. It has to be the work of something other than me." (Howard, 1980: 23).

By stating that we have a Sense of Ideas/ Thought and a Sense of Ego, which at present are scarcely recognised as such, Steiner draws attention to that which we take for granted and are oblivious of its true value. No doubt many objections and arguments can be raised concerning what has been stated above, but this does not concern me for a number of reasons. Firstly it is not intellectual arrogance that moves me, for although I may have clumsily expressed my ideas in the face of elegant, abstract postulations that fail to hit the mark, there is nevertheless in my remarks a nugget of pertinence that attempts to address the curious nature of Thinking when it is thought about. Secondly, by themselves logic and rationality can be deployed to prove that black is white and, conversely, that white is black, and these operative modes of Thinking remain unanchored unless tethered to a conceptual object such as 'what is thinking?'. Although I will take this no further, presently, Steiner emphasised the inter-related nature of the Sense of Ideas/ Thought and a Sense of Ego by placing them in the context of our Sense of Language and Sense of Hearing for both language and hearing open the soul to the world and community by enticing the soul out of the, at present, solitary, inner world of thinking.

Individual thinking as an aspect of Universal Thinking, which was in existence prior to an individual's existence, is able to make itself gradually manifest due to the material development of the brain. Just as my ability to drive cannot be made manifest unless I have possession of a car. Although these statements can readily be comprehended intellectually it takes much longer periods of concentration to understand their implications. Most important here it is that our individual, ordinary 'thinking' that knows us an object is indicative of a 'higher' (only in the sense of fuller) THINKING implicit to our individual, ordinary thinking, and because we are *only* able to know thinking associated with a being, then

THINKING likewise can only be associated with BEING. I would imagine that many readers of the arguments presented here will experience the same difficulty that I did when first encountering these arguments and gaining some understanding, namely - how does one conceive of the ontological existence of that which, although, it is real, and an absolutely essential, and a central aspect of our consciousness, is totally *invisible* to everyday consciousness. Traditional images are of little use with respect to this quest for they issue from a consciousness that has long been overtaken by our intellectual abilities, and cannot be accessed except by those who choose to transform their consciousness by long and arduous training, as with Goethe. If the thinking that we all possess makes an object of all that is other than itself in its higher form, including ourselves as temporary wielders of this faculty, then how is it possible to relate this to our lived lives, that is what place does this intellectual analysis of thinking occupy in relation to ourselves as living beings.

This can be approached by returning to the Imaginative Intelligence of childhood, which I stated never leaves us even though it is buried beneath our abstract, intellectual powers. The little understood achievement of Goethe is that he was able to bring a percept to the *invisible* concept 'growth' by consciously re-activating the Imaginative Intelligence of childhood, thereby effecting a transformed perceptual ability, the potential of which lies dormant within our corporeality. To appreciate this achievement we have only to consider the various stages of a plant that follow each other throughout the year that are driven, and linked conceptually, through an invisible process of development and metamorphosis that we name *'growth'*. This is true of all that is living, and Goethe's achievement was that he was able to transcend his immediate involvement with a plant and apprehend this *invisible* process of *growth* that governs a plant's coming-into-being. Through the power of his mind Goethe enacted a fertilisation between the Intellect and the Imagination that *compressed the time of the developmental course of a plant* into a perceptible event in his consciousness, something that I believe Bacon also achieved with respect to the human being and their various emotional states. Bacon through his intense contemplation of a human being *compressed the time of the developmental course of an individual's emotional nature* into a composite image, not just in his mind but as a tangible object.

Preliminary Remarks Showing the Interpretative Relevance of the Above.

Bacon's ability to *compress the time of the developmental course of an individual's emotional nature* is amply demonstrated by the works "Three Studies of the Human Head", 1953, (ill. 6) and "Three Studies of Lucien Freud", 1968-69, (ill. 7). It is immediately apparent that both these triptychs attempt to encapsulate in a single work (it is imperative that Bacon's triptychs are first viewed as a whole and only later as individual canvasses) the emotional states of a person over an extended time-period. The former is an early attempt to express this ability to compress time and evinces a linear quality that Bacon must have realised was at odds with his

38

aims, nevertheless he continued to struggle to express his vision and the later work displays an organic integration lacking in the first work, in this context all of Bacon's portraits, especially the triptychs, are similar attempts to express a simultaneity of emotional configurations by condensing the time differences of expression relevant to the subject of the portrait. The import of this ability is that both Goethe and Bacon were able to overcome the barrier that the episodic nature of our perceptive capacities of ordinary consciousness presents, based as they are upon abstract, intellectual reasoning, for a living realisation of the essence of what they surveyed. With our ordinary consciousness we 'live on the outside' of all that exists, it is as if we have been exiled from the very nature from which we have arisen. As I implied above the fact that we have displaced our responsibility for the search for truth from ourselves to technical instruments, and hypothesised elements in metaphysical realms, merely emphasises the breach with nature that has been brought about by the failure to comprehend the potential of our abstract, intellectual consciousness, and it is for me, fascinating. that Bacon raised similar questions with a remarkable series of paintings based upon x-ray photography, such as the triptych "Three Studies of Figures on Beds", 1972, (ill. 8). Armin Zweite in his book "the Violence of the Real" (Zweite: 174) attributes the circles surrounding the upper torso of the Figures in the three panels to Bacon's interest in x-ray photography via his ownership of Kathleen C. Clarks publication upon this subject. This in turn draws the text back to the whole question of the epistemological value of artistic cognition when there is an integration of the Intellect with the Imagination.

At first glance it may appear to be incongruous to bring postulations concerning **Thinking** to bear upon Bacon's work. However, any doubts are dispelled when those works are reviewed that contain 'newsprint', such as "Figure at a Washbasin", 1976, (ill. 9). Although the significance of the inclusion of 'newsprint' in particular works may indicate that Bacon wished to make the viewer aware of the more detrimental effects of mass-culture, I do not think that this is Bacon's strongest motive for including newsprint, although it does relate to my next comments. The painting "Figure Writing Reflected in a Mirror", 1967, (Ill. 10) unambiguously depicts a figure writing down his thoughts, and given that these two works were created in the same year, it is inescapable that Bacon at the time was intensely interested in the mystery of human thought, for although we take thought for granted it is, nevertheless, miraculous that an individual is able to create their own thoughts. One has only to consider the relative dumbness of the animal kingdom, of which we are a part, if not the vegetative state of the plant kingdom and the mineral kingdom, to realise the marvellous nature of our faculty of thought and speech. The 'speech' of animals is completely incomprehensible for the majority of people, even though their speech serves as a means of communication for particular species, and this fact points to an important conclusion regarding human speech, and that is that words through the development of our intellectual faculties have become abstract in nature. The infinite range of expressive possibilities of human speech is undeniable, but this does not alter the fact that the words we use no longer retain a direct connection with that which is expressed, as is so with animals, the connections are made, especially with the written word, through an intellectual understanding of the relationship between words and meaning. Is this what Bacon was referring to by placing pieces of discarded illegible, 'newsprint' in the work "Figure Writing Reflected in a Mirror", 1967, thereby stressing the expressive inadequacies of words, however, I will take this no further for the moment.

Steiner was well aware of this diminution of the expressive power of words in relation to our capacity for abstraction thinking, and we can gain an insight into this diminution by considering the opening statement of St. John's gospel - In the Beginning was the Word. Despite the fact that there is very little comprehension of such a statement to-day, it does point to a time when there was an understanding of the creative power of the Word. Steiner presented a series of relatively simple exercises designed to bring about a deepened awareness of thinking as an objective reality for the practitioner. At present we are aware of our capacity to think through the Sense of Ideas/ Thought referred to above. Nevertheless this awareness is only at rudimentary stage, and it is unacceptable at present to characterise our thinking as an independent realm, something that can only occur when we have intensified the experience of thinking. In his book "The Philosophy of Freedom" Steiner argued that Thinking, in all its forms, is the principal quality of our consciousness, without which we would not be aware of anything, and which, when grasped by the totality of our being, leads to freedom in the moral sphere. Steiner was well aware of how modern humanity was bewitched and beguiled by the promise that abstract, intellectual thinking could be a means of solving world-problems and a road to ultimate knowledge, and he was also aware that this belief was erroneous due to the fact that abstract, intellectual thinking only utilises a diminished portion of our total being (research into brain activity reveals that only a small part of its total capacity supports our everyday consciousness) and is incapable of giving an account of the qualitative dimension of life. If it is accepted that knowledge of phenomena derives from a joining of a percept and a concept then Howard makes a telling distinction between thinking and observation, in that with observation ('inner' as well as 'outer', and from any of our senses) we cannot prevent observation. That is once we are awake and our senses are fully functioning, then by the sheer fact of having a functioning body we automatically have sensory activity, but 'thinking' is not something we do automatically it is an activity that has to be *willed*. In everyday life we are so familiar with the parallel activities thinking and observation that we do not notice their difference, and this crucial difference highlights a fundamental aspect of our being, and that is we are determined with respect to our corporeality and observation but **free** in our thinking. It makes no difference if I choose to look at one thing or another, the basic ability of the body to sense continues, and any meaning to my situation can only be determined if, and when, I activate my thinking. This argues Howard indicates the unique nature of 'thinking', firstly it is an activity independent of the senses, and secondly it has a dual aspect, in that because we are self-conscious we able to observe that we have the ability to think,

40

and that this 'thinking' provides us with the capacity to ask questions about the essence of 'thinking' itself. This is the only dimension of our being that is able to make an object of its own subjective activity. Our instinctive self-consciousness, which is given by merely having a living body and an ego, is changed when we think about the sensory impressions we receive via the body, and this forms the content of ordinary, everyday consciousness. When we begin to think about the act of 'thinking' we initiate the beginning stages of a higher state of consciousness, in one sense both Goethe and Bacon focussed upon their own capacity for thought and thereby transformed their sensory capabilities.

The two works by Bacon "Figure at a Washbasin" and "Figure Writing Reflected in a Mirror" are clearly concerned with the effect of abstraction upon the human soul, due to the presence of discarded 'newsprint', and the fact that the Figure in "Figure at a Washbasin" appears to be vomiting into the washbasin, or at the very least cleansing itself, thereby indicating that the Figure is ill-at-ease for some reason. One interpretation of the ontological state of this Figure being ill-at-ease through the effects of abstraction, is that abstraction has induced a 'sickness of the soul' in this figure, which is manifested physically. Light is thrown upon this condition through the discourses on angst, alienation etc, a major theme of modernity and post-modernity, which Bacon would have been familiar with, and as such constitutes a major strand of the significance of Bacon's work. These comments are bolstered through the discarded 'newsprint', which, because it is crumpled and illegible, represents the failure of the written word to adequately express the intentions of the Figure. These two works demonstrate Bacon's acute Sense of Language, and through this sensitivity he draws the viewer's attention to the Mind, which because it is *invisible* cannot be depicted directly depicted only inferred, and through this strategy he highlights not just the central role to consciousness of language, but how it can be a force for good or bad right down to the physical level of the body. Although I shall not explore this in detail these two works evoke thoughts of what has been named by Jacques Derrida (1930-2004) as 'The Etiolation of Language', which refers to the manner by which language in modern times is becoming pallid and, to a large extent, vapid. Thus 'etiolation' may be perceived as referring to the breach between a concept and a percept that has been precipitated through our use of words now being founded upon the intellect and abstraction.

Interesting though Derrida's postulations are they only have a tangential critical connection to Bacon's work, in contrast to another theme of post-modernity that has an immediate connection, interpretatively, for Bacon's images, and that is ideas surrounding the issue of Indeterminacy. This is especially so because Gilles Deleuze in his book "Francis Bacon: The Logic of Sensation" (Deleuze, 2002:21) delineates Indeterminacy as interpretatively pertinent by linking it with his concept of 'a zone of indiscernibility, or undecidability', and as such it is, he argues, descriptive of those works by Bacon that depict individuals with animal heads, or features, such as "Study of Nude with Figure in a Mirror", 1969, (ill. 11). This principle also applies to those distorted Figures upon beds where it is not possible to determine their precise gender, such as "Triptych", 1970, (ill. 12). The subtle manner by which Indeterminacy pervades Bacon's imagery is demonstrated by "Portrait of George Dyer in a Mirror", 1968, (ill. 13). In this work Bacon undermines usual assumptions of the reflective properties of a mirror, by questioning the relationship between an individual and their reflection in a mirror. By undermining the mimetic assumptions of a mirror, by placing a question-mark over a mirror's reflective properties, Bacon underlines the uncertainty, or if you like Indeterminacy, of all imitative, naturalistic representation as possessing a one-to-one relationship to the subject. In essence Indeterminacy and Indiscernibility are concerned with those phenomena that fail to conform completely with either side of a Polarity, and a popularly used example to illustrate Indeterminacy is that of the zombie: is it alive or is it dead? Deleuze makes this principle specific by relating it to Bacon's imagery through the concepts of man and animal. There is no doubt that there is an absolute condition of death even if occasionally diagnosis is not clear cut, and by extending this argument it becomes clear that we use words with our abstract, intelligence to *point* to concepts, even if we cannot fully apprehend the concept pointed to by the word. Above I stated that there has occurred through the abstract, intellectual base of our thinking consciousness a breach between the concept and the percept, that is our abstract, intellectual powers have initiated a process of divorcing us from a living, immersion in, and interaction with, Nature that was the unknowing possession of our ancestors. In this state of consciousness the word, or a word, still had a living and vital presence in relation to the concept referred to, the development of our abstract, intellectual abilities has denuded language of its higher functionality, thereby reducing it to its mere phonetic and symbolic values. This is one consequence of the Fall, and is indicted by the statement that henceforth humanity will know only of the Tree of Good and Evil and not the Tree of Life. The Fall is indicated as being interpretatively apposite for an understanding of the significance of Bacon's *oeuvre* by Deleuze, (Deleuze, 2002:23). Bacon asks us to consider the question of the nature of Good and Evil in left-hand and right-hand panels of the triptych "Crucifixion", 1965, (ill. 14), where it can be seen that the presumably male, distorted figure is wearing an armband. There are complexities and depths to this work that defy simplistic assumptions, for instance is this a work that examines the consequences of the Fall (the left-hand panel has a female figure walking away from the figure on the bed) in relation to the event of the Christ. If this is so then the traditional narrative of assigning guilt to the feminine is de-railed, Bacon in this work points to the conundrums raised for the abstract and intellectual mind concerning a precise understanding of what is Good and what is Evil. This is a question that has vexed even the highest Initiates in their attempts to communicate on this question, and it is only Steiner, in the modern era, who was able to express ideas that make any sense of this question for the abstract, intellectual consciousness of modern humanity. To give an example that is pertinent to the above work - to say that in one context Good is Evil and vice-versa is almost incomprehensible - for how can the unimaginably, horrible events of Nazi Germany ever be considered Good?

In the world of Nature there are always hybrid, or indeterminate states, as phenomena come-into-being through a metamorphosis from one state to another and this is effected through an Intensification of Polarities, from this point of view a zombie is an artificial, imaginary, intensified resolution of the dichotomy between life and death. "Two Studies of George Dyer and Isabel Rawsthorne ", 1970, (ill. 15), illustrates both the principles of Intensification and Indeterminacy, through the brilliance of Bacon's technical skills. Distortion is deployed in this work to give the impression that the panels are in the process of 'leaking' into each other, thereby challenging everyday assumptions of the rigidity of borderlines between the Self and the Other. Instead we given the impression that these borderlines are fluid and mutable. As these borderlines are mental constructs this leads me to conclude, and is strengthened by my commentary upon "Figure at a Washbasin" and "Figure Writing Reflected in a Mirror", that a central element regarding the meaning of Bacon's images is that of the Mind, primarily the role it plays in the consciousness of everyday life, especially the repercussions of when it malfunctions. The evidence for this assertion is that the Figures of Bacon's work are, in the main, situated in dimensionless spaces and rooms, as for example with "Triptych - Studies of the Human Body", 1970, (ill. 16) and "Seated Figure", 1961, (ill. 17) respectively. (see chapter 6, "Between four Walls", of John Russell's book "Francis Bacon"). I have already provided an example of the malfunctioning of the Mind with the identification of a state of a 'Sickness of the Soul' as being interpretatively relevant to Bacon's *oeuvre,* and other examples equally relevant are Narcissism and Delirium. Perhaps less vividly we could define these conditions as being self-absorption and a state of heightened nervous tension, and if they are so characterised then we find a multitude of Figures in Bacon's work that conform to such traits, as for instance with "Study for a Portrait", 1977, (ill. 18) and "Two Studies for a Portrait of George Dyer", 1968, (ill. 19) respectively.

In contrast to the relative translucence of the thinking realm for our knowing, the emotional realm has a turbidity and opacity that denies thorough understanding. However an important distinction has to be made when considering our emotions between the nature of desires and yearning in contrast to our instinctual nature. Certainly an instinct as a drive can become a desire that is all-consuming, as with gluttony and sexuality. It is our inability to cope with the utter relentless force of the instincts, especially the reproductive drive, that leads to the ruination of dignity and self-respect for many individuals, and Bacon was fascinated by this fact. Bacon's work is fundamentally concerned with emotional states and Bacon illustrates the unabating, in some cases, certainly incessant overall, nature of the need for the release of sexual tension that demolishes all restraint with those works that depict entangled, garbled Figures on beds, such as the central panel of "Triptych - Studies from the Human Body", 1970, (ill. 20), and other instincts, such as the need for food and drink, with "Man eating a Leg of Chicken", 1952, (ill. 21) and "Man Drinking", 1955, (ill. 22).

The over-riding impression that we have in our ordinary consciousness is that the self-sentient I is somehow within the materiality of the corporeal body, this belief, however, is belied by our being unable to locate a precise organ, or body part, to substantiate this assumption. If one considers, as an example, the act of thinking characteristic of the self-sentient I, and assume that thinking is produced by the brain then this is much like thinking that my ability to drive a car is produced by the car itself. This is the error of believing an ability is produced by that upon which it is focussed, in other words, despite the fact that it cannot be denied that without a brain I cannot think, just as without a body I cannot be an I in this dimension, what exactly is the relationship between the brain and thinking?. The process of evolution has reached the point where consciousness has been drawn into a fuller association with the information derived from the corporeal base of our sensory abilities. Collectively we have, so to speak, been 'sucked' into an intimate correspondence with the ability to sense, meaning that the act of sensing is now immediate, and that we now have a one-to-one relationship with the material base of our sensory organs. One effect of esoteric training is to 'draw' an individual away from immediate responses, or learned behavioural patterns, to sensory stimulation, and so it may be argued that having secured a foothold in the world of thinking, we are embarking upon a similar venture into the world of emotions and feelings. One primary mood of Bacon's oeuvre is that of forlornness, perhaps tinged with melancholia, as if the Figures sense their own fallen-ness and loss of something valuable; their failure to live-up to their better 'selves' marks them as fallen creatures in the grip of hopelessness. But Bacon was never didactic or judgemental in his work and adhered to his stated aim which was to avoid story-telling, that is he was determined to eschew any narrative element to his images, and this applies above all to his triptychs. I would propose that Bacon's strong Sense of Language meant that he was fully consciousness of the deadening effect upon consciousness of our abstract, intellectual language, especially as the written word, and so strove to make the Language of the Imagination explicit in his work. The manner by which Bacon executed his work gives it a strong palpable, almost tangible, affect upon the viewer, and there is no doubt that he intended this, for as he stated he wished to 'unlock areas of sensation'.

What this BEING is associated with THINKING, referred to above, cannot be ascertained at this point, but it does imply that there is being associated with thinking that is other than ourselves, and this implication has a definite relevance to Bacon's work. In the first place through his extraordinary portraits of George Dyer. "Two Studies for a Portrait of George Dyer",1968, (ill. 19), immediately engages our curiosity for it is stated that there are *two* studies of Dyer in the work, and in view of the construction of the work these two studies can only be the two Figures depicted. But what is the Figure depicted in the black oblong? Is it a mirror-image? Is it another rendering of Dyer? Are the two depictions even related in time? Is the Figure in the black oblong how Dyer appeared to Bacon in the past or the present? What cannot be doubted is that the Figure in the black oblong has a ghastly, demonic appearance, and seems to be haranguing a terrified and distraught Dyer at the end of his tether. As far as I am concerned it cannot be simply 'glossed over'

44

that Bacon made definitive comments concerning the actual existence of the Furies, and that he painted unearthly, distorted beings, for that is what the Furies are arising as they do from the consequences of our actions, and are not merely figurative as Peppiatt sheepishly admits in the case of Bacon. Given Bacon's declaration concerning "The Furies" could Bacon have perceived a similar entity pursuing Dyer? Whatever it is that Bacon has depicted he has endowed it with elements of volition. Furthermore this work, because of its spatial and time ambiguities, hints that Bacon possessed an enhanced a level of consciousness which is at ease with such ambiguities. This will be further explored below in relation to Bacon's work. Another work that suggests the presence of extra-dimensional beings is "Triptych May-June", 1973, (ill. 23). This triptych which depicts the moment of Dyer's death in Paris, in 1971, is a cryptic work for it raises the question as to what is *real* and what is *imaginary.* Bacon was not present at the time of Dyer's death, (Peppiatt, 1996: 235), so although this work was created after the event are we to assume this was a totally imaginary reconstruction or did Bacon have some sort of visionary access to these events. Absurd as this will sound to many readers there are some anomalous features to this triptych. If we focus upon the central panel then there is painted a shadow emanating from Dyer that bears virtually no relation to what we would expect of a shadow thrown from the Figure in the panel. There is a light-bulb drawn to the upper-right of Dyer, but is it on or off? In addition even if the light-bulb were turned-on the 'shadow' falls in the opposite direction of a shadow thrown by a light-bulb in that position. For the shadow to conform to expectations it would have to be placed behind Dyer to the upper-left of Dyer. If we now turn the central panel upside-down then this shadow-shape is shown to have the attributes of a traditionally conceived demonic entity - horns and bat-like wings - and when considered in conjunction with "Two Studies for a Portrait of George Dyer",1968, (ill. 19), the conclusion to be arrived at is the distinct possibility that Bacon perceived spectral, wraith-like hostile entities accosting a beleaguered Dyer.

The question of what Bacon perceived is obviously unanswerable, as it is with regard to anyone else. Nevertheless through the manner by which he constructed his images clues are given as to the nature of his perceptions. Bacon stands in a long line of artists from the Renaissance onward that chose to focus exclusively upon depicting the Human Body. The rapid development of intellectuality at the time of the Renaissance was accompanied by an acute, objective insight into the composition of the material world, and so we see, starting from Giotto (1267-1337), attempts to depict the Human Body realistically as an earthly being. By the time of the close of the 19th century an anatomical knowledge of the human being was largely complete, even if it had a mechanistic bias, and from this time onward artists strove to delve deeper into the mystery of the human being from perspectives other than the corporeal. Marcel Duchamp's, (1887-1968), " Nude Descending the Staircase, No. 2", 1912, (ill. 24), which transcends its Cubist and Futuristic references is a good example of this new approach, where Duchamp attempted to depict not just the movement of the body *in toto* (compression of time), but attempted to integrate the *spatial changes* as the figure moves down the stairs into the depiction of the figure itself. Bacon also attempted to integrate a series of movements into one image, as is shown with the works "Figure Turning", 1962, (ill. 25), "Figure Turning", 1962, (ill. 26), "Turning Figure", 1962, (ill. 27), "Turning Figure" , 1963, (ill. 28). Bacon in addition to this also attempted to *compress the emotional disposition relevant to this compression of movement* into the construction of the Figure. All of this indicates that Bacon was attempting to express something very different from any other artist, he was in effect attempting to express in a composite picture the fluctuations of feelings pertinent to an individual situated in a particular space. In other words he was attempting to make *visible* the *invisibility* of emotions. The question of the exact nature of the emotional impact of Bacon's images is controversial, to say the least, and some commonly made observations revolve around issues concerning violence and sexuality.

Gilles Deleuze tackles the issue of a graphic representation of violence head-on right at the start of his book "Francis Bacon: The Logic of Sensation",

"Francis Bacon's painting is of a very special violence. Bacon, to be sure, often traffics in the violence of a depicted scene: spectacles of horror, crucifixions, prostheses and mutilations, monsters. But these are overly facile detours, detours that the artist himself judges severely and condemns in his work. What directly interests him is a violence that is involved only with color and line: the violence of a sensation (and not of a representation) … When Bacon distinguishes between two violence's, that of the spectacle and that of the sensation, and declares that the first must be renounced to reach the second, it is a kind of declaration of faith in life." (Deleuze, 2004: x).

This insight by Deleuze based upon Bacon's own admission to avoid any narrative element in his work, brings us to the hub of any meaning that may be attributed to Bacon's images for Bacon's interest is not with the particularity of instances of 'violence', or 'horror', or even 'sexuality' but with those forces, those 'sensations' that are bound up with such situations. Of course it cannot be ignored that these 'sensations' have a particularity, but in the process of reaching these 'invisible' forces Bacon had to resort to a complete pictorial re-evaluation of what it means to depict the human figure. Otherwise one collapses into the narrative and 'story-telling'; that is one starts to read in sequences of cause and effect in the works that relate to events as they occur in everyday life. If Bacon had allowed this to happen we could then accuse him of 'sensationalism', but he did not and strived on every level to prevent this from transpiring.

Deleuze explains this distinction between the 'spectacle' and the 'sensation' as a difference between the figural and the 'Figure', where the figural refers to the attempt to create an isomorphic copy of a human being through a tried and tested formula of pictorial codes - the mimetic - and is that which appears 'realistic' to our ordinary vision, and where, in contrast, the 'Figure' is a dismantling of these codes, after which there is a re-assembling, so as to create that which is analogous to a more profound expression of the reality of a human being pictorially - the 'Figure'. The purpose of which, for Bacon, was to lay bare, to make palpable and tangible, the invisible but all-powerful range of emotions a person is capable of experiencing. As Deleuze reminds us this attempt to make visible the invisible had been a concern of painting from the mid 19th. Century up until the present, for instance with Cézanne, Van Gogh, and Kandinsky. With the artists, including Blake, so far mentioned this desire was an unquenchable thirst that could not be relinquished until some success was achieved, regardless of whatever form it took. Paul Brunton echoes Deleuze's sentiments when he states of the visual arts that,

"When they fulfil their highest mission, painting and sculpture try to make visible the invisible, unimaginable mystery of pure Spirit." (Brunton, 1987: 21)

This is not to say that human distress is irrelevant to Bacon's intentions for what is the significance of the mouth? As Bacon puts it, and this is true anyway, the mouth and how it changes shape reflects a person's inner state of being and Bacon was particularly sensitive to this. So for Bacon the mouth was a visible doorway that could be investigated so as to gain insights into that which is invisible - the emotional state of the person viewed – if you like their soul. Bacon confirmed this in an unedited extract from a film that no longer exists shot in Wheeler's restaurant in 1958 when in conversation with Daniel Farson he stated

"…there was a very interesting thing that Valery said … that modern artists want the grin without the cat and by that he meant that they want the sensation of life without the boredom of its conveyance … how can I draw one more veil away from life and present what is called the living sensation more nearly on the nervous system…". (Farson: 115-117).

These comments on the mouth need to be further investigated in the light of Bacon's statements concerning this subject. If an artist's comments are to be taken seriously, and there is no reason not to do so in this case, for what stands out in Bacon's conversations is a consistency and candour over a long career that lacks any pomposity, self-aggrandisement and, importantly, artifice, then one is obliged to look to other factors for the appearance and affect of his work. This is particularly true when it is almost implied that Bacon had a morbid interest in 'violence', and so can we really naively assume that the famous open mouth that is a salient feature of his early period is purely a terrified figure screaming and nothing else? When questioned on this subject Bacon had the following to say

F.B. "…I did hope to make the best painting of the human cry. I was not able to do it … I think probably the best human cry in painting was made by Poussin … a second-hand book which had beautiful hand-coloured plates of diseases of the mouth; and they fascinated me …"

47

D.S. "The open mouths – are they always meant to be a scream."

F.B. "Most but not all. You know how the mouth changes shape. I've always been very moved by the movements of the mouth and the shape of the mouth and teeth…"

D.S. "So you might well have been interested in painting open mouths and teeth even if you hadn't been painting the scream?"

F.B. "I think I might. And I've always wanted and never succeeded in painting the smile."

Similarly when asked about the violence and horror that is associated with his images Bacon had the following to say:

D.S. "It seems to be quite widely felt of the paintings of men alone in rooms that there's a sense of claustrophobia and unease about them that's rather horrific. Are you aware of that unease?"

F.B. "I'm not aware of it. But most of the pictures were done of somebody that was always in a state of unease, and whether that has been conveyed through these pictures I don't know. But I suppose, in attempting to trap this image, that, as this man was very neurotic and almost hysterical, this may possibly have come across in the paintings. I've always hoped to put over things as directly and rawly as I possibly can, and perhaps if a thing comes across directly, people feel that that is horrific. Because, if you say something very directly to somebody, they're sometimes offended, although it is a fact. Because people tend to be offended by facts, or what used to be called the truth." (Sylvester, 1987: 34-35, 48-50)

It is clear that aspects of Bacon's personality have the propensity for engendering accusations of 'bad taste' and morbidity. His fascination with diseases of the mouth is certainly outside what most people would describe as 'healthy', and the same is true of his fascination with blood (he posed a number of times with sides of beef hanging from butcher's hooks in the background) and his interest in physically deformed children. There can be no argument over this, but the important point is that he transcended these aspects of his personality, gruesome and macabre as they are, so as to investigate their deeper significance. I have no intention of writing an apologia for Bacon in this respect. For instance his interest in the mouth was transformed in his work from a focus upon distortions of the shape of the mouth alone into an investigation of the causes of such distortions. With the works "Head I", 1948, (ill. 29) and "Head II", 1949, (ill. 30), which plainly depict distorted mouths within misshapen heads, we have images of individual torment caused by mental anguish. Because the Figure has clothing redolent of clerical garb we are lead to conclude that Bacon is challenging the assumption that any form of Religion offers any protection from terrors of the soul afflicting modern humanity.

48

Similarly his fascination with blood was transformed into issues concerning the Ego, and his interest in physically deformed children into an examination of how locomotion is affected by extreme distress, and by focussing upon locomotion in this manner Bacon makes us aware of the importance of our Sense of Movement and Sense of Balance, as referred to above. Works that display how our Sense of Movement and Sense of Balance work in harmony are "Portrait of George Dyer Riding a Bicycle", 1966, (ill. 31) and "Three Studies from the Human Body", 1967, (ill. 32).

Sundry Topics and Comments.

Number from the perspective of Sacred Geometry has a creative, qualitative function as opposed to its purely utilitarian value for the calculation of operations within a material context, and this factor points to an important aspect of Art History, that of Iconography. A vast subject but I will refer to one of the seminal individuals within this field - Erwin Panofsky (1892-1968). When considering a work of art Panofsky contended that the historical environment within which the work was produced could not be ignored , and that understanding this historical environment was essential if one was to define the significance of a particular work in the broadest of terms. However, this cluster of cultural and social factors had a dual functionality for Panofsky in that at a deeper level the artist could do no other than express the historical environment in their work, albeit through their particular individuality

"It is apprehended by ascertaining those underlying principles which reveal the basic attitude of a nation, a period, a class, a religious or philosophical persuasion - qualified by one personality and condensed into one work."

This assertion by Panofsky is immediately related to the concept of 'Intentionality' with regard to the motives for production. In the case of Bacon he stated that he wanted to 'unlock the valves of sensation' in the viewer, and he certainly achieved this for even after the passage of many years his work still has the power to shock and disturb, meaning that it has retained a strong affective power, thereby indicating that the work touches upon something fundamental to the human psyche. From another direction if we consider the 'angst' of the modern age from the late 19th century until today, which could be described as a disturbance of the soul due to social effects industrialisation etc, then there is definitely an exploration of this by Bacon in his work as will be shown later. The question of Intentionality becomes more complex when we consider Symbolism, which is undoubtedly tied up with Iconography, and leads directly to Esotericism. Below in my examination of Bacon's work based upon Van Gogh the power of Symbols that have a powerful psychological significance, accrued over centuries, comes to the forefront. The power of Symbols cannot be attributed to the conscious mind alone, and there is one simple reason for this and that is they cannot be fully comprehended by the abstract, intellectual dimension of our thinking. This was not a problem pre-

Renaissance as humanity, in general, thought in pictures, and despite the fact of the tremendous achievements of Classical Greece with regard to thinking logically and rationally this was not a wide-spread ability in humanity. These achievements only came to fruition with the dawning of the Renaissance, thus, for me, there is a problem with Iconographical studies for they stop short at the intellectual, rather than probing the system of thought, which deploys a different aspect of our psychic abilities than the intellectual, and which in turn gave rise to the import and significance of these Symbols. What I am implying is that the implication of Iconography/ Symbolism studies with respect to the meaning of a particular work of art eludes intellectual examination alone.

The genius of Goethe, who was a supreme artist, and familiar with the theoretical underpinning of such abstract, intellectual empirical methodologies as Isaac Newton's, (1643-1727), Theory of Colour intuited this fact and was determined to present a different methodology for his Theory of Colour that overcame the bias towards the abstract and intellectual, that is he determined to make both the Intellectual and Imaginative dimensions of his being co-partners in the quest for knowledge. As stated Bacon is fellow traveller of Goethe even if he took a different path. In this context there will be explored in this text the understanding that the Mind has not always been exclusively focussed upon the brain, but that the Mind is able to utilise differing aspects of our corporeality for the purpose of knowing the world, as is demonstrated by infancy and early childhood. From this perspective the body is that which provides the means for the Mind to become manifest, and that by studying our developmental path from infancy to adulthood an insight is gained into the development of humanities consciousness from time's immemorial past up to the present day. By *compressing the developmental time of a plant* into a single imaginable, conscious event, Goethe points to an important maxim which is that the Arts, ideally, draw the future into the ambit of our consciousness, whereas the present state of Empiricism refers to the past, such as the utilisation of the Ancient Greek concept of the Atom. Because the meaning of the original context of this concept was misunderstood it received, during the 19th century, a definition which was in itself materialistic, and is thus reactionary. For Blake who, similar to Wordsworth, was able to recollect incidents from his infancy, I have found no indications that they adopted anything approaching Goethe's methodology, rather they appear to have been endowed at birth with the ability to have access to the 'forgotten self' referred to above. Bacon, as I will demonstrate, combined a natural ability to access the 'forgotten self' of childhood with a quasi-Goethean methodology. For me it is a tragic fact for Epistemology that Goethe's methodology, together with his other ideas, have been overshadowed by a rampant, biased Empiricism, and are largely forgotten and ignored.

The above has outlined the rudiments of my methodology for an interpretation of Bacon's *oeuvre*, and as such will be expanded upon in the various parts below. Because Projective Geometry provides a formal explanation of the *modus operandi* of the *invisible* realms concerned here, then an objective bench-mark, albeit descriptive, is provided by which to assess my conjectures concerning the significance of Bacon's work. Thus the invisible, emotional dimension of the Soul, the workings of which fascinated Bacon, is brought, through mathematical thinking, into the ambit of personal understanding. Although this not an actual perception of this realm it is, nevertheless, a means by which an individual can familiarise themselves with the realm in question. In one sense, and for the purposes of this text, Initiation involves actively fertilising the interaction of the two hemispheres of the brain related to the Imagination and the Intellect, through various meditative exercises. When this is achieved the Mind's sensory capacity is expanded, exponentially, through a transformation of those configurations within the etheric body that give rise to the physical, sensory organs of the corporeal body. Is there any 'scientific' evidence that there is a factual basis for an individual's claim to possess extraordinary powers? In answer to this question I will refer to Dean Radin, Ph.D., a highly respected figure within American academia, who has spent a life-time researching paranormal abilities displayed by individuals, ("The Conscious Universe: The Scientific Truth of Psychic Phenomena"). By conducting a thorough investigation into experiments designed to test for the evidence of psychic abilities in individuals, he has demonstrated by using the latest statistical models, that although it is undeniable that humanity, as a whole, possesses psychic capacities it is not possible to prove that a particular individual is in possession of such powers, or in some cases is even aware they possess them. Whilst this is not an earth-shattering conclusion it does imply that there is a realistic foundation for an enquiry into humanities psychic powers, and for seriously considering the statements by those individuals who do claim to have such powers. Although much more could be said on this subject that would indicate that it is the intransigence of the scientific community, in general, as an authoritative body that prevents further progress this is not my concern, rather I am interested in the interpretative possibilities of the theorists I have chosen as a means of unravelling the significance of Bacon's images.

The question inevitably arises as to the nature of what Bacon perceived: were they genuine visions that revealed essential aspects of the human being, or were they hallucinations engendered by pathological states of mind? There is no evidence that I have found that Bacon suffered from any of the mental illnesses that give rise to hallucinatory states of mind, quite the opposite for he appears to have been as well-adjusted to modern society, as anyone can be, and was able to effectively manage his career as a successful artist. The distinction here is that hallucinations, in general, are caused by the projection of images lying in the unconscious into the imaginative aspect of the Mind, due to severe mental distress. If, therefore, Bacon had extraordinary perceptual abilities that revealed dimensions of reality hidden from ordinary consciousness then this in itself raises a number of important points. Firstly, when discussing the evolution of human consciousness, in general terms, Rudolf Steiner stated that it was now the case that humanity was in the process of 'crossing the threshold'. This is a complex subject. However, one crucial aspect is that since approximately the middle of the 19th century humanity, as a whole, is in the process of becoming aware of the spiritual worlds into which we are inextricably inter-related, however for the majority of people this is a totally unconscious event. Sergei O. Prokofiev states on this subject the following

"Now, the problem of the Threshold is connected with something that has even greater significance, and that is in fact true for all human beings. According to Rudolf Steiner's spirit-research around the middle of the nineteenth century humanity unconsciously crossed over the Threshold of the spiritual world. He even names a precise point in time for this - the years from 1842 to 1879." (Prokofiev, 2012: 31).

If this is the case then it is entirely possible that Bacon was born with a propensity to be able to perceive the dimensions of phenomena denied to ordinary consciousness, and that he honed this gift through intense concentration upon his subject-matter (to be discussed below). Going hand-in-hand with this possibility is the fact that Bacon, by his own admission, received very little formal, intellectual schooling until his late twenties:

"I think the analytical side of my brain did not develop until comparatively late - till I was twenty-seven or twenty-eight." (Sylvester, 1987: 71).

This would mean, returning to Bortoft, that Bacon retained the capacities of the imaginative, receptive mode of our early years well into adulthood, and provides an evidential support for my contention that the 'forgotten self' of childhood, which pervades Bacon's imagery, cannot be ignored as an important interpretative tool. As Rudolf Treichler puts it in his book "Soulways: Development. Crises and illnesses of the soul"

"Childhood powers that have been retained and transformed give the adult an independent creative mind" (Treichler, 1996: 110).

The next point to be considered is the calibre of Bacon's abilities, and on this point only the briefest of references can be made at present. When considering the relationship of the invisible realms of the ether body, astral body and thinking with the corporeal body it has to be said that this is a truly complex subject upon which only general references can be made here. To start with both the ether body and the astral body have a multi-dimensional character to, not only themselves, but to the corporeal body, that is the ether body and the astral body can metamorphose into differing modes depending upon the circumstances, for instance the formative forces of the etheric world have four principle manifestations, that of warmth ether, light ether, chemical/ sound ether and life ether. In their work of building up the corporeal body each of these realms has a principal basis in the physical body, hence thinking focuses upon the brain, the astral body upon the kidneys and the etheric body upon the liver. Whilst this is only a general distinction and has only a tangential interpretative value for understanding Bacon's images it is, nevertheless, important. Its importance relates to those images by Bacon that have as their theme what can only be described as an evisceration of our corporeality, for instance both "Painting", 1946, (ill. 33) and "Triptych Inspired by the Oresteia of Aeschylus", 1981, (ill. 34) are images that display a turning inside-out of the physical body, and both these works have a highly-charged emotional atmosphere. It is not possible to state that any particular organs of the body are referred to in these images only that the emotional atmosphere is depicted as having a vital relationship to the inner working of the human body, that is the emotional atmosphere is depicted as being something more that a surface phenomenon (turning white with fear, red with rage). This demonstrates both the depth and limitations of Bacon's psychic abilities, considerable though they were with regard to those of the general population.

The purpose of this *critique* is, principally, to expand the interpretative landscape within which the significance of Bacon's *oeuvre* is evaluated, and through this to rehabilitate the epistemological value of aesthetic cognition. The many books that I have read, and consulted, regarding Bacon's work have been both illuminating and frustrating, and have only provided a partial insight into the ramifications of Bacon's images. This is not to say that I believe my text to be complete or superior, this cannot be so for there is no end-point with regard to the significance and interpretative value of an artist's work, and if any end-point is regarded as definitive then this only reveals the bias and limitation of a particular group. A salient feature of the existing texts, regarding Bacon's work, is that the authors only select those works which are in harmony with the flow of their text, and interpretative trajectory, and ignore, or only briefly mention, unconvincingly, those which are not. The implication of this is that Bacon had brief lapses from the motivations for creativity those authors have identified, that is he had an unclear understanding of his own creative impulses and occasionally drifted into incongruous creativity. This I do not believe is the case, after his success in the 1940's Bacon's work displays an intentional drive that never wavered from his chosen subject the psychic well-being, or otherwise, of modern-day humanity with respect to the inseparably, intimate integration of the individual and the social context, from the perspective of their own state of soul.

The complexity of Bacon's apparently simple images (rooms with Figures and a limited range of objects, chairs, mirrors etc), presents a challenge for anyone attempting to read his work. Problems arise when authors find that discourses arising purely from a social context prove to be inadequate, or have a weak interpretative force when applied to Bacon's images, and the reason for this is that these authors have reached the point, through their reasoning, that can only be addressed as the Spiritual. This an interpretative obstacle for the only, if now widely discredited within the Anglo-Saxon world, and in sharp decline as a social force, spiritual programme that has an official sanction in this area is the Church, and dogma is of no use here as Bacon ably demonstrated with his images of the Pope from the early 1950's, a prominent example being "Study after Velazquez's

Portrait of Pope Innocent X", 1953, where we perceive a defenceless, terrified Pope petrified by either witnessing some ghastly scene or experiencing excruciating inner pain, perhaps both, despite his being the head of the Catholic Church. If one desires to approach the spiritual from any other direction then one's options are severely limited by the obscurity, and intractability, of the majority of alchemical and occult doctrines, they simply have no appeal for modern-day thinking. Apart from this they have no resources that could be utilised for a sustained, rational *critique* as is attempted here. The value of Steiner is not just that he elucidates the thinking that gave rise to the vast range of occult documentation (alchemical or otherwise) in existence, a mode of consciousness that has now been transformed into our present abstract, intellectual abilities, but further than this he has presented a paradigm of the human being that accounts for the vital roles played by, and interaction of, the spiritual and the material in the genesis of our being. It does not matter how outlandish an artist's assertions appear to either the author interpreting the work, or the viewer, there is an obligation to at least investigate the claims, and at least Preppiatt was honest in this respect. A researcher would have no difficulty unearthing a multitude of references to unearthly beings both demonic and heavenly within occult and arcane literature, but of what interpretative value are they if they cannot be evaluated by something other than hearsay, and lacking an interpretative context that accounts for the totality of Bacon's *oeuvre*. At least Steiner places his allegations within a framework that can be followed logically, admittedly this is no guarantee of the veracity of any claims, but it does go some way in eliminating any capriciousness. What is presented here is a barebones description from which it is possible to progress to a fuller understanding of those invisible realms, which although imperceptible to ordinary vision, are absolutely essential to our being, and which crucially provide an insight into Bacon's *oeuvre*.

Rudolf Steiner's work now means that there is a scientific approach to the spiritual that is based upon clear and precise empirical observations of such invisible, but absolutely essential, dimensions of our being such as growth, emotions and thinking that avoids all the obscurity and obfuscation of traditional occult texts, and the fantasy and sensationalism of popular culture. This means that any open-minded person can examine Steiner's ideas in freedom, for there is no compulsion or pressure to have any particular beliefs, or pre-conceived notions, in order to do this. The various ideas by Steiner touched upon in this Introduction will be further expanded upon during the course of this text, in conjunction with a demonstration of how they relate to ordinarily known phenomena. When having recourse to the principles of Projective Geometry for explanatory purposes it is the fact that these can be shown to have an integrated, rather than ad hoc, relationship to Bacon's work that proves most telling. For instance the triptych "Three Studies for a Crucifixion", 1962, (ill. 35) clearly evinces the processes of contraction and expansion, with left panel displaying contraction, through the slabs of meat pointing to the Figures, and right panel referring to expansion, through its ring of bones, whereas the central panel has a clear relationship to intensification. These are three basic principles of Projective Geometry, and the fact that Steiner stated that Projective Geometry describes the *modus operandi* of all invisible forces, in the first instance those of growth, means that there is an objective, scientific basis for an intense exploration of soul conditions and psychological conditions with respect to Bacon's *oeuvre*. As a final point for this Introduction I would like to emphasise that there is no bias towards either the spirit, the soul or the body in terms of their importance, for they constitute an integrated whole, and neither is there a bias towards the spirit, soul and body in relation to a social context, again they are an integrated whole, and one cannot be considered without the other, as will be made plain.

Chapter 1. The Prodigal Son.

After his initial success Bacon created a visual record of a remarkable spiritual/ psychological journey that he undertook, an understanding of which is essential in determining the significance of his work. This journey had the effect of freeing Bacon from specific psychic and sociological dilemmas. The nub of this journey revolves around the question of Authority, both in the sense of the Father and the weight of a cultural inheritance within which one wishes to make one's Name. It is remarkable because it is the only record that I am aware of that illustrates a fundamental component of spiritual development widely-known, culturally, as the story of the Prodigal Son. Although the central theme of this story concerns the relationship between Father and Son enacted through a process of rebellion and reconciliation, there is another dimension that Bacon makes explicit, and that is the weight of a cultural heritage upon the aspirations of an artist yet to make his Name. Bacon's disastrous relationship with an abusive father and liaisons with older men during the 1930's and 40's are sufficiently well-known as to require no further comment (see Peppiatt), It is less well-known the role that Roy de Maistre played as a mentor to Bacon during this period.

When Roy de Maistre (1894-1968) arrived in London in 1930 he already had an international reputation and met with some success in London. He was also from a family of high social standing and curiously enough his father was also a racehorse trainer (so was Bacon's see Peppiatt). Although he had a somewhat troubled relationship with his family he had close links with his mother and he, like Bacon, appreciated the benefits of social standing and connections. De Maistre was also an homosexual. By 1936 when he met Patrick White de Maistre had already met Bacon with whom he exhibited and most likely shared a studio. White himself was an homosexual but insisted that he and de Maistre were not lovers but firm friends, and I think that White's summation of his relationship with de Maistre is equally applicable to de Maistre's relationship to Bacon: "He became what I needed most, an intellectual and aesthetic mentor". Given his reputation de Maistre's circle included such persons as Graham Sutherland, Henry Moore and the aforementioned Patrick White, and there can be little doubt that Bacon benefited from contact with these fellow artists. Rudolf Steiner has commented extensively upon Joseph de Maistre, 1753-1821, (who was a Savoyard philosopher, writer, lawyer, and diplomat, and whom defended hierarchical societies and a monarchical State in the period immediately following the French Revolution), from whom Roy de Maistre claimed he was descended. Roy de Maistre made many references to Joseph de Maistre, and Joseph de Maistre inflammatory writing-style has been seen by some as the source of apocalyptic visions etc of society and humanity deemed by others to be a feature of Bacon's images. Nothing could be further from the truth Joseph de Maistre was a highly cultured figure at the time of the French Revolution who was a highly influential reactionary. His desire was to see France basically returned to the authority of the Catholic Church, and in many ways abhorred the egalitarian principles of the revolution. Certainly he used inflammatory language, but was no different in this respect from other writers of his day, and it stretches credence that Bacon, an highly intelligent and savvy man, would have been swayed by such rhetoric. No Bacon's vision is exclusively his own and his manner of depicting it unique, which is why he made the impact he eventually achieved. Perhaps the most lasting influence of Joseph de Maistre was to reinforce both Roy de Maistre's and Bacon's own sense of innate conservatism.

It is perhaps the difficulties that he began to encounter in his relationships with older men, compounded by the fact that he was growing older, that precipitated in Bacon a remarkable spiritual journey that is documented through his images. He found the space to do this both socially and spiritually through his meteoric success during the 1940's, which gave him sufficient funds and reputation to wean himself of his prior behaviour. The reasoning for me stating that Bacon had a protracted struggle integrating the Father into his psyche is based primarily upon the world-renowned 'Pope' series of the 1950's. One reason why these works had such an impact is that the integration of the Father into an individual's psyche is of vital importance to both sexes and as such may be viewed as an archetypal mental process of humanity. However, there is a definite prologue, in the latter part of the 1940's and early 1950's, before a particular theme gathers force in Bacon's work. "Painting", 1946, (ill. 33) and "Figure in a Landscape", 1945, (ill. 36) depict what may be regarded as ominous and deadly elderly masculine Figures that threaten mayhem upon their surroundings.

Nevertheless this in itself was not enough to for me to state that Bacon had something of a psychic problem regarding his psychic integration into his mental landscape of the Father. Rather, what convinced me was a series of quite outstanding paintings that are little known, and the significance of which is rarely commented upon, revolving around William Blake's life-mask and Vincent van Gogh's work "The Painter on the Road to Tarascon (the Painter on his Way to Work)", 1888, (ill. 37). The importance of these two series only becomes apparent when they are considered as constituting one series, with the Blake works performing a quasi-prologue to the Van Gogh works. Although both the artists were dead during Bacon's lifetime, the death of Van Gogh was, however, within living memory, an important fact discussed below. Blake's death was long enough ago for it to be a historical event, in contrast to the near contemporary death of Van Gogh, thus meaning that Blake's life and work represented for Bacon the force of Tradition. I do not think there is any doubt that Bacon was aware of Blake's poetry and art-work, and that Bacon understood the relationship of Blake's work to Blake's unusual perceptual abilities. By focussing upon Blake's work Bacon was able to integrate Tradition into himself in a non-confrontational manner, and also find a validation for his own unique perceptual abilities through the fact that Blake was a famous and world-renowned figure, thereby strengthening his own mental resolve. The importance of the paintings Bacon produced focussed upon Vincent van Gogh's "The Painter on the Road to Tarascon (the Painter on his Way to Work)", is that Bacon condensed, and thereby resolved, his hero-worship of famous painters, and to a large extent resolved his mental conflicts with the Father. This had two effects for the theme of the *Prodigal Son* is not only concerned with the reconciliation of father and son, but is also concerned with the consequences of abandoning a secure and safe situation for a future that is uncertain. After these two series Bacon radically revolutionised his style to one that led eventually to the production of works that made him the internationally renowned artist that he remains to this day. Perhaps he realised that with the works prior to these two series he had reached an *impasse* beyond which he could not progress, artistically, and had the strength of will and character to leave aside a style through which he had achieved a moderate local success, so as to explore the deeper ramifications of what he perceived. It is not out of the question that his own developing perceptual abilities impelled him to take a path through which he resolved his own inner conflicts concerning the Father, Authority and Tradition.

The Prodigal Son

During the 1950's Bacon produced several paintings around one theme that are a complete contrast to the earlier, more renowned, 'Pope' paintings, and yet there is a very precise connection to these earlier 'Pope' paintings. The theme that Bacon was working upon in this series of images and the 'Pope' paintings is that of the Father. Although it will not be considered here in great length here it cannot be ignored that there is a rural/ agricultural setting both for the story of the Prodigal Son and Van Gogh's work "The Painter on the Road to Tarascon (the Painter on his Way to Work)", and further to this the theme of labour/ work is common to both. Although Bacon's work is primarily focussed upon the soul-state of the human being and for the large part deploys a room as a metaphor for the mind, there is in the early period until the end of the 1950's, references to nature, in the broadest sense, as a contrast to overly, urbanised and disturbed Figures. "Figure in a Landscape", 1945, (ill. 36) depicts a murderous Figure manning what appears to be a machine-gun (gunfire flash from a barrel on the middle right-hand side) set in a nondescript natural environment that has overtones of a municipal park, in complete contrast is "Elephant Fording a River", 1952, (ill. 39) where we have an almost idyllic and lyrical depiction of a natural environment. This polarity between the natural world and urbanised environments is by the end of the 1950's side-lined in favour of the kind of work for which Bacon is rightly famous, although this theme of an unsullied natural environment does re-emerge during the period of the late 1970's and 1980's, with such images as "Landscape", 1978, (ill. 40). Notwithstanding this the polarity between the rural and urbanised environments is an important theme, interpretatively, for Bacon's work, and this connects to the 'forgotten self' of childhood already referred to, and in some ways evokes thoughts of 'lost innocence', as I am sure occurred to Bacon as he surveyed the soul-state of humanity, especially in view of the number of Crucifixion works he painted.

The works I will now consider that make explicit Bacon's psychological journey, centred upon the Prodigal Son, are "Study for a Portrait of van Gogh II", 1957, (ill.

41), "Landscape after van Gogh", 1957, (ill. 42), "Landscape after van Gogh", 1957, (ill. 43), "Van Gogh dans un passage", (1957), (ill. 44) "Study for a Portrait of van Gogh III", 1957, (ill. 45), "Study for a Portrait of van Gogh IV", 1957, (ill. 46), "Study for a Portrait of van Gogh V", 1957, (ill. 47) "Study for a Portrait of van Gogh VI", 1957, (ill. 48) and Bacon produced this series in response to Vincent van Gogh's "The Painter on the Road to Tarascon (the Painter on his Way to Work)", 1888, (ill. 37). Prior to 1957 Bacon had demonstrated a propensity to make use of particular 'past masters' works that he felt embodied characteristics he was presently concerned with, a famous example being his "Study after Velazquez's Portrait of Pope Innocent X", 1953, (ill. 49) based upon Velazquez's "Portrait of Pope Innocent X". There is however a radical difference with this series founded upon Van Gogh's work, for in the first place there is a stricter adherence to the van Gogh work than there was with the Velazquez work in the execution of subsequent images. Secondly this is virtually the last time that Bacon makes use of an iconic image of the past as the basis for his own creativity except for one or two exceptions, and as such this series represents a turning point in his own creative arc, and a decisive break with his own past production. Bacon in re-working Velazquez's "Portrait of Pope Innocent X" completely subverts the magisterial calm of authority and precedence emanating from the Velazquez work Instead what we have is an 'authority figure' reduced to a state of absolute terror in the act of issuing an agonised scream and this work, along with "Painting", 1946, (ill. 33) where the Figure exhibits extreme malevolence, are seminal works of Bacon's early period.

Van Gogh's painting "The Painter on the Road to Tarascon (the Painter on his Way to Work)" is a bright composition of predominately yellows and browns with the figure of the painter situated between two trees with the one behind possessing more foliage than the one in front. The tree in front also has more branches as if implying that the way forward consists of a number of, as yet, unexplored choices, whereas that which Van Gogh has left behind has now reached a 'fullness' due to the preponderance of foliage on the tree. Alternatively it may be that Van Gogh realised that he had reached a point-of-no-return beyond which there is only uncertainty, an uncertainty that he felt compelled to embrace given the direction of his own life and personal circumstances. Although this is a self-portrait, in that Van Gogh is painting himself, it is a curious self-portrait for it can be nothing other than a reconstructed imagination of an action he had already undertaken, or which he was about to undertake, for in reality there is no way that Van Gogh could have painted himself walking. It is not the place here to investigate Van Gogh's mental powers, but there is a condition known as Autoscopia, which is the ability of individuals to be able to consciously perceive themselves from the outside of their body. For the majority of those not trained to integrate this experience into their soul-life this is can be an extremely disturbing experience. The fact that many people have this experience relates to the 'crossing of the threshold' spoken of in the Introduction, and as such it is one possible effect of the new powers that are becoming available for humanity. Van Gogh was undoubtedly an unstable personality, who suffered from his remarkable gifts, and this could hardly be otherwise within a world that has no understanding of our mental possibilities, and eventually succumbed to his undoubted 'mental illnesses'. However, I would argue, that Bacon had similar out-of-the-body experiences and recognised a fellow-traveller in Van Gogh, hence his fascination with his work, and a painter of Bacon's subtlety could have hardly failed to notice the paradoxical nature of "The Painter on the Road to Tarascon (the Painter on his Way to Work)" as a self-portrait that was in fact a depiction of Van Gogh's own spiritual state.

So it is that Van Gogh could not have posed for himself at the moment of the work's creation, but it is perfectly possible that in reverie he saw himself taking this path. The setting is rural and in the distance behind the figure is what is presumed to be a farmhouse, and this being so we can assume that the figure is leaving behind, or by-passing, a place of relative civilisation and security for the unknown. This image was created in July at the height of summer and reflects Van Gogh's hopes and expectations at the start of his time at Arles, as is indicated by the fact that he is setting out to start painting. Bacon is known to have described this work as 'haunting' and is also known to have been deeply affected by Van Gogh's *oeuvre* and philosophy even to the point of quoting a passage from one of Van Gogh's letters to his brother Theo: " …real painters do not paint things as they are – They paint them as they themselves feel them to be ".

Naturally when an artist describes himself as going to work, the artist is not undertaking work in the usual sense of paid employment performed at a specific place according to predetermined objectives and tasks. Although the artist may have specific intentions there is no knowledge as to what the end-result will look like exactly, and so the production of an art-work, in this sense, is a spiritual act that occurs at the moment of creation. Both Bacon and Van Gogh may have had certain ideas and philosophical intentions with regard to methodology but at the moment of creation, regardless as to whether this was indoors or outside, creativity was spontaneous. So for both Bacon and Van Gogh there is with the works referenced a sense of anticipation with regard to their respective output, and these works reflect a desire in both artists to evolve from the known and secure towards that which is unknown. Although Van Gogh is known to have produced a prolific number of sketches, there is no evidence that Van Gogh in his painting out-of-doors mechanically reproduced from sketches. It seems that for Van Gogh the sketch was a way of testing ideas before, for him, the crucial act of spontaneous creation. This seems at variance with Bacon until we consider that throughout his life Bacon named the majority of his canvasses as Studies, thus indicating that he was condensing a particular creative process when he painted. In fact the first three paintings above are landscapes where there is no figure and are designated as studies, as were those works that contain a depiction of a Van Gogh Figure. I think that there can be little doubt that Bacon projected his own concerns onto the figure of Van Gogh in the above works, just as Van Gogh projected his own concerns onto an 'imaginary self' in his work.

Further examination of the Van Gogh picture reveals that because the figure is placed between the trees it appears to have walked through them from the fields. This impression is heightened through the hesitancy displayed by the figure which has one foot partially raised as if to move towards the viewer. Is the figure appealing to the viewer on some level? Thus we have a figure that has been deliberately placed between two trees, but which displays an indecisiveness that is at odds with the precision of the pictorial composition. The trees thereby function as limits to (or guardians of) the figure's erratic behaviour, and from this we are able to assume that the figure has walked across the fields from the farmhouse through the trees and onto the road, but is now unsure as to both the decision it has taken and as to whether to go left or right. This work demonstrates the effectiveness of Van Gogh's genius for he has created a magnificent, solidly constructed image that combines the determination that he possessed to pursue his artistic goals whatever the consequences despite the utter desolation and insecurity that he must surely have felt, given the nature of his death a few years later. What makes this an outstanding work for me is the seamless manner by which Van Gogh has been able to combine opposites, or polarities, into a monumental and convincing image. The polarities here are between the impoverished material conditions of his physical existence in contrast to the fierceness and richness of his spirit, a polarity that is counterpoised with the psychological polarity of decisiveness and indecisiveness that was intrinsic to this psychological make-up. Further to this these polarities are placed within the fundamental polarity of the richness of the landscape in comparison to van Gogh's own circumstances. These facts lend this work a subtlety and complexity that is entirely missed by a casual perusal of this apparently simple picture.

Bacon prefaces his actual portrayal of the Figure of Van Gogh with the three known landscapes referred to above where there is only a vague, barely noticeable, indication of a figure. This seemingly bizarre act on Bacon's behalf is clarified when we realise that the three landscapes are focussing upon the two trees and thus the circumstances, or context, of the actual decision made by van Gogh to go to work. I would suggest that Bacon was thereby attempting to empathise with van Gogh as van Gogh projected himself in his work. The locale is primary, for here the cultivated fields of the van Gogh original are played down in favour of a more exuberant and wild natural setting. These three works by Bacon have a turbulent character with the human figure only a spectral presence, which can be read as the helplessness of human beings before the majesty of natural forces or how the human being is enmeshed within, or surrounded by, inexorable natural forces. Bacon's preliminary handling of a portrait of van Gogh in these landscapes brings out another aspect of the van Gogh's work and that is that an individual despite all the advice and help they may be privy to has in the last resort to rely upon their own capacities and abilities when acting. Although I would be loath to start discussing 'alienation', (as commonly understood as relating to industrialisation, modernity etc), upon any level with these works it is a fact, from my perspective, that the evolution of an intellectual apprehension of the cosmos has alienated us from just not ourselves but from the nature that produced us. From this point of view Bacon's three landscapes depict a kind of pre-Fall state of consciousness that is imbued with premonitions of the Fall.

Although the aura of abjection that hangs over these landscapes precludes any exact corollary, nevertheless, the following quote from Goethe's Hymn to Nature evokes something of the emotional effect of these works

" Nature! – we are surrounded and embraced by her: we cannot draw back from her, nor can we penetrate more deeply into her being. She lifts us unasked and unwarned into the gyrations of her dance and whirls us away until we fall exhausted from her arms …… all men are within her and she in all men …. We are obedient to her laws even when we would fain oppose them ….."

This pervasive mood of abjection is also to be discerned in those works that contain a Figure and if we now turn to those works it can be seen how Bacon transformed the original. Only one of them closely follows the posture of the figure in the van Gogh work where Bacon's Figure displays the hesitancy of the van Gogh figure and is firmly placed between two trees. The other two that mimic this format have the Figure reversed and more 'sideways on' and definitely walking down a lane/ path or road. Any suggestion of hesitancy is removed from the final two which have a mournful Figure walking along a track, where in ill. 47 the Figure is looking at the viewer from a slanted position with no trees, whilst the other shows a Figure that is absorbed in its own thoughts placed between two trees, and is staring at the ground whilst walking somewhat dejectedly along the path. This last image exhibits the resolution and thoughtfulness that is necessary to carry through a decision whereas the slanted figure with no trees represents the realisation that your resolve has been carried out and that there is no turning back.

Before entering more deeply into the symbolism of the 'prodigal son' there will be a preliminary comparison of the van Gogh painting with an image of the Prodigal Son by Hieronymus Bosch, "The Prodigal Son", 1487-1516, ill. 50. At first glance there does not appear to be any consonance in posture between the two, although other images related to the Prodigal Son such as "Christophorus" by Joachim Patinir show a greater affinity to the van Gogh work. However both the figure of himself by van Gogh and Bosch's 'Prodigal Son' possess three almost identical artefacts: a stick/ club, a knapsack on their backs and a hat. Despite compositional differences it is striking that van Gogh's figure has the same air of impoverishment as the Bosch figure, and crucially both are tied to a farmhouse. Having established that there is some justification for considering the van Gogh work in the light of the Prodigal Son, and so consequently the Bacon images referenced, it is thus necessary before proceeding to contemplate the larger, cultural significance of the 'Parable of the Prodigal Son'

The parable is related in the Gospel of St. Luke (Authorised Version, 11-32), and along with the 'Parable of the Lost Sheep' and the 'Parable of the Lost Coin', is concerned with the theme of loss and redemption. Whilst the latter two parables deal with the loss of something valuable (a tangible material object) the recovery of which restores the status quo, the parable of the prodigal son is concerned with loss, restitution and reconciliation within a family, that is it refers to the dynamics of family relationships and as such directly relates to the spiritual in contrast to the indirect reference to spiritual matters in the first two. The subtlety of the first two parables is that they demonstrate how the spiritual is related to the mundane physical world whilst the prodigal relates to spiritual dimension of our relationships to each other, specifically father to son but also of brother to brother. The parable of the prodigal son does not have only a Christian background but has a universal dimension in that virtually the same tale can be found in other religions, and a striking example is to be found in Buddhism.

The story dealing with the same subject matter is part of the writings of Mahayana Buddhism and the differences between the two tales highlights the different approaches to theme of Christianity and Buddhism (see Ernest Valea at www.comparativereligion.com/prodigal.html). These differences have no immediate relevance in this context and indeed much could be said of the significance of the parable itself for humanity as a whole: does it refer to some pre-Eden paradise or Golden Age when the spiritual worlds responsible for our genesis and the material world of toil and hardship were unified? I will not dwell on the pertinence of such a question for the van Gogh image, except to point out its relevance with respect to physical work. This and many other questions are raised by this tale but on a fundamental level the parable is concerned with reconciliation. This abstract conclusion is useful in that it gives direction to our thinking, but one could ask what is the nature of the reconciliation enacted? A basic aspect of this reconciliation is the harmonising of a greater power of fullness, the Father, with a subsidiary power bereft of that fullness, the son, who has come to ego-consciousness within the constraints of the Father and, subsequently, wishes to act. This is the situation of any family that has children regardless of number and gender, and psychological theorisations concerning the harmonisation of relations between the male and the female with their parents is one attempt to interpret this familiar dilemma for modern consciousness, albeit one structured on the narrow base of the mundane. However in broader terms the parable refers to the reconciliation/ harmonising of a lesser power with a greater one, so that in this context that could mean the reconciliation/ harmonising of an artist's individual powers of creativity with that accumulated reservoir of past creativity that constitutes the artists cultural background. This a familiar enough theme – 'we stand on the shoulders of giants' – but it is rarely made so thoroughly explicit by an artist as is the case with van Gogh and Bacon. It goes without saying that there will be a commonality and difference of motives between Bacon and van Gogh, but Bacon makes this theme clear and unambiguous by choosing to produce works based upon van Gogh's painting that deals with the same subject-matter. It has already been hinted that Blake possessed extra-ordinary psychic and perceptual abilities and that it is my intention to demonstrate that Bacon also possessed such powers, however in this context it is also the case that these abilities were also possessed by van Gogh as well as Blake.

Having sketched out some similarities between both the van Gogh work and Bacon's paintings with the 'Prodigal Son' by Hieronymus Bosch I will now continue with a deeper analysis of the Bosch work, and for this purpose I will resort to the book by Clement A. Wertheim Aymes 'The Pictorial Language of Hieronymus Bosch'. One of the first comments Aymes makes of this image is that it depicts

"Man on the Threshold between life and death, between here and hereafter." (Aymes, 1975: 18).

The death of the corporeal body is the final, absolute transformation of one state into another after which there can be no further transformations on Earth for that individual, so death's significance in a broader sense can refer to any process where one state is changed into another. The principal characteristic of a death-process is that the preceding condition undergoes utter metamorphosis. Thus a change of consciousness and understanding, as per Initiation, whereby one's prior consciousness and understanding is completely illuminated so as to be unrecognisable to that prior consciousness may be referred to as a death-process, because one's former consciousness has had to 'die' so that the new can arise. Such a process of transformation of consciousness is one that if it is self-initiated can only occur through self-examination as Aymes states of the Bosch image:

"For a picture such as this to portray more than mere allegory, i.e. to portray real experience, it must bear the stamp of a quite impersonal and objective kind of self-examination and evaluation. One can only examine *oneself* quite as thoroughly as this." (Aymes, 1975: 18).

It is known that both van Gogh and Bacon were extremely self-critical in the sense of examining their motives for creation and production. This is amply illustrated by van Gogh's letters and by Bacon's many interviews with David Sylvester and comments he made to colleagues, in fact such self-examination and self-criticism is a pertinent characteristic of virtually all famous modern painters for it is only by such an attitude that an individual's creative potential can be truly accessed so that production transcends the limitations of time and place. Aymes' further comments illustrate this point

"It certainly is not an everyday experience for anyone to reach a point where really objective self-judgment has become possible. Such knowledge depends upon the qualities and power of concentration of the individual, on the degree of self-consciousness he has developed. Consciousness is inner light. The more strongly it burns and the wider it casts its light, the more accurate and true the objective picture of the self will be; it becomes more than mere intellectual self-criticism; it becomes illuminated in a quite concrete way. The self begins to be seen by the individual as though he were looking at it from the outside." (Aymes, 1975: 18).

For both van Gogh and Bacon the fact that they were nearing such a point is demonstrated by their respective works referred to, and relates to the above mentioned Autoscopia. After this work van Gogh produced some of his greatest works in the short time before he tragically committed suicide, whilst Bacon's style underwent a radical change after producing the series highlighted above. And this interpretation is underlined by Aymes' further commentary on the Bosch work with respect as to what time of day is depicted:

"The mood of the painting expressed in the lighting appears to be of eventide – or is it the beginning of the dawn? ...... The prodigal son stands in the centre of the picture. He looks back with a melancholy and somewhat glassy stare. The expression is intensified by a slight pallor around the mouth. His thoughts hover between past and future. The soul can apprehend the inevitability of what is to come." (Aymes, 1975: 18 - 19).

With the van Gogh work we can assume from the shadows that the time of day is around noon, however as I previously commented, the figure of van Gogh has a hesitancy and uncertainty that could easily be interpreted as an apprehension about the future. Although some of Bacon's Figures show more resolution in its act of walking there is with some an air of melancholic and abjection as they pause for reflection upon their course of action.

Bacon emphasises in his works, apart from the final one, the encompassing of the figure with two trees, and thereby he deemed this to be an important aspect of his design. The trees in the van Gogh painting symbolically evoke a gate that divides one area of the image (background) from another (foreground) and thus function to regulate comings and goings between these two spaces. As commented upon earlier von Gogh's figure of himself could have emerged from the fields through these trees from the farmhouses/ buildings and onto the path/ lane. With reference to the gate in Bosch's work Aymes states that

"A gate, door or portal, always divides yet unifies different spaces. A threshold also exists at meeting-point of different spheres, although it may not be outwardly perceptible. .... Here there is no logical explanation of the presence of the gate, no continuation to left or right, whether in the form of hedge or fence. Standing thus by itself, this gate can only be taken to represent a dividing-point, a threshold." (Aymes, 1975: 20).

The trees that act as gateways for, and restrictions of, the figures in both van Gogh's and Bacon's paintings also appear in virtual isolation evoking not only the inevitability of a course, or direction, but the threshold between not only differing spaces but differing times: past, present and future perhaps. In these images by both artists this threshold also denotes a transition from the fecundity of nature to the relative stoniness of the path/ lane. Although there is more of a wildness to the nature depicted in Bacon's paintings there can be little doubt that in the van Gogh work the background is of cultivated fields. I would argue that the manner by which nature is depicted by both artists metaphorically refers to their own instinctual, creative natures, thereby creating a contrast between the essentially practical, worldly dimension of painting with its canvasses, paints etc (stony path/lane) and the primarily inward contemplative mood of these works by both artists. The presence of a 'gateway' depicted by both van Gogh and Bacon in their respective works clearly indicates that both van Gogh and Bacon knew that they were approaching a turning-point in their particular artistic careers and lives.

A further significance of the two trees forming a 'gateway' is that they are symbolic of the tress in the Garden of Eden; the Tree of Life and the Tree of the Knowledge of Good and Evil. As has been noted the right-hand tree in the Van Gogh work appears to be blossoming more than the one on the left indicating that it has more to offer immediately than the left-hand tree, and could perhaps be understood as the Tree of Life. The other tree would then, because it is depicted without leaves, represent the arid, dry intellectual aspect of consciousness (Tree of the Knowledge of Good and Evil) in contrast to the fecundity of imaginative powers. Even though it is not possible to definitively state that the tree with leaves is an apple-tree in the van Gogh work, interpreting it as such, or perhaps as a tree about to give fruit, as with the Bosch work, harmonises with the symbolism of the staff, for as Aymes points out with respect to the apple-tree there is more to its symbolism than is commonly realised

"From the botanical aspect , the apple is pseudo-fruit, for the fruit is not developed from seed capsule only, as in a true fruit, but it also incorporates the structures immediately below it, i.e. it grows both upwards and downwards. It seems to give a concrete picture of an ambivalent situation …Man's spiritual individuality (ego) can be regarded symbolically as a pseudo-fruit with higher and lower aspect …. Life on earth for man is intended to enable him to gather knowledge." (Aymes, 1975: 24).

One of the three elements common to all these figures depicted in these works is the staff/ club which is also a traditional part of the attire of wayfarers or travellers, and of which Aymes states that

"The significance of the staff can be grasped through a study of the myth whence the symbol is derived, the story of Theseus and the Minotaur (man/ bull literally translated). …. Theseus's weapon is the club. It is also the weapon of Herakles, another hero. The club is a symbol of the man ….. who is able to act out of his personal individual decision (will) rather than because he is driven by his impulses. In ancient times, it was only the hero, or initiate, who was empowered to act by means of this force. Today everyone must learn to act through it." (Aymes, 1975: 25).

Even though there are no blossoming trees in Bacon's images Aymes's description of the symbolic dimensions of a staff does have a specific connection with Bacon. For Bacon produced a number of works based upon the Bull, and he emphasised in these works how the human being exists within the orbit of passions, desires and instincts that are so powerful that once they are activated take-over the human beings rational behaviour. Is the implication of these images that we only become *human* by controlling such passions, desires and instincts. "Portrait of Isabel Rawsthorne Standing in a Street in Soho", 1967, (ill. 51), is one such work where we can see that alongside Isabel Rawsthorne there are odd bull-like shapes in what appears to be mirrors, or the reflecting surfaces of buildings. This is an ambiguous image concerning our instinctual desires and there public expression, for we do not know whether or not Rawsthorne is in the act of soliciting – kerb-crawler (technological intrusion into desires) in the background – or just behaving coquettishly. If there is a sexual dimension to this work then it is referring to the self-consciousness that we have of our sexuality, irrespective of whether we are manipulating our sexuality for financial gain or merely displaying and enjoying it. The odd, bull-like forms of this work relate to other works where a bull is featured as in "Study for Bullfight No. 1", 1967, (ill. 52), which was produced shortly after the above work. The significance of the bull, and this connects with later commentary, is the struggle that the human being has in subduing their 'animality', and not specifically to violence. This is an instance where Bacon suppresses the spectacle so as to draw out the inner meaning of the symbol of a Bull, which traditionally is related to the Mithraic mysteries and our coming-to ego-consciousness. Van James in his book "Spirit and Art" makes the following comment " … the bull forces are also a picture of the instincts and will-power in human nature" (Van James, 2001. 55), and Albert Schutze states that

"When a man comes to the stage of consciously experiencing for the first time his own inner being , he sees that this 'I', or ego, stands against everything that does not belong to it and so [that which does not belong to the 'I'] can therefore be called the 'not-I'. He discovers that the 'not-I' comprises not only of other people, the external world and so on, but also his own bodily make-up, his dispositions, capacities, weaknesses, the whole complex of his desires, inclinations and temperament. With all this he is certainly connected, but it is not himself. To all of it he can say 'I have it', not 'I am it'. All of this 'not-I' was known to the ancient Mystery-wisdom as 'the Bull'. Through his individual activity man must set himself the goal of transmuting in a spiritual sense the 'not-I', the purely natural, in himself. He will then be himself a 'Mithras', who has overcome the bull." (Van James, 2001. 55).

Thus it is that only by confronting, overcoming and transforming, our animal instincts and all the passions and desires we associate with our soul life that we find our true humanity, for we can be neither free nor human, only 'Determined', whilst we are under the thrall of them. From this it is possible to state that both van Gogh and Bacon, though aware that they were approaching a turning-point in their lives, equally realised that they had to have a firm resolve with respect to their future action, and be able to overcome and transform the hindrances that were germane to their own Self.

The other two items commonly carried by wayfarers or travellers, a hat and a knapsack, will now be discussed and considered in conjunction because of their inter-relatedness. Aymes describes the *hat* as representing the earthly thinking of an individual: " … a hat denotes what the wearer has *inside* his head"(Aymes, 1975: 39). Whereas Aymes indicates that the meaning of the basket on the prodigal son's back, which in shape resembles those carried by the figures in the van Gogh and Bacon works, relates to the lived life of that individual:

"This man …. drags the whole of his past life along with him as burden. Its content remains hidden from his fellow human-beings, but it lies heavily upon and hampers him in undertaking new tasks. Bosch also uses the wooden spoon to indicate the individual's having a profession, a means of earning his livelihood." (Aymes, 1975: 37).

Although the Bacon works are bereft of anything that relates to earning a livelihood it is quite clear that the van Gogh figure is carrying what are presumed to be materials for painting.

By considering the significance of the stick/ club, hat and knapsack it is evident that both van Gogh and Bacon portray in the images listed that they were on a *spiritual journey* which had brought them to the threshold of a new understanding of themselves and their creativity. It is highly significant that Bacon was following the lead of van Gogh in this instance. It is presumed that Bacon had the opportunity to study van Gogh's work during his three month stay in France, bearing in mind that Van Gogh's death in 1890 was not that distant, culturally, from Bacon's own time. It is not known with whom he conversed with over artistic affairs but he did meet Yvonne Bocquentin a pianist and connoisseur, and stayed with Madame Bocquentin and her family in order, according to Bacon, to improve his French during his stay in France before the Second World War. I would hazard that the impact of van Gogh's work lay dormant in his unconscious until his late forties when he found himself undergoing, as a palpable fact, the same spiritual journey van Gogh had taken earlier in 1888. This journey for Bacon was a reconciliation with the Father and Authority. The coming-to-terms for him with his own father is surely demonstrated through the 'Pope' series, and this also had the further effect of reconciling Bacon with his own cultural heritage so that he was henceforth a free agent. It is also noteworthy that although Bacon was forcefully removed from the family home he nevertheless undertook a peripatetic journey for a number of years before returning home (London) and a series of relatively 'good' surrogate fathers.

Although this theme of reconciliation with the Father is of immense importance to anyone's psychic health and well-being, and was of utmost importance immediately to Bacon, it is a sign of Bacon's greatness as an artist that he also realised the importance of reconciliation with the Mother. Basically, for the feeling realm, this revolves around forgiveness and not bearing grudges towards our biological parents for having been brought into this 'vale of tears', which is one dimension of our world we inhabit, and is of great significance during puberty and adolescence when such earth-shattering, (for the individual) existential questions as Who am I? Why am I here? etc have a clear and insistent immediacy. It is also pertinent that a coming-to-terms psychically (that is harmonising the two aspects of consciousness that relate to the two hemispheres of the brain: the Masculine and the Feminine) can lead to the acquisition of higher powers of comprehension as indicated by the commentary upon Goethe in the Introduction. There is very little doubt, for me, that Bacon understood this in his treatment of the Feminine Figure, which will be discussed below. Whatever one may think it is an absolute fact that by the end of the 1950's Bacon had inaugurated a style of painting that was utterly unique and different from his earlier mode of production, even though it had evolved out of that work, and any self-respecting critique has to account for this radical change.

Chapter 2. Self and the World.

Central to an understanding of the spiritual journey that both van Gogh and Bacon undertook is the relationship between the 'self' and the ego, as well as how the individual 'self' interacts with the 'World-Self'. The 'World-Self' refers here to the consciousness of humanity as a whole and not to some particular civilisation, and the reason for this is that the basic corporeal, soul and spiritual structure is the same for everyone even if there are differences of 'self', personality and spiritual impulses according to the widely differing geographical locations of the planet. The individual self from this angle is thus all that which accrues from our own state of soul, the corporeal germ inherited from our parents and how we transform them in maturing. As we mature our personalities, character and thinking are clearly under the sway of the culture within which we are born. Rudolf Steiner expressed aspects of the inter-relationship of the 'self' and the 'World Self' in the following verse

Soul of Man!
Thou livest in the beat of heart and lung
Which leads thee through the rhythmic tides of Time
Into the feeling of thine own Soul-being.
Practise *Spirit-mindfulness*
In balance of the soul,
Where the surging
Deeds of the World's Becoming
Do thine own I
Unite
Unto the I of the World
Then amid the weaving of the Soul of Man
Thou will truly *feel*.

In particular this verse makes clear the striving of the individual ego/ self in its 'lower' and 'higher' aspects to that which is 'higher' than itself, the outcome of which is to be able to 'truly *feel*'. Implicit in this verse is the understanding that the *soul* and the *self* are integral is to each other.

In the previous chapter it was examined how both Bacon and van Gogh, by default, came to an understanding of themselves through their ability to free their consciousness from its normal embedded existence within the particularity our corporeality and the subsequent place that corporeal being occupies within a specific cultural and social setting, about which Aymes stated

"The self begins to be seen by the individual as though he were looking at it from the outside." (Aymes, 1975: 18).

This raises many questions as to the ontological nature of such a condition, and with the Aymes statement we may well ask who is the individual, in this instance, that is able to perform this action. For me consciousness is intimately related to our corporeality, however due to the changes of consciousness resulting from consciousness being focussed on other aspects of our corporeality than in ancient times, i.e. consciousness is now focussed upon the materiality of the brain with the consequence of abstract, intellectual thinking, we now, because of this intimate association, believe that consciousness is centred in our corporeality. My answer to the question concerning the Aymes statement is the 'individual' referred to is the 'higher ego' that has freed itself from its entanglement with the 'lower ego' that has a more direct relationship with our corporeality. Some people have a natural ability to do this, others by way of training. Bacon's principal concern, which as stated is the soul-state of the human being, and at present humanity is, in general, involved in the process of transforming and purifying what has been named here the soul, or the astral body, and this is a multidimensional endeavour. In the first instance there are those desires and passions that are related to our drives and instincts, and in this respect the sexual drive is exemplary for although it is an instinct its consummation is largely bound up with our desires and passions. With our other instincts there is mainly a one-to-one relationship with the pertinent object, e.g. hunger and food. This is not to say there are not passions and desires associated with hunger - this is obvious, but the difference is that these passions and desires are connected to instincts that by their nature, again for evident reasons, are hard-wired into our being. With passions and desires that arise from within ourselves from our characterlogical disposition and personal preferences there is a difference, for these are not hard-wired. This personal world of passions and desires that constitute a large part of our soul have an impact upon the Formative Forces, through our habits as learnt behaviour. I would characterise this by saying that in distinction to the instincts, which are in-built, hard-wired behavioural impulses, our passions and desires 'mark' the surface of the realm of Formative Forces, and depending upon the individual can become deeply etched and engraved habits that develop into *addiction*. Extreme addictions, in particular here to alcohol and chemical, recreational drugs, are very difficult to cure because of their effect upon the chemical ether, referred to in the Introduction, aspect of Formative Forces; which is responsible for the complexity of chemical action with the body, and which has become severely imbalanced, thereby necessitating drastic measures to restore equilibrium and health.

Bacon focussed on those individuals in crisis, and so depicted the corporeal and facial distortions inflicted on the human form through the emotional impact of suffering over time in the Figure. The Figure is, as already stated in the Introduction, the means by which Bacon expressed the results of his examination of the emotional state of an individual from the perspective of his exceptional visual abilities, in effect, as stated, he was able to *'compress the time-span of an individual's emotional state'*. Through the Figure Bacon depicted how we are our own worst enemies, with respect to our well-being - how we ruin ourselves through our drives, desires and passions. By examining the path of Bacon's career it is possible to determine the course of the development of the Figure as an expression of his ability to mentally 'compress time'. The triptych "Three Studies of the Human Head", 1953, (ill 53) was a turning-point in this respect, for although we have three separate panels the overall impact of this triptych is to condense the emotional turmoil of the individual depicted into a 'single' image from the viewer's perspective, which was Bacon's intention. I say this because with this work Bacon demonstrates another artistic achievement and that is the ability to express the **NOW.** This will be further examined below, but for the present the **NOW** is important when considering either Goethe's or Bacon's ability to 'compress time', because the state of mind, or consciousness, of a person with this ability is such that our normal awareness of past, present and future are perceived as a reduced understanding of the fullness of **TIME.**

From his unique point-of-view Bacon recorded in his work the suffering caused by the pursuit of our desires, drives, passions, and instincts within the context of our mental well-being. The esoteric implication of Bacon's endeavour is that he recorded the struggle that the higher 'self/ ego' has with the lower 'self/ ego', a theme already touched upon with the reference to the apple-tree in the previous chapter. This is a terrible struggle that eventually all human beings have to engage in, regardless of whatever beliefs they presently entertain. Bacon by living where he did and frequenting the places he did had, so to speak, a front-row seat from which to observe this battle in particular individuals. He was painfully aware, for instance, of the effects of the addiction to drugs through the tragedy of his lover George Dyer, as will be discussed below. It would have been impossible for him, given his life-style, to be unaware of the negative effects of the addiction to alcohol, even though he drank copious amounts himself he seems to have been to have been able to control its effects upon him. From this I believe that it was the characteristics of obsessive and addictive behaviour in general that caught his eye, and which he later expressed in his images.

The following description of Bosch's abilities by Aymes is an assessment that equally applies to Bacon:

"It would be erroneous to merely classify Bosch as a 'symbolic' painter in the modern sense. What Bosch painted was the content of his spiritual imaginative vision; it was the result of direct, inner pictorial experience, not an abstract, calculated representation of theoretical ideas and dogmas." (Aymes, 1975: 11).

What is being alluded to here is that Bosch had a direct inner experience of that which he depicted, and did not come to abstract conclusions concerning the world which he then illustrated with pictures. What was painted was first known to him as 'living' imaginations, much as with the above description of Goethe, and this is an important point to bear in mind with respect to the epistemological value of artistic cognition. The same is true, I believe ,of Blake and van Gogh, and with Bacon who can argue against this, for his Figures have a delirious, other-worldly exactitude born of the Imagination that is in complete contrast to the usual prosaic and intellectualised renderings of the human figure that are commonplace. Aymes continued his commentary as follows

"In a real, imaginative vision which is usually the product of concentrated meditative activity, a man can grasp the spiritual aspect, the living entities, of the outer and inner world of experience in such a way that an inner picture arises for him which truly represents the essential content of the subject of his meditation."(Aymes, 1975: 11).

This statement by Aymes introduces a topic that is crucial to understanding Bacon and his methodology the significance of which cannot be stressed enough. No doubt some readers will be surprised to learn that Bacon, the apogee of sensuality and *bon vivant par excellence,* indulged in concentrated meditative activity as a vital part of his working methods. This theme will be taken up later, but for now I will concentrate on another aspect of Bacon's methodology, for it is a fact that Bacon very rarely painted his portraits in the presence of the subject, instead he relied upon memories and photographs of the individual concerned. Bacon's approach to his work is drawn out in a series of conversations that Bacon conducted with the art critic David Sylvester, which have been printed as "Interviews with Francis Bacon":

F.B. I think it's the slight remove from fact, which returns me onto the fact more violently. Through the photographic image I find myself beginning to wander into the image and unlock what I think of as its reality more than I can by looking at it. And photographs are not only points of reference: they're often triggers of ideas. (Sylvester, 1993: 30)

F.B. I think that you said somewhere that, when you were sitting for a portrait I was trying to do of you, I was always looking at photographs of wild animals.

D.S. Yes, I never knew quite how to take that.

F.B. Well, one image can be deeply suggestive in relation to another. (Sylvester, 1993: 32)

D.S......But in recent years, when you've planned to do a painting of somebody, I believe you've tended to have a set of photographs taken especially.

F.B. I have. Even in the case of friends who will come and pose, I've had photographs taken for portraits because I very much prefer working from the photographs than from them. It's true to say I couldn't attempt to do a portrait from photographs of someone I didn't know. But, if I both know them and have photographs of them, I find it easier to work than actually having their presence in the room. I think that, if I have the presence of the image there, I am not able to drift so freely as I am able to through the photographic image. This may just be my own neurotic sense but I find it less inhibiting to work from them through memory and photographs than actually having them seated before me.

D.S. You prefer to be alone?

F.B. Totally alone. With their memory.

D.S. Is that because the memory is more interesting or because the presence is disturbing?

F.B. What I want to do is distort the thing far beyond the appearance, but in the distortion to bring it back to a recording of the appearance.

D.S. Are you saying that painting is almost a way of bringing somebody back, that the process of painting is like the process of recalling?

F.B. I am saying that.(Sylvester, 1993: 38-40).

D.S. When you're painting a portrait, are you at all conscious of trying to say something about your feelings in regard to the model or what the model might be feeling, or are you only thinking about their appearance.

F.B. Every form you make has an implication, so that, when you are painting somebody, you know that you are, of course, trying to get near not only their appearance but also the way they have affected you, because every shape has an implication.

D.S. Are you conscious of that implication as you make it.

F.B. Yes.

D.S. That it might be aggressive, might be tender, and so forth?

F.B. Yes.

D.S. In painting self-portraits, is there a radical difference in approach from the one used when painting other people?

F.B. No.(Sylvester, 1993: 130).

There is a dimension to these extracts that is easily overlooked that revolves around Bacon's statement concerning appearance and facts, and which has an intimate relationship to the interaction of imagination and reality. When Bacon stated that he distorted 'appearance' in order to return to *the* 'appearance', this cannot mean to the original appearance otherwise there would be no need to distort that appearance in the first place. The implication is that through his working practices Bacon discovered facts that are occluded by mere appearance alone, and which when known rendered a completeness to the inadequacy of just painting surfaces. The return to the appearance would then be necessary so as to interweave that which his meditations have ascertained as being vital to the appearance, but which only revealed itself over the course of his meditations. Thus another dimension emerged as being essential to the original appearance during private moments of meditation, and which, crucially, did not change the corporeal features of the person involved, rather it led to a perception of the completeness of that individual. This is another aspect of his ability to 'compress time'. Thus a photograph provide Bacon with the raw physical data with which to begin his meditations, and this is the case for all meditative practices whereby something ordinary is chosen upon which to focus the mind. It goes without saying that a camera because it is a machine cannot capture this dimension of an individual, the fact that we project onto a photograph that which is not there through familiarity will be examined later.

The implication is that there exists subtle factors intimately related to the original appearance that only reveal their significance when there is not a concentration upon immediate appearances alone, and which because of their nature, as stated, cannot be captured by a camera. Bacon also states that he wished to get at the facts and that photographs because they are removed from these facts, serve to 'violently' bring him back to this factual reality. One interpretation of this is that it is what is lost in a photograph that served to bring him back to what he had perceived as being essential to the person photographed in distinction to being fixated upon the physical resemblance of a photograph to that person. In this sense the photographs acted as an 'external master', or regulatory reference point, for Bacon in their 'slight remove from fact', for although they record the raw perceptual facts of a person they in effect belie that person by freezing them in a moment of time within which there is only a trace of the fullness of that person's soul life. A 'slight remove from fact' is further illuminated by considering a mathematical analogy, for a photograph only records the 'lowest common denominator' inherent to all objects. What a camera cannot do, because it is a mechanical device, is record the 'highest common factor' of all that is living, which is their differing relationships to the soul and spirit, anything that is perceived in a photograph is projected onto it by the human being, and the ability to do this has to be learnt. So for Bacon photographs, by recording raw data, served to bring him back to the *actual* person through processes of memory and imagination. Bacon stated that this process is freer without the presence of the person than when they are present, and could be characterised as a sort of 'free remembering', rather than 'involuntary remembering'. Steiner made the point that the reason memory cannot penetrate into childhood (the 'forgotten self' of infancy when we were in the '**NOW**'), is that the child does not have self-awareness, and that it is only when the I makes it presence felt that there can be any memory and knowledge of the 'reflections' of the self that exists upon the 'plane of time' back into the ego thereby inducing self-awareness. (Steiner, 1999: 142).

This is a complex process that is related to the body of formative forces that only makes its presence known, i.e. plays an active part rather than subsidiary one, around the time of the change of teeth at approximately seven years of age. Steiner explained this as follows,

"At the moment a child attains self-awareness as the result of the I entering the etheric body, the I mirrors itself inwardly. From that point on, all soul life is a co-reflecting of experiences and impressions. And this also explains why we are unable to remember anything that happened before the I gained its mirroring capacity. A child's earliest impressions are not remembered. The important thing is that the human I – to the extent that it has entered the etheric body or to the extent that it receives mental images from the past – becomes, through this, a mirror within the soul. After that, it is open to whatever appears in its mirror." Steiner, 1999: 142.

In addition to this we have to acknowledge that in the majority of cases the ego in an adult is usually not powerful enough to penetrate deep enough into the psyche to uncover the 'forgotten self' of a child's earliest impressions, as denoted in the above statement by Steiner. Upon the nature of our mental images Steiner gave the following comments

"You can easily see that mental images live a life of their own in our souls when you consider, for example, that the soul is powerless to easily call a previously formed image back into memory. A mental image formed only yesterday may sometimes refuse strongly to allow itself to be recaptured. In ordinary life we then say that we have 'forgotten', that it simply will not rise to the surface resists recall. A battle takes place between something that lives within us as an undeniable soul power wanting to force an image to the surface and something else that is also present within the soul. A battle is waged in our souls with the mental image, though it will eventually return without any external cause. It was present all the time, but refused to reveal itself at the desired moment. You know further that this battle between our own soul forces and the image to be called up is different with different individuals. The mental images live in the soul, but as opponents, so to speak, of our own soul forces. The difference between these two is frighteningly great."(Steiner, 1999: 98).

Anyone who has endeavoured only the simplest of concentration exercises let alone the intensity of focussed meditation will acknowledge the pertinence of the above, for the moment one starts there is a welling-up of images and thoughts that appear to have a life and a will of their own in that they appear completely opposed to permitting the individual to concentrate upon their chosen subject-matter. This is how things are to start with. Steiner proffers some insights into this surging sea of images and emotions

"We also pointed out that sensations, given through our senses, emerge and fill the soul life like waves that continually rise and fall on the sea…..We experience these sensations when we have contact with the outer world; they then transform themselves in such a way that they live on in us." (Steiner, 1999: 93).

"Essentially, human soul life is anything but unified. It is more like a dramatic battlefield, where opposites struggle continually. Anyone who listens with sensitivity and feeling to this soul life will certainly notice its dramatic character. When confronted by these opposing forces in the human soul, people in fact feel a lack of control, a passivity." (Steiner, 1999: 94).

"The soul cannot be a homogeneous entity; it would be unable to progress further. It is vital that we begin by gaining a feeling for this polarity, or contradiction, in the soul life." (Steiner, 1999: 95-96).

"As we progress inwardly, we must look at the dramatic contradictions of our soul life. We need to recognise that we are subject to a master there, just as we are in the external world – a master who makes sure we have a different soul life at the age of seven, for example, than at twenty, thirty, or later…..it is important to note that mental images really do have an existence of their own in the soul life; they have their own life. Please understand the full significance of that statement. Visualisations are like parasites, like living beings in the soul that lead their own existence there." (Steiner, 1999: 97).

As stated, anyone who has attempted even the simplest concentration exercise immediately experiences the force and will of that which dwells in the depth of the soul, and which even though it is *invisible* has the power to disturb our focus. At present it is utterly unacceptable to state that the *invisible*, as images and sensations, within our soul is capable of volition and being and can, not only disrupt concentration, but can make an individual mentally and physically ill- **how can the invisible and insubstantial (in comparison to material phenomena, such as stones) do this?** It goes without saying that this question is of the utmost importance for our continued evolution, and all the intellectualising and theorising will not alter this fact, and if not addressed then the situation can only be exacerbated.

These characterisations of the soul-life of humanity by Steiner, in general, have a number of ramifications - one of which is that the simple act of using our sensory abilities to be merely aware of the world is in itself a complex affair. Given the fact that we also have an aspect of ourselves that is a seething cauldron of egotistic desires and passions that often work against our best intentions it is not difficult to see how chaotic our inner soul-life is for the majority of individuals. If these egotistic desires and passions, and the results of sensory impressions, becomes too insistent it is also not difficult to understand how there is an ensuing condition of suffering as the **I** (the block capital refers to the 'higher' ego) struggles to maintain its balance. Steiner's statements also provide a theoretical background by which to understand how the **I** strives to prevent itself from being swamped by these lower, egotistic desires and passions that constitute the 'lower' self (i). If the **I** succumbs then it is as if we have no **I** and merely become the 'animalistic' expression of our egotistic desires and passions. An individual thus becomes fettered and chained to those egotistic desires and passions to the point of enslavement and loses all sense of its 'higher' self.

Through these statements by Steiner we are made aware of the role of the **I** in recollection and memory, and that our ability to remember depends upon how strongly we are able to activate our **I**. Steiner also stated how remembering a slice of our soul life at a particular point in time changes our perceptual abilities if the exercise is repeated regularly. The difficulties in achieving this remembrance adequately is due to the fact that we do not have sufficient control, to start with, of these attention-grabbing, swarming, life-filled images that fill our inner being. Bacon had prodigious abilities in this area for he possessed an unusually strong will and was thus able to activate his **I** to such an extent that the reluctance, or recalcitrance, of mental images to be pliable to our ordinary soul life was overcome. As an aid for achieving this extra-ordinary act Bacon made use of photographs so as to relate and focus a whole series of memories and recollections that are by their very nature transitory and difficult to pin down. This was done to fully permeate and understand the nature of the individuals he wished to portray, for Bacon knew that this was not revealed by immediate appearances, and that he had to penetrate to those worlds immanent to immediate appearances whose presence was signalled by 'a slight remove from facts' of a photograph. Furthermore Bacon also achieved this whilst accounting for his own emotional responses to the subject. But it is also important to give full weight to the fact that Bacon states that this process had to take place with someone he knew, that he had met, and this points to another area of understanding: the role that 'after-images' play in our soul life.

Day-dreaming and Reality.

It is well-known that Bacon spent long periods of what is commonly called 'day-dreaming', during which we can assume that he would spend long periods contemplating mental images of people he knew and that these were stimulated by photographs of those people.

"....we know enough about 'day-dreaming' to be quite sure that in Bacon's case it is a working-name for something purposed and constructive...It is a common and universal experience of everyday life that if we forget something, we cannot recapture it by knitting our brows and concentrating; but if on the contrary if we let the mind go limp, the missing fact will find its way back of its own accord."(Russell, 1997: 22).

Russell's words recall Steiner's statement above with regard to memory and

78

indicate that in his opinion Bacon was performing something more than what is usually meant by day-dreaming. The 'something purposed and constructive' here is that Bacon used a photograph as an *aide de memoire* of a person he was familiar with, and with whom he socialised in ways other than a studio-setting (this is undoubtedly true of the portraits he produced of individuals comprising his social circle). This is interesting because it means that Bacon knew these people intimately and was able to compare his observations with that information of them which was petrified within a photograph. Anyone with insight into the usual process of portraiture knows that a similar petrifaction occurs in the studio as the sitter strikes a 'pose' etc. Thus a photograph by itself was meaningless to Bacon, it only had a function when he had met someone and was able to carry a *living image* of them within his soul; then the photograph served to sharpen that image, and its higher implications, in his periods of reverie.

It is interesting to experiment in this area and it soon becomes clear just how pallid, fuzzy and lacking in detail these images are that we carry of people intimate to us – how woefully inadequate these images are in comparison to the infinite nuances of mood, shades of light and variety of viewing angles that constitute the actual person. But this is exactly what Bacon attempted, to so fully know his subject that he was then able to paint the unique gesture of their soul life as a *compression of time*. In their book "Learning to Experience the Etheric World" Baruch Luke Urieli and Hans Muller-Wiedemann present a thorough investigation of the 'after-image' and the role that it performs in our soul life. The formation of after-images is, when practised conscientiously, a complex process that comprises four stages: Taking an interest in another person, the inner perception of the other person, the return, and the reading of the resonance. The above authors thus present a detailed analysis of the ability we have of inner visualisation, and here we are speaking of holding an image in one's mind of someone known to us, and have been familiar with for long periods of time, and then awaiting the resonance of this familiarity and visualisation upon the mental planes. To approach a human being in this manner, to treat them as a spiritual being and not a physical object, is by no means unusual and appears in the best-selling book "The Tenth Insight: Holding the Vision" by James Redfield. In this book a process is described whereby one closely examines a person's face in order to by-pass all those strategies and defences constructed during the course of life, so as to perceive that which is fundamental to that person – their 'higher' self. This mode of approaching a human being concurs with Gilles Deleuze's comments (to be examined below) upon the 'face' being a construct whilst the 'head' is the fundamental.

Bacon possessed this ability in a highly-developed form and continued to hone his performance of this skill throughout his career, and the above process outlined by Urieli and Muller-Wiedemann indicates why Bacon painted the same individuals over and over again, sometimes in completely different situations than a formal portrait, and why, given the difficulty of the process, Bacon resorted to photographs and felt inhibited by the presence of the sitter. The following quote serves as a guide and context for that which has been stated in this chapter on Bacon's working-method and his approach to his subject-matter;

"If the ethereal formative forces, of which the theory is here propounded, are a reality, they will be there not only in the growing plant and animal, the outer object of our researches, but in our own thinking activity, inasmuch as our own forces of life and growth have gifted us with the power of imagination. If then our knowledge of the organic world, transcending the merely empirical and descriptive stage, is to penetrate the *idea*, the underlying force and essential 'law' of what is living, we are in a different situation than when examining the laws and forces of the inorganic world. We are a stage nearer to the primal font, not only of the outer world but of our own thinking about this world." (Adams and Whicher, 1980: 88-89)

The above statement also makes it clear that there is an intimate relationship between our ability to Think and Formative forces, and that as well as gifting us with the ability to think rationally we also received the gift to Think Imaginatively (Imaginative Thinking mentioned in the Introduction that never leaves us), and that Bacon, by instinctively making use of this technique, penetrated beyond the immediately perceptible to reach the primal font of his own Thinking and Imaginative abilities.

Thus Bacon's working methodology involved intense concentration upon his subject-matter for protracted periods of time, and there is ample evidence that Van Gogh spent virtually all of his adult-life intensively focussing upon his painting. Both these artists had phenomenal will-power enabling them to concentrate upon their work, absolutely, for hours on end. Aymes' commentary upon Bosch's images makes a reference to what he referred to as referred to 'an inner picture':

"This 'picture', however, forms itself in terms of outer percepts which are experienced by the individual in everyday life. Because this picture contains the essential content rather than the outer happenings of the original subject of meditation however, it may form itself out of outer percepts which appear to be arranged in a very bizarre way."(Aymes, 1975: 11).

What Aymes is alluding to here is that although we can hold an image of some phenomenon of the 'outer' world in our mind, such as for instance a dog, when through meditation we have pierced the outward appearance of this phenomenon, by *compressing the time-sequence of a number of observations*, then the inner essence of 'dog-ness' is revealed, a revelation that completely alters the original mental, inner experience of, in this example, a dog . It has also to be considered that what we perceive straightforwardly with open eyes is also an 'inner' experience, the 'outside' does not project into our minds a ready made image of the world that we passively receive, but we actively create this image of the 'outside' from sensory input. There is no question that Bacon's images appear extremely 'bizarre', and also that at the time of their execution van Gogh's images appeared outlandish and fantastic to the general public, even if they do not appear so strange to us now. As a further comment upon this theme Aymes adds,

"Curious combinations of form and substance appear which are not the product of abstract fantasy, but of a creative pictorial faculty. This faculty in fact lies dormant in all men, but to activate it, it must be cultivated. Many modern artists are experimenting with a new use of form and substance to reactivate visual pictorial faculties. Bosch painted out of a direct inner experience of visions which arose through a particularly vivid creative faculty." (Aymes, 1975: 11).

For me there is no doubt that van Gogh and Bacon 'painted out of a direct inner experience of visions which arose through a particularly 'vivid creative faculty', and, furthermore, I have provided evidence that Bacon undertook instinctively a meditative path that leads to enhanced perceptual abilities. Since Bosch was associated with a stream of esoteric wisdom he was able to clearly and consciously evaluate that which he perceived, however this was not the case with van Gogh and Bacon. By the late 19th century such esoteric streams no longer had the social influence they had in Bosch's time, consequently both van Gogh and Bacon had to deal with their experiences in their own way, and what a difference in character and circumstances between the two. Bacon was by time of 1957 a relatively successful and well-known artist, at least in London, whereas, as is generally known, van Gogh created in total obscurity. Van Gogh was an unstable character who was driven to commit suicide because he did not possess the social skills to incorporate his work into the fabric of the society he inhabited. Maybe this would have been impossible in any event, however this is not the case with Bacon who was able to integrate his experiences into his work through the drastic stylistic changes after 1957 and, as stated, was a worldly and commercially successful artist.

The Now.

I have already referred to the 'Forgotten Self' of childhood with respect to Bacon's Figures as an important attribute to investigated. However this attribute cannot be considered as having the same ontological status as adult consciousness in relation to time. Our understanding of the world and time, as past, present and future, is based upon the intellect, but this is not the case with an infant under the age of three simply because they have not developed the brain so as to support intellectualism. The human being at this stage of consciousness lives within the **NOW,** that is the *time-less*. Our acquisition of the intellect has torn us out of the living fabric of the world so that we now experience life in a *'one step remove'* mode. Bacon struggled to find the necessary technical means to be able to depict his Figures as being in the **NOW,** this is one of the implications of his spiritual journey during the 1950's.

An evaluation of some of the aspects as to what is to be considered the **NOW** is absolutely crucial for an understanding of the affective power of Bacon's images. Firstly, what we consider to be the 'outside' world is an 'inner' experience stimulated by the impressions we receive through our senses, and through concentration and meditation it is possible to achieve a level of consciousness that expands this 'inner' picture so that other aspects of the perception under consideration are revealed. Henri Bortoft in his book "The Wholeness of Nature – Goethe's Way of Science" makes it clear that this is not a discovery of worlds that lie behind the phenomenon as separate metaphysical realities, but a case of revealing what is already present in the phenomenon, or experience, by shifting the focus of consciousness to the **NOW**. Below through an analysis of Bacon's triptychs I will demonstrate how Bacon made the **NOW** an active ingredient of his work, thereby shattering the illusion that we live in the *never present 'present'* of our ordinary consciousness, so that the viewer effectively becomes embroiled not only in the picture-space but inhabits a space that becomes transformed by the work itself. I have no idea if the readers of this text have considered just how much a work of art changes the spaces within which it is displayed, or that works posses what is traditionally known as the 'aura', a phenomenon that radiates from the work under consideration. Great works of art emit a powerful 'aura' and it cannot be ignored that Bacon's images had a similar influential 'aura'. A theorist who produced significant thoughts in this area is Walter Benjamin, albeit his ideas were tinged by dialectical materialism, somewhat against his will I suspect, but that is a matter for another occasion. I will only say at this juncture that the 'aura' of a work has a considerable part to play in bringing the **NOW** into the ambit of the viewer.

Alan Howard in his booklet 'Thinking about Knowing' provides an intellectual framework for the relationship between the Ego, Self and the World. From his perspective our everyday lives, and all the events concerned with this, take place upon the *'plane of time'* governed by the Laws of Cause and Effect and Growth and Decay, which is the world of which our *self* is a part and within which our *self* acts. The self in this instance comprises all we know ourselves to be as an individual - our personalities, character, ideas, opinions, likes and dislikes and so on. Within this multi-faceted organisation our ego attempts to bring some order into this totality, and of itself issues from the **Eternal** - *the timeless*, and the ego may be thought of as a pole that intersects with the *'plane of time'* at a right-angle. The place where it intersects the *'plane of time'* is designated the **NOW**, although in ordinary consciousness we are rarely aware of this fact. Its involvement at its lower end with the *'plane of time'* creates what we name our *'self' (i)* and this is what we are usually conscious of in our everyday lives. We all know that we live in the World, and that this World is an organisation that is larger than us, and which encompasses our being, and everyone knows in that in their ordinary consciousness they cannot possibly cognise this all-encompassing totality. From this it is argued that there follows, logically, if one speaks of one's limited *ego* and *self* that there is a **Self** and *Ego* immanent to humanity that includes our limited *self* and *ego*, that in fact our *self* and *ego* are secondary, or subordinate, bearing in mind this is not meant pejoratively, instances of the categories of **Self** and **Ego**. Just as a particular *dog* does not make fully manifest all the possibilities of the category **Dog**, so the same is true of our *self* and *ego*. Admittedly if this is so then **Self** and **Ego** are for ordinary consciousness *ideal* categories but this does not make them any less *real*.

Through meditative exercises a person transforms their 'lower' self into the 'higher' self thereby giving them greater access to the potential of the **Ego.** In effect one rises up the pole of the **Ego** to that which comprises the totality of the **Ego**, meaning that an individual touches upon the **Eternal** and gains what might be describes as a sublime overview of themselves and the world they inhabit in the **NOW**. However this is a schemata, and is as such lifeless, and does not encompass how we live, and although Bacon's work is, in part, representations of the **NOW** he impregnated his images with such an emotional charge that the viewer experiences an activation of their own **NOW** together with all the reactions that such an activation produces. To continue with my analogy, it can be stated that where the *ego* touches the 'plane of time' thereby engendering our 'self' *the ego* is to begin with swamped and controlled by all the unbridled passions, desires and instincts etc that make up the 'self'. In this respect the Ego is overwhelmed by the ferociously powerful instincts and drives, and these powerful instincts and drives are largely responsible for the *desires* and *passions* that comprise our own emotional (astral) body. But a human being has a **WILL** and it is through exerting this will that the astral body is purified and the *self*, as the i, gradually encompasses more of the potential of the **I**. In one sense this rising up the pole of the *Ego* is an expansion of consciousness so as to include some knowledge of the composition of the **NOW**.

That the Ego is *timeless* is appreciated when we consider the *knowing* aspect of our consciousness, the ability to know something remains unchanged from early childhood to old age, and it is a given fact that the content of *knowing* changes dramatically over time but the actual ability does not. In contrast the *self* is conditioned by time, and it can easily be acknowledged that the *self* I had as child is utterly different from the *self* I possess as an adulthood. The difference between the two is illustrated by the fact that I say 'I know' and not the 'self knows', and this is further emphasised by my knowing that for the **I** the *self* is the *non-I*. The *self* is the vehicle through which the **I** acts, just as the Soul is the vehicle for the *self*. The implication is that the *self* is shaped through the flux of events characteristic of the world of space and time, whereas the **I**, which is timeless, only has a tangential relationship, to start with, with the world of space through its connection to our 'self'. In contrast to the *timeless*, the world that we know through our ordinary consciousness is dominated by time, and this becomes apparent in the forward flow of time from past to present to future. This raises the question as to whether it is ourselves that is moving, or whether movement is intrinsic to the 'plane of time'? However, as well as having a *knowing* dimension to ourselves we also have a *doing* ability, and when we are in the mode of 'doing' all awareness of the **I**'s connection to the *self* is overshadowed in the *act of doing*. 'I am doing this, I am doing that etc', and so in our lived lives the 'self' comes to the front and the **I** is subsumed into, and held in thrall to, the 'self'. The manner by which an act of will becomes a deed is a process that is very little understood, and Bacon demonstrates such an awareness with "Painting 1978", 1978, (ill 54). In this work we have a truncated Figure attempting to open a door with its foot - is this Figure trying to gain access to some secret behind the door?

Our ordinary consciousness of the 'plane of time' is that the future is constantly becoming the present, and that the present is constantly becoming the past, and that we exist in this 'present' through which time only flows in a forward direction. This is how things appear with our ordinary consciousness. This forward flow we assume is also characteristic of Law of Cause and Effect and the Law of Growth and Decay. The 'plane of time', as with all the other planes referred to in the Introduction, is a whole that is dimensionless, in contrast to a geometrical plane that is only so ideally, in understanding this it will be realised that what we call the past, present and future is only a local event pertinent to ourselves as appreciated through the limitations of our ordinary consciousness. Distinctions have to made when debating 'timelessness', **Eternity** or the **Eternal** for although in some circumstances they are interchangeable in effect the **Eternal** and **Eternity** are very different from 'timelessness', for the **Eternal** and **Eternity** are not merely non-time but something more than this. The **Eternal** and **Eternity** are completely 'other' than time as they include everything associated with time within themselves. Through the fact that the ego issues from **Eternity**, and the **Eternal**, it is thus able to transmit impulses from the **Eternal** to every manifestation of the 'self' in the world of 'space and time'. A fundamental aspect of the **Eternal** relates to that which is **Moral**, and that which is **Moral** can only enter the 'plane of time' by an individual freely absorbing moral impulses from the **Eternal** and acting upon these impulses. So when an individual freely absorbs these moral impulses there is the possibility of *freedom* through the action of the ego in contrast to the determination of Cause and Effect/ Growth and Decay that rules the coming into being of all that we know. If *freedom* were not made possible through the **Ego** then no-one would have the possibility of changing themselves, and so because we all have an ego anyone can change providing they have sufficient will-power to exert their ego-forces to initiate change, and it is in the **NOW** that this takes place.

We all assume that we live in the 'present', however careful examination reveals that this is not completely true. For instance with thinking if we are aware that we have a thought, or an idea, in our consciousness then this is not the original act of thinking but solely the end-result of thinking - thinking takes place with absolutely (in our ordinary consciousness) no awareness that it is taking place. One aspect of Steiner's comments upon 'Thinking about Thinking' is bring about an awareness in the individual of the actual act of thinking by removing attention from an absolute focus upon the end-results of thinking. The same is true of emotions, we are certainly aware of their presence, but where they came from and how they blossomed into the feelings we now have, of that there is no awareness. Again when we look at our willing we are aware that we have done something but a comprehensive awareness of how we acted is never the case. Normally we believe that we dwell in a *never present 'present'*, which is in fact the past, and which obscures us from realising that we do in reality exist in the **NOW**. It is only possible in our ordinary consciousness to be aware of what we have thought once we have thought it, that is fairly obvious and one of the purposes of meditative exercises is to bring awareness of the act of thinking and harmonising this with our overall consciousness, thereby transforming the *never present 'present'* into a realisation of the **NOW**. Outside of Initiation it is perfectly possible to have super-sensory experiences for whatever reason and to focus upon them, as is the case with Bacon who made use of his experiences for the purposes of his creativity. So Bacon was able to enter into the **NOW,** through his meditative activity, where he was able to experience not only his own 'self' at that moment but the condition in the **NOW** of others. This I believe, and will be arguing as such, is the key to understanding Bacon's bizarre imagery and its powerful affect upon the viewer, for in reality we are all in the condition being in the **NOW** but of not being able to experience this due to the nature of ordinary consciousness where the *never present 'present'* is a dead reflection of the **NOW**.

Howard then goes on to investigate the relationship of the individual *'self'* to the **World**, and again this is relevant for Bacon's imagery because of the Crucifixion triptychs. The *self* may be seen as the vehicle through which the **ego** interacts within the world, and as such there is unconsciously embedded within the *self*, not only knowledge of that which results through an individual interacting with the world, but a knowledge of all things appertaining to a human being *in toto*, and this is especially true with respect to our corporeality. This point is illustrated by the fact that we have a **'sense of life'**, or well-being, and if we feel healthy then it follows that we must have an unconscious sense of the functioning of the body to know that all is functioning correctly, otherwise one would never to be able to know if one were ill or becoming sick. Once consciousness has been expanded the individual has access to the autonomic system and is able to survey how this system operates in maintaining the functioning of the corporeal body.

Howard makes the crucial point that the body I possess along with its sensory organs is created by nature/ the World, and, furthermore, that I do not create my sensory perceptions, they are simply occur through my being conscious and having healthy organs. I open my eyes and see my surroundings and this happens instantaneously. From this perspective it can be said that the **World** reflects itself into me through my bodily senses and *knows* itself through the thinking of an individual **I**. What I know of what is reflected into me depends upon the range of concepts I possess and the sophistication of my perceptual capabilities. We can only speculate as to the nature of a babies' consciousness, however it is possible to state that if all its sensory organs are healthy that a babies' embryonic consciousness is flooded with sensations of every possible kind. Sounds, vision, smells, touch, to name a few, all of which can only be consciously cognised through the development of the brain and ego. Thus right from the moment of birth a 'self' is in the process of developing that has one aspect dependent upon its experiences within the World, in particular the social context within which it is born, and this includes everything that comprises a society, education, the press, television and cultural/ religious values, a family environment to name a few that to start with are determinant of the 'self', and which, furthermore, are instrumental in establishing who we are.

It is permissible to state that to begin with an individual is determined by the World they are born into and are able to cognise. If we now take into account that the World was in existence before an individual was born then it follows that the determined 'self' cannot know the fullness of the World at inception and into adulthood - there is no consonance between the two to begin with - and individuals can only change their conception of the World by changing themselves. At the moment of birth there is only consciousness and not knowing, which can only be acquired through thinking. By this argument the 'self' resembles a 'house' within which the I can dwell and which is supported by the corporeal body, and which only knows a portion of the World through its own particularity. **World** and **Self** are a polarity through which our reality comes into being, and where **'World and Self'** encompasses not only all the individual *'world and self'* configurations but all that which has not achieved our level of development. It is fascinating to see how these are treated by Bacon and Bosch respectively. Bosch is mainly concerned with the interaction of the individual *'world and self'* within the context of the all-encompassing **'World and Self'**, although he does not neglect issues revolving around how the individual comes to knowledge of the larger picture, whereas Bacon mainly focuses upon the involvement of the *'world and self'* with *it's self*, so to speak, as Russell aptly illustrates when he entitles one of his chapters as "Between Four Walls". Again Bacon does not wholly neglect the interaction of **'World and Self'** as is demonstrated by his Crucifixion triptychs, it is a matter of emphasis according to the character of the artist in question, for neither **'World and Self'** nor *'world and self'* exist in isolation from each other. Because the 'real' World existed before I came into being it is naturally, although this is largely unconscious to begin with, the standard by which an individual judges the 'truthfulness' of the contents of the 'self', and there comes a point for some individuals when they challenge the 'truthfulness' of the account they are given of the 'real' World from whatever source. Even if an individual was to experience every culture extant upon the planet they would still only be contemplating flux and change, and it is only when an individual is able to grasp those *truths* which are *'timeless'*, and which remain overshadowed to begin with within their own consciousness, that they begin to understand the essential nature of 'reality'. Primarily this means transforming ordinary consciousness from the *never present 'present'* to the **NOW**.

One of the ways of achieving this to become aware of the *percept* that belongs to those concepts that are 'real' but which at present we cannot perceive, such as growth, digestion and love. The concept of growth is absolutely real and knowable and is not an abstract, imagined concept, used to explain organic life, that is conjured as an illusory, distillation from all that grows, after all, we all have experience of it as a 'real' force that relates to our bodily health. The same is true of other concepts of this nature, such as 'love', and what is important here is that by attempting to find a percept relevant to these concepts we begin to feel our way into a higher order of knowledge that can eventually become wisdom. This is a gradual process until ordinary consciousness is transformed and an actual perception of these realms is achieved. Apart from exercises that result in an individual being able to perceive the Formative Forces of growth there are at present two principal methods for the transformation of ordinary consciousness. These are the transformation of thinking and the transformation of our soul, that is the purification of our passions, desires and urges. Through this arduous process the 'self' itself is transformed and the individual is then cognisant of an entirely new relationship of itself to the **World Self**.

It is almost banal to state that a human being is a complexity beyond present human understanding and the above is only a stunted schemata of this complexity, however it serves to illuminate a crucial difference between Bosch and Bacon. Bacon is entirely correct to state that his work has fundamentally nothing to do with Bosch, for both are working from opposite ends of a polarity. Bacon's comment was made in response to those who sought an explanation as to appearance of his Figures by recourse to Bosch's paintings, and were thus projecting the past onto his work as an explanatory cause. Notwithstanding this I believe Bacon was pointing to a far deeper reason for the difference between them through his declaration.

The work of Hieronymous Bosch has as one of its themes the relationship between the personal self and the World Self. To start with every individual is utterly enfolded within the World Self - and it is only with their development through the stages of life, from childhood onwards, that an individual begins to realise that they are one of many within the World. In the majority of cases this realisation is fully realised by the time they are approximately 21 years of age when the ego comes fully into its own as that individual's **I**. This is a process of maturation that is not fully conscious with regard to its implications, and for the greater part of humanity their further development proceeds after this point in a haphazard, barely conscious manner, governed mainly by instincts, drives and passions. Bosch was a fully conscious initiate who had perceived the nature of his own 'self' and its relationship to the society he inhabited, Bosch depicted the spiritual state of individuals who composed that section of European society that interested him, as well as indicating the overall spiritual condition of European civilisation. Bacon was certainly conscious of his own abilities and the information they provided of his own 'self' and others within his social circle, and of the specific connections between this information and the World, but he was unable, as far as it can be known, to place his experiences within an authentic and tested conceptual framework such as the Rosicrucian traditions that Bosch was privy to. Nor, in my opinion, would he wanted to have done, for Bacon was an instinctive painter who lived life to the hilt, and was in many ways driven by the very drives, passions, desires and instincts that Bosch himself had largely transformed. I will explore in another place evidence that Bacon was privy to esoteric knowledge to a far greater extent than is currently entertained. The fundamental difference between Bosch and Bacon is that there is to Bosch's work an instructional, didactic quality that is entirely lacking in Bacon's imagery, instead Bacon wished to jolt the viewer out of any complacency they may entertain regarding who, and what, they thought they were. It may be that Bacon had no desire to explore anything other than the dimensions of the human being that his abilities revealed to him.

This somewhat belaboured analysis of the relationship between the world, self and the ego has been necessary to create a platform for the further progression of this *critique* of Bacon's deceptively uncomplicated images. For in the majority of cases there is just the Figure juxtaposed to a bare minimum of objects. It is the manner of this juxtaposition and demeanour of the Figures that creates the complexity that has baffled so many viewers of the work - which is the question as to why this work retains such an affective power?

A Very Special Gift.

There is little doubt for me that both van Gogh and Bacon had abilities that are not to be commonly found, and which point to the possibilities of humanities' future development. The implication of these abilities, which revealed the essence of that which they both perceived, for both van Gogh and Bacon is that the ego has to be particularly strong so as to able to compartmentalise these experiences when going about their everyday business – this Bacon was able to achieve but van Gogh was not. This is the advantage of being associated with an occult school of training, as Bosch was, because through the guidance of those 'who have gone before' the pupil is guided in a beneficial manner. With Bosch we have a clear separation in his images of the 'body' and the 'self'. In his 'Prodigal Son' Bosch presents an image of the journey that his physical body - the support for his soul/'self' - has taken during the course of his life, and through the symbolism of the various parts of his work Bosch depicts the pit-falls and triumphs of this path. This is couched in a recognised system of symbols which were, authenticated by, and intrinsic to the Rosicrucian school of knowledge which Bosch undoubtedly subscribed to (see Aymes). In the work 'The Temptation of St Anthony' Bosch depicts the situation of his soul with respect to the world after he has achieved initiation, and throughout his artistic career Bosch demonstrated how he was able to keep separate what he perceived through his psychic abilities from his everyday life. Without the support and guidance that Bosch received an individual is plunged into a world of confusing experiences because they have not learnt how to integrate these experiences into their lives in a logical manner.

Apart from William Blake and Hieronymous Bosch there are many individuals who have come to public attention who claimed to possess remarkable psychic powers. Two of these individuals are Charles Webster Leadbeater, 1854-1934, one of the principals of the Theosophical movement around the turn of the 19ᵗʰ century, who undoubtedly had considerable psychic powers, and the Swedish scientist Emanuel Swedenborg (1688-1772). Much could be said about these individuals, and others, but a common theme is the struggles they had to endure in order to make sense of their experiences, and even a brief insight into these struggles is instructive with regard to Bacon. Bacon's work, even though he was able to make manifest the **NOW** in his triptychs, is at first meeting a confusing mixture of insights into our corporeal being and the soul-state of modern humanity, indicating, possibly, that he was not able to clearly identify and distinguish that which he perceived. In this sense Bacon provides a contrast to van Gogh who although he had similar abilities to Bacon was unable to translate his experiences not only into his work, as the following statement in a letter to his brother Theo makes evident,

"I have painted seven cornfields and still to my sorrow, they are only cornfields.",

but was also unable to integrate them into his public life.

I do not wish to develop this psychological theme any further at this juncture, but I would add that apart from van Gogh and his influence upon Bacon there is, as mentioned in the Introduction, the influence of Blake upon Bacon, and Blake again is an individual with remarkable mental powers as the verse that opened the Introduction demonstrates. Bacon was absolutely correct when he said that Bosch's work had nothing to do with his work – technically I doubt Bacon found Bosch's work very interesting as Bosch's symbolic style had very much fallen by the wayside with regard to modern styles - apart from which the narrative style of Bosch' work would have been contrary to his own stated intention of ridding his work of story-telling. Bosch's work is contemplative in the sense that it refers to what has been achieved, whereas as stated Bacon's was concerned with the **NOW** and not principally with what was past. Thus Bacon wanted to palpably express the psychic state of humanity so that it had a visceral impact upon the viewer, and strove to make this as real as possible – Bacon was certainly more passionately involved with his work than Bosch was in this respect. Nevertheless, I do not believe that Bacon was an 'action painter' in the art historical sense and will leave that issue until another time.

There seems little doubt that Bacon had life-changing spiritual experiences around the period of 1956/ 1957, and the painting "Man Carrying a Child", 1956, ill.14, marks a high-point in the visual record he created of his experiences, for this work demonstrates that Bacon experienced the condition of childhood with full self-consciousness. This work has undeniable resemblances to the Christophorus, and the main Figure is enclosed in what I will designate as an 'impossible frame'. The decoding of these 'impossible frame' is essential to the unlocking of the import of Bacon's work and will be fully analysed below. However, to start with Bacon used such frames as a metaphor for changes of consciousness required to achieve a deeper insight into the nature of 'reality'. The fact that Bacon painted such an image as "Man Carrying a Child" that is redolent of a modern rendering of the Christophorus, a widespread and popular mystical theme of the 14ᵗʰ and 15ᵗʰ centuries, can only mean that Bacon was living through perhaps if not absolutely overwhelming, then certainly intense spiritual experiences during the period of 1956 to 1957, for the Christophorus is a symbol of someone who has attained profound spiritual insight. I do not wish to explore all the ramifications of the Christophorus at this point, but I will provide one quotation from Steiner upon the subject:

"And so he knew to what extent he bore within him the force of the spiritual Sun, for he had seen it in his vision. He had gained a consciousness of how he bore the spiritual forces of the Sun within him, and this in effect was the degree of Initiation whereby man became a Christ-Bearer, that is to say, a bearer of the Sun Being, not a receiver of the Sun Being, but a bearer of the Sun Being. Just as the Moon itself when it is Full Moon is a bearer of Sunlight, so man became a bearer of the Christ, a Christophoros.".(Steiner: The Easter Festival in relation to the Mysteries, Lecture Three).

This statement certainly provides some illumination into why Bacon deployed the symbolism of the Crucifixion, and he did this in a manner that rejected the dogma and commentary of the Church upon this theme. Bacon from the perspective of the coming-to-terms with himself and the **World** implicit to the spiritual journey of the mid 1950's previously referred to, confronted particular traits of his personality and character connected with his own maturation into adulthood. Primarily this concerned the Father (the 'Pope' series) and, this as an artist, was complicated for Bacon by his having to deal with the authority of the past as embodied within Western culture. For Bacon to be able to make an impact and be successful, and he was a very determined person who desired success as an access to the standard of life he was not only used to but wanted, he had to develop a style that not only carried on from that which had brought him success but which embodied that which he perceived. Thus, in a sense he had to overcome, or transcend not only himself, but also the past in terms of what was expected of him so as to be truthful and sincere as an artist, without endangering his own financial prospects. A delicate balancing act he achieved with aplomb. As stated he had a troubled relationship with his natural father but whatever psychological needs were bound up with this and continuing needs, he was shrewd enough to realise that he could exploit his own needs and sexuality to get the funds necessary to maintain his lifestyle from wealthy older men. However by 1957 and at the age of 48 he must have realised that this method of conducting his private life was finished, and combined with the pressure from his own intensely creative nature, he knew he had to change and 'step up a gear', so to speak. Thus for Bacon 1957 was kind of epiphany that, to return to a use of biblical symbolism, was akin to seeing the light on the road to Damascus.

The evidence for this assertion is to be found by comparing the stylistic changes of the pre-1957 period with the post-1957 period. There is a difficulty with this period of the 1950's for assessing Bacon's output because he is known to have destroyed many of his works from this period, however recently a large number of sketches have been found that are now on display in the Tate Gallery. So we can conclude that for Bacon both van Gogh and Blake represented the 'past', literally, in cultural terms and that by absorbing them through reworking them in his own work he neutralised the paralysing effect that the past can have upon an artist's own creativity – which can aptly be described as the 'Gaze of the Gorgon'.

Chapter 3. Movement and Dynamism in Space.

There can be no questioning of the fact that Bacon's work exhibits unusual forms of movement, and after overcoming the emotional disturbance that results from a first viewing of Bacon's paintings it is more than likely that one begins to notice the movement, or more specifically the change and metamorphosis, of the Figures depicted by Bacon. In reply to M. Archimbaud's question "Do you like Gericault?" Bacon states

" Yes. The impressive thing about Gericault is the sense of movement in everything. Especially the representation of the human body and of horses; everything is captured in an incredible sense of movement. But when I talk about movement, I don't mean the representation of speed, that's not what it's about at all. Gericault somehow had movement pinned to the body. He was fascinated by it." (Archimbaud, 1993: 41).

The implications of Bacon's statement that 'Gericault somehow had movement pinned to the body' is worth investigating with respect to my contention that Bacon possessed unusual sensory abilities. One difference immediately noticeable to someone with these abilities is how movement, or dynamism appears, for, as my commentary upon the **Now** above indicated, time is no longer understood in a linear fashion. Instead, also indicated above, the person possessing these abilities gradually becomes to understand time as a *whole*, and not extruded into a past, present and future sequence. We normally perceive movement as the rate of change of a body within three-dimensional space – Cartesian space. The element of speed (rate of change) has a dramatic and stirring impact upon our consciousness, and evokes within us a wide range of emotions and sensations. Yet Bacon is adamant that this is not what he is talking about and, further, that Gericault's images capture the quality he is referring to. For a person with Bacon's perceptual skills linearity is now appreciated as only one facet of time, and consequently rate of change is no longer seen to be the exclusive mode of expression of movement, or dynamism. Instead movement is perceived as a *whole* and as acting *within itself* as though it were in fact referencing itself. The reason for this is that in states of higher consciousness the demarcation between *self/I* and the **Other** is not as defined as it is in ordinary consciousness, but is permeable and porous. So that one begins to merge into the other, and in this case *speed* is appreciated for *itself* and not as a phenomenon to be *observed*, this again has been referred to in the Introduction. There is when viewing Bacon's Figures the feeling that although they have an energetic quality to them this is being expressed in a way that is hard to comprehend. The only clue we have is Bacon's enigmatic phrase that 'Gericault somehow had movement pinned to the body'. By denying the concept of speed Bacon is implying that it is not dynamic, linear, mechanical movement that concerns him, but rather that he has perceived, and is concerned with depicting, some other type of dynamism and movement that is intrinsic to the body, and it can be appreciated how radically different Bacon's depiction of movement is when it is compared with, for example, how motion is depicted by the Futurists.

Bacon's attempt to capture in his Figuration a movement, or dynamism, of the body that is very different from that which is linear and mechanical is emphasised in a conversation with Michel Archimbaud.

M.A. "Nevertheless, the analysis of movement through photography has been very helpful to painters, such as Degas, hasn't it? For example, in studying the way horses gallop?"

F.B. "Yes, but not for me…". (Archimbaud, 1993: 15).

From this it is understood that the reason that Bacon was interested in photography –examples of Muybridge's photography are known to have been in his studio – was not for information concerning mechanical movement. I believe that Bacon was fascinated by Muybridge's photography not for their reflection of how they captured actual movement as ordinarily perceived, but for how they belie the actual perception of movement for someone with Bacon's abilities. In this respect Bacon displayed an unusual sensitivity to our **'Sense of Movement'** and our **'Sense of Balance'**, as referred to in the Introduction. Furthermore, it is possible, that the grotesqueness of Muybridge's photography provided Bacon with a starting-point for depicting the difference from ordinary consciousness of how the human form appeared when in a state of meditation. Nevertheless, this creates a problem for in the course of everyday life we are only normally aware of movement as mechanical and linear. Daniel Kurjakovic (an Art Historian who has published various articles in a number of publications) presents an important insight into the triptych "Three Portraits: Posthumous Portrait of G. Dyer, Self-Portrait and Portrait of L. Freud", 1973, (ill. 55), of which he says that the triptych's space is not 'expressly three-dimensional', and that the relationship of the Figures is marked by their being on a different axis to that of the background. This Kurjakovic believes allows them to perform an *'impossible simultaneity'* where they can hypothetically substitute for each other. I have already stated that Goethe achieved, through enhancing the resonance between his Intellect and Imagination, a *compression of time* when perceiving the plant world, and an 'impossible simultaneity' is another way of expressing this, there is thus a correspondence between Kurjakovic's *'impossible simultaneity'* and my contention that Bacon *compressed time* when viewing the human body, especially with respect to emotional states. Kurjakovic's insight is thus suggesting that Bacon's Figuration records that which we consider to be impossible for our ordinary consciousness, namely that individuals are not separated out from each other discreetly in space and time, but that they have a commonality in that they can, from a particular viewpoint, be perceived as inhabiting, or dwelling within, in some manner, one common space. Naturally from an ordinary corporeal viewpoint we are discrete bodies in space, but this is not the case on other levels of being already referred to, and from that viewpoint we exist in simultaneity with all beings. I have already, in the Introduction, pointed out that there is no such thing as an inner world that is separate from an outer world (dualism). The 'mind' is not distinct from the world but integral to it, and when it is transformed, as indicated, then the absolute inter-connectedness of all that is corporeal is apprehended, i.e. there is no longer a strict *them* and *us* (self and other). Clearly such an insight by Kurjakovic implies that we have to reconsider our normal understanding of the Cartesian space-time continuum when viewing Bacon's images. In fact Kurjakovic in the rest of his commentary states that we can only really understand Bacon's work if we take into account Bacon's disruption of Classical Perspective; where Classical Perspective is the technical means developed, by artists, for the pictorial rendition of objects in what we call the Cartesian space-time continuum. Additionally Kurjakovic is implying that this was so important to Bacon that Bacon went to the lengths of producing a triptych that not only expressed the connections he perceived, but that in so doing he felt it necessary to subvert common assumptions as to how we perceive and relate to others in everyday space. (Dumas, 1995: 62-69). *Simultaneity* is a basic tenet of events in the spaces of Projective Geometry, however a far more simple example of simultaneity is to be found in everyday life. Whilst awake during daylight we all receive through our eyes the light-of-the world, and in doing so we are all unconsciously simultaneously connected for **Light** is *indivisible* and *invisible.* The import of this is that we are *simultaneously* connected to everyone whilst awake, or contemplating the stars, through the medium of the **Light**. Even from this basic example, which can be extended endlessly through commentary upon holograms and the like, it is realised that simultaneity is an important but hidden and largely ignored aspect of our cognition. It is not suggested that these are the only explanations of the simultaneity that Kurjakovic perceived in Bacon's triptych, but it is indicative of levels of consciousness where simultaneity of being is endemic to our ordinary consciousness. **Light** is simply more than its quantification as wavelengths and photons, and although it is acknowledged that without the sun there could be no growth this understanding is conjectured from a material base.

*

Gilles Deleuze notices a correspondence between Bacon's use of line and that of the line in Gothic Art. In Gothic Art although the line traces out organic forms it escapes this functional subordination through the decorative (as opposed to the ornamental), for within Gothic art the patterns produced by the interaction of the lines aesthetically affect our sensibilities so that we are drawn away from the portrayal of objects in space into realms that are generative of the real-life organic forms depicted. This is what Deleuze states, and the uplifting effect of the Gothic is well-known and documented. Deleuze then goes on to argue that with the evolution of the optical-tactile space of Classical perspective the line became subjected, as a contour to the codes for depicting objects in everyday space, and that in order to achieve his aims Bacon, and this also applies to a great number of other artists, had to prise the line away from such a utilitarian function.

" ...it is not by outlining a form, but on the contrary by imposing, through its clarity and nonorganic precision, a zone where forms become indiscernible. It also attests to a high *spirituality*, since what leads it to seek the elementary forces beyond the organic is a spiritual will. But this spirituality is a spirituality of the body, the spirit of the body itself, the body without organs… (The Figure of Bacon would be that of the Gothic decorator)". (Deleuze, 2004: 46-47).

A 'zone where forms become indiscernible' is an apt description of how forms metamorphose in to, and out of, each other, which is one of the first impressions of 'realms that are generative of the real-life organic forms', until these fleeting, evanescent forms become more discernible as an individual improves upon their ability to follow this metamorphosis in its many guises. Deleuze understood the 'line' in Bacon's paintings to be a 'spiritual' line, in that it raised awareness from the organic form depicted to forces generative of the organic:

" … lines of flight that pass through bodies, but which find their consistency elsewhere …. lines that are 'more' than lines, surfaces that are 'more' than surfaces ... It is out of chaos that the 'stubborn geometry' or 'geological' lines first emerge ... this frenetic line: it is a life, but the most bizarre and intense kind of life, a *nonorganic* vitality …" (Deleuze, 2004: 54, 111).

Deleuze presents here a paradox for what could a 'nonorganic vitality' possibly be, what is he referring to? I would argue that in the first instance Deleuze is referring to Formative Forces, for these forces are nonorganic, and certainly full of vitality, in the sense that they are responsible for directing material to the right place within the corporeal body so that it can evolve and grow, and they do this according to a schemata that is projected into their field from the astral realm. This statement will be explored in depth below, but for now it provides an insight into Deleuze's enigmatic phrase. Furthermore, they are nonorganic in that they are completely and utterly different from earthly forces, but, nevertheless, they bring life and form to that which is to begin with lifeless through the 'living' ideas they carry within themselves (which Goethe was able to perceive). In this sense a 'nonorganic vitality' may be spoken of, especially when considered alongside the commentary upon movement above. From this it is apparent that Deleuze, and Bacon, by default, spoke of and depicted 'lines' other than as they are understood through Euclidean geometry. Deleuze struggles to find words descriptive of these other lines, and his 'stubborn geometry' is an elusive concept. As far as it is known neither Deleuze nor Bacon were aware of the existence of Projective Geometry. Still Deleuze's description above concerning lines and geometry bear a similarity to Steiner's statements

" … One receives an 'imagination' of the whole cosmos, One receives a counter-image of …. the three geometrical space dimensions. What one receives can take a variety of shapes … One receives the idea of space which I can only indicate figuratively. If I indicate the ordinary space by three lines at right-angles to one another, I should indicate this space by drawing everywhere sets of figures or configurations, as if surface-forces, or forces in surfaces were approaching the earth from without, from all directions of the universe, and were working plastically on the forms upon its surface ...". (Whicher, 1989: 41).

"...these mutually supporting forces in space were recognised as they streamed hither and thither. They were felt and perceived by those in whose soul the idea of the Greek temple arose. They did not 'think out' the forms, but they could perceive the force streaming through space and then worked the stone accordingly...Thus the Greek temple is a material representation of forces working in space. Such a temple is a crystallised percept of space, in the purest sense." (Steiner, 1987: 19).

Deleuze proposed that with Bacon's Figuration specifically with how line is deployed, there is a movement away from merely registering the corporeal form of the human body as it appears to our ordinary, intellectual consciousness in favour of a search for those fundamental forces that give rise to our flesh and bones. This is an absolutely crucial insight and its ramifications will echo throughout this text, for a line is capable of expressing more than the outline of a form. Proclus, a fifth century A.D. Neoplatonic philosopher, gives an idea of this power of line when he describes his experience of the *Ars lineandi*:

"*Ars Lineandi* is the recaptured memory of the invisible ideas of the soul: it gives life to its own cognition, awakens the spirit, purifies understanding, and brings the formative element, which is part of our being, to light. It eliminates the baseness and ignorance that clings to us from birth, and liberates from the bond of unreason. It rouses the soul from sleep and impels it towards the spirit. It makes us a true human being, allows us to behold the spirit and guides us towards the gods." (Kutzli, 1981: 8).

*

Steiner's description of a temple as being 'a crystallised percept of space' is an apt analogy for some of Bacon's images, and Proclus' comment of bringing 'the formative', which is part of our being, to light' further illuminates Steiner's and Deleuze's comments above. The statement by Proclus also serves to remind us that with our coming-into-earthly life at birth our consciousness, after the first years of infancy, suffers a 'forgetfulness' of its relationship to the light-filled higher members of our being (body of formative forces, soul and spirit) and the Cosmos. During these early years, which end with our learning to speak and think with an earthly language, we are in absolute, undivided communion with the Cosmos. The *Ars Lineandi* according to Proclus is thus a way of resuscitating this lost memory so as to regain our humanity. It is also apparent that Deleuze was aware of such 'invisible ideas of the soul' as described by Proclus, and that these could be expressed through lines, and that with Francis Bacon he recognised an individual who had the ability to make these 'invisible ideas of the soul' visible. However it still remains to indicate how this concept of 'lines in space' can be approached from everyday experience. A particularly good example is with the fields of electro-magnetic force and sound. It is well-known that it is possible to make these invisible force-fields perceptible through the use of iron filings which reveal the patterns of these forces in space. We never see the 'lines of force' of these fields but they are nevertheless present permeating the space surrounding us in our daily lives. These, however, are mechanical force fields and as such are related to the inorganic world, whereas the focus here is with those forces that are related to the organic living world, and it has to be clearly stated, again, that they are of a completely different order to mechanical forces and consequently make themselves manifest through an entirely dissimilar manner.

Heaven's Geometry.

Through the development of Euclidean geometry we have now become such masters of the spatial world of our waking consciousness that we are able to send men to the moon. But at the same time that Rene Descartes, (1596-1650), put forward his brilliant mathematical insights that eventually made such a feat possible Girard Desargues, (1593-1662), pursued a different and equally brilliant line of mathematical enquiry into what is known as Projective Geometry. Euclid's theorems and Descartes' mathematics concern the inorganic and earthly dimension of the world that we inhabit, and how we can measure this and predict movements within it. The Cartesian Space-Time Continuum has been developed as a model so that we can orientate ourselves within, and negotiate, the world of wide-awake ordinary consciousness. This is the inorganic world of matter that we cognise, whilst awake, through the auspices of a mineral, corporeal body. The Law of Cause and Effect and the Law of Growth and Decay, which order the course of events, and the force of Gravity are primary to this world of matter. We perceive how through the force of gravity matter interacts and masses are built up through a process of accretion or how masses are worn away either through collisions or through erosion.

This is one side of our consciousness, but as we are all aware we do not spend all our time awake but have periods of sleep during which we dream and have spatial experiences that are contrary to those of being awake. There are experiences of floating and flying; there are also experiences to be had where one event seamlessly transforms itself into something completely different. Experiences of time are also contrary to everyday expectations, events can interrelate to each other and appear natural, which on waking-up we realise relate to different periods of our lives. Past, present and future interact in a different manner during sleep than the linearity of waking consciousness. The volatility of time and space during sleep in comparison to being awake finds expression in the tenets of Projective Geometry which although logical and orderly do effect rapid changes of form. The depiction of sleep is an important, vital and easily over-looked aspect of Bacon's iconography, an example being "Lying Figure", 1958, (ill. 56). "Painting", 1946, (ill. 33) displays an ambiguity due to the occluded eyes of the Figure and grimacing mouth - is this a macabre nightmare in a slaughter-house? Is this a Grand Guignol allegory of pantomime proportions due to the intestines festooning the top of the picture in the manner of Christmas decorations? Whatever the conclusion it is apparent that due to the distortions of space the work depicts an altered state of consciousness, and this is emphasised by representing the corporeality of the Figure inside-out. As far as I am concerned this is a rendering of the Lesser Guardian of the Threshold who appears to every individual upon the point of Initiation. This will be examined in more detail later.

Bacon's work "Painting, 1946", explores the juxtaposition of wakefulness and sleep, for the central Figure has its physical eyes occluded thus indicating that the Figure is possibly 'sleeping' or 'dreaming'. The triptych "Triptych Inspired by the Oresteia of Aeschylus", 1981, (ill. 34) reveals what can only be described as weird Figures performing bizarre acts of will, and where once again the Figures have occluded sight even though they have a purposefulness. The import of these 'sleeping', apparently, wakeful Figures is that they exhibit wakefulness during sleep. They inform us that the lack of consciousness we have during 'sleep' cloaks the fact that we are active in another space, and indeed our experiences of 'dreaming', chaotically infused as they are by our desires, indicates such a fact. So if it were possible for everyone to be as self-conscious during sleep as when awake, particularly of the middle deep-sleep part, of which there is *no* consciousness, what would we experience? One immediate consequence would be that such an individual would have consciousness of the space relevant to each state described - wakefulness and dreaming - and there are individuals who claim to be able to invoke this ability at will. Accordingly we have much first-hand information concerning the state of being fully conscious during deep-sleep (lucid dreaming), and one particularly noteworthy example is quoted below.

*

The postulations of Projective geometry are such that they theorise about properties of simultaneity, inter-relatedness, metamorphosis, floating and non-linear time sequences, and in this sense connect us symbolically with the experience of dreaming. However, it would not be feasible to provide an in-depth exposition of all the facets of Projective Geometry here, but this is to be found in Olive Whicher's books "Sunspace" and "Projective Geometry". Nevertheless, I will explore those fundamentals that are pertinent to Bacon's work. The primary reason for deploying Projective Geometry as an interpretative tool is encapsulated by Whicher's statement that

"Projective geometry is not merely a geometry of created forms, but the geometry of the relationships between form-creating entities." (Whicher, 1985: 49).

When "Painting, 1946", is contemplated it is clear that Bacon has eviscerated the standing Figure to expose some of those parts of our anatomy essential to our corporeal constitution. This image provides a starting-point, in the first instance, interpretatively for Projective Geometry for as Whicher states Projective Geometry concerns *'the geometry of the relationships between form-creating entities'*, that is what is the relationship between the Figure and eviscerated flesh and organs. The fact that these eviscerated body-parts lie outside the Figure points to an important facet of Projective Geometry, and that is Counter-Space: initially Counter-Space may be thought of as the inverse of Cartesian Space. The conjunction of these two types of space will be referred to here as Lemniscatory Space, (ill. 57), and the point that marks the transition from one to other will be referred to as the 'cross-over point of lemniscatory space', and everything that is inside one of the spaces, either Cartesian Space or Counter Space, is then outside in the other as it passes through this point. It will be demonstrated below that Bacon had an intuitive, as opposed to a rational and intellectualised, grasp of these two types of space. This is one example of how Projective Geometry may be applied interpretatively, and the relevance of other concepts of Projective Geometry for an understanding of Bacon's work will be investigated below. Projective Geometry theorises about the inter-relationship of the two spaces already delineated, therefore it may be postulated that the space of *dreaming* is in fact that of Counter-Space, and that in going to sleep we pass through the 'cross-over point of lemniscatory space', and then dwell in the invisible realms of the astral world and the Spirit. The actual focus of the 'cross-over point of lemniscatory space' is Infinity, which plays a crucial but unrecognised role in our daily lives. This behoves an introductory examination of our assumptions regarding Infinity.

What is the Point of Infinity – A Question of Balance?

The practical value of Cartesian Geometry, and its associated mathematical models, is that it enables us to understand how the force of gravity and other mechanical forces radiate out, and operate, from points in the world of matter with which we are so familiar. Clearly for the majority of people there is no familiarity with the properties of Counter-Space simply because there is no conscious awareness of our ontological circumstances when sleeping, or of the hidden dimensions of reality. Nevertheless it is perfectly possible whilst awake to cognise the role that Counter-Space plays in the growth of plant-life with our ordinary powers of reasoning and observation. This possibility is another facet of Goethe's methodology for enhancing the manner by which the Intellectual and Imaginative aspects of our being resonate together, a methodology he named as 'Exact Sensorial Fantasy', and which has already been referred to above. Goethe,s methodology, Bacon's work and the meaning of Blake's verse can be familiarised by a number of imaginative exercises relating to colour, plant growth and so on, specifically here there are geometrical imaginative exercises that enable one to become familiar with Projective Geometry, and importantly with Infinity. To be precise there is an exercise where one imagines what it would be like to travel to the point-at-infinity.

To do so appears at first to be, literally, a 'pointless' exercise, for where is Infinity and where could such a point be located? One way to initially of coming-to-terms with this exercise is through Classical Perspective. Perspective allows us to abstractly internalise the spatial world of ordinary consciousness into which we are physically embedded. Through perspective we possess this spatial world as an inner reality, albeit it in an abstract, shadowy form. There is no longer an outside or inside through this mode of representation, but the full implications of this cannot be grasped because this imaginative mode of thinking is in a sense 'unreal' and possesses no substance. One reason for this is that ordinary consciousness only allows access to the lowest order of space. I will not at this juncture refer to those forms of Perspective that attempted to rectify this situation by formalizing aspects of enhanced perception. Since its inception Perspective now has a commonality of understanding for the vast majority of people, and is not the exclusive property of small section of society. Classical Perspective, which is a form of geometry, is thus an intimate and precise, abstract knowledge of the Cartesian Space of ordinary consciousness.

One of the fundamental achievements of this system is that it encloses infinity within it as something cognisable, this is achieved by having the 'vanishing' point as that which logically organises the representation of the spatial disposition of phenomena. That is, through the 'vanishing' point a 'realistic' representation is possible for the inter-relationship of phenomena in space with respect to size and distance. So as we view a perspective drawing we see objects getting smaller and smaller the further into the distance and nearer to the 'vanishing' point they are, and these 'vanishing' points, for there can be any number of them, lie upon an horizon the importance of which will become apparent later, and which has already been referred to in the Introduction. The primary function of the horizon is that it sets the limit to that which can be visualised and represented, and thus echoes our own experience. The fact that the globe of visual experience given to us by our ordinary senses can be so represented means that, socially, perspective is inclusive and democratic. The horizon from this reasoning is in fact a multitude of infinities arrayed all over the inner surface that is the limitation of our visual field. Infinity therefore has an ambiguous status as both 'real' and 'unreal', and as such this borderline of innumerable infinities sets the limits of ordinary consciousness. Thus this abstract representation is analogous to our own experiences of, let us say, an avenue of trees receding into the distance. In this system 'vanishing' points act as masters that regulate and order the representation of the object-filled world of our wide-awake consciousness. How different this space was represented by artists prior to the creation of perspective drawing; people, buildings, and sundry other phenomena are haphazardly depicted regardless of their size in relation to their relative distances from each other in a dream-like manner, and this is because at that time everyday consciousness had not uniformly become centred upon the Intellect alone with the Imagination playing an increasingly, and unregulated, minor role. There is no doubt that for present epistemological purposes the Imagination is the inferior and impoverished handmaiden of the Intellect, and this situation is not altered by the Imagination being subjected to ungoverned and ungrounded fantasy - this is the value of Goethe for he demonstrated how the Imagination could be fruitfully woven into our everyday consciousness by accessing the Imaginative Intelligence of infancy. The system of perspective we are commonly familiar with reflects the dry arid world of the Intellect alone, and it would be too much of a diversion to examine other perspective systems that attempt to capture a greater range of our lived experiences - it is this aridness that Bacon, and other artists, tried to counter through their disruption of Classical Perspective.

In the material world we all regard ourselves as a centre, but what do we mean by this? If we abstractly regard our centre as a point how big is this, is it large or small, and what is it? If we regard our ego as this point, and this is not unreasonable for it is from the I of our thinking that we orientate ourselves in the world, then speaking of Infinity has a clear reference to the fact the ego was described as at right-angles to the plane of time and stretched upwards into the **Eternal**. It requires no further elaboration to realise that this ego-point within ourselves must in itself be, in *reality*, an **Infinity** from which we orientate ourselves and to which we aspire. It is only by realising that any point (a representation of infinity) when expanded to any great degree becomes a globe that we gain any awareness of how our world has issued from the Infinite, and this relates to the globe of experience described above. The peculiarity is that the horizon, when stretched in all directions, up and down etc, becomes the inner surface of our visual world as a globe. If the expansion from a point to a globe is infinitely large then its surface would appear as a plane, made up of infinities or points, because we would be unable to detect its infinitely small curvature.

If we were then able to travel, in consciousness, along a line from our point to the surface of the infinitely distant globe and be able to stop just before we reach the surface of this infinitely expanded globe, and then be able to look back we would see the infinitely distant point that was our centre. Clearly if this was actually happening then one would be able to perceive one's own self from the outside, and thus be undergoing what is termed an out-of-the-body experience. Bacon's work "Painting 1946" is an image that attempts to depict such an experience, and I shall argue that much of Bacon's imagery is concerned with the ramifications of this experience. This also reflects upon the need for guidance, as Bosch received, when experiencing the higher levels of these exercises for what is described here are only the rudimentary beginnings. Through practising this exercise eventually our consciousness is transformed so that in the words of Blake we are able

> To see a world in a grain of sand,
> And a heaven in a wild flower,
> Hold infinity in the palm of your hand,
> And eternity in an hour.

But we can also imagine ourselves to be travelling towards a 'vanishing' point, and if we remain within its strictures, we witness an ever-diminishing world until we reach the 'vanishing' point, or the point-at-infinity. If we then imagine we pass through this point, and still remain within its strictures, what do we now see? If we stay true to the exercise we can only say that we perceive the smallest closer to us with the largest further away as our visual cone expands to, shall we say, the 'plane-at-infinity' of our infinitely distant globe, there has thus been a reversal of our condition at the start of this exercise. This exercise gives one a first-hand experience of an extremely important aspect of Projective geometry and that is the 'cross-over point of lemniscatory space', which is the point at which Cartesian space and the Counter-Space perceived upon passing through the vanishing-point transform into each other. We start the exercise in the Cartesian Space-Time Continuum and end up experiencing the Counter-Space of *invisible* forces and **Levity**. Repetition of these exercises brings about a mobility of thinking and seeing that felicitates an enhanced awareness of the transformation of forms in the living world. It is also equally possible, so as to develop this experience, to imagine that one is on a plane that is moving towards 'the plane-at-infinity' and that the closer this plane we are on comes to the 'plane-at-infinity' so it expands until it becomes infinitely large when it reaches the 'plane-at-infinity', and we able then to experience a state of absolute instantaneous inter-connectedness with all other possible planes originating from every conceivable point. By doing this exercise one's consciousness has encountered an absolute focus and an absolute expansion - a systole and a diastole - and realised their inter-relatedness whereby one is the other perceived from either position. Given that the plane-at-infinity is infinitely large it includes, as stated, all possible planes that one could have started from, and all that could have been inscribed on any particular original starting plane is simultaneously connected with all that which is inscribed on any other plane that any other person could have chosen to start with. Contemplation of these fundamental facts - who can deny that a point that contracts into itself continuously does so to infinity, or that a point that expands goes through the stages of ball/ sphere to an infinitely large globe and is thus infinitely large - provides an abstract understanding of the underlying inter-connectedness of the Cosmos, despite the fact that to our ordinary, untransformed intellectual consciousness everything seems utterly distinct and unconnected upon first appearance.

Whicher emphasises the fact that Projective Geometry theorises from the plane-at-infinity to the point, whereas Cartesian geometry does the opposite theorising from the point to the plane-at-infinity. Thus to have any practical value Projective Geometry has also to provide a similar service, i.e. it has to indicate to which phenomena in the world its tenets are applicable for waking consciousness. As stated it is Steiner who provided the insight that it is with the organic world, with that which is living, that such an endeavour should start. He also indicated that the forces associated with the plane-at-infinity were formative, moulding forces that worked from this plane, in a hovering, floating manner, through the force of **Levity** to create the living. To claim that there is a force, named Levity, that is equal and opposite to Gravity will no doubt be greeted by some with incredulity, my own particular journey started out thus, and I have no intention to mount a defence for this claim, and I direct the reader to Ernst Lehrs book "Man or Matter" for a discussion based on scientific principles, especially when it is considered objectively that there is no logical reason for there *not* being a force equal and opposite to gravity within the bi-polar universe of our experience. (See Ernst Lehrs Book "Man or Matter" for an introduction upon the properties of Levity and arguments for its existence. Pg. 190, then *passim*). Further discussion of the effects of Levity, which is the primary force of the space of Formative Forces, is to be found in Georg Adams' and Olive Whicher's book "The Plant between Sun and Earth". In the Introduction I pointed out that **Gravity** and **Levity** are related to *absolute darkness* and *absolute light*, respectively, and are in fact the same force acting in the direction of either, both of which are unknowable, in themselves, for ordinary consciousness Clearly these invisible forces allied to concepts that have no percept must exist somewhere, for they are utterly and inseparably a part of the world we inhabit and within which we live and work. All that can be said at this point is that there is a 'hidden-ness' to our everyday cognition of nature - a part that does not fully reveal itself to ordinary consciousness.

When we look at a living organism what we perceive is the interaction of *absolute darkness* and *absolute light*, making themselves manifest as either **Gravity** or **Levity**. Where the Formative Forces, emanating from the plane-at-infinity of ethereal space, penetrate into the *gravity-bound matter* of the material world so as to create that which lives, then we bear witness to the interaction of the two spaces described as Counter Space and Cartesian Space. Initially familiarisation with Projective Geometry's principles and their relationship to Formative forces and the life forms of nature erodes the picture of nature as a collection of separate phenomena standing side-by-side that are mechanically related. Instead it is felt, and perceived, how nature is an inter-related whole where particular forms that appear in lower life forms appear again, but transformed, in higher life forms.

Lemniscatory Space.

An abstract appreciation of how these two spaces (the earthly and the heavenly) interact in any living organism, is gained through the Lemniscate (ill. 57), which illustrates the cross-over point of Lemniscatory space (Cartesian space interacting with the Ethereal/ Counter space of Formative forces described by Projective Geometry). As can be seen this is a fascinating figure for if one traces a route from the inside of a line on one side then one emerges on the surface of this line on the other side, properties that are enhanced by viewing the Lemniscate in three-dimensions. This figure gives a feeling for moving in and out of spaces and is of immediate importance in attempting to understand Bacon's Figuration, and so it is worthwhile exploring how Bacon displayed in his works an innate, intuitive understanding of the cross-over point of Lemniscatory space.

To initiate this discussion attention is drawn to those illustrations that have a curiosity value because of their reversibility, Gestalt figures. Here we have figures that display within a single form the possibility of being interpreted in two different ways, and so we have two contradictory readings the potential of which resides, even if we can only view them sequentially, within our consciousness *simultaneously*. There has to be a movement in conscious cognition away from one to the other whereby all the qualities of the parameters that condition one interpretation are rejected in favour of the other. The significance of the elements of these figures are volatile and do not appear fixed until we decide upon a particular interpretation. This invokes Heisenberg's Uncertainty Principle, whereby only either the position or the movement of a particle can be determined at a specific moment. The example of Gestalt figures indicates that the way the world appears to us is the result of our what decide it to be either consciously or unconsciously. Although through these figures we simulate a traversal across the cross-over point of Lemniscatory Space mentally, it has to be remembered that they are static, whereas with Projective geometry and Formative Forces all is movement and change, even if this is only implied in the figures of Projective Geometry, nevertheless, we are able through our imagination to follow these implied transformations logically. Thus these Gestalt figures become an instructive analogy of how an individual such as Bacon, Blake and Goethe, turned their thinking inside-out so as to perceive hidden dimensions of that which is normally perceived, and in this respect the Lemniscate provides a geometric expression of this ability by demonstrating how it is possible to move from one state to another that has as its fundamental note a turning inside-out. To normal observation a plant is a static organism (even if in an abstract, intellectual manner we know it is not), however as implied this is not its true nature, for a growing plant is always undergoing transformations, as when it is producing flowers, fruit or seeds. The only time a plant approaches something like being stationary is during the winter, for during this time the Formative Forces have retreated into the seeds and buds and lie dormant awaiting the return of the Sun in the Spring.

*

A viewing of Bacon's images reveals that from the start of his career he embedded his Figures within cube-like structures, particularly in the 1950's, but the striking feature of these structures is that they rarely make sense as objects typical of Cartesian space, for they are impossible shapes. "Three Studies of Lucien Freud", 1968-69, (ill. 7) is a particularly refined example of a Figure embedded in a cage-like structure. This triptych displays from the viewpoint of 'focalisation', where focalisation refers to spot where the viewer's vision is focused in an artwork, an unusual characteristic. In traditional Western perspective there may be any number of vanishing points in a work, but there is usually only one dominant point to which attention is directed in accordance with the action of the work in question. This is not the case with this particular triptych, for the viewer's attention is split between the panels. In this triptych "Three Studies of Lucien Freud", we see that the tubular framework that surrounds the figures divides the head completely in the outer panels whereas it only partially does so in the central panel. Therefore we have only one complete head that has a damaged, or divided, head on either side of it. The effect of this visual device is to disrupt the habit of reading from the left to right, or any other sequential time-mode that is predicated upon past, present and future - in Bacon's words to avoid 'story-telling'. The viewer is thus drawn into this triptych and away from any disinterestedness and is emotionally conjoined to the work regardless as to whether they are fully conscious of this fact or not. Bacon had thus found the technical means to make manifest the **NOW**, and it is worth discussing this further.

Fundamentally, reflection in Bacon's work is to be understood in the light of mimetic representation, and so there is with Bacon's reflections that do not reflect a questioning as to what it is that constitutes a truthful, or for that matter faithful, rendition of reality. In this sense there is a 'debunking' in his work of the commonly held assumption that mirrors, x-ray photography and photographs, in general, present a true record of individuality or of reality. X-ray photography is a diagnostic tool for medical purposes and tells us no more concerning the mystery of a living human being than does an autopsy of a dead body, or any other surgical procedure, for these furnish no more than a glimpse into the surface of the bodies' basic functioning. Likewise photographs and mirror-images are mechanical illusions created by inanimate objects that only display the Lowest Common Denominator, and so this questioning of photographs and mirror-images by Bacon is an essential facet of his refusal to produce mimetic portraits, even though he was technically perfectly capable of doing so, so that he could concentrate upon the Highest Common Factor with regard to the human being. As he stated in conversation with the art critic David Sylvester

"I can quite easily sit down and make what is called a literal portrait of you. So what I'm disrupting all the time is this literalness, because I find it uninteresting." (Sylvester, 1987: 121).

Bacon in his portraiture questions whether there is any value whatsoever, as a record of a person's individuality, in mimetically produced portraits. So as to distance himself completely from narrative and descriptive portraits, so as to refute the cliché, Bacon made use of the triptych. The triptych, along with the diptych which he also made use of, is a format that we associate with the middle ages and religious themes, and which had rarely been favoured by artists since the middle ages let alone the twentieth century until Bacon utilised its hidden potentials. The religious themes portrayed in traditional triptychs illustrate stories from the life of Jesus Christ, but Bacon was perceptive enough to note the oddities that occur with time sequences when attempts are made to depict various scenes in a linear fashion over three panels. Various conventions were adopted so as to create a coherent and plausible narrative that also emphasises the deep and profound events concerning the life and death of Jesus Christ, and the reason for this is that humanity in general still had glimpses of how the world looks from the plane-at-infinity intermingled with their everyday consciousness, something that I am arguing that was also pertinent to Bacon.

Bacon treated the triptych as merely three canvasses, however if they are blank and hang in space there is clearly no linearity implied to the three panels, for they are merely *present*. A triptych, therefore, has a number of implications that are important for an understanding of Bacon's use of the format, and his use of the triptych functions primarily to erase the distinction between past, present and future by presenting all three panels to the spectator *simultaneously*. By doing this Bacon attempts to erase the traditional linearity of narrative stories, for if all three panels are presented simultaneously there can be no beginning, middle and end: "there is only duration, the force of eternal time, the eternity of time, brought about through the uniting-separating that reigns in the triptychs …" (Deleuze, 2004: 63-64). This in effect means that time can no longer be perceived in Bacon's triptychs as operating in a linear manner towards the future. Through this method of presentation Bacon's deployment of the triptych thereby has an inherent 'impossible simultaneity', which Bacon exploited by combining this with his adaptation of the technique of 'focalisation' in conjunction with the dispersion of linear time in his triptychs that echoes the inherent reversibility implicit to his Figuration, thereby strengthening the impact and effectiveness of his triptychs. It is not possible to fully comprehend Bacon's triptychs, and those single canvasses that also display similar time characteristics as the triptychs, without accounting for how Bacon disrupted the assumption that time sequences are always linear. As we know in our lived lives we are rarely, if ever, in the present for our consciousness is always focussed either upon the past or the future, and consequently existence is played out in a kind of stasis of the *never present 'present'*.

The ego constantly plays into the 'self' and that is one reason why Deleuze speaks of 'duration' with respect to Bacon's triptychs in the above quote. Duration is from one viewpoint the Eternal making its presence felt in ordinary consciousness without becoming fully manifest. The *never present 'present'*, referred to above as unconsciously characterising our normal consciousness, is thus this hybrid state brought about by the fact that because we exclusively deploy purely intellectual means for cognising our state of being we are deflected from the point where the ego plays into the 'self'. Normally we are aware of the present becoming the past and the future becoming the present in, for our intellect, an inter-related forward flow of being concerned only with the mundane, and we are completely unaware of the presence of the Eternal. If, however, we were to become aware of the interpenetration of the Eternal into the Mundane then we would be in the **NOW**, and would thus be able to cognise how reality is conditioned by the timeless together with the time-determined World of Space that is subject to both the Law of Growth and Decay and the Law of Cause and Effect. Returning to Bacon's triptychs, the manner by which Bacon constructed his triptychs sets up the conditions for the viewer to have such an experience of the **NOW**. This is a process that starts as soon as one focuses upon Bacon's work, in this instance a triptych, and is one reason why Bacon's work is so unsettling for the viewer is, in a sense, being transported into an unfamiliar state of consciousness that is not completely benign.

The properties of simultaneity and lack of focalisation are emphasised in this triptych, "Three Studies of Lucien Freud", through the fact that the outer left and right parts of the head in the two outer panels can be joined, imaginatively, to form a full face that may, or may not be that of the central panel, likewise we can speculate as to whether the inner right and outer left of these two panel's divided heads are in fact mirror-images of each other. In deciphering this deceptively complex triptych it is useful to bear in mind the exercise one can perform with a mirror, whereby one stands in front of a mirror and holds up a mirror in front of one half of the face so that one half of the face is reflected in the mirror thus creating an imaginary whole face from one half, and repeating this with the opposite half – the result of which is astonishing with respect to how we usually envisage ourselves. Do the two halves of the face which can look so different to each other when viewed in this manner reflect the functioning of the two hemispheres of the brain already referred to? So although there is no particular spot to which the viewer's attention is drawn in this triptych nevertheless focalisation is implicit to this work, but on an *imaginative* level, having been stretched over the three panels to emphasise the work's simultaneity.

By doing this Bacon is able to incorporate into one work differing viewpoints of Freud and thereby depict, in the triptych as a whole, what he believed to be a fundamental note of Freud's character at that time. There is with this work an almost crystalline atmosphere as if Bacon was attempting to construct a magical lens through which he could adequately focus upon a subject that was always just beyond his grasp. Bacon has with this work completely revised Western portraiture away from a representational technique concerned only with the subject's vanity and social status, yet he did this whilst retaining the psychological depth that constitutes a worthwhile portrait. In constructing this frame that surrounds the Figures, Bacon 'pinned down' the movement between all the possible interpretations of his subject which he perceived as moving in and out of one another as a composite image that is a triptych - in effect he *compressed the time* inherent to these divers interpretations into a single event. Bacon attempted with this triptych to record the differing emotional conditions of Lucien Freud some of which, as with any individual can be diametrically opposed to each other, and in this sense we experience something of the movement from one reading to another typical of the reversible Gestalt figures referred to above. Through this triptych Bacon made visible his ability to *compress time*, and he achieved this through his manner of deploying the triptych to express the NOW, and the use of a tubular frame that defies the rules of Classical Perspective. Thus we have a rendering of the emotional disposition of an individual, which by its very nature expresses itself over time, and so Bacon made the *invisible* visible in this work. The far-reaching implications of this is that Bacon has down-played the importance of corporeal appearances in favour of that which is essential but invisible - primarily our emotional disposition.

There is with this triptych a tension between a 'coming' and a 'going' of something from some unknown point, or place, and by doing this Bacon has imbued the whole of this triptych with a definite rhythmic quality that augments the emotional turbulence of the figure. Our normal experience of Cartesian Space is that it is, typically, a colourless, seemingly empty medium in which we find objects or phenomena, inorganic and organic, in varying degrees of solidity. However Bacon has in the above triptych rendered space *palpable* and made it integral to the depiction of Freud, and indicated, through the use of frames, that space is permeated and activated by the *invisible forces of emotions*, a fact that, as will be seen, is particularly noticeable around the human being. Consequently my experience as a viewer is that the space in Bacon triptychs is not merely a subsidiary medium in which objects are located, but is alive and plastic. Through this technique Bacon has gone a long way in making *visible* that which is invisible, and the crucial point here, and this cannot be repeated enough, is that these realms which are spoken of are not separate from everyday space – a separate metaphysical dimension – but are thoroughly entwined within ordinary, Cartesian Space. The above commentary on Bacon's triptychs demonstrates how Bacon makes such an understanding explicit by surrounding his Figures with 'tubular constructions' that are rooted in ordinary, Cartesian Spaces, such as rooms.

The primary signifier that Bacon's frames, or 'tubular constructions', relate to a space other than that of Cartesian space is the fact that they are impossible shapes – they do not cohere as Cartesian three-dimensional objects. So the conclusion is drawn that these frames mediate between the two types of space that Bacon was aware of, that is they depict the point where forces move from one type of space to another, and within Projective Geometry this is the 'cross-over point of Lemniscatory space'.

A Spiritualised Pictorial Space.

Through this study of "Three Studies of Lucien Freud", it has been provisionally established that Bacon was aware of two types of space; one related to the world we are normally conscious of, whilst the other is related to the space within which emotional, and other, invisible forces reside. From another point-of-view one could characterise these spaces as related to the inorganic and the organic worlds. It has been proposed that the reason Bacon embedded his Figures within geometric structures was that this was a technical device to represent how forces move from one type of space to another within the same space, meaning that these geometric frames relate to the 'cross-over point of Lemniscatory space'. This assertion is validated through a further consideration of how Bacon integrated these two types of space within "Three Portraits: Posthumous Portrait of G. Dyer, Self-Portrait and

Portrait of L. Freud" and "Three Studies of Lucien Freud". Both of these works show Figures in rooms. In the former work it is three different Figures whilst in the latter it is three different versions of the same Figure. In "Three Portraits: Posthumous Portrait of G. Dyer, Self-Portrait and Portrait of L. Freud" there are no tubular frames, however as Kurjakovic noted, the Figures exist on an axis separate from that of the room, which represents ordinary everyday space, the implication of this axis for these Figures is that it demonstrates that they possess a *simultaneity of being*, in that they are not only discrete and distinct corporeal beings but that they are inter-related on another level that is just as important, if not more so. By doing this Bacon highlights that which we take for 'granted' - our very life and being - and demonstrates that it is essential to do this in order to cognise the Human Condition. These Figures also have a 'sameness' to them in how they have been executed, for each one of them appears to be emanating from its 'shadow'. But these *shadows* only loosely reflect the seated Figure, and these shadows give the impression that they are **voids** within the fabric of the three-dimensional space of the room. The overall impact given is that the Figures appear to have emerged from some other dimension. By constructing this triptych in this manner Bacon has depicted the separateness characteristic of the material world in conjunction with the *simultaneity* characteristic of our spiritual being – **simultaneously**. In addition it cannot be ignored that this is a posthumous portrait of Dyer, (Bacon produced several posthumous images of George Dyer and they strike one as odd for practically all of them show Dyer performing actions characteristic of ordinary human beings and seemingly having interaction with the living), perhaps Bacon was implying by depicting Dyer in this way that the connection between the *living* and the *dead* in Counter-Space is one of continuity, connection and simultaneity.

*

So why are there no tubular frames in "Three Portraits: Posthumous Portrait of G. Dyer, Self-Portrait and Portrait of L. Freud"? Examining why there are geometric frames surrounding Lucien Freud in "Three Studies of Lucien Freud" provides one answer to this question. In this triptych Bacon was attempting to depict Freud trying to cope with the onslaught of various emotional states and forces, as a composite image, that is to *compress time* . However, there is a triptych that has precisely the same theme, but without the geometric frames and that is "Three Studies for Portrait of Lucien Freud", 1966, (ill. 59). In this work we merely have a Figure uneasily writhing on a bed of some kind, and what could be three moments in a linear sequence of events. There is a 'looseness', a sort of irresolution, to this work that lessens its impact upon the viewer. With "Three Studies of Lucien Freud" the geometric frames give cohesion to the triptych, and by their construction indicate that the emotional forces afflicting Freud not only have a common source but do not correspond to linear time sequences alone. The geometric structures around Freud make it plain that Bacon's concern was with attempting to depict how emotions rise and fall with particular intensities over time as one decisive event. Thus the geometric frames serve as mediators between the invisible realms of emotions and the visible realm of substances, and as such are metaphors for the 'cross-over point of lemniscatory space' as outlined above.

So the essential difference between "Three Portraits: Posthumous Portrait of G. Dyer, Self-Portrait and Portrait of L. Freud" and "Three Studies of Lucien Freud" is that the former relates to a social situation, and as such required a different treatment to the latter that deals with an individual's private feelings, otherwise the use of a geometric frame would have become meaningless as an artistic device, degenerating into just an affectation, or stylistic convention. Another reason, and perhaps the most telling, is that with Three Portraits: Posthumous Portrait of G. Dyer, Self-Portrait and Portrait of L. Freud" there are no frames because Bacon is attempting to depict how the *past* appears from the *plane-at-infinity*, from which invisible forces issue into our world, whereas with "Three Studies of Lucien Freud" Bacon is attempting to demonstrate how both the *visible* and *invisible* have a logical interpenetration of each other. This is a point to be taken up later. However, as implied, Bacon attempted to go further than this and definitively depict how the human being is an amalgamation of both these types of space and their associated forces, this is why we have Figures, painted principally from the viewpoint of solid bodies in space, ensconced within the geometric frames and other Figures, to be discussed, that appear to be dissolving outwards. The impression given is that Bacon was attempting to represent how through being alive we bring these two spaces into a living, vital conjunction and that we are, in a manner of speaking, suspended between these two entirely different realms. The triptych "Three Studies for a Crucifixion", 1962, (ill. 35) strikingly depicts this in a clear and unequivocal manner.

In this triptych Bacon's illustrates, as a polarity, the two understandings of space he has so far deployed, for the l. h. panel clearly shows the point-to-periphery understanding of space as the two sides of meat are radiating out from one of the Figures - this is Cartesian space under the influence of gravity – where this Figure has all the solidity we expect of bodies in our everyday space. The r. h. panel, however, shows the opposite - the periphery-to-point understanding of ethereal, levity-orientated space (Counter-Space). This is indicated by the 'ring of bones' for all the bones of this *ring* are interconnected and appear to support the flesh of a Figure that is disgorging itself and dissolving, in a way not dissimilar to "Painting, 1946". These 'rings' that occur in both these works are interpretable as being related to an understanding Bacon had of ethereal space, because the perception of a 'ring' is an important experience of ethereal space. Olive Whicher had such an experience and describes its nature,

" … In a waking dream, I was once poised, high up above the earth, which was far below me. Vertical, arms by my side and toes pointing earthwards, I was slowly descending. Far away in the blue distance, at shoulder level, there was an 'infinitely' large ring of light, which appeared to belong to me. The horizontal ring of light grew smaller as I descended, coming closer and closer on a level with my

110

shoulders, the nearer I came to the earth below; until, at the moment when it merged into, and closed around my shoulders, my feet touched the earth below…". (Whicher, 1989. 48).

Whicher's description of a 'waking dream' must not be confused with ordinary dreaming and has more the nature of 'lucid' dreaming where the individual is fully aware of their circumstances but in a 'higher' state of consciousness. (Whicher, 1989. 48). In effect Whicher is describing how she was conscious of moving from the Counter-Space of deep-sleep and entering the space and consciousness of everyday life prior to waking up, that is she was conscious of the change in consciousness from one not dominated by the Intellect to one under the sway of the Intellect.. It is also known, as stated above, that Bacon spent much time 'day-dreaming'. It is therefore perfectly possible Bacon had experiences of this kind, especially when we consider how there is a hovering quality to both the r. h. panel of "Three Studies for a Crucifixion", where the 'ring of bones' undulate in an manner that is uncharacteristic of ordinary bones, and to the floating flesh on the circular rail in "Painting, 1946". Whicher's description of her experience is also applicable to "Three Studies for a Crucifixion", if we just look at the bare facts. The r. h. panel shows a figure closely associated with a ring, and there is a hovering, floating atmosphere that contrasts with the heaviness of the l. h. panel, that is there is a contrast of how the world looks from an exclusively, intellectual perspective to how it is conceived without the intellect dictating cognition.

Whicher states that when her feet touched the ground she was now totally back within the Cartesian Space of ordinary perception, but until that point she retained a perception of Ethereal Space, or Counter Space, and that the closer she came to the cross-over point of lemniscatory space the closer the 'ring of light' came to her shoulders. When the central panel of "Three Studies for a Crucifixion" is examined there is seen a mixture of extremely distorted figures. This panel is a more graphic rendition of the interaction of forms at the 'cross-over point of lemniscatory space', where there is a movement from one space to the other that involves an apparently chaotic merging and interaction of forms, than depicted in "Three Studies of Lucien Freud". These panels of distorted, jumbled figures that occur throughout Bacon's career are clear indicators that he had an enhanced consciousness, for as I have pointed out above a person possessing enhanced perceptual powers does not perceive discrete separate figures, or phenomena, but how they move in and out of each other. Through the depiction of a turning inside-out in this panel there is a pictorial description given in this triptych of the descent from ethereal space to earthly space, or vice-versa the ascent from earthly space to ethereal space and the change of consciousness and perspective that accompanies such an experience. Intellectually this experience of a 'ring' has a formal counterpart in the mathematics of Projective Geometry, thus mitigating any purely subjective connotations that a personal experience of it may have.

"With practice, though, it is possible to see the common line of the two planes moving all over the fixed plane, reaching the infinite when the parallel situation is reached and flashing in from it one side or another, according to the way the pivoting plane moves. In any direction at any moment, the common line of the two places can disappear from the world of measure, but this does not mean that it then ceases to exist; it is still attainable in thought! Rudolf Steiner uses the word 'Umkreis' for this invisible line, a term George Adams translates as 'the Encircling Round'." (Whicher, 1989: 19).

In looking at "Three Studies for a Crucifixion" it cannot be ignored that this is a crucifixion and the significance of this is, perhaps, not that of a formal, traditional religious icon for Bacon, but rather that of the theme of *sacrifice*. Although Deleuze does not speak of sacrifice in his commentary on how Bacon handled his subject-matter, we appreciate that so as to get away from all the associations, connotations and narrative conventions attached to 'crucifixion' scenes, when portrayed realistically, Bacon had to completely revise its Figurative format. It may be that at a basic level Bacon found that descriptions of the light-filled resurrection body of Christ had a resonance for his own extra-sensory experiences of the human body (a point to be taken up below). Quite apart from the religious significance of the Crucifixion it is astounding to consider that human beings can be so selfless as to sacrifice themselves for others, and such acts do occur, and on many other levels sacrifices take place – it is not an exaggeration to say that without the *sacrifices* of other beings we would not exist – the earth has as its primary motif acts of sacrifice and love, the significance of which cannot be overrated. In ordinary everyday terms it is clear that without the sacrifices of the plants and animals we would be unable to function – plants allow themselves to walked upon without reacting to this indignity and similarly animals permit themselves to be abused and maltreated by us without rising up against this ignominy.

*

However Bacon's interest was not to be didactic, morally or otherwise, and so this contrast of two types of space serves to introduce his understanding of how these two types of space function within the constitution of human beings, suspended as we are between Levity and Gravity. Thus Bacon uses the Figure in the l. h. panel of the above triptych, to the right of the Figure from which the sides of meat radiate, to point to the central panel. This central panel contains, as stated, what can only be described as a garbled Figure, or Figures, lying on a bed, and there is an unmistakable air that an act of reconstitution, or coming-into-being, or dissolution is taking place - the ineffable interaction of birth and death in everyday life. The pointing Figure's outstretched arm directly connects the central panel to the r. h. panel, and it is possible to discern fleeting embryonic animal-shapes in both the r. h. panel and the central panel, and so the import of the pointing figure, is amongst other things, that it draws attention to metamorphosis as a salient factor in considerations of how the human being develops. Such Metamorphoses of Forms are, as has already been indicated, fundamental to Projective Geometry, and in consequence to ethereal spaces. Christ's sacrifice, although it permits us to continue with our existence, also points to a reconstitution (central panel) at an higher level, and further indicates that there is a relinquishing of something at a lower level that allows something to come-into-being at an higher level, and this is aptly described by Lehrs

"Whatever type of metamorphosis is followed by a plant … they all obey the same basic rule, namely, that before proceeding to the next higher stage of the cycle the plant sacrifices something already achieved in the preceding one … he saw the plant develop through Metamorphosis and Heightening towards its consummation. Implicit in the second of these principles, however, there is yet another natural principle for which Goethe did not coin a specific term, although he shows through his utterances that he was well aware of it, and of its universal significance for all life. We propose to call it here the principle of Renunciation." (Lehrs, 1985: 84-85).

In the light of this with "Three Studies for a Crucifixion" Bacon is perhaps giving expression to his own experience of moving between these two spaces, and how he felt on being 'reborn' ('sucked into') in another place. There is a rhythmic quality to this triptych and this is expressed primarily through the contrast of the corporeal condition of the Figures in the two outer panels (a polarity). The Figure to the left in the l. h. panel appears to be 'sucking' in its flesh as joints of meat thus evoking contraction, whereas in the r. h. panel the figure's flesh is expanding outwards. This rhythmic contrast of expansion and contraction, more appositely described by extensive and intensive, is echoed by the movement of the semi-conscious, somnambulant figures in the l. h. panel that appear to be mechanically participating in an unknowable ritual that has an air of something more ancient than the time of Christ's Crucifixion. It has the feel of harking back to the beginning of time itself and being performed in a manner that is almost automated. This rhythmic quality did not escape the attention of Deleuze who states of Bacon's figuration that

"Everything is divided into diastole and systole. The systole, which contracts the body, goes from the structure to the Figure, while the diastole which dissipates and extends it, goes from the Figure to the structure. But there is already a diastole in the first movement, when the body extends itself in order to better close in on itself: and there is a systole in the second movement, when the body is contracted in order to escape from itself…" (Deleuze, 2004: 33).

Deleuze perceives the presence of rhythm in Bacon's work as extremely complex and operating on many diverse levels, but it is not necessary to examine them all. Primarily Deleuze delineates a 'passive' and an 'active' rhythm and that these are attenuated by other Figures in the works that act as attendants, as with the two seated Figures in the right-hand panel of "Crucifixion", 1965, (ill. 14). (Deleuze: 74-75). The delineation of a receptive rhythm and an active rhythm has an echo with the receptive mode of consciousness of a child and the action mode of consciousness of an adult as described by Bortoft in his book "The Wholeness of

113

Nature", and draws attention to discoveries made in Developmental Psychology concerning how there are changes in modes of consciousness as we grow out of infancy into adulthood;

"Psychologists have discovered that there are two modes of organization for a human being: the action mode and the receptive mode. In the early infant state, we are in a receptive mode, but this is gradually dominated by the development of the action mode of organization that is formed in us by our interaction with the physical environment…The result is an analytical mode of consciousness attuned to our experience with physical bodies. This kind of consciousness is institutionalised by the structure of our language, which favours the active mode of organization. " (Bortoft, 2004: 15-16).

This adds another dimension to these 'Crucifixion' scenes by Bacon for the presence of witnesses, or attendants, are an extremely important feature of the events surrounding Christ's Death and Resurrection.

This rhythmic quality that pervades Bacon's work also relates to the feeling system that mediates between thinking and willing, and is characteristic of everything within our organism that works rhythmically from breathing to pulsations of the blood to cycles of emotions. Ernst Lehrs describes the condition of consciousness of this realm as one that is half-awake, or semi-conscious.

"Our observation of the functional systems of the human being would be incomplete without taking into regard a third system, again of a clearly distinct character, which functions as a mediator between the other two. Here all processes are of a strictly rhythmic nature, as is shown by the process of breathing and the pulsation of the blood. This system, too, provides a direct foundation for a certain type of psychological process, namely feeling….As one might expect from its median position, the feeling sphere of the soul is characterised by a degree of consciousness half-way between waking and sleeping." (Lehrs, 1985: 34).

Given the analysis above it is not difficult to see that the figures of the l. h. panel are 'characterised by a degree of consciousness half-way between waking and sleeping'. In "Three Studies for a Crucifixion" Bacon developed the qualities of extensiveness and intensiveness ('issuing' and 'sucking') through a polarity to show how polarities intensify (or heighten) to a third state or condition that dramatises the theme of Renunciation, but this work also shows, as indicated above, that these qualities have to be understood alongside the principle of metamorphosis.

"Modern Geometry provides a way of experiencing space and spatial forms, so that the importance Goethe attaches to *polarity* in nature – light and darkness in the *Theory of Colours*, expansion and contraction in the *Metamorphosis of Plants* – may be approached through the transparency and exactitude of mathematical thought … the discovery in modern geometry of the Principle of Duality – better expressed as the *Principle of Polarity*- which bears on all ideas concerning space and spatial formations, the relationship of 'Centre and Periphery' can be experienced in quite a different way than before, and the needs of biology are met with an exact, scientific mode of thought." (Adams and Whicher, 1980: 35-36).

After this work Bacon went on to produce a number of triptychs in this vein where he explored the ramifications of "Three Studies for a Crucifixion", such as "Crucifixion", 1965, (ill. 14), where Bacon approached the notion of morality without making any judgements. In this work we are presented with a contrast between the figure in the r. h. panel bearing the Nazi arm-band that is being 'sucked' into itself in an excruciating manner and the Figure in the central panel, which, although wounded, is opening itself up to the world in the manner of a supreme sacrifice, or renunciation. This contrast has immense ramifications for an understanding of human morality, but it is the difference in how Christ has been depicted that is immediately important. In the first work there is almost an atmosphere of resurrection, or at least reconstitution, given the embryonic animal shapes that can be perceived, and whilst joyful is the last word I would use to describe the overall impact of this triptych it has a markedly lighter air than the second work. There is the evocation of a devotional tone in the first triptych whilst the tone of the second, which although not as 'heavy' in one sense, is one of desolation and loneliness that surely must have been felt by those who witnessed Christ's death. Bacon with this triptych made allusions to the contrast between the air of desolation at the actual crucifixion and the joyful, light-filled atmosphere of the resurrection. The bandaged legs of this work have a decidedly root-like look to them as if they were the roots of a plant that have been shorn of their tendrils. This is reinforced by the upper part of the body resembling unopened blossoms, as if this is the moment when Christ left his earthly body. A flower uprooted from this world and cast aside in some dingy alleyway. Perhaps, also, this is Adam and Eve besides the Tree of the Knowledge of Good and Evil after the Fall. To bring these notions into play when reading this triptych is not as preposterous as it might at first appear for Deleuze notes that there are quite definite sensations of 'falling' in Bacon's images:

"We can see here the importance of the *fall* [*chute*] in Bacon's work. Already in the crucifixions, what interests Bacon is the descent, and the inverted head that reveals the flesh." (Deleuze, 2004: 23).

So Bacon developed the relatively simple geometric structures of the 1950's that surround his Figures to the complexity and sophistication they display in 1969, as in "Three Studies of Lucien Freud". In the process Bacon deepened his understanding of the forces he perceived as playing a vital role in the coming-into-being of a human being to such an extent that by 1962 with "Three Studies for a Crucifixion" he had made himself conversant with the *modus operandi* of these forces, and this has been demonstrated through the texts referenced.

Once this conclusion is reached it becomes apparent that Bacon's images abound with examples of polarities, intensifications and metamorphoses. Further polarities are to be found in "Three Studies of Lucien Freud" and "Three Portraits: Posthumous Portrait of G. Dyer, Self-Portrait and Portrait of L. Freud" between the non-human geometric structure and Lucien Freud in the former, and between the living and the dead in the latter. Stylistically, a metamorphosis is to be observed with the development of the geometrical frames from the 'curtains' of Bacon's earlier period that also served to enclose the Figure, so that the effect of 'invisible' forces upon an individual could be assessed. The centrality of this transformation of the 'curtains', stylistically, is pinpointed by Deleuze:

" ... the large fields of color on which the Figure detaches itself - fields without depth, or with only the kind of *shallow depth* that characterises post-cubism ... It often seems that the flat fields of color curl around the Figure, together constituting a *shallow depth* ... The Figure of the screaming Pope is already hidden behind the thick folds (which are almost laths) of a dark, transparent curtain: the top of the body is indistinct, persisting only as if it were a mark on a striped shroud, while the bottom of the body still remains outside the curtain, which is opening out. This produces the effect of a progressive elongation, as if the body were being pulled backwards by its upper half ... At its simplest, the position behind the curtains is combined perfectly with the position on the ring, bar, or parallelepiped, in a Figure that is not only isolated, stuck, but also abandoned, escaping, evanescent, and confused .... The dark curtain falls, but in doing so it occupies the shallow depth that separates the two planes, the foreground plane of the Figure and the background plane of the field, thereby introducing the harmonious relation between the two..." (Deleuze, 2004: xi & 29).

One important point of this statement is that Deleuze elucidates yet another polarity between the foreground and the background in Bacon's imagery, and Bacon retains the integrity of his vision by allowing the tubular, geometric structures to retain a 'flatness', as can be seen with the work "Three Studies of Lucien Freud". Bacon instinctively deployed elements formally known through Projective Geometry, and he did this not as a self-conscious manufacturing but because to anyone with Bacon's perceptual capacities it is seen that they are inherent to that perception.

The inference taken from the above is that Bacon attempted to find ways of depicting how the human being - the Figure - is situated between the two spaces delineated above, and that this had to done in a manner that was in agreement with that which he perceived. But this was not done as an academic exercise but with a keen eye for exposing factors that compose the emotional substrata of our public lives, together with those forces related to our corporeal genesis. Bacon throughout his life was able to combine a rigorous, scientific approach to his subject-matter – the human being – with a profound empathy for those he studied and painted. Bacon developed his technique so as to avoid the cliché, to get away from the representational and narrative so as to 're-present' his subject-matter in a fresh

116

light, and this is particularly important when considering a 'Crucifixion' scene and the centuries of significance it has accrued—how does one approach such a subject and paint it so that hidden dimensions are revealed that tell something about the way we are now?

The 'Animal' Within.

In Chapter 2 there was an investigation of the relationship between the *self* and the **World Self** of Humanity, and this is a theme that played a prominent role in Bacon's work in the late 1940's and into the 1950's during which time he developed the technical means to make pictorially explicit his life-long fascination with the emotional disposition of a person in crisis. Bacon sporadically returned to this theme for a while after 1960 as with "Crucifixion", 1965, (ill. 14) which is a portrayal of the relationship between the *self* and the **World Self** of Humanity at the highest imaginable level. No doubt there are those for whom the notion of a **World Self** is an abstract fantasy, however it cannot be doubted that crowds and large masses of people display behavioural characteristics that subsume the individual in favour of actions that transcend individualism. From a cultural perspective there is also no doubt that Civilisations display qualities synonymous with those of organic life - there is a birth, development and metamorphosis, maturing, decline and death. A knowledge of the **World Self** is the ability to consider all of this from a planetary standpoint. Given the complexity of this subject, as for instance, with regard as to why crowds act as they do etc, I can only discuss how this theme relates to Bacon's *oeuvre*. By introducing thoughts concerned with the notion of 'evil' into the triptych "Crucifixion", Bacon indicates that what may be considered the **World Self** is a collective responsibility. That is no-one can shirk, or hide-away from the fact that we all, every individual, are accountable through our actions for the state of the **World Self**. Such thoughts relate to the comments already made of how we have a 'higher' and a 'lower' self, and it is readily apparent that our 'lower' self has a distinct connection to our propensity to become debased - those passions and desires that arise from our instincts can be so degraded that an individual can sink into a state of perverted animality. A large portion of the 'lower' self is founded upon a distortion of the basic instincts that we share with the animal kingdom. These hard-wired basic drives for food, shelter, reproduction, warmth and so on are clearly open to abuse by human beings. It is not logically supportable to accuse an animal of being greedy, depraved or making any other moral judgement of their behaviour. The reason for this is that our difference from the animal kingdom is that we are *ego-endowed* beings, and so have self-consciousness and responsibility for our actions which is not the case for animals. Because we are **ego-centric** to begin with, and not aware of the higher dimensions of the **Ego**, this means that an individual can develop habits and drives based upon these instincts that are antagonistic to the society they dwell within. A human being clearly takes pleasure in the satisfaction of their instincts and pleasures, and so the Emotional body (Soul) we possess is susceptible to distortion through our **ego-centric** cravings, and consequently these distorted desires, instincts and passions constitute a significant part of the lower aspect of our 'self'. The assumption of everyday, ordinary consciousness is that instincts and drives together with their associated sensations are not visible to the naked eye, but is this the whole truth of our experience? If animals are considered as being the pure and unsullied expression of specific sets of drives and instincts it can be said that instincts and drives are made manifest through the particularity of animals, and so can be observed.

*

The function of the geometric structures Bacon used to surround many of his Figures has been discussed above, however there is another dimension to Bacon's deployment of geometric structures and that is they can be seen as cages and in fact Bacon produced a number of images that feature animals in cages. Firstly it should be stated that one implication of Bacon's use of a 'cage' refers to how we are 'entrapped or ensnared' within not only our corporeal bodies but upon a mental level by those desires and drives that constitute our personalities. This could be expanded to those philosophical and religious commentaries on how the human being is confined to, and limited by, its corporeality whilst living, in contrast to the potential freedom experienced in thinking. However human beings mainly live within social structures and so Bacon's 'cages' could refer to how human beings are constrained between impulses that have their derivation within the individual and the mores, rules and regulations that issue from society at large. This is not to say that we have not created social conditions that are inimical to our survival and continue to do so, this is patently the case, and this fact has a direct bearing on Bacon's work if it is viewed under the general term of 'environment'. In this sense the Figures seem to struggle against, or writhe within their environments, in rooms (metaphor for the mind) where " … walls twitch and slide, chairs bend or rear up a little, cloths curl like burning paper". (Deleuze, 2004: 59). So, initially, it can be theorised that Bacon with his 'animal' paintings wanted to show that the state of society largely relates to our inner nature, specifically with how we have come to terms with our 'animal' nature. Whereby in meeting the instincts and drives that constitute this 'animal' side of our nature we have egotistically contorted and twisted these drives from their original function to our own desires, and that the unnaturalness of this act makes itself manifest as social conditions.

The argument so far has suggested that there is no reason for not assuming that an animal lives in anything other than a seamless connection with its environment where its instincts and drives are unproblematically expressed within its environment. Bacon's handling of this theme, what it means for a human being to have an 'animal-ness' of which it is conscious falls into three distinct categories: animals by themselves in their natural habitat or in cages, such as "Elephant Fording a River", 1952, (ill. 39) and "Study of a Baboon", 1953, (ill. 59), people with animals, and individuals with heads that have animal characteristics. In works of the first type Bacon is, perhaps, inviting us to consider the effect that the placement of an animal in artificial surroundings has upon that animal's well-being, and by default our own, deprived as the animal is of the space to act out its normal behavioural patterns. Bacon intensified this polarity by indicating how animals become demented in such environments as zoos, however he did not stop at such an unremarkable conclusion, because in those paintings of animals with people he depicted some where human beings initiate contact with the animals in cages, thereby indicating a kinship between the caged animal and the contestable freedom of the person outside the cage. We can also speculate, by extrapolating from the fact that as these works were produced within the same time-period as the 'Pope' works that Bacon is alluding to the effect that the artificial conditions of modern civilization have upon our instinctual nature. From this the conclusion is drawn that these 'animal' works by Bacon reflect his struggle with such questions as to whether or not we are absolutely founded upon our instincts and drives (Determinism), and whether as a result of being self-conscious we have access to capacities that are capable of mitigating, and transforming, the seemingly inexorable force of instincts and drives.

This point is substantiated by the works produced during this period that have as their subject-matter the satiating, or satisfying, of elemental, instinctive drives - eating and drinking for instance - but the demeanour of these figures is one that suggests that this is done in an 'animal', pejoratively, manner rather than the natural, uncomplicated fashion they are performed in the animal kingdom, such an image is "Man Drinking", 1955, (ill. 60). If this is so then Bacon indicated that it is the manner by which we deal with our instincts, individually and socially, that is paramount and not merely that we have them. When these works are considered alongside the terrorised 'Pope' it implies that this animal configuration if not exacerbated by the artificiality of civilised living, maintains a precarious existence that is unaffected by skin-deep, civilised customs and behaviour, but which has the propensity to break out in a ferocious and unruly fashion if overly maltreated or distorted. Consequently it could be said that these works imply that Bacon thought that it is essential that these instinctual and elementary aspects of our psyche be smoothly integrated into our personalities as members of a society. We know that this is not always the case and on this simple level these works examine the contrast between the natural, uncomplicated instincts we posses as an 'animal', and the, sometimes, thoughtless manner by which these instincts are gratified and distorted in artificial environments.

Apart from examining how the health of a society is partially determined by the morality of its inhabitants, Bacon extends this concern by considering how artificially constructed social conditions affect the mental health of the individual, through pondering upon the implications, for our inner self, that the generation of non-natural, synthetic personalities has upon us in order to fit into a wider social agenda. This interpretation is exemplified by the images of 'Businessmen' produced by Bacon, an apposite example of which is the triptych "Three Studies of the Human Head", 1953, (ill. 53). The figure of a businessman is an archetypal image of conformity and obedience to artificial norms. This figure represents with its regulation suit and tie the suppression of inner desires, instincts and animal vitality so as to serve the non-human and non-vital, in the form of corporations, or bureaucracies, with all their rules and regulations as to how one has to behave and conduct oneself, and it is not inadmissible to also view the Church, and thus the 'Pope' paintings from this perspective. So in "Three Studies of the Human Head" we witness the degeneration of a smiling, self-satisfied, smug 'businessman' in the l. h. panel, pleased with his situation in life, to that of an agonised and distraught individual in the r. h. panel. The progression of the triptych from the left to the right demonstrates the inadequacy of this social veneer in the face of virulent inner forces. Such meditations are fairly run-of-the-mill and widespread in our present time, but they were noteworthy in the 1950's for the pungency of the psychological analysis that these works contained. Noteworthy as these 'Businessman' triptychs are, Bacon must have found them unsatisfactory for they have the linearity of 'storytelling' something that he wished to expunge from his work.

"Figure in a Landscape", 1945, (ill. 36), shows an incomplete be-suited figure operating a machine-gun that is indiscriminately firing within a grassy landscape. The landscape has overtones of the controlled and regulated public space of a municipal park, (Russell, 1997: 28), and thus complements the similarly socially controlled and regulated figure of a businessman or bureaucrat, but the figure is only partial and, therefore, because the machine-gun is firing it is legitimate to state that a brutal and murderous repressed spirit, or temperament, has virtually swept away this Figure's flimsy, insubstantial socially contrived surface to reek its vengeance on whatsoever is in its vicinity. This work also evokes a terrible dream where a murderous will has been unleashed for the Figure's head is missing thus evoking the condition of sleep as with "Painting, 1946", (ill. 33). Metaphorically a machine-gun represents an unfettered, slaughtering will that has no other aim than to cause death, but it also represents technological innovation. With this image, and other similar ones, Bacon wove into the above themes an extra dimension in that not only is the present mode of technological development inimical to our humanity, but it is also releasing devastating and ruinous forces previously slumbering in our sub-consciousness. Surely such an image is a wake-up call to be cognisant of the fact that with the technological rush, and dash, into Modernity/ Post-modernity controlled as it is by corporate lust and greed and an amoral, (professed with pride), unethical science, we have sold short essential elements that make up our soul and spiritual constitution, with the result that these elements of our being have become 'rancid' and 'soured' capable only of displaying antipathy to humanity at large.

The third category where Bacon produced images of individuals with animal characteristics represents an intensification of all that he has learnt concerning the accommodation of our 'self' to our 'animal' roots within a dysfunctional social environment. This is brought down-to-earth and given a particularity, as for instance in "Henrietta Moraes", 1966, (ill. 61). In this work we perceive an integrated and refined fusion of animal and human characteristics. These works occur in a period when Bacon was drastically revising his depiction of the human figure in general – this will be further addressed below. The intent here is to depict the manner by which the human being strives to maintain its dignity and composure in-between two opposing equally, compulsive poles - those urges related to our instincts with their concomitant desires and our own personal desires and passions - within a social setting. With "Portrait of Isabel Rawsthorne Standing in a Street in Soho", 1967, (ill. 51), an image already commented upon above with reference to the Bull, we can see that her head has a decidedly ape-like appearance with the exaggeration of the lower face and jaw.

Gilles Deleuze devoted considerable effort in examining the 'heads' in Bacon's work:

" … Bacon is a painter of heads, not faces, and there is a great difference between the two. For the face is a structured, spatial structure that conceals the head, whereas the head is dependant upon the body, even if it is the point of the body, its culmination. It is not that the head lacks spirit, but it is a spirit in bodily form, a corporeal and vital breath, an animal spirit. It is the animal spirit of man: a pig-spirit, a buffalo spirit, a dog spirit, a bat spirit ... the extraordinary agitation of these heads is not derived from a movement that the series would supposedly reconstitute, but rather from the forces of pressure, dilation, contraction, flattening, and elongation that are exerted on the immobile head." (Deleuze, 2004: 20 & 58).

These are profound insights, but for now it is what Deleuze means by stating that 'the face is a structured, spatial structure that conceals the 'head' that has import. So far it has been suggested that we live within a fragile amalgamation of contrary psychic strands that have the potential for disaster. Thus one aspect of Deleuze's comment, and he also speaks of Bacon's portraits in the same vein, is that this 'face' covering the head relates to that side of our personality formed in response to social and inner demands, whereas the head is a dependency of the body that is derived from our corporeality, which in turn is created by the spirit. The distinction between the two is that our 'face' reflects the influence of invisible forces (emotions, desires, passions etc) upon our physiognomy and is thus something we are intimately tied to, whereas, although the head also derives from invisible forces, the head is inherited and so to begin with largely outside our making. The process of socialization that starts as soon as we become ego-conscious as children marks and forms our immediate appearance, our *face*. Given Bacon's desire to get away from the representational there would be little point in him producing mimetic portraits in a traditional manner for this fails to capture the key person. It is not that Bacon did not value immediate appearance but he realised that if one creates a portrait in the traditional manner then one has to exert much effort resisting how the sitter wishes to be portrayed. Implying that the essential aspect of a portrait is how an artificial 'face' intertwines with a corporeal, 'head' bedrock, and this would be compromised by the a reliance upon the ephemeral and contrived alone. This is an important point to bear in mind when considering how Bacon compressed the *time-span of an emotional disposition into a single image*, for through the above commentary Bacon displayed an acute understanding that it was necessary to take into account the skeletal structure of an individual when creating that single, unified image. There is, therefore, no question of arbitrary or specious distortions to Bacon's portraits, or studies, of individuals, like Isabel Rawsthorne, and that for Bacon to have created a portrait in any other way would have been for him to produce a 'nothing' that ultimately does violence to the truth of that person's individuality.

From the images so far reviewed it is possible to arrive at a number of conclusions. Firstly there is no hint of a condemnation of our instincts in Bacon's depiction of the animal, rather Bacon focuses upon how we have allowed our instincts to define ourselves through abusing them. Secondly although Bacon sees the human being under pressure from particular 'invisible' forces that we cannot immediately cognise, the spaces from which they issue are not approached as a separate order from the space of wide-awake, everyday consciousness, they are depicted as thoroughly interwoven into that space, this will be made clearer later. The impetus of these images is to make us aware that the instincts are inextricably bound up with what it means to be a human being – it is impossible to conceive of human beings without instincts. And for Bacon any consideration that there is an unbridgeable void between the person and there instincts would be an indulgent intellectualism spinning idle fantasises.

An Essential Bond.

The absolute inter-relatedness of the human being is indicated by L. C. Mees in his book "Secrets of the Skeleton". Mees' exposition points to the sheer fusion of desire, form and environment that is inherent to an animal, but which is lost to our present intellectual consciousness that fundamentally reduces this unity to individual parts, we are simply incapable of recognising the interconnectedness of everything at present.

"In the animal there is something that is continually changing its appearance. What is this 'something'? … Our 'something' works in the inner being of the animal, and when we ask ourselves what that 'something' is, we come to the surprising conclusion that it lets itself be seen in the mature form … We may describe the animal as the result of an urge working within it which becomes visible in the mature form. How must we comprehend this urge? To do this we have to see the animal in its own environment. Just as the plant lives between heaven and earth, the animal lives between itself and the environment. This animal life can be studied by everyone and can only be spoken of as desire … The animal is a unity of desire, form and environment." (Mees, 1984: 7).

Environment is not be confused with a particular spot, as a particular spot is

122

capable of supporting a vast number of greatly different environments that contain creatures ranging from worms to elephants. The change that has come about with the human being is that we do not passively respond to, and live within our natural environment, as do the animals. Instead we actively change our environment in manifold ways, and the reason for this is that we have a thinking ego-consciousness and a creative will, and are able from this to make decisions as to what we like and what we think is 'good'. Through this ability civilisations have come into being based upon cities that have evolved into states governed by democracies. All that comprises the natural order and habitat within which the animal dwells the human being has replaced with formations and operations produced by its own collective *thinking,* thereby bringing spiritual forces into play in the public arena. One has only to think of the number of radically different environments a city sustains; public, family and work to name a few.

The dialogue has so far argued, through examining Bacon's 'animal' paintings, that artificial and unnatural environments contribute to not only the erasure and debasement of the individual but to the production of agony and mental collapse, and that this is inseparably tied up with how we come to terms with the so-called 'animal' dimension of our being. Since an animal is a unified multi-sensible creature, that is to quote Mees, 'a unity of desire, form and environment', it can be assumed that we still possess such a dimension to ourselves as animals. An animal does not suffer the disturbance to its sensory awareness that we do due to our intellectual mode of consciousness, where in the attempt to cognise the world and come to knowledge we intellectually extract ourselves from the flow of cosmic creativity, thus creating the illusion that we do not have a 'one-ness' with our environment. This loss of a sense of unity with the Cosmos precipitates, amongst other issues, a sense of *angst* and alienation that is further aggravated through the championing of such philosophical postulations as Dualism.

It will not be missed that I am implying that there appears to be a similarity between our consciousness before the acquisition of language (a 'forgotten' self) and that of the consciousness of an animal. Is there any evidence for this assertion? Rudolf Steiner states of childhood that

"In the first epoch before the change of teeth, we may describe the child as being wholly 'sense-organ'. You must take this quite literally: wholly sense-organ." (Steiner, 1982: 33).

The fuller implications of Steiner's statement will be examined later, but for now I shall comment on a number of paintings that Bacon produced, which make this line of enquiry credible. These works are "Man Carrying a Child", 1956, (ill. 62) and "Man and Child", 1963, (ill. 63). The first of these is a remarkable image, already commented upon, for which there are no precedents. It shows a Figure that has an almost priestly presence as it glides across the ground whilst tightly holding a child. This pair is positioned in a geometric structure that instead of being tubular has been transformed into a crystalline structure, and where the man's head has been oddly rendered with a halo-like emanation on its crown. At the present stage of evolution the human being the physical and formative bodies virtually coincide. However, around the head region the formative body protrudes to a slight extent. The conclusion is that Bacon was able to perceive this protrusion of the formative body, and this work stresses how the human being although it evolves into adulthood still maintains an unconscious union with its childhood. If we now examine "Man and Child" we find that the other-worldly atmosphere of "Man Carrying a Child" has disappeared and instead we have a tension between the Figures that indicates strained relations. The Figures have been placed in the recognisable space of a room and are **not** surrounded by the crystalline structure as in "Man Carrying a Child". In this work Bacon paints the normal adult, intellectual state of consciousness that has been divorced from the imaginative faculties and unitary state of childhood, and so these two works examine how our adult sensory awareness arises from an originary, sensory unity of childhood.

Metamorphosis: Flesh and Bones.

L. F. C. Mees in his book "Secrets of the Skeleton" also presents an exposition that demonstrates how all the bones that comprise the human skeleton are in fact various transformations of each other. Thus in the chapter 'Metamorphosis in the Human Skeleton' Mees illustrates, with the aid of diagrams, how we are able to follow the paths of transformation from one skeleton part to another, for example

"In the first place, we can say that metamorphosed shapes from the axial skeleton can be recognized in the shape of the skull bones. Just as the girdles and the limbs were a metamorphosis of the vertebra-ribs unit...".

The bare physical dimension of nature abhors forms and sees to it that they are completely dissolved once the life inhabiting them has departed; nowhere in considering the physical aspect of nature do we find forces capable of producing forms. The opposite to this is the manner by which forms are built up through the birth of all that is living, apparently out of nothing. A Crystal is an exception in this respect, however it has to be said that the form of a crystal is not derivable from purely physical laws even though physical laws operate within it. With the crystal we have, from a purely external aspect, the striking of a primordial note of life from which the symphony of living beings that inhabit our planet develops. The crystals are the first and most basic action of Formative Forces that we are able to perceive in our world, and from this primitive base Formative Forces act to create the diverse living forms that constitute Nature. John Ruskin's phrase 'Always stand by Form against Force' to which he added 'Discern the moulding hand of the potter commanding the clay from the merely beating foot as it turns the wheel', (Ethics of the Dust: lecture X.), succinctly reminds us that in our search for meaning in Nature Form is paramount and not the forces associated with them.

Bacon's growing understanding of how the Formative Forces function made him realise that it is only through mobility and transformation, the coming-into-being, and not the finished and the rigid, that the human body can be understood, and this realisation led him to depict Figures that were plastic and in states of metamorphosis. The r. h. panel of "Three Studies for a Crucifixion", 1962, (ill. 35), shows a figure in a state of transformation from the pelvis upwards in a manner similar to Mees' description. The work "Triptych Inspired by the Oresteia of Aeschylus", 1981, (ill. 34), is a complex work where we have images relating to transformations of the skeleton in the central panel, and to the Formative Body in the r. h. panel, with what looks like a 'monstrosity', with respect to the ideally depicted healthy human being, made up of distorted organs in the l. h. panel. The Figure in the central panel has been ruthlessly dissected to reveal its skeleton and, again, it is seen that the Figure is in a process of transformation. All the examples of skeletal parts to be seen in the works referenced so far are depicted in a manner that suggests that they are not rigid and lifeless but are animated and able to change. However if the human being is to be considered as an integrated whole in which all is related and capable of transformation and not as a mechanical assemblage of parts, then we have to do just that. Additionally it is not only the skeletal framework that can be viewed as possessing possibilities of metamorphosis, it is also possible to perceive how one organ transforms into another.

Mees in his book presents an exposition of these principles for the general public in simple and easy to understand language, however it has to be acknowledged that Steiner's teaching on this subject penetrated to the deepest level it is possible for us to imagine, and Steiner demonstrated the absolute mutability of human organs from a unitary principle, by showing how all our organs can be understood as transformations of the brain. This reminds us of Deleuze's 'body without organs', (to be discussed below) especially as he described it as an infinitely mobile and 'indeterminate organ' that is 'living, and yet nonorganic' (Deleuze, 2004: 47). With this understanding Deleuze comes close to a knowledge of the Archetypes which because they have an ideal existence, as far as we are concerned with respect to our ordinary consciousness, are indeterminate before they become manifest. Goethe when describing the Archetypal Plant that he perceived as dwelling within the plant realm, and governing the growth and development of plants, stated that it appeared to infinitely mobile, and never assumed one definitive form. It is argued, because of the plasticity and mobility of Formative Forces, that this is one reason why we perceive such a bewildering, dynamic interpenetration of flesh and bone in Bacon's work, of which the triptych "Triptych, Inspired by the Oresteia of Aeschylus" is a sophisticated example. Steiner's radical proposition can be familiarised together with the stringency of Bacon's examination of the human being by returning to Bacon's 'animal' paintings.

When referring to the plasticity of Formative Forces Steiner, through a series of blackboard drawings, illustrated how if you removed portions of the human head and distorted others it was possible to create any animal head imaginable. Through this exercise Steiner indicated that from a particular perspective the human being bears, potentially, the whole of the animal kingdom within it. Steiner thus gives precise descriptions of the extreme mobility and malleability of Formative Forces but more importantly demonstrates how this is approachable from a purely external, physical perspective. This again recalls Deleuze's definition of the 'body without organs', particularly when speaking of the 'head' as the culmination of the body: 'a pig-spirit, a buffalo-spirit, a dog-spirit, a bat- spirit'. (Deleuze, 2004: 20). We can now say, in general, that from the late 1950's and the beginning of the 1960's Bacon struggled to create Figures that were more plastic and mobile, so as to record his growing awareness of the absolute plasticity of the human form that is always in states of transformation. It has also been seen how in the 1950's Bacon examined a process of mutability between human and animal heads. Although we cannot go so far as Steiner and say that Bacon shows how 'man bears the whole animal kingdom within him' we can say that he was very close to this understanding for the animal forms that we find in various works, such as "Henrietta Moraes", 1966, (ill. 61), relate to no *specific* animal. The impression given is that Bacon is implying not that the human being attempts to eradicate the animal, but that the human being works in such a way as to transform and integrate, any distinct animal specificity, into its own particular form.

Chapter 4. Body of Formative Forces.

The first part of this chapter will relate what has been stated of Formative and Emotional Forces with concepts and postulations that are to be found in the Public Domain. This will create a platform for a more esoteric exegesis of these forces in the latter part of the chapter. If it is accepted that the principles of Projective Geometry shed light upon how Bacon structured his canvasses and triptychs, and that these principles are also descriptive of how emotions function and the forces of growth unfold, as depicted by Whicher and Adams in their books, then it has to acknowledged that through the language of art Bacon expressed his own discoveries of the critical role these 'invisible' forces of growth and emotions play within the human being. The principles of Projective Geometry describe how emotions and growth forces function through polarities, metamorphosis and intensification. By deploying Projective Geometry as an interpretative tool it has been demonstrated that Bacon was aware of the attributes of the space from which formative and emotional forces issue, that of Counter-Space. By highlighting how with the concept of growth we have a concept that we know is absolutely real but for which we have no percept, I have directed attention to a point where that which is *invisible* to ordinary perception impinges upon our present understanding of the world. Growth simply cannot be perceived in our present state of consciousness and we have to transform that consciousness along with our physical, perceptual capacities to perceive the reality of Growth. However, it is also true to state that we can 'sense' the presence and absence of growth in a deeply, unconscious instinctive and intuitive manner - most people know when the life-forces are ebbing in an organism - and this is triggered by all sorts of sensory clues, principally visual and smell. It is possible for sensitive individuals to 'feel' the state of health of an organism even if they are unable to actually perceive its state of health. Formative Forces not only promote growth but are also responsible for maintaining the health and 'wholeness' of an organism, and so it becomes a question of whether or not it is possible with ordinary awareness to find some phenomenon, commonly known, that indicates the existence of a body of Formative Forces as postulated here.

The Body Schema.

Although it is not strictly relevant to this critique it is as well to provide further information concerning Formative Forces. In the first instance there are known, as has been stated, to exist four principle ethers: Warmth, Light, Chemical and Life. Despite the fact that they are not identical to each other, rather each expresses an aspect of the fullness of Formative Forces, they do work harmoniously together and are known, collectively, as the Body of Formative Forces. I was reading an article, a while ago, where a scientist, who worked upon various technical issues at the molecular level, was exclaiming how miraculous it was that the molecules, etc of the human body knew where to go in the human body, and that this was achieved with unbelievable precision. There is no doubt that this is miraculous, and the miracle of the human body, behoves us to think that there is an intelligence that is responsible for the literally billions of 'messages' etc that are transacted within the human body every moment with the sole purpose of keeping us alive. There is no such thing as chance in this area (in respect to how the body evolved in the first instance and how it maintains its functioning) as many scientists are now beginning to realise. It is the case that the wisdom of **Nature** far outstrips that of human intellectual reasoning, and will always do so. At present the scientific community, and for that matter the human race, is sleep-walking into the primordial dimensions of existence driven on by, fundamentally greed, and are blinded by the allure of short-term technical innovation. No doubt some who read this will consider it extreme 'ranting', but just think for a moment who funds this research, that is where does the money come from that supports this activity and who thinks it is a 'good' idea in the first place.

So where can a start be made for an examination of the possible existence of a Body of Formative Forces in everyday life. One salient area for research is the experiences of amputees which has led to postulations that there must exist, somehow, within ourselves a knowledge of the form that the physical body takes, and Elizabeth Grosz considers that 'phantom limbs' are the most convincing evidence for the existence of a 'Body Schema', a sort of plan that maps where everything goes within the body, and furthermore that this is not just related to our external limbs (Grosz, 1994: 70). Grosz states that the connection between the Body Schema and the actual physical body only came to prominence with S. Weir Mitchell, an American Civil war physician, who originally coined the term 'phantom limb'. Following on from Weir Mitchell a number of neurologists became interested in this phenomenon, of whom John Hughlings Jackson and Sir Henry Head are the most prominent. Grosz points out that a conclusion Head came to was that this Body Schema, Postural Body or Postural Scheme in the way it works 'cannot be conscious, but neither is it purely neurological' (Grosz, 1994: 65). This is an important point when considering Formative Forces, for Grosz goes on to say that Head considered that the Body Schema is three-dimensional and capable of recording and organising information concerning a bodies location in space, that it is extremely plastic and pliable and is able to maintain a record of the last posture or movement undertaken (Grosz, 1994: 66). Whatever else may be said about the 'Body Schema' or 'Postural Body' (or Body of Formative Forces for these are different names for the same thing) it is undeniable, from Grosz's analysis, that it does have a phenomenal existence even if it is not normally perceived. From my perspective the Body Schema is a Body of Formative Forces that contains a plan, or *living imagination*, that regulates how a human being grows into the form that it does by directing substances to their appropriate place, and the *chemical ether* is instrumental in achieving this. Goethe's Ur phenomena is a *'living imagination or idea'* that he perceived through refining his thinking, feeling and imagination during his empirical studies, and a *'living idea/imagination'* is a projection from the Astral World into the body of Formative Forces so that these forces have a template from which to operate.

Even a cursory and superficial glance of Bacon's *oeuvre* would reveal a wealth of images that contain Figures that are only partially complete, and which, in some cases are attempting to perform actions that are impossible given their physical state. Works of this nature are "Study from the Human Body", 1981, (ill, 64) and "Study for a Human Body (Man Turning on the Light), 1973-74, (ill. 65), but many others exist. All these works depict Figures performing various actions, and as such they are concerned with the deportment and positioning of bodies in space. In some cases there are Figures that are incomplete and in other cases Figures that appear to be emanating from, or disappearing into an unseen space, begging the question as to what aspect of the Figure is co-ordinating the action performed. Nevertheless these incomplete Figures are performing these actions with aplomb and an efficiency that belies their perceived inadequacy. There must be some reason for Bacon constructing Figures in this manner and by suggesting that he was aware that the physical body is co-ordinated by an 'invisible' Body Schema is one such reason. From a different angle Steiner's statements concerning childhood indicate that it is only through a gradual process that the child learns to distinguish its own being from the phenomenal world,

"…does not yet distinguish between the lifeless and the living…considers everything as a unity, and himself as also making up a unity with his surroundings. Not until the age of nine or ten does the child really learn to distinguish himself from his environment." (Steiner, 1982: 48).

Childhood is a time of intense activity for the growing child as the physical body is developed, and the child whilst learning how to manipulate its corporeal body, also has to learn to distinguish it's body from its surroundings, a process that is never fully completed even into adulthood; one has only have to think of the number of times objects are blamed rather than ourselves when we bump into them. Within the field of Developmental Psychology many studies have been carried out on how young children develop their awareness of space. To quote Andrew Wellburn from his book "Rudolf Steiner's Philosophy",

"It is significant that perspective begins to be understood at around the age of nine …For, if the ordering of things in perspective were simply a matter of sorting out how to judge elements in our perceptual field, one would actually expect children to master it much earlier. Experiments show that in fact children younger than nine, who do not yet grasp perspective, nonetheless already have very good judgement concerning the apparent sizes of things….Yet perspective is understood only later: so that it clearly does not derive directly from perception – from direct comparison of apparent sizes." (Wellburn, 2004: 110).

Foremost in this field is Jean Piaget, (1896 –1980) a Swiss psychologist from whom Wellburn quotes the following

"In fact', Piaget writes, 'the concept of projective space…requires a co-ordination

129

of viewpoints and consequently an operational mechanism of transformation much more complex than the perceptions corresponding to each these viewpoints considered in isolation." (Wellburn, 2004: 111).

Meaning that as we become ego-conscious we have to create a perceptual construct of the world (perspective) that takes account of the ego-consciousness of others. Is there any evidence of this understanding in Bacon's images? Well Van Alphen's commentary in his book "Francis Bacon and The Loss Of Self" on Bacon's work also includes a reference to M. H. Abrahms' book "The Mirror and the Lamp: Romantic Theory and the Critical tradition", where Abrahms contests that we can begin to know how our minds function through two metaphors: The Lamp and the Mirror, where the lamp acts as a symbol for ego-consciousness, for how we project out from ourselves when cognising the world whereas the mirror refers to how we reflect the world in ourselves and act as receivers. (Van Alphen, 1992: 60).

*

There is no evidence that Bacon knew of either Steiner's or Piaget's ideas – none of the biographies of Bacon, nor his statements, point to him having such interests – yet through the tenacity of his observation, and the rigour of his thinking, he produces the work "Study for a Human Body (Man Turning on the Light)". Given what has been stated of the Body Schema, and how when as children we become ego-consciousness we then develop a perspective vision, then this work indicates that the acquisition of this ability is not merely a concern of the physical body alone, but relates to the development of an organisational, sensing ability within the consciousness of the individual. If it was not known otherwise the assumption would be that Bacon was merely illustrating particular theories on human development, for "Study for a Human Body (Man Turning on the Light)" is an image that records the moment of becoming ego-conscious in relation to spatial awareness, and this is made plain through the Figure switching on the light.

Bacon's subversion of classical perspective was not an arbitrary act or whim, but serves the purpose of dismantling the assumptions of our adult perception of the world so as to indicate the consequences of an intellectual cognition of nature; namely how we have become estranged from the world and our environment. By investigating motion in relation to posture Bacon demonstrates that he was conscious that there is an 'invisible' formation underpinning our physical bodies that has a shape analogous to that physical body, a Body Schema or Formative Body, and that it is only with time, through learning how to control our physical and Formative Bodies, that we realise that we are different to our surroundings as an ego-conscious fact. Bacon also demonstrates with these works how there are Senses of Movement and Balance operating in conjunction with a Body of Formative Forces and Body Schema.

Strikingly Bacon's Figure as it developed from 1950 onwards appears to have gained the ability to float, or glide, over the ground – it appears to have an inner buoyancy. Thus those Figures that display these characteristics give the impression that they are being co-ordinated by an unseen order and resemble puppets that are choreographed by an invisible hand. Even the eviscerated flesh and bones to be seen in his works have a liveliness and animation that is at odds with their 'lifeless', in the sense of being separate body-parts, condition. These Figures, therefore, act in a gravity-defying manner whilst giving the appearance of conforming to injunctions that are hidden from the gravity-influenced space in which they are placed. There are examples that make this clear, in particular, "Portrait of George Dyer Riding a Bicycle", 1966, (ill. 31). In this work we see George Dyer furiously peddling his bicycle and appears to have taken off in the process, and to be free-floating through space. We are given the impression that Dyer is performing such a spectacular stunt that the effort is causing parts of his body to unravel and protrude.

From this commentary upon the 'Body Schema' it is clear that we are dealing with a phenomenon that permeates the whole of the body, which even though it is invisible to ordinary perception has so much vitality and life that individuals believe their missing limbs are present. Indeed one is justified, because of this, to state that it is more primary than the physical body itself, for it continues to function even when its physical counterpart is missing. From this perspective Head's empirical observations highlighted by Grosz come close to a definition of the Body of Formative Forces, or Formative Body. Furthermore when she quotes Head that 'This co-ordination cannot be conscious, but neither is it purely neurological' this also is an apt description of the intermediate position that the Body of Formative Forces occupies between our physical body and the other higher members of our being, the Astral Body and the Ego.

Deleuze's sustained analysis of Bacon's Figure led him to theorise it within the terms of his own concept of 'the body without organs':

" A wave with a variable amplitude flows through the body without organs: it traces zones levels on this body according to the variations of its amplitude … An organ will be determined by this encounter, but it is a provisional organ that only endures as long as the passage of the wave and the action of the force, and which will be displaced to be posited elsewhere. 'No organ is constant as regards function and position … The entire organism changes colour and consistency in split-second adjustments'. In, fact, the body without organs does not lack organs, it simply lacks the organism, that is, this particular organization of organs. The body without organs is thus defined by *an indeterminate organ*, whereas the organism is defined by determinate organs." (Deleuze, 2004: 47).

It is true that Bacon did not depict specific organs in any of the Figures he painted, even though as we look at these Figures we suspect that they are somehow present. Thus Deleuze sees in Bacon's Figure an attempt to bring to light forces that underpin these organs of the physical body. The Body Schema as defined above merely registers the lack in some part of the body, however it must have an indeterminacy and inter-relatedness to the corporeal body in *itself* in contrast to the specificity of its functioning with respect to the multiplicity of actions, and differing constructions of, the organs that comprise the corporeal body. To take this thought further Ernst Lehrs states that

"We have seen that the presence of waking-consciousness within the nerve-and-senses system organism rests upon the fact that the connection between the physical body and the etheric body is there the most external of all. But precisely because this is so, the etheric body is dominated very strongly by the *forces* to which the head owes its formation…What can now be added is that, in consequence, the physical brain and the part of the etheric body belonging to it – the etheric brain – assume a function comparable with that of a mirror, the physical organ representing the physical mass and the etheric organ its metallic gloss. When, within the head, the etheric body reflects back the impressions received from the astral body, the I becomes aware of them in the form of mental images." (Lehrs, 1985: 453).

For the time being the important part of Lehrs' statement is the fact that there is an 'etheric brain' (*living* imagination) as the counterpart of the physical brain. This statement also makes clear that the Formative (etheric) forces assume a specificity as the 'etheric' brain. When thinking of the Formative and Emotional bodies it is perhaps difficult to visualise that these bodies are in constant flux and movement, whilst being capable of creating definitive forms. A flowing river gives an inkling of the Formative Body in that it has different intensities and levels to the flow, (there are flows beneath the surface as well), and that precise forms are created in this flow according to the physical terrain it flows over, which change completely when these circumstances alter. Another example is that of Air for within the Air there is a constant movement of forces, brought about by temperature and pressure gradients, that, for example, transport water-vapour around the globe resulting in the various weather-patterns typical of the continents, all of which is invisible apart from the end-results. From this example we have an insight into how the invisible forces pertinent to our being can act as both transmitters and reflectors, for we know that under certain conditions those constituents of the Air can act as both transmitters and reflectors when a rainbow appears in the sky.

It is suggested that Deleuze's description of a 'body without organs' comes close to an understanding of how Formative Forces act under the influence and direction of *living imaginations* by having their actions determined. If this accepted, then there is a congruence and correspondence between three factors: Bacon's Figure, Deleuze's 'body without organs', and the 'Body schema' all of which I argue bear similarities to what is known of the working together of Formative Forces and Astral Forces to create the human body. What the 'Body schema' and 'body without organs' lack as models and concepts is that they do not have a *modus operandi*, that is there is no explanation for how the substances of the physical body are moved around so as to create its complex organs, bones, flesh, skin, nerves, and so on. This achieved for Formative Forces through a *living* image of the human body radiating into these forces from higher spiritual dimensions, and this acts as a template for these Formative Forces, so that substances are guided to there correct place in the physical body. This should cause no difficulty for an 'idea' regulates and determines a machine's working, and this 'idea', in its pure form, we never perceive under normal circumstances, but which, nevertheless, we carry within our thinking. To start with, either consciously or unconsciously, it is only the inventor, who in a flash of inspiration, sees the founding idea of a machine, which afterwards acts as a template for future models. The most important aspect of a machine is this founding 'idea' and not the physical substance of it later manufacture.

To dramatically characterise this it can be said that all that is living is basically a Formative Form/ Idea cloaked in physical substances, a combination that would be unaffected by the loss of its physical counterparts, just as the 'idea' of a machine is not compromised if a part of the machine malfunctions, but where the physical construction of the idea, a machine, ceases to function if a part of it is missing. These *living* images that direct the Formative Forces and create the forms of life we see in the physical world are known as Archetypes, or Ur-images, to use a Goethean terminology, and are described by Lehrs in his book "Man and Matter. (Lehrs, 1985: 390).

A Fundamental characteristic of Formative and Emotional Bodies is that they are *bodies of light* and this is brought out by Olive Whicher when she relates in her book "Sunspace: Science at the Threshold of Spiritual Understanding" that

"It is not through my physical body that I experience being in reality a body of light. Living in a body of darkness; I experience this with another member of my being, of which I can learn to become aware. It is the ether-body, or body of formative forces, which forms, in its relationship to the nerves-senses, the rhythmic system and the metabolic-limb system, the basis for the soul forces, which are also threefold in nature – thinking, feeling and willing." (Whicher, 1989: 50).

In this vein Deleuze indicates just how integral light is to Bacon's Figuration with the following comment,

" ...the maximum unity of light and colour for the maximum division of Figures .. It is light that engenders rhythmic characters … Everything becomes aerial in these triptychs of light …" (Deleuze, 2004: 84).

Body of Light.

Bacon's Figuration is composed of different orders of Figures, and there is an order of Figures that so widely diverges from normal expectations of painted figures as to appear literally fantastic. These Figures lack the density and rigidity of a human being's corporeal constitution instead these Figures are evanescent and translucent in comparison, and with these Figures there is the impression that they have an internal dynamism, as though permeated by a mysterious, inner light that is in constant movement. By comparing "Study for a Pope, VI", 1961, (ill. 66) with "Study of Red Pope", 1962, (ill. 67), it is apparent that the latter has the hallmarks of a traditional representation of the human figure whereas the former lacks the solidity and substance we associate with figuration that attempts only to capture the physicality and heaviness of the human form. The Figure in this work has an evanescence and translucency, as though permeated by an inner light that has given it a plastic, bubbly quality as though its bones have dissolved into light.

It becomes apparent that Bacon in this period was experimenting to find novel ways of depicting his new understanding of the human being. The evanescent and translucent nature of Bacon's Figuration has to be considered alongside Whicher's comments above that the Formative Body (ether body) is light-filled, luminescent and in constant movement. Bacon's Figures have a high degree of distortion, however, this is only a first impression, for when we examine these Figures we see that, in many cases, this distortion is the merging of two types of metamorphosis, one of which concerns the inner constitution of the body, as with the Figure in the r. h. panel of "Three figures for a Crucifixion", whereas the other is concerned with the surface of the Figure. It sometimes appears that the skin of his Figures has acquired volatility giving it an animated life of its own. This relates to the 'sucking' effect of Formative Forces already remarked upon.

"Leichte works *centrifugally*, drawing or sucking living substance upward and away from the all-relating point or relative centre of the living process, towards the Leichte-plane......*The peripheral, Etheric forces work inward and unite with the physical, but in doing so, the levitational force draws or sucks the physical outward.*" (Adams and Whicher, 1980: 105).

"In one lecture, he even used the words 'surface-like' and 'planar' to describe the forces working inward from the universe, and he described the 'Gegenraum' as a 'plastically formed space'. 'It is only possible to study it, if we think of it as being formed from out of the whole cosmos; if we can understand that these *planes of forces*, approaching the earth from all sides, come towards man and plastically mould his formative-forces body from outside." (Adams and Whicher, 1980: 89).

There is thus a reversible process where Formative forces work in from the periphery, the infinitely distant plane, meet the physical forces, under the influence of gravity, and in so doing draw physical substances outward, and this occurs at the cross-over point of Lemniscatory space, thereby giving rise to the rhythmic movements inwards and outwards that are characteristic of any living organism.

Analysis of the composition of Bacon's Figures thus reveals a tendency to get away from viewing the human body strictly in terms of the rigidity that the skeleton produces within the body, for Bacon realised that attempting to cognise the human form purely from the rigidity of the skeleton, the most mechanical and mineral aspect of the body, distorted one's vision as to how the rest of the body functioned. For Bacon the apparent solidity of our corporeal bodies, and it has to be taken into account that our corporeal bodies are predominantly liquid, was an illusory assumption, and that it is only when an individual wrenches themselves away from being entranced by only the mineral dimension of its surface, that they realise how far from the mark that their normal perceptions and assumptions are concerning our corporeality. It is then seen how plastic and mobile the human body is, for an individual then perceives the utter mobility of Formative Forces, working within the fluid element, as they direct the small percentage of highly-reflective mineral particles (that so entrance us) to their designated place within our corporeality. When referring to the plasticity of Formative Forces Steiner, through a series of blackboard drawings, illustrated how if you removed portions of the human head and distorted others it was possible to create any animal head imaginable. Through this exercise, already referred to, Steiner indicated that from a particular perspective the human being bears, potentially, the whole of the animal kingdom within it. Steiner thus gives precise descriptions of the extreme mobility and malleability of Formative Forces but more importantly demonstrates how this is approachable from a purely external, physical perspective. This again recalls Deleuze's definition of the 'body without organs', particularly when speaking of the 'head' as the culmination of the body: 'a pig-spirit, a buffalo-spirit, a dog-spirit, a bat- spirit'. (Deleuze, 2004: 20). We can thus appreciate the intensity of the struggle Bacon underwent during the late 1950's and the beginning of the 1960's to create Figures that were more plastic and mobile, so as to record his growing awareness of the absolute plasticity of the human form that is always in states of transformation.

Study of Bacon's translucent, mobile Figures reveals another striking quality and that is that they have no end-point to their process of change, they have an implicit reversibility where there is the feel of a movement from one state to another and back. The oscillatory condition of these Figures illustrates from one angle the confluence of Formatives Forces and Mechanical Forces when they meet at the cross-over point of lemniscatory space, and also relates to the statements on the reversibility of the Gestalt figures in respect of Bacon's geometrical frames. But we cannot definitively say with these Figures that there is a development from animal to human, or that the human being is in the process of regressing to a state of bestiality, we can only say with these works that there is a state of flux between the two, this recalls Deleuze's identification of 'a zone where forms become indiscernible'. Additionally everything seems to be taking place at the same moment in a way that recalls Kurjakovic's 'impossible simultaneity'. The overall impression is that if it cannot be said that time has stood still, it can be said that with these Figures time is behaving in a highly unusual manner. That time is somehow moving in and out of itself as if, to use Deleuze's phrase there is a 'vibratory, rhythmic transformation', and significantly such unusual time-sequences are characteristic of Formative Forces.

A Body of Time.

The assumption that Bacon had the ability to *compress the time span* of an individual's emotional disposition into a single image has a number of consequences. Of prime importance is the fact that the vision from which this single image, as the Figure, devolves is not static but enlivened, that is it has a dynamism that is at odds with cognition of movement in our ordinary state of consciousness. When viewing Bacon's images it is not an exaggeration to state that virtually all of Bacon's work contains Figures that have an implied dynamism, or movement, which takes the form of a kind of unravelling or binding together – there is no indication as to which mode is taking place. A particularly good example where there is a pronounced expression of this ambiguous dynamism to Bacon's Figures is "Studies from the Human Body", 1975, (ill. 68). This is a fascinating image due to the disposition of the Figures. For instance although we can identify the standing figure to the right as female – what is the sexuality of the Figure that is lying on its back that gives the impression that it is emerging from a mirror? Is the import then of this work a concern with the relationship between the outer and inner dimensions of a human being, or the mutability of our sexuality with regard to pleasure? I ask this question for given the prior commentary linking theorisations concerning the Etheric Body, or Body of Formative Forces, interpretively with regard to Bacon's images it is a fact from this perspective that whatever the gender of a particular individual is then their etheric body is of the opposite gender. So that the female has a masculine etheric body and vice-versa. I shall not at this juncture explore the implications of this statement.

If this process of flux and reversibility to be discerned in Bacon's figuration appears not to have any evolutionary overtones then what is its import epistemologically, i.e. what does it tell us? To answer this there has to be further exploration into the characteristics of 'simultaneity', and it has to be taken into account that the elements of flux, reversibility and metamorphosis play a precise part in the actions of Formative Forces. This is revealed by the fact that a plant's development, as a living process from leaf to flower, cannot be understood by considering that it takes place within a purely linear time mode of mechanical development - to understand a plant's development there has to be a re-evaluation of how plants develop and the time-mode of that development. Thus to quote from the book "Toward a Phenomenology of the Etheric World"

"Plants like ferns, which in their formative movement show only expansion, not contraction, also do not form flowers. Their reproduction remains in the vegetative realm…. In only a few ferns (e.g. the Ostrich fern) does the sporophyll contract at all and these are therefore rightly seen as transitions to the flowering plants." (Bockemuhl: 158).

From this it is realised that something special and complex has to occur with leaf development for a flower to appear:

"Whatever type of metamorphosis is followed by a plant … they all obey the same basic rule, namely, that before proceeding to the next higher stage of the cycle the plant sacrifices something already achieved in the preceding one … he saw the plant develop through Metamorphosis and Heightening towards its consummation. Implicit in the second of these principles, however, there is yet another natural principle for which Goethe did not coin a specific term, although he shows through his utterances that he was well aware of it, and of its universal significance for all life. We propose to call it here the principle of Renunciation."

Renunciation has already been discussed in relation to Bacon's crucifixion images. It has also been discussed how the principles of Projective Geometry are ideally suited to cognise the coming-into-being of the plant realm. Thus through processes of expansion and contraction, starting immediately after germination, forms arise and disappear within loops and spirals of leaf development, so that hints of a mature form may fleetingly appear at an early stage then disappear, before arising again as that mature form. Bockemuhl states of these spiralling and looping actions that

"Where the inner spiral meets the counter movement of the periphery, there stands the mature leaf. Every leaf originates as the product of these two movements. If the path along the outer loop is short, then the path along the spiral is long and sharply curved." (Bockemuhl: 158).

Thus we all, if we spend any time contemplating the plant-world, unconsciously perceive the *compressed developmental time-span* relevant to the Archetypal Plant that governs the overall development of the plant, but we do this as a *linear series of snapshots*. Ordinarily we lack the capacity to integrate into a single image this extruded series of snapshots, which was not the case with Goethe and Bacon. This commentary makes clear that the manner of a plant's coming-into-being expresses the characteristics of dynamism, metamorphosis, intensification and reversibility (expressed as counter-movement). This latter quality of reversibility is no stranger to those scientists studying Quantum Mechanics and is formally named as Retrocausality, which is a philosophical consideration of the proposition as to whether 'an effect can occur before its cause'. The problem of time-sequences in the sub-atomic world has long been struggled with and is illustrated by Wheeler and Feymann who proposed what is known as the Wheeler-Feymann absorber theory. This theory deploys Retrocausality with regard to particular solutions to Maxwell's equations so that a 'charged particle' would not have to act upon itself for the Maxwell's equations to function, for if a particle were to act upon itself it would then posses 'infinite self-force', which is clearly an unacceptable conclusion because of its implications. The theory arose out of Feymann's earlier work, in conjunction with Stueckelberg that indicated that in some instances it was only possible to consider a positron as an electron moving backwards in time. With regard to the levitational action of Formative Forces this is also no stranger to modern scientific methodologies, for it is now known that levitational effects are associated with m-state powders of the platinum series of the Periodic Table (both light and heavy members) in conjunction with the Meissner effect of superconductors (see also ORME: orbitally re-arranged mono-atomic elements).

The fact that a plant's coming-into-being does not follow a linear time sequence, even though to the intellectual, analytical mind there appears to be a succession of forms appearing one after the other, has implications for how time is considered with regard to the organic and living. The inorganic world of separate phenomena follows such a linear mode, but a plant's forms arise from within one another in a more complex way, as the fact of the form of a mature leaf appearing at an early stage of development then disappearing until later stages of development demonstrates. As is well-known every living organism has a specific life-span that denotes its birth, maturation and decline and is identified as the *signature of time* for that particular organism. These thoughts are encapsulated in the following quotation from Adams and Whicher's book,

"Just as in the human soul experiences of the present moment – joys and sorrows – live together with memories reaching back through the years and decades, so it is in the space-time existence of Nature. Things which co-exist in space and in the immediate flow of the present time – especially when it is a question of different orders of size – can correspond to different cosmic times. It becomes a matter of recognising the *signatures of Time* at every stage."

The *signature of time* thus characterises how, for instance, the Archetypal Plant makes its presence known for each and every type of plant in existence, and the same is true of every other organism. However, the concern here is with the time implications of a plant's mode of development for an understanding of the modality of time expressed in Bacon's Figures. Through an exact observation of the actual forms, and changes occurring in leaf development, it is perceived that there are spirals that move inwards and outwards consisting of many differing leaf formations. There are spirals of leaves that hark back to the earliest leaf forms of the plant, whilst others contain nascent forms of the mature leaves. A plant is constantly recapitulating earlier stages through intensification, metamorphosis and renunciation and does not come-into-being by merely filling out an already predetermined forms that exists in some metaphysical space separate from the sensed world. Thus time is not an abstract nothingness through which the plant grows in a linear fashion, but has a palpable, real existence that is capable of expressing different modalities in particular circumstances. This is why Bockemuhl states that 'through the constantly changing spatial body, we apprehend the expressions of a '*time-body*'. Therefore, Bacon's Figures are not arbitrarily distorted and consist, in some cases, of quite definite spiralling movements and a reversibility redolent of Bockemuhl's characterisations of plant growth, since

Bockemuhl is speaking of attributes common to all that lives and Bacon's concern was with the living then it is possible to discern hints of such a 'time-body' in the reversibility of Bacon's Figures. Thus there is with the 'time-body' of anything living a kind of 'stasis', and this can be readily observed with a plant, for at any particular moment a plant appears to be static even though we know it is in the process of growing, this was referred to earlier. This stasis is a 'simultaneity' where there is an instantaneous working together of all the parts visible, none of which are superfluous but all of which are necessary, which is an **'is-ness'** that produces through emergence that which is immanent to the plant's development. To follow Bockemuhl, and others, this 'stasis', or 'simultaneity', may be described as the *'correlate'*, for the 'correlate' implies all that is knowable of a plant is working in conjunction with each other at the moment of viewing. One implication of the *correlate* is that there is no definitive teleological or evolutionary function to be ascribed to the immediate appearance of a plant. The 'time-body' of anything living is thus that specific entities particular way of relating the **Eternal** to the **Earthly**, and overall time-bodies are expressive of modes of incarnation into the **Earthly**. The correlate is a useful term to bear in mind when considering Kurjakovic's identification of 'simultaneity' as an aspect of Bacon's work, and for Bacon's integration of a Counter-Space into a Cartesian Space-Time setting, because the correlate is descriptive of how differing elements act upon each other simultaneously.

Deleuze makes us aware of the importance of temporal issues in his analysis of Bacon's images and this investigation begins with the 'body without organs', as already referred to above:

"In short, the body without organs is not defined by the absence of organs, nor is it defined solely by the existence of an indeterminate organ: it is finally defined by the *temporary and provisional presence* of determinate organs. This is one way of introducing time into the painting, and there is a great force of time in Bacon, time itself is being painted. The variation of texture and colour on a body … is actually a temporal variation regulated down to a tenth of a second …. Can life, can time, be rendered sensible, rendered visible? … Bacon seems to have done this twice. There is the force of changing time, through the allotropic variation of bodies, 'down to a tenth of a second' which involves deformation: and then there is the force of eternal time, the eternity of time, through the uniting-separating that reigns in the triptychs, a pure light." (Deleuze, 2004: 48 & 63-64).

Deleuze's question 'Can life, can time, be rendered sensible, rendered visible?' is clearly answered positively here, and it is also the opinion of Deleuze that Bacon was capable of doing this, and in keeping with the logic of my argument is powerful evidence for Bacon's extraordinary powers of observation. In keeping with this if we take Deleuze's 'deformation' to mean metamorphosis then it can be appreciated with the above quotes that Deleuze indicates that 'time itself is being referenced' in Bacon's work, and that time is as real as any tangible object even if it cannot be experienced as a tangible object- that time itself is *alive* and acts like an organism in which things happen, rather than being a subsidiary, abstract measurement. Although Deleuze does not make this fully clear he does explain how Bacon paints time as something real and living, and that is through the conjunction in his work of eternal time - pure light of the triptychs - and the time that is involved in the coming-into-being of organs - *temporary and provisional presence* of determinate organs - that is expressed through the 'allotropic variation bodies' 'down to a tenth of a second', which means that Bacon has depicted through his Figures the *time-body* already discussed. Deleuze thus provides the insight that Bacon's Figures are different forms of a 'Figure'.

Observation of a plant at any particular moment discloses a totality of parts that we instinctively know are relevant to that type of organism and no other. For instance if a snail is perched on a leaf we do not associate that as a part of the plant even though snails and plants have a relationship to each other, and we also know that these parts of the plant are not mechanically linked. So what is the character of the 'wholeness' that a plant possesses? For a reply to this question I return to Bortoft's book "The Wholeness of Nature: Goethe's Way of Science". In all that has been stated so far concerning our perceptual abilities it is apposite to state that 'there is more to seeing than meets the eye', and what is meant by this is that what we normally consider to be our ordinary vision of the world is *already an act of cognition*, meaning that what we normally perceive as adults is not pure vision, but sensory perceptions that have already been 'worked over' and internalised during the progress from birth to adulthood, and as such are a kind of reverberation from the original act of cognition. If there were no act of interpretation upon whatever enters our various senses in the first place we would only be aware of a bewildering confusion of sounds, light, smells etc, which would be completely unintelligible until sense was made of them. In infancy it is our Imaginative Intelligence that makes sense of this world of sensory impressions, and this is a process of which we are absolutely unconscious of, it only becomes a conscious process as our Abstract Intelligence develops and we learn to separate ourselves from our environment, but once this happens that which had been cognised through our Imaginative Intelligence is now coloured by the Abstract Intellect. Until an individual decides to rediscover this original interpretative core to our sensory impressions provided by the Imaginative Intelligence, they habitually repeat the later colouring by the Abstract Intelligence. Thus when we attempt to understand something we perceive as adults through our Abstract Intellect we are only overlaying the abstract with the abstract.

The primary act of interpretation is that of cognising our sensory environment for the first time in the early years of life before we learn to speak, something that has long disappeared from consciousness and been refashioned by our Intellect. As adults due to this memory-loss of the original primary act of interpretation we now mistakenly presume the colouring given to this primary act of interpretation by the Abstract Intellect to be the original. The import of this is that interpretation is always an intentional act, even if we were unconscious of it being performed as infants, and there is no better way of illustrating this than by following Bortoft's example of how we construe the meaning of a text. In order to speak and read we have to learn the alphabet both phonetically and as written symbols, if this is not achieved then we can neither understand speech nor read. Once this is achieved it takes many years before an individual becomes fluent in these abilities, but upon becoming fluent the original acts of learning become unconscious abilities. Thus when reading a text we are no longer aware of interpreting the symbols but are focussed upon trying to decipher the *meaning* of the text. But meaning, although it is the most important part of the text, is not an empirical object and cannot be perceived or handled in the usual manner we manipulate the object world (much the same as growth and other concepts referred to that have no perceptual counter-part). **Meaning**, is thus another concept that has no percept, and is something that we bring to the text and, although, *invisible* is an intentional act that has the power to transform that, which is meaningless to those who do not understand the symbols (letters) in the first place, succession of symbols (a text) to a higher level. Although somewhat long-winded this is a process that we enact with all that we perceive, and so in order to be able to recognise the phenomena of the world (as a tree, dog stone etc) we have to have undergone a process of recognising, and learning them, in the first place just as we do with letters of the alphabet, something that we are no longer aware of as we attempt to cognise the deeper structures of existence.

If we apply the above understanding to the plant-world then we have to be able to read the 'alphabet' of the plant before we can say that the totality of that which we perceive is a plant, but what we normally see as a plant is only the adulthood dead, intellectual cognising of the plant as a totality that is a refashioning of the original, 'living' act of perceiving a plant that occurred in childhood. Bortoft makes the distinction between two types of totality - **wholeness** and **unity**. Where one is associated with our intellectual abilities, alone, which he names as *'unity in multiplicity'* and one associated with the 'Intellect and Imagination' working together which he names as *'multiplicity in unity'*. The former unity is achieved by abstracting what is common to a series of related phenomena, such as plants, thereby creating particular categories, a methodology that we now know as the Linnaeus system of classification. The other unity that Bortoft describes is that of 'multiplicity in unity' which is derived from Goethe's scientific methodology. Goethe's scientific methodology is a process of immersion within the phenomena of nature so as to ameliorate the illusion of separation from nature that results from an intellectual comprehension of the Cosmos. This involves intensively contemplating the relationships that exist within a particular plant, such as that between the petals and leaves, and then reconstructing these transformations within the imagination (described as Exact Sensorial Fantasy by Goethe). This is by no means easy to begin with but after a while one begins to notice differences in one's responses to nature, and the reason that this is not easy is that it requires *activity* on behalf of the individual to transform the habits of our usual mode of consciousness.

It is my contention that through his working-methods Bacon instinctively followed Goethe's path of knowledge.

Goethe persisted in this methodology and eventually reached the stage where he perceived a *living* imagination that was capable of giving rise to all of the plant kingdom, but this was an imagination in a state of constant metamorphosis and not a dead and lifeless image as is the abstraction derived from 'unity in multiplicity'. This Ur-plant is within every different part of the plant as a partial manifestation and never fully manifests itself to sensory perception. Through this methodology the human being heals the shattering of the Cosmos into many parts which results from an intellectual comprehension of the world by intensifying the interaction of their intellectual and imaginative abilities. The example that Bortoft provides of how a *whole* can be immanent in its parts is that of a hologram. When a hologram is broken into any number of parts each of these separate parts contain the image that was on the original hologram, notwithstanding the fact that as the parts become smaller so does the image lose focus but not identity. This analogy applies to the plant, however the interest here is with the dynamism of Bacon's Figures and his statements referenced above that it was not linear movement that interested him but a different mode of movement altogether.

It has been stated that this *living imagination is in constant motion*, and that this motion is a **correlate.** Bortoft explains how this type of motion that is distinctive of a *compression of time*, and which is so different from that of our ordinary perception of movement, can be understood through the example of a bird in flight by bringing the inherent motion of flight to the foreground of consciousness as a single perceptual event. Bortoft characterises this understanding as follows,

"Thus, lacking the necessary experience, or perhaps just not having noticed it we try to imagine elements which are experienced simultaneously as if they were present together in a static way, as in a snapshot of a changing scene. In fact the experience of simultaneity and relationship in the holistic mode of consciousness is the opposite of this, inasmuch as it is inherently dynamical. Whereas we imagine movement and change analytically, as if this process really consisted of a linear sequence of instantaneously stationary states (like a sequence of snapshots), when movement and change are experienced holistically, they are experienced dynamically as one whole. The elements which are experienced simultaneously in this mode are thus dynamically related to each other, and thus *dynamical* simultaneity replaces the static simultaneity of the analytical mode….Similarly, if we watch a bird flying across the sky and put our attention into seeing flying, instead of seeing a bird which flies (implying a separation between an entity 'bird', and an action 'flying' which it performs), we can experience this in the mode of dynamical simultaneity as one whole event. By plunging into seeing *flying* we find that our attention expands to experience this movement as one whole that is its own present moment." (Bortoft: 63-64).

Later in his book Bortoft expands on the ontological status of this dynamism

"We see the separate leaves as united by a movement – which is the dynamic form. Indeed, we can see this so strongly that we begin to see in a *reversed* way. We have the impression that the *movement* (which is not a physical movement) is the reality, and that the individual leaves we see with the senses are no more than single snapshots of this movement – as if they were transitory markers making the movement visible. This movement is certainly not made of the visible foliage leaves, as if it were a material sequence of these leaves – what is evident to the senses is discontinuity, not continuity. Yet it is surprising how easy it becomes to see the movement in this reversed way, with the leaves which are visible to the senses appearing as abstractions from the movement which is not visible to the senses as such but which we can see." (Bortoft: 284)

What Bortoft is suggesting is that when viewing a bird flying, or a plant growing, our abstract, intellectual consciousness focuses upon only the material surface of the phenomena in question. There is no doubt that we see a simultaneity of movement and object, either the bird or the plant, but that this is a *static simultaneity* because we only unconsciously acknowledge any dynamism pertinent to the phenomena being observed. In effect our Abstract Intellect shatters the **wholeness** of phenomena into separate parts, in this case the entity, of either a plant or a bird, and the actions of growing and flying respectively. By sensitising our consciousness to the dynamism of the phenomena we raise that which is unconscious to a conscious acknowledgement, and thereby restore the **wholeness** by compressing a linear sequence of snapshots of static simultaneity into a *dynamical simultaneity.*

There is no doubt, for me, that Bacon possessed this ability to see in a *reversed* way, where there is an overturning of visual priorities from the visible to the 'invisible' so as to make the 'invisible' visible, except that for Bacon the focus was upon not just the dynamism of emotions over a period of time, but the locomotion of the subject as well. So rather than focussing upon a particular emotional instance, let us say rage and how it is expressed, Bacon strove to discern how a particular emotion originated and evolved over time. Naturally this also meant taking cognisance of the physical deportment inherent to such a process. Thus Bacon *compressed the time* of both the *invisible* (emotions) and the *visible* (the physical body), bearing in mind that he took into account the difference between a *static simultaneity* and a *dynamical simultaneity,* in the creation of his Figures. It is of the nature of things that as one becomes aware of this holistic 'whole', or Ur-phenomena, referred to here there is no change in the content of sensory perception as this dormant faculty asserts itself, for what occurs is that which had been previously unconsciously acknowledged now comes within the purview of the individual, and is recognised as being an essential element for an understanding of the phenomena observed. With this radical and unorthodox review of the coming-into-being of a plant, or a human being, we have theorisations that provide a

143

context within which to cognise the reversibility, metamorphosis and dynamism of Bacon's perplexing and bizarre Figures.

To summarise, clearly a plant follows a cyclic seasonal pattern from seed to leaf to flower to seed and this takes place within what at first appearance is a linear time sequence, a series of snapshots of *static simultaneity*, but is actually a *'correlate'/ time-body* that matures and wanes through the seasons. This cycle also has expansive (to the flower from the seed) and contractive phases (to seed from the flower), but in essence a plant is a unity of its parts and transitions, and the coming-into-being of each of the phases and transitions in this cycle occurs through a *'correlative'* mode, where time references itself as a *dynamical simultaneity*. Once the *static simultaneity* of ordinary consciousness is transformed into a *dynamic simultaneity* we recognise the **wholeness** of the phenomena and consequently its *'time-signature'*. From this we understand that ordinarily we have an intermediate understanding of time that is neither purely the **Eternal** nor the **Earthly**, but which has the potential for cognising how the coming-into-being of the living from the **Eternal** proceeds, and this process of coming-into-being is *never* finished, otherwise the World would long have been atrophied and dead having succumbed to the Past and Necessity.

There is, however, another aspect to the dynamism and metamorphosis of Bacon's Figures that complements the above commentaries, and that is there is a quality of 'turning inside-out' pertinent to how his Figures are perceived. In essence Bacon attempts with his Figures to paint how there is a metamorphosis from the 'inside to the outside' as well as a transformation from one state to another. Assessment of this characteristic to be found in Bacon's paintings will give a concrete understanding to statements concerning the cross-over point of lemniscatory space, for as discussed above, there is with this point a process where the outer becomes the inner and vice-versa. A concrete understanding of this is absolutely necessary to fully comprehend how the human being develops from conception onwards, and also demonstrates how thoroughly Bacon integrated a *'time body'* into his Figures. Firstly though it is necessary to investigate how Bacon depicted the presence of the Emotional, or Astral, Body in his Figuration.

The Emotional Body.

I will start this section on the Emotional Body by reviewing Van Alphen thoughts concerning an interweaving of inside and outside to be perceived in Bacon's images. Van Alphen's focuses his analysis upon the works "Painting 1978" (ill. 54) and "Three Studies of Isabel Rawsthorne", 1967, (ill. 69), when speaking of "Painting 1978" he states

"..a naked figure tries to lock (or unlock) the door with his foot. This extremely artificial pose seems to express the danger and anxiety involved in this simple act. It remains unclear whether the danger is caused by something inside or outside, or by the act of drawing a line between inside and outside." (Van Alphen 1992: 148).

"We see a female figure inside and outside a room; we see her as a shadow on the white door, and in a drawing or painting nailed on the wall. This image encapsulates the tensions produced by the painting it is part of..... it is as if the represented figure is coming out of the image; or perhaps it is the other way around and a figure is being sucked into an image. The figure is both inside and outside the image on the wall." (Van Alphen 1992: 152).

We could go further with "Painting 1978", for there is the back of a Figure to the far, middle left, and there are no indications as to the status of this figure – is it a mirror-image, is it a painting or is it a window into some other space abutting the room – it seems to be both in and out of the room simultaneously. The head of the protagonist is positioned against a black space – is this a painting, or is it just a head silhouetted against a blacked-out window? These works initially relate to how we distinguish ourselves form the environment we inhabit, but Van Alphen's comments have made us aware that Bacon is not merely referring to a functional process alone but to its psychological dimension as well, and this relates to the 'outpouring' of the self to be commented upon below with regard to mirror-images. Although we largely complete the process of physically distinguishing ourselves from the environment by the time we reach late childhood, this is not true psychologically. When speaking of dreaming as pertinent to Bacon's images, and there is a dream-like, or nightmarish, atmosphere to "Painting 1978", it will be readily acknowledged that during sleep we are more susceptible to our desires, and find ourselves performing actions as if propelled by unconscious will-forces. During sleep the astral body and the ego leave behind the combination of a physical body and the formative body, which continue to exist in a vegetative condition (i.e. non-consciousness of the outside world), and are as such free of the constraints of this combination. But what is the relationship of the body to the ego and astral body during sleep? There is certainly, to start with activation of the physical body during sleep in response to the emotional events experienced during periods of dreaming. However a reconsideration of the three principal dimensions of our Soul - thinking, feeling and willing - will take us deeper into this work. Of these three it has been stated that we are least conscious of our *will*, we are certainly able to exercise our will but as to how something which is contemplated becomes an act of will we have virtually no consciousness. That is we are utterly 'asleep' in the metabolic system, which is where the will is focussed, and this can be appreciated due to the fact that the metabolic system fuels our limbs. During sleep we cannot make use of the brain for thinking because the ego and astral body have removed themselves from our corporeal body. This means that the space we inhabit during sleep is cognised without the help of the brain, but is instead cognised through the auspices of the metabolic system. The condition of being able to be conscious during sleep is achieved through an individual, either through birth (crossing the threshold) or esoteric training, possessing the requisite organs of perception that enable cognition not only through the brain whilst awake, but within the metabolic system whilst asleep. Given that such an individual, and I include Bacon amongst these individuals, has a deeper and more thorough understanding of the human being from every aspect then "Painting 1978" is commenting upon inner, psychological conditions regarding our will (of which in everyday life we have no consciousness of) through the depiction of a Figure that is attempting to open the door with its leg and foot. This highly unusual action that has a pathetic tone, which emphasises the limb system and metabolic system, raises questions concerning the nature of consciousness whether asleep or awake. It is a fact that the line between sleeping and being awake is deliberately blurred by Bacon in his work, as evidenced by the ambiguity of his Figure's ontological condition – are they awake or are they dreaming?

These reflections upon the inter-relationship of outside and inside in Bacon's work are further developed by considering the work of Julia Kristeva. Julia Kristeva, (born 1941), is a Bulgarian psychoanalyst, linguist and writer who has studied the theories of the French psychoanalyst Jacques Lacan, (1901-1981), and has advanced her own psychoanalytic postulations concerning the nature of the mother and child dyad which bring a more intimate quality to the themes of inside and outside and the 'forgotten' self. Kristeva's analysis of this dyad concerns conditions both before and after birth, and although this analysis is one that is detailed and in depth I will only be referring to two aspects of her dialogue – the Chora and the Abject.

The Abject results from the inevitable separation of the mother and child, where the mother and child relationship is characterised by the lack of any clear distinction between Self and Other both before and after birth. For instance all the bodily functions relating to fluids and solids are marked by being both inside and outside the bodies of the mother and child at once during pregnancy. The result of this can be an ambiguity for the mother and child, before birth, with regard to these bodily secretions that sustain the life of the child; i.e. are they me or not me, us or not us - inside and outside are blurred and confused. The consciousness of a child before birth is a total mystery to us, and yet it must be conscious in some manner because it is alive, indicating that even though the sensory organs are in a rudimentary, but constantly maturing, state they must be functioning on some level.

Kristeva sees the time of birth and immediately afterwards (when separation has occurred and the child, if healthy, has developed to the stage of being able to start cognising the world) as marked by a mood of deflation for mother and child, a sort of crestfallenness, and whilst it cannot be said that this time is one of desolation it has a mournfulness associated with loss, and the combination of these is to produce an effect that is profoundly deep and spiritual. This is commonly well-known as post-natal depression. The period of pregnancy is thus unique for it is a period of indeterminacy between being and non-being, and a pregnant woman engenders a inimitable aura of other-worldliness that is easily discernible. This is one side of the Abject, but there is another side and this has an almost demented and frenetic character. Here fascination and revulsion can occur at the same time and this simultaneity of emotions sometimes leads to a kind of delirium. At the time of birth both the mother and child are affected by this mood, but the child because it has no self-consciousness and ability to reason cannot conceptually absorb these experiences into it's nascent self, and so they remain uncontaminated and pure within the depths of the psyche. This mood of Abjection makes itself manifest in all those rituals of purification that occur between mother and child, and on a simple level this definition relates to Bacon's triptych "Three Studies of the Male Back", 1970, (ill. 70), a work that depicts scenes concerned with rituals that surround the cleansing and care of the human body.

J. Lechte in his book "J. Kristeva" describes the Abject as a situation where 'horror and fascination are entwined' and is a situation that can only be defused by apocalyptic laughter. (Lechte, 1991: 167). Furthermore Lechte states that the Abject is all that which is taboo, such as rotting flesh, defilement and pollution. By bringing these further dimensions to the Abject Lechte places an emphasis on the Abject as constituting a primordial note to our soul lives. There are thus moods, or soul conditions, associated with our birth that over-shadow, in intensity and depth, our later emotional responses. In effect we have no parallels by which to judge these moods associated with birth in adult life, unless we are able to re-live that time. The act of birth and the preceding pregnancy involves the whole of the Cosmos, and the fact that it is treated as commonplace does not alter its primacy and primeval nature, anyone who has attended the birth of a child knows the special, awe-inspiring atmosphere that surrounds the about-to-give birth mother, and how this persists afterwards and lasts for weeks never to be completely forgotten. One becomes part of this soul-condition and one's outlook upon, and attitude to, life are drastically changed, for witnessing a birth briefly rekindles *forgotten* memories of one's own birth. Lechte's point concerning apocalyptic laughter is pertinent for it is necessary to break-out of what can become an almost funereal soul-mood so that one can resume, or get on with, 'normal' life. The act of birth in our rational and technological society is becoming almost mechanical and perhaps part of the Catholic Church's appeal is the reverence and importance it attaches to the Virgin Mary. Be that as it may evidence of apocalyptic laughter can be found in "Painting 1946", (ill. 33) with its carnivalesque atmosphere, where the intestines of the eviscerated carcass are ghoulishly festooned in the manner of Christmas decorations at the top of the canvas, and in the right hand panel of "Three Studies for a Crucifixion", 1962, (ill. 35) where Bacon's customary circular, tubular railing has been mockingly replaced by the ring of bones.

The 'Abject' is a word that is difficult to precisely define, and as an emotion it is able to readily transmute itself into many forms, however, Deleuze sensed it as a quality of Bacon's work, and his description of it compares favourably with Lechte's comments above,

"… in short, a spasm. Perhaps this is Bacon's approximation of horror or abjection … An abominable smile, an abjection of a smile …. Where is the abomination or abjection of this smile? Presence or insistence. Interminable presence. The insistence of the smile beyond the face and beneath the face …. Abjection becomes splendour, the horror of life becomes a very pure and very intense life …. And he senses a certain abjection in his own love of the photograph …." 5.

The Abject is theorised by Kristeva as a soul-condition that is closely associated to the Chora, and so the identification of aspects of the Abject as being relevant to Bacon's work leads to the assumption that Bacon's images will be able to tell us something about the Chora. Kristeva describes the Chora, provisionally, as a receptacle or space that arises from the mother and child dyad that is the locus of the 'drives'. Although Kristeva states that it is almost impossible to characterise this space, she does say that it is similar to a thunderstorm in that there is a build up of tension (through the drives) that can be released unpredictably, and that like a thunderstorm it does not have a precise form and is a continuous process.

"...Here the drives hold sway and constitute a strange space ...that I shall name... a Chora, a receptacle." 3.

Kristeva does not fully specify what she means by a 'strange space', nevertheless by stating that the 'drives hold sway' she is indicating that this space is related to sensations, feelings and instincts and their dissipation, and as such she is referring to the Emotional Body which, as described above, exists within Counter-space - hence her description of it as a 'strange space'. Thus it appears from her descriptions that there is a close correspondence between Kristeva's postulations concerning the Chora and my portrayal of the Emotional Body. The Astral body, or Emotional Body, in its raw, unrefined state is just that: violent and unpredictable.

Kristeva's description of the Chora as a 'strange' space is highly relevant for the Emotional body operates from the same spaces as the Formative Forces, and will appear to anyone who first encounters this space and its forces as extremely 'strange', for there will have been nothing in their previous experience with which to compare this encounter of what has been described here as Counter-Space. The 'soul body' we possess is the basic configuration created out of astral forces so that we are able to have sensations and it is quite feasible to define it as a 'receptacle'. The fact that Bacon has not depicted his 'primal scenes', to be discussed, in a cosy, sentimental style, indicates that Bacon with these images referenced the emotional turbulence that characterises the soul body at this stage of development, consequent to which strong emotions and feelings have to be overcome and regulated. The principal factor in this ordering of the soul body's pristine state of 'violence and unpredictability' is the Ego, even though in our early years it is not fully integrated into our being. Through Kristeva's commentary on the Abject, and the light it sheds on the meaning of Bacon's images, the conclusion is that it is possible that Bacon unearthed feelings, experiences and memories of the events surrounding his own birth. This evidence from the public sphere serves to validate my postulations concerning the significance of Bacon's *oeuvre*, i.e. that Bacon's Figure is a painterly representation expressive of his investigations of the emotional disposition of human beings as a totality and not as a succession of emotions. Bacon's Figure is the *compression of the time-span of the progression of an emotional episode* within an individual's life, whereby he transformed the *snapshot quality of the static simultaneity* characteristic of our normal abstract, intellectual consciousness into that of a **dynamic simultaneity**. In this regard there are a series of images which reinforce this assumption, and these are extremely incongruous images, with respect to Bacon's output as a whole, and, importantly, feature extraordinarily *strange* spaces.

Beyond the Pale.

There are works by Bacon that are so incongruous in comparison to the rest of his images that they almost give the impression that they have been executed by another hand. The works that fall into this category depict what appear to be amorphous, unidentifiable shapes, or spaces. These paintings were produced fairly late in Bacon's career within a few years of each other, and these works are "Sand Dune", 1981 (ill. 71) and "Sand Dune", 1983, (ill. 72). These enigmatic works present interpretive difficulties for many authors, but Van Alphen and Deleuze provide the most sustained analysis of them. Van Alphen states of "Sand Dune" 1981, that it has

"..the softness and hairiness of a body. While the rest of the space is clean, cool and impersonal like a swimming pool, the sand represents an intrusion of bodily turbulence."

"..has the softness and roundness of a body, while the space is closed of..." (Van Alphen 1992: 147)..

Van Alphen concludes with an overall view of these works by stating that

"The conceptual categories of inside and outside, or innerness and outerness, seem to be evoked, but they cannot be attributed to a specific space within the picture...Put more radically, we are not even sure if there is something which can be defined as 'space', in which the body can be framed or embedded. Bodyscapes, then, offer no bodies and no landscapes but represent the impossibility of both." (Van Alphen 1992: 147)..

Van Alphen voices his perplexity with these images when he states that although 'innerness' and 'outerness' are evoked they are not attributable to a specific space, and that 'we are not even sure that there is something that can be defined as space'. It is well worth pursuing van Alphen's comments on the spatial organisation of Bacon's images, and so I will quote in full his statement on Bacon's work "Study for a Human Body (Man Turning on the Light)", a work that has already been encountered, above, when speaking of how we distinguish ourselves from our environment.

"The figure is entangled in a cage structure that renders the space of the representation confusing. If one starts looking from the bottom of the painting, the figure looks like half a reflection in a mirror - at the left side - and half a figure against a green wall. The foot which seems to stand on the green wall, cancels out this view....If we focus on the figure's head, it is almost as if we are looking into a box...on the floor of which the man is falling down...this is undermined by the lower part of the representation, where the figure's leg disappears behind the green wall/ floor. Every reading of the space is overturned." (Van Alphen 1992: 83)

As with Kurjakovic Van Alphen perceives in the way that Bacon has spatially organised his work a refusal to organise events as they would appear, and occur, in a Cartesian Space-Time continuum, and from Van Alphen's commentary Bacon was determined to make specific just how radically his vision of reality differed from common expectations. So from Van Alphen's remarks upon the 'sand dune' works Bacon is producing a rendition of a 'body' from some other viewpoint than what is customary of a corporeal body in space. From the statements made above concerning 'inner and outer' Van Alphen's analysis of the attributes of Bacon's paintings indicates a strong relationship to the Formative and Emotional forces of Ethereal space (Counter-Space) that have the capacity to create their own 'bodies', or receptacles, for the coming-into-being of a human being.

Deleuze sees the 'sand dune', and other associated works, in a not entirely different way from Van Alphen in that he perceives an attempt in these works to both evoke the body and erase it simultaneously,

"There will be …. reason to distinguish a very recent fourth period. Suppose the Figure no longer had only elements of dissipation, and that it was no longer even content to privilege or return to this element. Suppose the Figure had effectively disappeared leaving only a vague trace of its former presence. The field will then open up like a vertical sky …"(Deleuze, 2004: 84).

If Deleuze is correct, and there is also here a connection to Deleuze's 'body without organs', then with these works Bacon attempted to depict aspects of the physical body that are not immediately perceptible. That the corporeal body has entwined within it essential, invisible dimensions which he could only depict by demonstrating how they disrupt normal spatial expectations when their presence is sensed. In that case the 'vague trace of its former presence' would relate to the Formative and Emotional bodies as defined here, a view that is supplemented by Van Alphen's comments. In effect Bacon attempted a style of thinking and painting that is *sense-free* by eschewing a dependence upon what is transmitted by the physical eye alone. Given the comments in the Introduction of how Mathematics is

150

a *sense-free* language of the Abstract and Intellectual, then Van Alphen's remarks are very perceptive for it will be appreciated that I have been arguing that Bacon was attempting to create a *sense-free* pictorial language with his images, a pictorial language that is based upon a fruitful integration of the Imagination and the Intellect that was not dependent upon Abstraction.

Given the explanation here of Projective geometry and the Formative and Astral realms then the above authors' bafflement is understandable, and their difficulty to completely cognise the spatial organisation of Bacon's images indicates that a radically different understanding of space is necessary in order to come to grips with Bacon's images. Nevertheless we can see that Van Alphen's descriptions of the spatial organisation of Bacon's work come close to describing the experience of space as described here, and the same could be said of Deleuze. I would argue that Bacon is with these images activating aspects of the consciousness of the 'forgotten self' of our first years of life. The consciousness of space during these years is very different than in later years, for as highlighted above our internalisation of the Cartesian Space-Time continuum of space around the time of ego-consciousness overrides any earlier memories so that we may become members of the larger world.

A Forgotten Self.

Deleuze expands upon his 'zone where forms become indiscernible', and comes to the conclusion that the admixture of animal and human characteristics in Bacon's Figures displays a

"...*zone of indiscernability, of* undecidability, between man and animal...". (Deleuze, 2004: 21).

This is astute for it exactly describes the development of Bacon's animal paintings from their early beginnings to the sophistication of the Isabel Rawsthorne work and the Portraits, and we understand Deleuze's perceptive comment as alluding to how the human being is suspended somewhere between an animal condition and a higher, but as yet undefined state, and consequently exists in a sort of no-man's land, i.e. there is an existential and ontological bafflement as to the exact meaning of our admixture of human and animal characteristics. A confusion discernible at virtually every level of our civilisation. Through depicting the human being in this way Bacon placed a question mark over how we have evolved – do we really evolve from animals or have they devolved from us - what *is* our exact ontological status. Furthermore it could be argued that Deleuze's 'zone of indiscernability' is descriptive of how the 'face' is an amalgamation of a countenance adopted in response to social demands and a countenance determined by our response to our desires and passions, meaning that the response to social demands and the handling of our passions and desires are instrumental components of our *visage*. So if we have a 'face' and personality partially predicated upon passions and desires the implication of the commentary upon the Bull, is not to suppress the animal, as stated, which is perfectly natural, but to channel, direct and transform this elemental power into a form (our 'face', character and personality) that produces a 'self' that acknowledges the Other and works to enhance a community spirit that integrates the individual amongst the many. This theme of the Other in Bacon's *oeuvre* will be examined in depth later with a detailed analysis of Bacon's portraits, but for the time being an important point to note is that Deleuze's '*zone of indiscernability*' has a distinct connection to the cross-over point of lemniscatory space, and will be treated in this light henceforth.

*

Ernst van Alphen in his book "Francis Bacon and the Loss of Self" refers to Deleuze's comments upon Bacon's statements that there are 'levels of sensation', 'orders of sensation', 'domains of sensation' or 'moving sequences' to be discerned within Bacon's Figures. Van Alphen comes to the conclusion that these 'levels of sensation' are not concerned with the arousal of emotions but rather with how we perceive ourselves when sensing, (Alphen, 1992: 30-41). Van Alphen takes this further by saying that Deleuze interprets Bacon's statements to mean that Bacon is attempting, with his Figures, to paint an amalgamation of the senses in that 'he is putting a multisensible figure into the visual range of the eye' (Van Alphen, 1992: 32). The implication of this is that in Bacon's work the Figure becomes one integrated sense-organ, i.e. Bacon is making us aware, in actuality, that there is a unity to our sensing and that all the senses are interconnected. Van Alphen states of Bacon's Figures – multiplicity within unity -

"I see in Bacon's tormented figures the neutralization of the differences between the senses in order to emphasize their unity, through the acceptance of their responses, as an uncontrolled force or power in the body." (Van Alphen, 1992: 41).

What did Deleuze himself have to say about these 'orders and levels of sensation'?

"… Bacon constantly says that sensation is what passes from one 'order' to another, from one 'level' to another, from one 'area' to another. This is why sensation is the master of deformations, the agent of bodily deformations … At first, one might think that each order, level, or area corresponds to a specific sensation: each sensation would be a term in a sequence or series … this true. But it would not be true were there not something else as well … It is each painting, each Figure, that is itself a shifting sequence or series (and not simply a term in a series); it is each sensation that exists at diverse levels, in different orders, or in different domains. This means that there are not sensations of different orders, but different orders of one and the same sensation. It is of the nature of sensation to envelop a constitutive difference of level, a plurality of constituting domains … at a certain level, an organ will be determined depending on the force it encounters; and this

organ will change if the force itself changes, or if it moves to another level." .
(Deleuze, 2004: 30-31 & 48).

One aspect of my interpretation of Bacon's images is that they evoke the 'forgotten self', and if this is the case then regarding Steiner's statement regarding infancy

"In the first epoch before the change of teeth, we may describe the child as being wholly 'sense-organ'. You must take this quite literally: wholly sense-organ." (Steiner, 1982: 33).

we can certainly say that Bacon 'is putting a multisensible figure into the visual range of the eye'. In the Introduction I stated that our sensory organisation is not uniform with regard to its interaction with the 'material' world, that each of the senses has a differing immersion into material substances, with the eye being the least involved whereas the sense of taste directly impinges upon materiality in its most concentrated form. From this perspective we can appreciate that there are differing orders of sensation, however there is a difference between 'senses/ sensing' and 'sensation' even if they are ultimately 'part and parcel' of each other, the former applies to the bodily organs of the five commonly known senses, whereas the latter commonly refers to our ability to have sentience, that is the ability to actually be able to feel that we are here. Was Bacon when he spoke of 'orders' referring to the bodily organs of the five senses or differing levels of sentience? Neither of the above authors is clear on this point. One thing is clear though, and that is whatever we are referring to there is no doubt that there is unity within consciousness despite there being differing 'levels' or 'orders', and that Bacon encapsulated this unity in his Figures. Referring to earlier commentaries and Bortoft's delineation that a **Whole** may be conceived as a 'unity in multiplicity' or as a 'multiplicity in a unity', it is reasonable to assume that Bacon was trying to make explicit the latter with his Figures. Neither of the above authors appear to be clear on this point, and I have no idea if either of them acknowledged that such a difference exists. In addition there is little recognition of the twelve senses outlined in the Introduction, which is not surprising as there is virtually no public affirmation of their existence. Our abstract, intellectually based consciousness has the effect of 'atomising' all that is perceived through the senses, the wholeness that is inherent to phenomena is through this consciousness rendered into what are thought of as constituent parts, and this is an illusion that has to be overcome if we are to truly know the world we inhabit.

Furthermore our intellectually-based, ordinary consciousness effects the peculiarity that we have consciousness of both a sensory awareness that appears to have an 'external' origin and one that is 'internal'. Our assumption of an external world is etched into our thinking through the five commonly known sensory organs being 'sucked' onto the surface of the body, whereas our consciousness of an inner world is due to those senses, outlined above, of which we only have a dim awareness at present. To ordinary consciousness, which, as stated, has been 'sucked' into our corporeality through our reliance upon abstraction and intellectuality, there has been exacted an emphasis upon the supposedly external dimension of consciousness to the detriment of the supposedly 'internal'. All of this loses sight of the fact that all nerves whether 'internal' or 'external' terminate in the brain, which is the seat of consciousness for our present stage of evolution. It matters little whether there is agreement or not with this categorisation of the senses, for the important point in this *critique* is that Bacon made explicit an understanding of these, if you like 'levels' or 'orders', of consciousness and sensation with his Figures.

Deleuze emphasises in the above that the Figures are 'a shifting sequence or series (and not simply a term in a series)', that whatever changes are taking place in the Figures takes place in one exclusive space, and is not to be part of a linear sequential sequence. This agrees with aspects of this commentary in so far that I have characterised Bacon's Figures are devolving from his ability *to compress time*, and that within the Counter-Space of *invisible* forces there are no separate spaces and is a space where everything occurs within the **wholeness** of that space: *a multiplicity within unity*. The changes that take place in the manner by which the twelve senses listed above transform into each other is not something that is linear, but holistic, and as such the sensory capabilities of the human being are a 'correlate'. Deleuze's observations are, as such, very astute in their analysis of Bacon's Figure. So despite the fact that we have visibly separate sensory organs, which have their counter-parts in the Ether Body (body of Formative Forces), our sensory awareness is a unity, and is as Bortoft states a 'multiplicity in unity'. If Bacon was able to perceive the emotional structure of an individual, and evidence that he was able to do so is provided from Bacon himself and is referenced below, then he would be able to perceive the multiplicity of emotions within the unity of the emotional body. Bacon would then perceive the flow and ebb of emotions and how they intensified and dissipated within a particular individual as a *compression of time*. Together Van Alphen and Deleuze are stressing the importance of the fact that in his Figures Bacon is striving to express the unified nature of our sensing despite the fact that there is a multiplicity of sense-organs that operate through different 'levels', different 'intensities', so that at one moment when we become aware of a rose the sense of sight may be focussed upon its colour, whereas the next moment we may be more aware of its scent, both of which are unified in our consciousness as belonging to a rose by the ego. There are many examples that point to the fact that our senses are unified and inter-related despite their multiplicity, and that we do not function robotically as a 'sensing' machine, where each piece of sensory technology would be separate and discreet. One of these examples are individuals who have sensory experiences where when, let us say, they are listening to music they experience colours, a 'condition' or ability named Synaesthesia and that has found expression in German culture with the idea of the 'Gesamtkunstwerk', the total work of art.

The consequence of this is that Bacon is making us aware, through his Figure, that the sensory wholeness characteristic of the 'forgotten' self of infancy is not something that is lost but merely overlaid by the 'atomising' effect of our abstract, intellectual consciousness. Steiner stated, a child is 'wholly a sense-organ', and this dormant aspect of ourselves is capable of being reactivated not as something separate from our overall being, but as an essential and integrated aspect, that silently provides us with our unified sensory consciousness despite our sensory awareness appearing as separate organs to our ordinary consciousness. Bacon strove to depict how the senses are unified despite their apparent fracturing into separate organs in the corporeal body, and he attempted this by his allusions to the 'Forgotten Self' of infancy, this, as stated above, is the import of "Man with Child".

*

From this assessment of our sensory capacities it is possible to propose that there is a sensory unity to our being that underpins normal consciousness of which we have lost sight of, and which is shattered by our acquisition of intellectual powers at the time of learning to speak. As we develop into adulthood and accrue further layers of socialisation we find ourselves further removed from knowledge of this unity. This then would be a *hidden primary, foundational sensory and instinctual* **wholeness** that we have lost sight of, and which only faintly glimmers in our everyday selves which have long been fragmented into the piecemeal sensory awareness that characterises our normal adult state of being. Bacon provided clues as to where this **wholeness** is located, for there are numerous images painted by Bacon that depict distorted figures lying on beds. The importance of such a scene has already been commented upon above in the triptych "Three Studies for a Crucifixion", (ill. 35), and how it alludes to a change of consciousness, a sort of 'birth' upon another level of awareness. There are, however, a number of works that Bacon produced in the 1950's that are precursors to the above triptych's central panel, some of which have an explicitly sexual connotation. Two other works that have such scenes are "Triptych (inspired by T.S. Eliot's poem 'Sweeney Agonistes'), 1967,(ill. 73) and "Triptych – Studies from the Human Body", 1970, (ill. 16). In the former work we find that in the two side panels that there are figures depicted as lying on beds, whilst in the latter work we find them in the central panel.

It is not possible to state exactly what they are doing, or even what their precise genders are, but the salient feature is that virtually in all these scenes there is to be found an adult figure that is looking at the figures on the beds. It would appear that Bacon through these works that are redolent of a 'primal scene', is making a direct reference to the consciousness of infancy, and by doing this is offering clues to the nature of his own consciousness and perceptual abilities. We cannot know whether or not Bacon remembered his days as an infant, but this is not such an unusual occurrence generally - its just that such memories at present find no place within modern society, and by and large, because of their fragmentary nature, their import is misconceived. However, Bacon does, with the attendants that populate these 'scenes' as stand-ins for the 'higher self', clearly indicate the importance of recovering the 'forgotten' self of infancy with respect to how we cognise the world as adults. The important factor, here, is that of *memory*. the potential of which in regard to its imaginative capacity is poorly understood at present. Thus the somewhat hallucinatory mood of Bacon's triptychs signals that these works are concerned with altered states of consciousness in which a 'heightened' memory, or remembrance, plays a vital part. Bacon is drawing our attention to events of our early years with these 'primal scenes' as a time where there is/was a cohesion to our experiences, which lacked self-consciousness, of the world into which we have been born, and is indicating that he considered it was essential to take account of this stage of our development if we are to understand how we are as adults. This theme of the recovery of early states of consciousness to be found in Bacon's work is of such *interpretative* importance that it is worth repeating Steiner's depiction of infancy

"In the first epoch before the change of teeth, we may describe the child as being wholly 'sense-organ'. You must take this quite literally: wholly sense-organ." (Steiner, 1982: 33).

This categorical statement by Steiner confirms that which was stated above about a primary, sensory unity that only faintly glimmers in the fragmentary, sensory state of adulthood, and so we can say that the *intensification, or heightening*, to a third state in the 'primal scene' of the central panel of "Three Studies for a Crucifixion", (ill.35) and other works, refers to the *recovery, re-finding*, of a consciousness analogous to that we possessed in the first years of life. The hallucinatory, dream-like mood of these works is emphasised, and enhanced, through the interweaving of 'inside' and 'outside'. This very much recalls the ontological conditions of dreaming where the distinction between inside and outside is eroded, and this blurring of boundaries is fundamental to the *modus operandi* of the 'invisible' Formative Forces and Astral/ Emotional Forces referred to here, and which I argue Bacon was able to perceive as a unified image, the outstanding feature of which was a *compression of time*. This highlights an important point for Bacon with these 'primal scenes' is making explicit his own involvement with his subject-matter by demonstrating how he *compressed the time* of his own remembrances.

Inside Outside Revisited.

When viewing Bacon's Figuration a distinction has to made between those Figures that appear to be disgorging their innards, or unravelling their physical organs and flesh, and those that appear to be endlessly twisting and turning on an internal axis in a seeming constant metamorphosis, even if these two types are intimately related. Having made such a distinction it is also necessary to repeat and develop that which has already been stated above concerning Cartesian Space and Counter-Space. When we are in the former space, which is that of our normal, gravity-orientated consciousness, we perceive from a point to the infinitely distant plane, and this is a world where we predominately cognise the world to be composed of separate, discrete phenomena, however when in the latter space, intimations of which pervade our normal consciousness, the perception is an awareness of the interconnectedness of everything it is possible to know from the plane-at-infinity, and is thus the reverse of our normal consciousness, a reflection of which is experienced whilst dreaming. When we come to consciousness whilst dreaming a movement has occurred from a gravity-based awareness to a levity-based awareness where, from that infinitely distant plane, orientation is towards the infinitely distant point. As such this necessitates asking the question 'what happens when levity-based force systems come into contact with gravity-based force systems' and engender the world that we are aware of?

To answer this question, which has already been partially answered, the focus has to be upon what it means for something to turn itself inside-out. In the first instance it means that everything becomes its opposite and so engenders new forms. The books mentioned above on Projective Geometry provide detailed information on such processes and their ramifications, but the interest in this context is the cross-over point of lemniscatory space; this *'zone of indiscernability'*. At this point that which is levity-based has direct contact with that which is gravity-based, and vice-versa, thus meaning that there is a confluence and integration of each. There is no denying that this is a difficult concept to grasp, given that our customary mode of perception and thinking is one that is static, linear and lifeless, predicated, as it mainly is, upon the intellect and the mechanical. One way of entering into this way of thinking is by considering a pair of gloves that are exactly the same on the inside as the outside, such as a pair of surgical gloves minus the talc on the inside. A pair of gloves are mirror-images of each other, so that if either the left-hand glove or the right-hand glove is turned inside-out it becomes an exact replica of its opposite. One implication of this is that if I reflect my gloved hands in a mirror I perceive the glove of its opposite, and if I were able somehow to enter the mirror, see the 'great outpouring' referred to below, then I would be able to turn this inside-out and obtain the glove I reflected. This I am able to do in reality for if I am holding the other glove as I reflect one of them in the mirror then I can physically turn its reflection inside-out through turning its physical opposite inside-out thereby returning to the original glove reflected. This analogy provides an insight into the complex nature of reflection in relation to questions of inside/ outside and is certainly pertinent to Bacon's images as was demonstrated in the commentary upon "Three Studies of Lucien Freud", 1968-69, (ill. 58).

However it is possible to enliven and mobilize our perception and thinking by paying closer attention to how natural phenomena behave. Many instances are given by George Adams, Ernst Lehrs and Olive Whicher in their respective books, contemplation of which has the effect enlivening our perceptual capacities, and though these authors provide an insight into how Formative Forces function with respect to the plant kingdom, another understanding is necessary to conceive of how these forces manifest themselves in the human being. Mees' book has already been mentioned together with the relationship of his postulations to Bacon's

Figures, and this has been amplified through Deleuze's comments. Mees' ideas represent a movement away from conceiving the human body as a collection of separate organs that somehow come together in order to function as a human body, but rather moves towards perceiving the body as a living, integral whole that is constantly enacting change and metamorphosis. That which has already been stated concerning the Formative Body, and Formative Forces, intensifies when we begin to consider the deeper role played by Emotional Forces and Formative Forces during the development of the human being, for these forces are fully incorporated into ourselves in comparison to the predominately external nature of Astral Forces in the plant kingdom. Armin Husemann provides the conceptualisations needed in this respect in his book "The Harmony of the Human Body". Husemann's thesis, based upon Steiner's research, and his thesis is that we can understand the actions of the Emotional Realm in conjunction with Formative Forces by deepening our appreciation of music, and so quotes Steiner to this effect

"To begin with I want to say a few words about the relationship of the major to the minor key. If we want to understand the more intimate aspects of music we have to develop an awareness of the way music corresponds to subtle structures in the human being. In other words, what comes to expression in music responds in a certain way to the subtle inner constitution of human beings." (Husemann 2002: 34).

This quotation hints at the complex, simultaneous interaction of Emotional and Formative Forces within the human body, and Husemann makes plain how complex is the interaction of the above forces when he discusses the *point of fertilisation*, which he describes as a situation that is only concerned with the limb system and not the head. The head is formed by the whole of the cosmos, and is already pre-disposed in an unfertilised egg. (Husemann 2002: 28).

Certainly this postulation by Husemann, via Steiner, regardless of whether one finds it credible or not causes one to stop and think when we consider the large number of 'Heads' Bacon produced during the 1950's, such as "Head VI", 1949, (ill. 74), the majority of which appear in geometric structures that I have argued signify the presence of Counter-Space. These 'Heads' are marked by the fact there is very little reference to the limb system of the human body, and exhibit a sort of hovering quality whilst enclosed within their geometric structures in an ambiguous space that has a womb-like, all-enveloping quality that is almost maternal, and so the theme of coming-into-being remarked upon as a characteristic of Bacon's later work is to be found – dramatically - in Bacon's earliest period. The painting that Bacon produced from Blake's life-mask is a work that strongly indicates that Bacon was aware that Blake possessed similar psychic abilities to his own, and how from the viewpoint of these abilities the 'head' occupies a unique position, with respect to the rest of our body, in the genesis of our corporeal being. The animal heads/ skulls remind us of Deleuze's statement of the head being the culmination of the body and has the capacity to be 'a pig-spirit, a buffalo-spirit, a

158

dog-spirit, a bat-spirit', a remark that was investigated above in the light of Steiner's investigations. So what are we to make of this profusion of unearthly 'heads' created during the 1950's? What is it that Bacon is attempting to draw our attention to with these images? Since there are skulls and life-masks interspersed in this series our thoughts are drawn inevitably to the termination of life within the physical body, where the emphasis is thus upon the past. A life-mask emphasises such a view for the life-mask is an attempt, albeit morbid, to record some essence of the character and personality of an individual that can only ever refer to the past.

This reference to the past is pertinent from my perspective for a number of reasons, as for instance with how the processes of expansion and contraction co-ordinate the inter-action of Astral forces and Formative Forces so that substances are ordered and structured from the moment of birth, and onwards, for the creation of the maturing human body, and as such is not a process that can be understood by considering expansion and contraction side-by-side in a linear fashion. Instead an imagination has to occur whereby by they can be seen as mutually interacting so that an expansion is a contraction, and vice-versa. This is Deleuze's characterisation of such a process to be found in Bacon's images

"The rising-descending, contraction-dilation … A discharge, for example, is a descent, as well as a dilation and expansion, but there is also a contraction in the discharge …" (Deleuze 2004: 80).

This interaction of expansion and dilation, whereby they become each other, is a fundamental principle of how living forms develop, and during the nineteenth century through the work of Ernst Haeckel, 1834-1919, and others, the process of invagination was discovered as an essential process of embryonic growth. Haeckel described invagination as follows

"Now a very important and noteworthy process begins namely the invagination of the blastocyst. The sphere with its single layer of cells becomes a cup with a double layer of cells. At a given point the surface of the sphere begins to flatten and deepen into an hollow. This hollow becomes deeper and deeper. It expands at the expense of the blastocoel or cleavage cavity. The latter decreases to the extent that former increases." (Husemann 2002: 53-54).

Haeckel goes on to describe how cells change shape and size during this process and how the process continues right through to the other side of the blastocyst. Haeckel also eloquently describes how when forces responsible for the initial construction of the blastocyst further strike into this construction a simultaneous process of expansion and contraction then ensues that finally ends in a complete *inversion*, or *eversion*. Parts formerly on the inside are on the outside, and vice-versa. So as to make this process of inversion simpler to understand Steiner provided a number of sculptural exercises in clay-modelling which Husemann refers to in his book. The first part of this exercise is where one is able to feel, through working with the clay, the action of a force, one's own, that works from the outside and gradually makes it way right through the ball of clay to other side.

Contemplation of the course of embryonic development engenders a mood of deep humility as one witnesses the stupendous changes taking place within the womb, for here it is perceived – actually - the unfolding of life close to the cross-over point of lemniscatory space. The 'primal scenes' that have been spoken of have at first glance a 'garbled' appearance, but on closer inspection we see that there is an inter-weaving of the Figures as in the central panel of "Triptych – Studies from the Human Body", (ill. 20) as though the Figures are trying to get in and out of each other. Obviously we can give this a sexual overtone and I have no doubt that Bacon, like everyone else, entertained such thoughts, however as I have shown Bacon was a highly intelligent and multifaceted personality. This being the case, and the fact that a female egg has to be fertilised by a male sperm, then it is entirely plausible that Bacon with his psychic abilities intuitively realised the importance of invagination, and it does not require much imagination to imagine the difficulty there is in producing merely an illustration of invagination that does full justice to this process of turning inside-out, let alone the creation of an artistic rendition. Bacon's inspiration was to place his Figures within the impossible frames that have been much commented upon, whereby these frames that indicate the presence of Counter-Space, also intimate the turning inside-out of forms that occur in Projective Geometry thereby formally reflecting the complex and *real* process of invagination that is fundamental to our corporeal development. In his attempts to render an image of the process of invagination Bacon went to extreme lengths so as to make what he was painting visceral and unforgettable, as in "Triptych, Inspired by the Oresteia of Aeschylus", where the Figures' apparent acts of disgorging there insides, or more accurately turning themselves inside-out, is depicted in graphic detail.

The "Moebius Leaf", (ill. 75), is another example of an apparently 'impossible' form as with the Gestalt figures, except that here instead of simultaneous reversibility upon a flat plane, an illustration is produced of how three-dimensional space enfolds *itself into itself* according to the laws of Projective Geometry as with invagination.

"The lemniscatory quality of space was demonstrated towards the end of his life by the famous mathematician August Ferdinand Moebius, (1790-1868), to whom a great deal of mathematical discovery is due. His "Moebius leaf" is a familiar puzzle …The leaf is of course not continuous, but has edges, and the task was set at the beginning of the century to create a closed model of the projective plane, with its strange attributes. Werner Boy in Gottingen, setting out to prove it impossible, found that it was possible to create a surface that closes in upon itself without singularities. The model shows the lemniscatory quality which inevitably arises when the nature of space is investigated according to the laws of projective geometry." (Whicher 1985: 236).

The model demonstrates how it can be envisaged that space folds into itself and turns itself inside-out at the cross-over point of lemniscatory space. This folding into itself has been remarked upon as a characteristic of Bacon's Figuration, where Figures appear to be attempting to move in and out of themselves, and when the Moebius leaf is compared to Bacon's portraits as well as his Figuration then there is a remarkable similarity between the two. "Portrait of Michael Leiris", 1976, (ill. 76) and "Three Studies for Portrait of Henrietta Moraes", 1963, (ill. 88) are two examples that reveal this fact.

An Unimaginably Sublime Confluence of Forces.

This somewhat unfamiliar principle of inversion, referred to above, as a characteristic of natural processes within the human organism, is readily revealed through a simple observation that focuses upon the distribution, and comparative ratios, of flesh to bone throughout the human body. When this examination is conducted it is found that the lower body and limbs consist mainly of flesh that covers a lesser density of bone whilst the upper body, and head, shows a predominance of bone with the skull completely enclosing a fleshy brain; the complete reverse of the lower body. Between these two poles we observe that the central section of our bodies, around the ribcage, has a roughly equal distribution of flesh to bone.

This is a relatively simple and basic example of inversion but it serves as a foundation for understanding the complex processes of inversion within the human anatomy highlighted by Husemann. Husemann demonstrates how the principle of inversion is to be found within the nervous, muscular and blood systems, (Husemann, 2002: 59-67). From this we realise that a mechanistic paradigm of the human body where the human body is cognised as a system of parts mechanically related, or as a chemical/ genetic composite, are inadequate representation, no matter how refined these models are, for such a complex and miraculous organism as the human body. Instead there has to be mobility to our thinking in order to encompass the body's coming-into-being. In this respect Bacon's Figures that appear to be disgorging their innards, or turning themselves inside-out, present us with images from someone whose thinking was so enlivened, and who strained, on one level, to set down the results of his observations in a logical, scientific and *aesthetic* manner.

When this principle of inversion is viewed alongside what has been stated of the Formative and Emotional forces then the picture arises that the human body is in fact a confluence of forces that interact, as a *correlate*, in order to produce that which we ordinarily perceive as a human being. This is the picture given by Deleuze's descriptions of Bacon's images, and also by Steiner who elucidated such an understanding in his series of lectures known as "The Psychology of Body, Soul and Spirit". In lecture 3 of this book Steiner states

"Now let's go further. We can see that in human beings there is an interaction between the front and rear such that the sentient body and the sentient soul collide. There is a similar collision between streams that come from the right and the left. From the left comes the stream belonging to the physical body, while from the right comes the stream belonging to the etheric body. The physical and etheric bodies pour and thrust into each other, and that which arises at the place where they do so, where they work together, that is the sense-perceptible human being. An illusion, so to speak, appears before us. The stream of the physical body flows from the left, that of the etheric body from the right. They interpenetrate each other and build in the middle that which appears as the sense-perceptible human being. Just as there are streams from the left and the right and from the front and the back, so also is there a stream from above and one from below. The main current of the astral body flows upward from below and that of the I flows downward from above." (Steiner, 1999: 42-43).

"The Jews of ancient times really put all their most sublime wisdom into this Sephiroth tree. It would be fair to say that they have put into it their knowledge of man's relationship to the world. We have often said quite clearly that man is not only the part we see with our eyes but also has other, supersensible aspects. We have called these the ether body, the astral body the I or the I-organisation. People knew this instinctively in earlier times, not the way we know it today. This ancient knowledge has been lost, and today people think that something like the Jewish Tree of Life, the Sephiroth Tree, is simple fantasy. But it is not. Today we will consider what the ancient Jews really meant with their Sephiroth Tree. You see, they saw it like this. The human being is here in this world, and the forces of the world influence him from all directions." (Steiner, 1999: 163).

In another series of lectures Steiner speaks of the Sephiroth Tree, which is a symbolic representation from Ancient Judaism of the manner by which the human being is constituted by, and continuously acted upon by, supersensible forces. Through the symbol of the Sephiroth Tree Steiner shows how there is an unbroken chain in an understanding of the human being, but importantly reconstitutes this knowledge into a conceptual form that is suitable for our present powers of cognition. The vision that arises is of the light-filled human being working creatively with these levity forces against the mechanical forces of gravity as an 'unimaginably sublime confluence of forces', and in the process thereby redeeming that which has come under the influence of gravity.

Returning to Bacon's work there is now a better understanding of the different Figures within Bacon's iconography, between those that are disgorging their insides, or turning themselves inside-out, and those that appear to be spinning endlessly upon an axis and moving in and out of themselves, for they are the consequence of observing the human body from differing viewpoints. Thus, when we view the r. h. panel of "Three Studies for a Crucifixion", we perceive the upward movement Steiner refers to together with a turning-out, or disgorging, of the insides that is redolent of invagination. Bacon's Figures are therefore cognisable from the perspective of the human being as being constituted through a confluence of differing forces and that these swirling forces, in their actions, are characterised by invagination, where the time-mode of these forces at the cross-over point of lemniscatory space is that of *correlation*. And that correlation, initially seen as the reversibility of those works with animal characteristics, and those with Figures spinning on an axis, turns out to be utterly crucial for understanding why Bacon painted Figures in this way. Bacon's differing Figures thus present images from diverse angles of the same phenomenon, the cross-over point of lemniscatory space, and how this relates to the creation of a human being. By performing this investigation Bacon rigorously explored the complexity of the human being from a number of perspectives, and that, remarkably, his analysis is entirely in line with that which Steiner, and other researchers, have found to be the case. I offer one further example to indicate Bacon's awareness and investigation of invisible realms and that is "Water from a Running Tap", (ill. 96),1982. It is common knowledge that water is essential to life, however from the perspective of this *critique* the Etheric, or Formative Forces, that give rise to all that is living have water as their place of manifestation in the material world, and so with the above work where it can be discerned that in the outflow from the running tap there are a number of nascent animal shapes, surrounded by a frame which, as described above, is indicative of the cross-over point of lemniscatory space, it appears only reasonable to assume that Bacon perceived the coming-into-being of living forms from Counter-Space via Formative Forces. If it is not accepted that Bacon could perceive these Etheric realms from which life arises then why should he have created the above work which expresses this fact in his own inimitable manner? Below I will present an intensely esoteric examination of particular topics discerned as being relevant to Bacon's Iconography, and in doing so further anchor to Bacon's work the postulations I have already made concerning the significance of Bacon's images.

Mirrors.

It has been emphasised on a number of occasions, during the course of the above text, that for a person with the psychic abilities that Bacon possessed the human body reveals itself very differently from the image presented by our ordinary, intellectually based consciousness. I have provided numerous examples of how that which Bacon perceived of the human body is in alignment with the findings of Steiner, who possessed and refined this psychic ability to the highest degree possible at present. So as to underline these statements concerning Bacon's investigation of the human being I will present a few examples of how Bacon made explicit his vision of the human body from the perspective of his enhanced visual capacities.

There can be no doubt that mirrors and reflecting surfaces play an instrumental role in Bacon's Figuration. This has been tangentially referred to on a number of occasions, with mirrors that do not reflect faithfully, and with the mirror-relationships present in Bacon's work that exhibit attributes with the mirror-relationships inherent to a pair of gloves, for instance. Bacon's investigation, through his Figuration, of the intimate and subtle relationship between the supersensible and corporeal aspects of our being is conducted in the majority of cases in the presence of a reflecting surface of some sort that has an undeniable connection to the Figure in question. What I mean by this can be illustrated to begin with by a few examples: "Triptych – Studies from the Human Body", 1970, (ill. 16) and "Figure in Movement", 1978, (ill. 77). In the former work these reflecting surfaces can almost certainly be described as mirrors, even though they are rendered as doors, whereas in the latter the status of the surface is more ambiguous, for the black rectangle behind the Figure can be interpreted as either a sort of black mirror, that depicts the Figure as it would reflect in an ordinary mirror, or as a painting of the Figure from that viewpoint. In this respect it has to be remembered that an artist in creating produces a *mirror,* through whatever medium is deployed, of their own imaginative abilities. This however is a *'living'* mirror in that the actual act of mirroring **imaginations** in a medium by the artist transforms not just that which is being mirrored but the very substance of the medium that acts as a mirror. The fact of this volatility of creative processes and their interaction with the greater Cosmos points to, once it is cognised, immense possibilities - its potentiality is limitless, dependent only on the calibre of the artist. This specialised instance of mirroring has repercussions upon how it was described above that sense-impressions are reflected upon various aspects of being. One of these repercussions is that due to the fact that the 'lower self' is composed of many unconscious impulses and desires these distort the faithfulness of the reflections thereby leading to error. This ambiguity concerning mirror-images referred to above, in some aspects, revolves around the notion of the contrast between transparency and solidity, the illusory and the 'real'; an ordinary mirror gives the appearance of transparency because of the properties of glass but is actually solid, and the same is true of a skilfully mimetic painting, in that it appears *real* but is actually illusory. No doubt one could write several tomes on this observation from an Art Historical perspective, but I would like to continue with a far more, from my standpoint, profound critique and to initiate this I will quote from Alan Howard, where **i** refers to the point where the axis of the ego touches the plane of time, as described above,

"The **i** does not live in the physical body, at least not in the way we imagine. The **i** lives in the *self*. The physical body is throughout life a part of the world, the *real* world, and is governed by world processes and laws. What **i** *know* as the world, therefore, cannot be the *real* world. The real world is not what **i** become aware of by perception as a precondition of knowledge, *but what produces perception in me*. Perception is given **i** do not do a thing about its coming to pass, nor do **i** know how it is done. It just happens. **i** simply perceive," (Alan Howard, Thinking about Knowing: 14-15).

Having made this point Howard continues with

" a body existing in time and space. That body, however, being part of the world, has the property of reflecting in itself whatever may exist in that world. In this respect the body is like a lake set in a mountainous terrain, of which the lake itself is, of course, also a part. Like the lake, man's body is also a part of its terrain, the world, and, just as the lake mirrors the tree-clad slopes around it, and the cloud-filled sky above, so the body, by means of the senses, also mirrors the surrounding world. But the lake knows nothing of the world reflected in it; and man would know nothing of the world reflected in him if he were only a body." (Alan Howard, Thinking about Knowing: 26).

To understand Howard's comments we need to return to Lehr's statement above that 'the physical brain and the part of the etheric body belonging to it – the etheric brain – assume a function comparable with that of a mirror, the physical organ representing the physical mass and the etheric organ its metallic gloss'. The import of the physical brain being analogous to the physical mass of the mirror means that just like the glass of a mirror it offers no resistance, i.e. is transparent, to the stimulations from the outside world entering through our senses, the resistance is provided by the etheric formation supporting the physical organ, thereby creating a 'mirror', so that the **I** can then become aware of these stimulations. To take the example of the 'eye', the physical substance of an eye offers no resistance to the light entering it, and it is only when the light reaches its etheric counter-part that there is resistance and reflection, and this reflection is cognised by the **I** as vision. In passing it was part of the rituals of the Ancient Mysteries that a candidate was so trained that thy were able to witness the Midnight Sun, which in essence meant the transformation of the perceptual capacities of an individual so that they were able to perceive the Sun through the substance of the earth at midnight. I have already hinted at the mysteries of light and what we see, ordinarily, as reflections in the 'outside' world is the workings of the lowest order of light. From this commentary it is readily apparent that artistic creativity, of any type, is an instinctive act that attempts to unravel the mysteries of our sensory constitution. The only time there is resistance from the corporeal sensory organs is when they are malfunctioning. If this is the case, and there is a 'transparency' to our corporeality to impulses from the cosmos, then this can only mean that we live in undivided communion with the cosmos - there is no 'inside' and 'outside' except for our present consciousness. Furthermore as Howard indicates the metallic gloss - the ethereal organs - of themselves know nothing, in terms of human epistemology, of what they reflect, and it is only when our ego which dwells in the self becomes aware of the reflections that we become conscious of our presence in the cosmos as an individual. Therefore the physical body is created by the world for the world and for us to be in this world, but if we did not posses the supersensible dimension of thinking, *vis a vis* the ego, we would know nothing. Admittedly, because we have an astral body as do the animals, we are sentient, that is we are able to experience pain and pleasure, however we would not be able to know these emotions as a self-conscious fact without an ego. It is only when an individual transforms their way of 'seeing' the world, through a transformation of the sensory structure of the Etheric Body, that we can know through our thinking that our prior perception was only an intermediate state. The senses now become something more and 'reach out' into the world - they are now active as well as passive. Although as we know the reflection of ourselves in a mirror is an inert lifeless illusion that can only mimic our actions, Bacon explored through his works as to whether this reflection could become more than that, and "Portrait of George Dyer in a Mirror", 1967-68, (ill. 78), and "Seated Figure", 1974, (ill. 79), are good examples of this effort. In the former the mirror-image has taken on a life of its own in that it is reflecting a divided head rather than the unitary head, albeit distorted, of the subject, whereas the latter painting depicts the seated figure's head in the process of becoming a picture/ mirror and where its reflection is a distorted caricature of itself. Although on a general level these images question the empirical value of reflections as representative of reality, these images also question the border-line between the animate and inanimate and how the animate can infuse the inanimate with life. We have to ask ourselves did Bacon perceive how etheric organs reflect from a more profound level of consciousness, for another interpretation of "Portrait of George Dyer in a Mirror", 1967-68, is that Dyer in his attempts to understand his situation in life was doing this from a malfunctioning spiritual constitution, and was thus arriving at erroneous conclusions regarding his state of being.

Steiner refers to the profound depths of mirror images by referring to what is known as the 'great sacrifice', and this quote supplements the above:

"One may picture this "great sacrifice," the highest expression of will in divine nature, by imagining oneself before a mirror in which one's image is reflected. This image is, of course, an illusion, a semblance. Now carry over this image to the point of imagining yourself dying, sacrificing your existence, your feeling and thought, your very being, to inject life into that image. Spiritual science in all ages has called this phenomenon the "outpouring," "the emanation." If you could really make this sacrifice, it would be clear that you would no longer be here because you would have given up your whole being to this reflected image to imbue it with life and consciousness." (Steiner: The Lord's Prayer, An Esoteric Study)

It is not possible to analyse this statement in great detail, nevertheless let us consider that the above statement could refer to the reflective properties of the etheric organs. Such a thought would mean that Bacon, who was able to perceive from a 'higher' viewpoint than the intellectual would in effect be able to partially infuse himself into these reflective etheric organs. Evidence for this contention is that Bacon, in the above images, presents an inchoate intimation of a deep truth concerning our being and how we integrate ourselves into the world. I say inchoate because Bacon did not have a clear, cognitive understanding of the sublime process hinted at by Steiner but he certainly intuited it and deployed his intuitions for purposes of his own. As Bacon never spoke of his cognition of the world it is a moot question as to how deep his understanding of what he perceived was, and obviously cannot be pursued further at present. This question of an 'outpouring' or 'emanation' is a very noticeable attribute of particular Figures by Bacon, for instance in "Studies from the Human Body", 1975, (ill. 68), there is a clear impression of the reclining Figure on the bench outpouring/ emanating or being sucked into the mirror to which it is juxtaposed.

"Now imagine you are looking into a mirror. Your reflection is a faithful copy of your physiognomy, imitates your every gesture, resembles you in every respect, but it is a lifeless image of yourself. You stand before the mirror as a living being and are faced with your lifeless image, which resembles you in every detail, but is without the living reality, the essential self. Imagine that your will had developed to the point when it was able to make the decision to sacrifice your own existence, your own being, or to surrender it to your reflected image. You would then be in a position to sacrifice yourself wholly in order to endow your reflected image with your own life. Of such a will we say: it emanates, it pours out its own nature. What Christianity terms "the divine Will of the Father" is the highest expression of the will.

Today, therefore, the human will is the least developed member of the soul forces. It is however in the process of developing such strength that it is able to consummate the "Great Sacrifice". Volitional nature, in so far as it is an outpouring of Divinity, is the true nature of that which can develop as the power of Atma." (Steiner: The Lord's Prayer, An Esoteric Study).

I will not pursue the question of our future evolution into the sublime state of Atma, however as has been emphasised here Bacon had developed his will to an extraordinarily high degree in comparison to the general population. From the perspective of ordinary consciousness this intermingling of a mirror-image and the subject being reflected, together with the blurring of the distinction between a mirror-image and a mimetic rendition of the subject, can only appear as fantastic possessing no connection to 'reality'. However Steiner's statement from the above quotes, 'Imagine that your will had developed to the point when it was able to make the decision to sacrifice your own existence, your own being, or to surrender it to your reflected image' encapsulates the impression given by the Bacon images so far considered, and evidence of Bacon's concern with the 'will' is demonstrated by contemplating "Painting", 1978, (ill. 54). In this work we have a Figure that appears to be armless and which is trying to open the door with its foot so as to compensate for itself its inability to perform this task with its hands. The 'will' is related to the metabolic system, and this should be readily understandable as the arms and legs are the primary limbs for the expression of the 'will'. It has been stated that the etheric sensory organs that lie behind the corporeal senses of perception together act as reflectors, and that the *ego* which dwells within the *self* becomes conscious of these reflections, and the same is true of the astral world of sensations with the nervous system as indicated by Steiner

"Take man — without considering his blood — take him as being made up of the substance of the surrounding physical world, and containing, like the plant, certain juices which transform it into living substance, and in which a nervous system gradually becomes organized. This first nervous system is the so-called sympathetic system, and in the case of man it extends along the entire length of the spine, to which it is attached by small threads on either side. It has also at each side a series of nodes, from which threads branch off to different parts, such as the lungs, the digestive organs, and so on. This sympathetic nervous system gives rise, in the first place, to the life of sensation just described. But man's consciousness does not extend deep enough to enable him to follow the cosmic processes mirrored by these nerves. They are a medium of expression, and just as human life is formed from the surrounding cosmic world, so is this cosmic world reflected again in the sympathetic nervous system. These nerves live a dim inward life, and if man were but able to dip down into his "sympathetic" system, and to lull his higher nervous system to sleep, he would behold, as in a state of luminous life, the silent workings of the mighty cosmic laws." (Steiner: The Occult Significance of Blood).

Steiner further states that

"In past times people were possessed of a clairvoyant faculty which is now superseded, but which may be experienced when, by special processes, the activity of the higher system of nerves is suspended, thus setting free the lower or subliminal consciousness. At such times man lives in that system of nerves which, in its own particular way, is a reflection of the surrounding world." (Steiner: The Occult Significance of Blood).

It is a fact that Bacon, through his own admission, did not develop his intellectual side, which is a function of the higher nervous system, until he was in his late twenties, thus the above statement provides one possible reason as to why Bacon possessed the psychic abilities I argue he had. This evolutionary progress to our modern consciousness is explained further by Steiner:

"Certain lower animals indeed still retain this state of consciousness, and, dim and indistinct though it is, yet it is essentially more far-reaching than the consciousness of the man of the present day. A widely extending world is reflected as a dim inward life, not merely a small section such as is perceived by contemporary man. But in the case of man something else has taken place in addition. When evolution has proceeded so far that the sympathetic nervous system has been developed, so that the cosmos has been reflected in it, the evolving being again at this point opens itself outwards; to the sympathetic system is added the spinal cord. The system of brain and spinal cord then leads to those organs through which connection is set up with the outer world.

Man, having progressed thus far, is no longer called upon to act merely as a mirror for reflecting the primordial laws of cosmic evolution, but a relation is set up between the reflection itself and the external world. The junction of the sympathetic system and the higher nervous system is expressive of the change which has taken place beforehand in the astral body. The latter no longer merely lives the cosmic life in a state of dull consciousness, but it adds thereto its own special inward existence. The sympathetic system enables a being to sense what is taking place outside it; the higher system of nerves enables it to perceive that which happens within, and the highest form of the nervous system, such as is possessed by mankind in general at the present stage of evolution, takes from the more highly developed astral body material for the creation of pictures, or representations, of the outer world. Man has lost the power of perceiving the former dim primitive pictures of the external world, but, on the other hand, he is now conscious of his inner life, and out of this inner life he forms, at a higher stage, a new world of images in which, it is true, only a small portion of the outer world is reflected, but in a clearer and more perfect manner than before." (Steiner: The Occult Significance of Blood).

There is with Bacon's use of 'mirrors' in his pictures no attempt to produce clear-cut mimetic 'reflections', on the contrary what we are given are wispy and indefinite indications in many cases, for example "Study from the Human Body", 1981, that can either appear upon a 'mirror' surface or a square that straddles the definition between a mirror and a painting, as in "Triptych – Studies from the Human Body", 1970, (ill. 20), and "Two Studies for a Portrait of George Dyer", 1968, (ill. 19), respectively. All of these works are redolent of Steiner's statements above with respect to a 'dim consciousness' and the ability we now possess to create clear, inner pictures or representations of a reduced portion (in comparison to the sympathetic nervous system) of the outer world. With these 'mirror' renditions in his work Bacon gives the impression that he is intermingling the older consciousness with the new. This is bolstered if we consider further statements by Steiner upon the nature of the astral world, for then we are given an insight as to why Bacon created images where a mirror does not mimetically reflect the subject.

"The first thing to realise is that in the astral world, everything that exists is revealed as it were in a mirror, inversed. In the astral light the cipher 365 must be read backwards: 563. If an event unfolds before us, it is perceived in inverse sequence. In the astral world the cause comes after the effect, whereas on Earth, the effect follows the cause. In the astral world, the aim appears as the cause — proving that the aim and the cause are identical, acting in an inverse sense according to the sphere of life in which we are functioning. The teleological problem which no metaphysician has been able to solve by dint of abstract thought is thus solved by clairvoyance.

Another result of this inverse unravelling of things in the astral world is that it teaches man to know himself. Feelings and passions are expressed by plant and animal forms. When man begins to behold his passions in the astral world he sees them as animal forms. These forms proceed from himself, but he sees them as if they were assailing him. This is because his own being is objectivised — otherwise he could not behold himself. Thus it is only in the astral world that man learns true self knowledge in contemplating the images of his passions in the animal forms which hurl, themselves upon him. A feeling of hatred entertained against another being appears as an attacking demon.

This astral self-knowledge occurs in an abnormal way in those who are troubled with psychical illnesses which consist in constant visions of being pursued by animals and menacing entities. The sufferers are seeing the mirror images of their emotions and desires.

No psychical trouble arises in true initiation, but the premature and sudden flashing-up of the astral world may give rise to insanity. In clairvoyance, man is liberated from his physical body. Hence the dangers that may threaten the mind and brain of one who attempts this kind of training without being absolutely balanced." (Steiner: An Esoteric Cosmology, IX, The Astral World, June1906).

Thus if we contemplate "Portrait of George Dyer in a Mirror", 1968, and "Two Studies for a Portrait of George Dyer", 1968, it is not difficult to perceive how Bacon has subtly undermined our usual expectations with both mirror-reflections and the order of cause and effect. The latter part of the above statement readily applies to "Two Studies of George Dyer with Dog", 1968, (ill. 80), which is an image of the deterioration of Dyer's mental state. The ramifications of this image will be fully explore in the chapter on Portraits. In addition Steiner's remarks concerning the reversibility of the astral world, font of our emotions, provides further elucidation of the strange reversibility of Bacon's Figuration.

Digestion.

It may seem to be an otiose question, but 'why do we eat'? It takes little thought to assume that in the majority of cases the answer would be to keep ourselves alive, and importantly conscious. But let us look at the question from another point-of-view Steiner in his book "Theosophy" states the following of the human body,

"The human body is so built as to be adapted to thinking. The same materials and forces which are present in the mineral kingdom are so combined in the human body that by means of this combination thought can manifest itself." (Steiner: Theosophy, 1989: 25).

So, yes, the purpose of eating is to maintain the physical body but this purpose serves a higher cause, that of thinking. At our present stage of evolution the ability to be self-conscious and also to be aware of our thinking, which at present is based upon an abstract and intellectual apprehension of the world, lies at the heart of our consciousness. An abstract, intellectual consideration of the information provide by the senses is the foundation of the Western Scientific pursuit of Knowledge and Truth, and this is presented in the form of logically, manipulated concepts. The locus for thinking in the body is the brain which is completely covered by the bony structure of the head. As well as being the locus for thinking the brain is also the centre whereby all sensory activity is focused, as is shown by the fact that the majority of the senses are located upon the surface of the head and connected through openings in the skull to the brain. The brain, furthermore, is the locus for all the information that is gathered by the various parts of the nervous system. Thus when considered the head/ skull/ brain shows itself to be a contrast to the red-blooded chest/ heart system and the mobility of the limb system, in that it appears to be completely cut-off from the 'outside' world. This distinction is characterised by Walthur Buhler, M.D., in his book "Living With Your Body" as follows,

"What is the nature of the brain? It is an unusually pale, grey organ: if you ever have the opportunity of seeing the brain and how it is situated in the skull, you will be inadvertently reminded of the coiled appearance of the intestine…. But despite its appearance even the outward form of the brain is quite different from that of the intestine. For to our great surprise this organ does not move at all. All these convolutions are fixed with respect to one another. The millions of brain cells with their many fibres, ramifications and extensions – which we observe and call nerves and, which issuing from the brain, extend throughout the body - are absolutely immobile….. we observe here that the mobility that was characteristic of the metabolic-limb system has come almost to a standstill." (Buhler: 1979, 16-17).

Buhler then proceeds to describe how the bones in the skull are rigid and bowl-shaped in contrast to the tubular shape and mobility of bones within the limbs, and how the brain resists all that is material. This he demonstrates by indicating how the food we eat and the air we breathe are immediately transferred to the stomach and the lungs respectively once they enter through the mouth. Of the actual substance of air and food that enter the body through the mouth only the finer elements of taste, sound, smell etc associated with their material foundation are taken hold of by the brain. It is a well-known and established fact that taste and smell have an extremely minimal material content, and this is even more true of vision, Thus it is possible to state that for the functioning of our consciousness and the knowledge accrued through thinking (image-making and conceptualisations), the brain virtually dematerialises everything which it receives of the 'outside' world. That is the brain does not permit the gross materiality of phenomena to enter its sphere of operations for the functioning of all the dimensions of our conscious abilities, albeit that the brain receives nutriments etc from the rest of the body for the maintenance of its status as an organ.

However it is a fact that the information that the brain receives through the senses is not a passive affair, the materiality of the corporeal body is radically altered through the impact of the 'outside' world upon its sensory organs. Examination of the functioning of the eye clearly demonstrates this, but firstly it has to be noted that what we call the 'eye' is basically a combination of brain nerve tissue (retina) and skin (lens), that which will become the retina in an adult first grows out of the brain as a nerve-shoot during embryonic development. So in effect the eye has all the characteristics described above as pertinent to the brain in that the metabolic processes of the body have retreated from the eye so that it can selflessly receive the light from outside but, as stated, this is not a passive affair,

"..so each impression of light may be said to punch an hole in the retina. If the impression of light is especially strong, we become aware of this hole; we simply cannot see anything else, because – strange as it may sound – *all seeing destroys the eye!* Not the whole eye, of course, but a part of it; for in the retina something undergoes catabolism, is actually destroyed. And we know what it is that is destroyed in this way. On the retina, as on a photographic plate, there is a delicate, special layer called the *visual purple.* This substance changes chemically, decomposes and fades..." (Buhler: 1979, 91-92).

The visual purple is built up by the anabolic processes of the blood that flows to the brain, and this is a procedure that is true of all the other senses with regard to their specific configuration, so there is thus in the brain a constant interaction of catabolic and anabolic processes that enable us to have conscious perceptions. However, this is not the only instance of anabolic and catabolic actions working to maintain our corporeal body for the very act of being conscious and thinking whether in images or concepts causes a deterioration of the substance of the brain:

"We are able to see through our eyes only because a 'hole' is made in the retina; in the brain, too, when mental images are formed, nerve substance always undergoes catabolism. Whenever we have an idea, whenever we hold an image before us in our souls, a kind of hardening takes place in the brain; a minute hard structure, an organic counterpart seemingly of crystal or salt, is formed. So when you picture the square in your soul, a delicate impression, an organic, physical one, is left in the mirror of the brain. In time, such impressions begin to 'oversalt' the brain, as it were, making it more rigid and lifeless than it already is. These structures accumulate during the day, since we form an incredible number of mental images, all of which the brain must reflect. So the brain becomes increasingly over-salted and rigid. By the evening we begin to notice this process as a feeling of fatigue." (Buhler: 1979, 106).

From this description of the chemical processes taking place in the brain whilst we are conscious it is not over-dramatic to state that whilst we are conscious our consciousness 'feeds' upon the corporeal body in order to function, and that the metabolic system has to continually resist and renew the damage to our organism so as to maintain our existence as thinking beings. It is as though our consciousness is continually 'sucking' the life from our corporeality in order to maintain its existence. Two 'heads' painted by Bacon that immediately come to mind in connection with the above are "Head I", 1948, (ill. 29), and "Head II", 1949, (ill.

172

30). Both of these images depict Figures that appear to be collapsing into themselves, and given the prominence of the mouth in both cases we conclude that they represent instances of auto-cannibalism. In this respect Salvador Dali is evoked for he too produced two images in the same year of an equally gruesome nature with "Autumnal Cannibalism", 1936, (ill. 81), and "Soft Construction with Boiled Beans", 1936, (ill. 82). Thus both Dali and Bacon produced images that depict the corporeal body consuming itself, and I would suggest that it is perfectly possible that Bacon and Dali had an 'instinctive', if not clearly conscious, understanding of the interaction of body and consciousness as an underlying motive for the production of their respective images, that complements other reasons for production.

Such a comment is pertinent to Bacon for his two 'Heads' were painted shortly after "Painting", 1946, an image that clearly depicts the metabolic-limb system of the human being. In this work the mouth and its relation to digestion is unambiguously emphasised whilst the 'eyes', representative of the senses, are occluded thus implying that the consciousness of the Figure has retreated into the background. It has been noted that the ambience of this work is that of 'dreaming', albeit in a somewhat nightmarish mode, and the implied dynamism of the chunks of meat (limbs) and festooned intestines readily suggests the unceasing activity of the metabolic-limb system. In "Painting", 1946, if we concentrate upon the torso of the Figure ghostly animal-shapes can be observed, (ill. 83), there are no clear-cut, definitive animal forms but this would not be expected of Bacon. This raises the question of my 'reading into' Bacon's images that which I am predisposed to find, a danger for every individual interpreting an artist's images. Such a danger is deflected by my having indicated, above, the presence of nascent animal forms in several other works, and by the fact that in "Painting", 1946 there are to be observed a number of embryonic animal shapes. To the middle left, below the shoulder there is a bird-like form, whilst on the right what we presume to be the spine of the Figure that diagonally traverses the rail has the appearance of an insect of some sort. I will not develop this theme but within occultism it is acknowledged that the human form has been derived from the whole of the animal kingdom and that various body-parts are related to differ creatures, which in turn are related to the Houses of the Zodiac. Did Bacon have such an understanding? This cannot be answered at present but what is significant about these fleeting animal forms in Bacon's work is that that they are ever mobile metamorphosing into each other, as they are in reality. Of the metabolic-limb system Buhler makes the following noteworthy comments,

"When the infant receives nothing he cries, and when the stomach is not fed, it begins to 'growl', because its desires have not been fulfilled. Imagine a hungry living creature such as a cat, a dog, or even a baby, and picture it as a stomach – only then do you have the right idea of what the stomach is." (Buhler: 1979, 79).

If it is accepted that these ghostly creatures present in "Painting", 1946 are not a figment of my imagination, and that Bacon did not create them unconsciously by chance – an absurd notion at the best of times – then we have a remarkable agreement concerning our metabolic-limb system between two entirely unrelated individuals, one a doctor the other an artist. There are many images that demonstrate that Bacon was aware of how our metabolic-limb system has the propensity to operate autonomously despite the fact that it is inseparably intertwined with the thinking and feeling systems in a living human being. Clearly "Painting", 1946, is one such image and another is "Painting", 1978, which depicts a Figure in the act of opening a door with its foot. The metabolic-limb system is emphasised by the reduction of the Figure's functioning to its legs, whilst the will is stressed by the focus upon the keyhole of the Figure's gaze. The thinking dimension of the Figure is rendered explicit through the depiction of the discarded newsprint upon the floor, the subtlety of this metaphor for 'thinking' is that once a newspaper is read it is laid aside, and similarly once we have finished thinking upon a subject it is laid aside and partially retains a shadowy existence within the memory. Our feeling dimension is referenced in this work through the rhythms of the work which are integrated more complexly within the overall composition of this work than "Painting", 1946, and particularly by the overall ambience of the work which combines a mood of forlornness with excited anticipation.

If we now return to the fact that in order to be conscious we have to 'use' up the brain during the time whilst we are awake Steiner made the following comments upon the significance of this medical fact,

"It was necessary, then, for the human being to be involved in death, to know death. The ancient epochs, when men knew nothing of death …. Ideas were inspired from the spiritual world, not 'thought out.' There was no intellect as we know it. But the intellect had to take root and this is possible only because the human being can die, only because he has within him perpetually the forces of death. In a physical sense we may say: Death can only set in when certain salts, that is to say, certain dead, mineral substances deposit themselves in the brain as well as in the other parts of the human organism. In the brain there is a constant tendency towards the depositing of salts, towards a process of bone-formation that has been arrested before completion. So that all the time the brain has the tendency towards death." (Steiner: Exoteric and Esoteric Christianity, Dornach, April 2nd, 1922.)

These brief indications of the relationship between our consciousness and our corporeal body indicate that the 'will to survive' has to be exerted constantly if we wish to continue living, even though in the long-run the 'forces of death' we have internalised through our ability to intellectualise overwhelm our regenerative forces, but Steiner makes an even more telling comment with regard to the ability to think,

"We in modern times have the faculty of intellect; but intellect makes us inwardly cold, inwardly dead; it paralyses us. In the operations of the intellect we are not

174

alive in the real sense. Try to feel what this means: when man is thinking he does not truly live; he pours out his life into empty, intellectual forms and he needs a strong, robust sense of life if these dead forms are to be quickened to creative life in that region where moral impulses spring from the force of pure thinking, and where in the operations of pure thinking we understand the reality of freedom, of free spiritual activity." (Steiner: Exoteric and Esoteric Christianity, Dornach, April 2nd, 1922.)

It is undeniable that there is a morbid ambience to Bacon's *oeuvre* and for many viewers this obstructs the ability to view his work dispassionately, but if an individual stands back from their own emotional reactions then a work such as "Figure at a Washbasin", 1976, (ill. 9), acquires a new significance. If instead of focussing upon what appears to be a man in the act vomiting we concentrate upon the discarded newsprint then we are able to make the comment that the Figure appears to be trying to rid itself of something related to its past thoughts that is making it ill. Since there are no indications as to what form this past thinking took the only conclusion is that it relates to act of 'thinking' itself, which in its present form has the deadly effects described by Steiner.

Blood is a Very Special Fluid.

This title is a statement taken from Goethe's work, "Faust", (Act I, Scene 4), and it highlights the profound function of blood within our corporeality. The first glimmerings of life are to be found in the mineral/ crystal realm where we have definite, ordered structures created by the 'shining' into the earthly of Formative Forces. Above the crystals we have the plant realm that has drawn the Formative Forces completely within themselves. Whereas the mineral/ crystal realm can only multiply through a reflective process the plant is able to propagate itself through the seed. The next level of complexity is the animal which has within itself the Cosmic Astrality, and this is made evident through the animal possessing a nervous system which is closely aligned to the airy element. Because the mammal (ourselves included) has drawn the element of heat into itself the ego now has the opportunity to function through the medium of the blood, and so we now have an animal that, potentially, is able to think, feel and propagate itself and which also has the capacity to become self-consciousness, as is demonstrated by ourselves. From realms of unimaginable beauty and sublimity we have descended into corporeal bodies that also include water, air and warmth bodies with their respective corollaries to the Formative, Astral/ Emotional and Ego forces, the presence of which is signalled by the creation of the cell, nervous system and blood respectively. The ego in making itself manifest transforms various fluids within the 'animal' and 'plant' realm into the blood, so that firstly cold-blooded animals arise, then the warm-blooded mammals, both of which we have transformed, during our descent into the earthly, into our present human form. It can be readily perceived how the ego, through the blood, is intimately connected to emotional forces, through such examples as to how the blood immediately rushes to our faces when we are embarrassed, or when we are frightened, or shocked, our blood seems to disappear and evaporate leaving us white and pallid; the list is almost endless. It can thus be said that blood has a sensitive and intimate relationship to our emotional state and well-being as well as to the ego, but it is also a fact that this sensitivity can be controlled by those individuals who have sufficient will power to so control the effect of the emotional realm within themselves, so that they do not display embarrassment, fear or any other emotion upon the surface of their corporeal bodies.

It has been explored with relation to theories of childhood development by Piaget and others how the discovery of perspective enabled an individual to rationalise their relationship to the 'Other', particularly within an urban environment. The desire to disrupt the confines of Classical Perspective from the 19th century onwards reflects a need to go beyond the purely formal societal, integration of egos for merely functional and utilitarian reasons to something different, what one might name as the necessity 'to become the Other'. This relates to the profusion of, contrary to normal expectations, mirror-images in Bacon's work where there is a confusing of the boundaries between Self and Other. One effect of this is to give the impression that there is an 'outpouring of the human being' into these mirror-images, and one reason for this peculiarity was supplied by Steiner's profound comments on this subject. Bacon had an intense drive to understand not only the psychological aspects of a human being but also the deeper features of our corporeality, and it is Bacon's disruption of Classical Perspective which first alerts us to this fact.

Our modern wide-awake consciousness is a direct effect of an evolutionary development of our higher, nervous system which came to the fore through the expansion of the frontal lobes of the brain. With the development of a higher nervous system humanity's consciousness no longer leads a dull, inward life, as in ancient times, when it was restricted to the sympathetic nervous system but now opens itself to the surrounding environment. The state of consciousness of ancient peoples (atavistic clairvoyance, see the Figures in l.h. panel of "Three Studies for a Crucifixion") was a dreamy, semi-conscious awareness that lacked the wide-awake self-consciousness that we possess, but they had a natural ability to perceive the realms spoken of above that are invisible to modern humanity, and this ability of the ancients was related to the metabolic system, via the sympathetic nervous system. If we consider the works "Three Studies for a Crucifixion", (ill. 35), "Triptych Inspired by the Oresteia of Aeschylus", (ill. 34), and "Three Figures and Portrait", 1975, (ill. 84) we see that the spinal chord, via the depiction of the spine, plays a prominent role in these paintings, specifically the r. h. and central panels of the first two works and the l. h. figure of the third work. The interesting element of these works is the depiction of the head in relation to the spine. In the first work the head is almost unrecognisable consisting principally of a mouth and an eye, whilst in the second work although there is what appears to be an ear the head is still severely distorted, whereas in the third work we have a complete head, replete with collar and tie. It is interesting to note the implied locomotion of the Figures which, because the limbs are the outward expression of movement, draws attention to the digestive, metabolic system of the human being. The subject of the portrait in this latter work is Michel Leiris, and he appears as the head in the background and as the head of the Figure on the left, and was a well-known academic in France. The impression these works give is that in the first two works Bacon stressed the metabolic functions of the body and so they are to be read in relation to the atavistic, clairvoyant stage of humanity, (when a higher nervous system had not developed), whereas with the third work he stressed the dead intellectualism, which shrouds the spiritual world in darkness, that is characteristic of our present stage of development, and which predominates in the head and brain.

One outcome of the addition of a higher nervous system is that the blood now occupies a mid-way role between the 'inner' and the 'outer' - our inner world of imaginations and an external world of form. But the blood, the bloodline into which we are born is the repository for all of that which relates to our ancestors through our parents. Steiner clarifies these complex relationships with the following

"When evolution has progressed so far that the sympathetic nervous system has been developed, so that the cosmos has been reflected in it, the evolving being again at this point opens itself outwards; to the sympathetic nervous system is added the spinal chord. The system of brain and spinal chord then leads to those organs through which connection is set up with the outer world." Steiner, 1926: 28.

"Hand in hand with this transformation another change takes place in higher stages of development. The transformation thus begun extends from the astral body to the etheric body. As the etheric body in the process of its transformation evolves the astral body, and as to the sympathetic nervous system is added the system of the brain and spine, so, too, does that which - after receiving the circulation of the lower fluids – has grown out of and become free from the etheric body, now transmute these lower fluids into what we now as blood. Blood is, therefore, an expression of the individualised etheric body, just as the brain and spinal chord are the expression of the individualised astral body. And it is this individualising which brings about that which lives as the ego or 'I'." Steiner, 1926: 29-30.

"…the blood stands mid-way, as it were, between the inner world of pictures and the exterior living world of form. This role becomes clear to us when we study two phenomena, viz., ancestry – the relationship between conscious beings – and experience within the world of external events. Ancestry, or descent, places us where we stand in accordance with the law of blood-relationship. A person is born of a connection, a race, a tribe, a line of ancestors, and what these ancestors have bequeathed to him is expressed within his blood. In the blood is gathered together, as it were, all that the material past has constructed in man; and in the blood is also being formed all that is being prepared for the future." Steiner, 1926: 33-34.

From this we are to understand that it is against this ancestral inheritance that we struggle to establish our own particular ego-consciousness and identity. There is waged in a newly born child a struggle to overcome all that is inherited both temperamentally and physically from its parents.

"I pointed out yesterday how the child's development undergoes a radical change with the loss of his first teeth … If the individual who comes down out of the spiritual pre-earthly world is weak, then the second life organism is similar to the inherited one. If the individual is strong, then we see how in the period between the change of teeth and puberty, from seven years to about fourteen, a kind of victory is gradually accomplished over the inherited characteristics. Children become quite different and they even change in their bodily outward appearance." Steiner, 1982: 33.

This struggle is one that is profound and difficult to complete, and any success is heavily dependent upon the strength of an individual's ego and the nature of their 'lower' self. Steiner explained the crucial role that the blood has in relation to our individuality, and indicated that for any entity, and this includes those entities we create in the emotional world through our own passions, to take control, or affect us, they have to take control of the blood for only by doing so do they gain a mastery over the ego.

"Whatever power it is that wishes to obtain the mastery over a man, that power must work upon him in such a way that the working is expressed in his blood. If, therefore, an evil power would influence a man, it must be able to influence his blood…For whoever has mastery of the blood is master of the man himself, or the man's ego." Steiner, 1926: 40.

If one is to understand Bacon's personality and his portraits of George Dyer then this commentary upon the relationship between blood and the ego is absolutely essential. Bacon as a personality had a somewhat morbid interest in physical blood to the point of visiting various meat markets so that he could immerse himself within its atmosphere. I do not wish to dwell upon this aspect of Bacon's behaviour at present, however it is a fact, as referred to above, that Bacon focussed upon the ego in various works, for example "Study for a Human Body (Man Turning on the Light), 1973-74, (ill. 65). If there is any doubt over this statement then one has only to view "Blood on the floor - Painting", 1986, (ill. 85), for in this work Bacon made absolutely explicit his understanding of the connection between blood and the ego. The light-bulb in this work has been identified as a metaphor for the ego above with Abrahms's commentary upon the mirror and the lamp as metaphors for how our consciousness functions, and it is significant that Bacon included the light-switch so as to leave no room for doubt as to the meaning of the image. If one has the ability to perceive the realms referred to here then it is perfectly possible to observe those entities which are created through, amongst other things, our passions and to study how they are inimical to an individual's well-being. Such a seemingly, fantastic assertion will be investigated in the next chapter in relation to Bacon's images of George Dyer. It will be pointed out that in his various images of Dyer Bacon explored such a possibility, and that given the nature of Dyer's demise it has to be taken seriously, for it is clear that something in Dyer's inner life compelled him to take the actions he did.

Chapter 5. Portraits.

Without the foundation of the previous chapters it would have been impossible to even begin to approach the profundity of Bacon's portraits of George Dyer. In my opinion the works to be considered are a supreme land-mark in the progression of Western culture, the fact that they are not considered as such does not alter this fact. Bacon, perhaps, because of his intimacy with Dyer produced with his portraits of Dyer an empirically, truthful exposition of Dyer's psychological and spiritual state that was grounded in an overwhelming compassion for the fate of that individual. These works are not merely outstanding but without parallel, because, as I will demonstrate, Bacon condensed into these images every imaginable nuance that concerns an individual's psychic struggles. As a forerunner to reviewing these works I will appraise Bacon's portraiture from a general viewpoint, so as to outline some of the salient features of his portraits of George Dyer.

Bacon's work, as Kurjakovic identified, refuses conventional representations/ identifications as a response to the encounter with the Other. The Other in my use of the term means that which is radically 'non-I'. What I mean by this is anything which I consider not to be me, and it rapidly becomes evident that the only thing I can call me is my self - I am. Paramount in the effect upon us of the non-I is the I of another person, and in this meeting with the Other it is possible to find ourselves severely alienated and desolate in their company. The ego from this perspective behaves in two principle modes - rejection and surrender. The actions and behaviour issuing from the rejection/ antipathy pole are only to plain to observe, but the surrender pole is far more subtle, as is shown by the fact that in order to listen, or to be sympathetic, to another person our own I has to be completely dimmed down in its functioning. From our intellectually-based consciousness we only perceive the world, and our own self, in terms of discrete essences, the baseline of which treats individuals as physical objects in space to be numbered, weighed and counted. In "Three Portraits: Posthumous Portrait of G. Dyer, Self-Portrait and Portrait of L. Freud", (ill. 28) Bacon has presented us with an integrated vision of community and alienation. The figures, as Kurjakovic perceived, are on a plane that expresses the inter-relatedness and synthesis, characteristic of Counter-Space from which our life-forces issue, and this plane is placed within a room that stands for the exclusivity engendered by the mechanical forces of the inorganic world. Although the placement of the three figures in separate panels indicates our individual, self-awareness, they have as Kurjakovic pointed out, 'impossible simultaneity', thereby showing how the ego functions in two modes – the individual and the social, and how we oscillate between the two poles of individuation and assimilation. Bacon through his manner of constructing this triptych demonstrates his awareness of these two poles of the Ego, and further implied that our identity is not specifically something that clings to our body surface. The 'impossible simultaneity' of this work indicates that identity is not a fixed and impermeable state with precise borders, but rather is in constant flux, and in this work identity is effectively is spread over all three panels further implying that identity is bound-up with the presence of the Other, thereby undermining the assumption that our identity is something that is solely a personal construct that completely conforms to our bodily structure.

Bacon's portraits, as triptychs or diptychs, only approach the 'being-ness', duration or 'now-ness' of a subject, or subjects – the relationship between time and space here is not something that is mechanical and linear and external to ourselves but is something that we create through our congress with others - and is something that is 'organic and living', meaning that time and space are as integral to our being as is our blood to the physical body. Through Bacon's portraits we come to understand that we are not empirical objects that can only be weighed, numbered and counted so that fictional 'norms', or for that matter individual, mimetic portraits, can be constructed relating to our behaviour and interaction. The appositeness of Bacon's style of portraiture can be appreciated by returning to the subject of Projective Geometry for there is a crucial *social* element to Projective Geometry that is largely lacking with Euclidean Geometry. This is expressed by the inter-relatedness and metamorphosis of the elements of Projective Geometry as opposed to the solitary, static and exclusive existence these elements have in Euclidean Geometry. Yet again it is seen how in "Three Portraits: Posthumous Portrait of G. Dyer, Self-Portrait and Portrait of L. Freud", 1973, (ill.55), Bacon has expressed the conditions of the cross-over point of lemniscatory space except here it relates to the psychic dimension of our individuality and socialisation. There is thus no correct way to view a Bacon triptych except possibly to be aware that despite our habit of 'reading' linear, narrative stories concerning individual events and people into the images we view, there is another mode of perception that concentrates upon inter-relatedness and non-linearity, as described above, and that Bacon combines the two without ever regressing into 'story-telling' or utter abstraction.

Turning to "Three Studies for Portraits (including Self-Portrait)", 1969, (ill. 86), we find a highly unusual presentation that has as its focus the inter-relationship of the 'Self' and the 'Other'. In this work the faces appear to be fracturing, as if being viewed in a broken mirror, and melting into each other thereby suggesting that there is a commonality to the subject's identities. If it is accepted that the constitution of self-identity is in some respects dependent on an 'Other', this work implies that something essential of Bacon's Self is bound up with the presence of the Other. Since Bacon's opposite is wearing a collar and tie that has become unbuttoned in the l. h. panel, the implication of this is that we have to by-pass, or remove, the artificial layers of social conformity to discover the layers on which we actually relate to each other. The other person in this work bears striking similarities to Michael Leiris, Bacon's close friend, and so Bacon thereby acknowledges how through the Other an aspect of himself comes to life and finds expression through his friendship with Leiris that otherwise would have remained hidden and silent. But the process of social inter-action is a mutual and simultaneous process for any individuals involved, and so Bacon investigated how if we really want to understand how we relate to each other we have to overcome the illusion that we are only separate, discrete, individual beings. The forces, energies and materiality that comprise our corporeality are common to everyone and it is only because we have an ego that we can have a sense of identity, but as pointed-out above the ego itself acts in the two modes of internalisation and externalisation, meaning that we both reject and absorb the Other who is also ego endowed. When we view ourselves as individual beings then the constitution of self-identity has a dimension of remembrance that rests upon complex memories and mental representations of the Other, and this is particularly emphasised in the triptych "Three Portraits - Triptych, Posthumous Portrait of G. Dyer, Self-Portrait, Portrait of Lucien Freud". This appears straightforward enough but what is the nature of this remembrance, what is it that is remembered and what is it that has made such an impression that it becomes memorable? It is this that Bacon explored in his meditations, during which he strove to remove his own subjective reactions to the subject, so as to focus upon that which defined an individual as that person uniquely. Bacon was acutely aware that every person is a mystery who can only be approached tangentially if one was going to accept that person and not take them for granted through familiarity. This is yet another reason for the production of multiple portraits of the same individuals, however the inclusion in "Three Portraits - Triptych, Posthumous Portrait of G. Dyer, Self-Portrait, Portrait of Lucien Freud" of photographs in each of the side panels that are not of the subject of that particular panel, but appear to be of the subject of the another panel, highlights the complexity of the mutability and inter-connection of identity in relation to the Other. In particular by referencing a photograph Bacon evoked the power of memory in relation to how we view the Other, and all of this is coupled with an ambiguity of time sequences between past and present that has a disorientating effect upon the observer's own sense of identity by jolting the viewer out of their usual perceptual habits and assumptions into the **NOW**. The over-riding impact of this is that Bacon in this work made explicit the fact that physical proximity has very little to do with how we relate to each other, and that the actual wellspring of our relationships occurs within subtle mental planes of memory, time and feeling. From this the conclusion is drawn that Bacon with these works urged the viewer not to confront the Other but to enter into a process of *becoming the other,* to so enter into the being of the Other that one is able to feel and think as they do.

I make no apologies for the complexity of this argument concerning Bacon's portraits, or for that matter Bacon's *oeuvre* in general, simply because Bacon's work is complex once one starts to contemplate it, and not merely try to explain it. This is one reason why I have adopted the interpretative strategies I have in this *critique*. I am not alone in recognising the complexity of a body of work that on the one hand first appears to lend itself to a straightforward critique because of its apparent simplicity (with regard to content) only to find, on the other hand, one's attempts at a satisfactory *critique* evaporating thereby precipitating the interpretative difficulties that ensue. Bacon's *oeuvre* is complex because he compressed into his deceptively simple images a life-time of contemplating the essential forces that comprise a human beings mental and corporeal constitution.

He recorded into these images how these forces effect the changes that can be perceived in the particularity of a specific person. Thus for Bacon the surface had no intrinsic value in itself except as an indicator of the presence of, and the handiwork of, absolute forces. Consequently Bacon's work is a highly impacted condensation of manifold dimensions crafted in such a manner that each image, or set of images (diptych/ triptych), is its own key to understanding once insight into the generality of his oeuvre is gained. It can now be appreciated why Bacon vigorously rejected the flaccid, bourgeois self-satisfaction and smugness, or flattery etc, which constitutes the meagre psychological penetration of vast swathes of portraiture to be observed in the Western world.

The arguments I have put forward concerning the forces that imbue all that is living are internally coherent and an understanding of them starts to emerge once one abandons the paralysis of thinking that is the outcome of accepting Anglo-Saxon Empirical interpretations of the Cosmos, this is demonstrated by the reference to such authors as Deleuze. Meaning does not arise from contemplating so-called pure phenomena/ sensory perceptions because as I have made clear above there are no such things as pure phenomena/ sensory perceptions, for anything perceived is already interpreted in the first instance, albeit that this primary act is now unconsciously accepted. To take the analysis concerning a pair of gloves above, one can sit staring at the gloves all day long and no meaning will arise, it is only when thinking is activated that something happens, and when this happens then a process is started that is infinite. I have outlined some of the usefulness of considering a pair of gloves for an understanding of how 'wholeness' is immanent to *all of* the phenomenal world, but I have no doubt that others who consider this presentation will find further dimensions pertinent to this analogy.

Portraiture Revised.

As well as producing portraits in a triptych format he also made use of the diptych for this purpose as in "Two Studies of George Dyer and Isabel Rawsthorne", 1970, (ill. 87), where there is a direct face-to-face depiction of the subjects from a side-on viewpoint. The two panels in this work appear to be 'leaking' into each other, as with "Three Studies for Portraits (including Self-Portrait)", 1969, (ill. 86), as though the identity of each of them had become enmeshed with the other. What is to be made of this diptych that echoes the husband and wife diptychs of the 16th and 17th Centuries? Although it is known that Dyer indulged in homosexual activities is Bacon implying that Dyer was bi-sexual, or given the panels 'leaking' into each other is he implying that each of the sexes is not monolithic, and possess within them something of the other sex, as in a Jungian sense (this has already been alluded to with respect to the Ether, or Formative, Body). Or yet again we may speculate given the inter-connectedness of the two panels that Bacon perceived a similar psychic structure to both Dyer and Rawsthorne, or that Bacon suggested in this work that focussing upon gender, and sexuality exclusively, obfuscates any attempt to uncover the essence of an individual, or of human beings, in general.

However, given the commentary above upon *memory* this work examines how we relate to each other, as individual beings, by presenting the most basic polarity there is with respect to our corporeal bodies, and the role of this polarity in the constitution of identity. It is not extravagant to interpret the expressions of Dyer and Rawsthorne in this diptych as being redolent of an aspect of 'yearning', especially given the incomplete and damaged portrayal of each of them. If this is accepted then because they are facing each other this yearning is concerned with 'completeness' and 'wholeness'. Thus this work makes explicit the fundamental yearning for completeness, through the Other, that is basic to all human beings, who by their very nature, are since the Fall in a state of splintered and shattered reality, the crux of which is the division of the sexes. This pre-Fall wholeness is encapsulated by Sacred Geometry where the pre-numerical 1 is the absolute 'wholeness' of the Cosmos out of which the numbers 1 to 9 have devolved, and where the condition of 2 within this understanding is incomplete and constantly strives towards, and yearns, for the pre-numerical 'wholeness' of non-division. Thus Bacon alludes in this diptych to the abjection and despair that is one consequence of humanity being divided into the two genders of male and female, and also in this diptych, and his work in general, indicated that sexual desire is the most primitive, but necessary, attempt to restore this lost unity, however I would also comment that Bacon is perhaps also alluding to the fact that when sexual gratification is pursued purely for itself it can only lead to despair, loneliness and dissoluteness.

It has also been stated how the encounter with the Other can be productive of self-understanding, and with "Two Studies of George Dyer and Isabel Rawsthorne", the implication is that the encounter with the Other can lead to a mitigation of the sense of isolation and separation we experience as ego-conscious, gendered individuals – our commonality is stressed rather than our separateness. But Bacon was also capable of expressing more complex emotional states concerned with friendship, and this demonstrated by "Three Portraits: Posthumous Portrait of George Dyer, Self-Portrait, Portrait of Lucien Freud". As highlighted this is a posthumous portrait of Dyer, but Bacon implied, by rendering Dyer in the same manner as Freud and himself, that Dyer's death was no impediment to their shared friendship. This work was executed a number of years after Dyer's death and so as previously indicated cannot be considered in the light of a standard memorial, instead it implies that there is something immortal about friendship that transcends, in reality, the limitations of the flesh. As with Bacon's 'Crucifixion' works Bacon's portraiture is capable of expressing profound depths that have scarcely been broached to date.

With "Three Studies for Portrait of Henrietta Moraes", 1963, (ill. 88) there is presented three different images of the same person that have the plasticity that is a hallmark of Formative Forces. This plasticity is also to be seen in "Three Studies for Portrait of Isabel Rawsthorne", 1965, (ill. 89). In these works Bacon literally gets 'beneath the skin' to show in these works how the I remains ever-present through the multiplicity of changes of mood and countenance that occur within a person from day-to-day, and demonstrates how this, the 'I', remains unchanged through the flux of time and emotions. The **I** thus acted, for Bacon as a centre upon which to anchor the multitude of fleeting impressions that constitute the time-span of an aspect of a person's emotional disposition, so that he could then create the Figure as a representation of his ability to *compress the time* of the 'coming and going' of these fleeting emotions as the composite image of the Figure. Through this technique Bacon makes a complete break with the tradition of static, stylised portraits we are accustomed to, and demonstrates how the changes of psychological disposition over periods of time, which are inherent to any individual, can be encompassed in the Figure. The above comments concerning Bacon's portraiture are fully borne out by investigating the series of remarkable portraits/ studies that Bacon produced of George Dyer, an investigation that demonstrates that Bacon was fully aware of the powers he possessed.

Portraits of George Dyer.

If Bacon possessed the powers I assert he had then his statement concerning emanations around the human being,

"But there are always emanations from people whoever they are, though some people's are stronger than others." (Sylvester, 1987: 174).

acquires a deep significance when considering his portraits of George Dyer. Normally if someone makes such a statement we assume they are speaking figuratively, or metaphorically, but as Steiner indicates these emanations are visible to individuals who have developed, or posses the requisite cognitive faculties.

"The precise thought of a thinker appears itself as a formation with definite outlines; a confused idea as a wavering, cloudy formation. In this way the soul and spirit of man appear as the super-sensible part of the *whole* human being. The colour effects perceptible to the eyes of the spirit which ray out around the physical man when observed in his activity, and which envelop him like a cloud (somewhat in the form of an egg) are a *human aura*. The size of the aura differs in different people….The most varied tones of colour ebb and flow in the aura. And this ebb and flow is a true picture of the inner life of the man. As this changes, so do the colour-tones change. But certain permanent qualities such as talents, habits, traits of character, express themselves also in permanent and basic colour-tones." (Steiner, 1989: 121).

There is evidence that Bacon had considerable psychic abilities for when speaking to George Peppiatt (Peppiatt, 1996: 92), he spoke of how he could see the Furies pursuing him, and he indicated that he did not mean this figuratively. Given that Bacon was patently not insane and there is absolutely no evidence that he suffered from hallucinations, or was in any way deranged, then we can only conclude that Bacon perceived aspects of human beings and hidden realms invisible to others.

The fact that in the series of portraits he produced of George Dyer he portrayed Dyer being harangued by a harrowing demonic being similar to the Furies indicates that this is the case. Such beings do not have a tangible existence but emerge from dimensions of the soul hidden to ordinary consciousness. For as Steiner states:

"Thus it is only in the astral world that man learns true self knowledge in contemplating the images of his passions in the animal forms which hurl, themselves upon him. A feeling of hatred entertained against another being appears as an attacking demon. This astral self-knowledge occurs in an abnormal way in those who are troubled with psychical illnesses which consist in constant visions of being pursued by animals and menacing entities. The sufferers are seeing the mirror images of their emotions and desires." (Steiner: An Esoteric Cosmology, IX, The Astral World, June1906).

Bacon had a prolonged and intense relationship with Dyer right up to the time of Dyer's death, which occurred in the bathroom of the hotel where they were staying just before the opening of Bacon's 1971 exhibition in Paris. Dyer was in many ways a disturbed and, in some senses, unstable character on whom Andrew Brighton offers the following information in his book "Francis Bacon"

"George Dyer who died alone, full of booze and pills, sitting on the lavatory in their hotel room in Paris. Bacon told with variations the story of Dyer, the handsome uneducated petty criminal with a speech impediment he met in 1964; Dyer became his lover and drank himself to death on Bacon's money….After Dyer's death in 1971 Bacon returned to Dyer's image repeatedly over the next four years. He is the subject of three triptychs, is portrayed in a fourth and appears in a number of other paintings." (Brighton, 2001: 68).

George Peppiatt in his book "Francis Bacon" is in agreement with this view of Dyer's habits, and there are indications that his death was not accidental. (Peppiatt, 1996: 211-212). It is a commonly known fact that negative emotional conditions have the ability to deepen and develop and behave as if they have not only a volition but an objective towards which they gravitate if left unattended. Since they behave as if they were 'alive' by developing and intensifying their effect upon an individual then they must be considered as having some form of being of which we are presently ignorant. The situation is similar to the concept of 'growth' which although it is real because we can perceive its effects we cannot perceive its actuality. There are thus individuals who appear to be incapable of controlling there actions because they are in the grip of something, which although it is invisible, has the power to manipulate their mental processes and physical actions; a comment that relates to the observations on the 'Blood' at the end of the previous chapter. If we are content to believe that abstractions are in fact realities, then no-one need die of thirst for they only have to conjure up the abstract image of a glass of water and their thirst will be quenched. Clearly this is not the case, and so these characteristics that comprise negative emotional conditions cannot be considered to be mere figurative, metaphorical or symbolic assignations because of the damage done in reality to individuals within the grip of such emotional configurations. Meaning that some reality has to be ascribed to these conditions, of and for themselves.

There is an epistemological hiatus here for intellectual *thinking* has reached a certain point and conclusions, and this hiatus is that because there are no intellectual structures within which it is permissible to theorise the possibility of ascribing a 'living' volition to that which cannot be seen, no palpable reality can be ascribed to that which, although invisible, is patently real and 'alive'. What is needed is a new vision and approach to epistemology that takes account of the conundrum that is presented by the ability of emotional configurations to intensify and develop with a seeming volition of their own, even though they are invisible, and central to this issue is the part that a human being plays in the worsening of these conditions, and here Bacon's portraits of Dyer are instructional. These are the bare facts about which one can have whatever opinion, but it is also a fact that Bacon had great depth of feeling for this tragic character, George Dyer, and through a continuous series of portraits Bacon performed an unparalleled analysis and examination of the destructive forces that afflicted Dyer. Bacon is unique amongst Western Painters in this respect. Parallels of a similar depth of insight into the spiritual realities of our soul-life are to found within literature, in particular Oscar Wilde's "Portrait of Dorian Gray" and R.L. Stevenson's "Dr. Jekyll and Mr. Hyde". Wilde's work, which concerns an individual who although he leads a dissolute life never shows the effects of ageing or his dissolution, rather it is his portrait that displays these effects. From one angle Wilde's work relates to the destruction that occurs to the soul through particular habits but which cannot in general be seen, it is also the case that the deleterious effects of such behaviour only appear physically after prolonged periods of indulgence. Stevenson's work revolves around the balance between the 'higher' and the 'lower' self and how this can be disturbed. Both of the above have a connection to Bacon's portraits of Dyer, and in effect these portraits record the effects of Dyer's actions upon Dyer's own soul, a process from which no-one is immune either positively or negatively. Both, Stevenson's and Wide's books, are outstanding works that concentrate upon those forces that are destructive within ourselves. However, these works are based upon fictional characters, and so are crucially different to Bacon's portraits of George Dyer that concern a real individual whose life-history is partially known to us.

There are a large number of portraits that Bacon created of George Dyer, of which only five works will be reviewed at this stage: "Portrait of George Dyer Staring at a Blind Cord", 1966, (ill. 90), "Portrait of George Dyer Crouching", 1966, (ill. 91), "Two Studies of George Dyer with Dog", 1968, (ill. 80), "Portrait of George Dyer in a Mirror", 1967-8, (ill. 92) and "Two Studies for a Portrait of George Dyer", 1968, (ill. 19).

A Profound Meditation upon Spiritual Realities.

There is an ambiguity with the last three of these works for what is presented is two images of George Dyer within the same work, and in all three cases one of the images is one step removed from the Figure that would normally be assumed to be the Figure that is the portrait. For instance in "Two Studies of George Dyer with Dog" there is an image of Dyer within the dog in the foreground, (Steiner: 'images of his passions in the animal forms'), whereas with the other two we find, what we assume to be, an image of Dyer within a mirror and a black rectangle respectively. What does this mean? Is the mirror-image a reflection of Dyer or is the black rectangle another painted portrait of Dyer alongside him? One assumption to be made is that Bacon leads us to believe that both the secondary images are just as 'real' as the seated Figure in both these works. The subtlety here revolves around whether or not Bacon is giving us a rendition of how Dyer appeared to himself, how he appeared to an observer, or how he appeared to Bacon. Also the mirror in "Portrait of George Dyer in a Mirror" itself raises questions as to its status as a reflector, for if it is a reflector then it is malfunctioning. What strikes one about this malfunctioning is that the half of the face that is missing in the seated Figure has miraculously reappeared within the mirror. A mirror when it reflects normally is in itself a fascinating object, for we are presented with a reversed world that tantalisingly offers a glimpse into another counter-world we could enter if only we were able to penetrate its surface (Steiner: The Great Outpouring'). But Bacon has placed George Dyer in this mirror-space, and through the juxtaposition of the seated Figure and this image we are led to believe that one is the reflection of the other, but which? Also this is a mirror with a life of its own that has the remarkable ability to make missing parts of George Dyer reappear. Given the complete disparity between the two images of Dyer in this work can we even assume that the two images are in the same time zone, and obey the same laws of time, i.e. the 'mirror-image' could be a rendition of Dyer from an earlier time when whatever it was that caused him to be the way he is now as the seated Figure- severely damaged – was only in its beginning, echoing the statements above concerning how time can reference itself, but just as importantly precipitating the viewer into the **NOW**. With this work Bacon demonstrated his ability to *compress the time-span* of events that are disparate in time for ordinary consciousness, or another way of stating this is that for a person of Bacon's psychic abilities is that when these events are viewed from the stand-point of Counter-Space they are perceived as one integral event.

In that case this 'mirror' is an example of Bacon's use of a mirror as a sort of recording device that records Dyer's life history, and here the 'device' is deployed in an ingenious and decisive manner that blurs the distinction as to whether it is Bacon who remembers Dyer as he was, or whether it is Dyer looking back upon himself as he was in earlier times. Thus we are in fact given two portraits in this work of George Dyer, the seated Figure that is unsettled and anxious, expressed by the Figure's distortion and agitation, and the so-called 'mirror-image', separated in time and space, either of which could be the 'true' George Dyer. Through this device Bacon invites the viewer to question what they consider as *real* and *unreal* with regard to people who are emotionally close to them, and the implications of this work are raised to a higher stage and intensified with the work, "Two Studies for a Portrait of George Dyer", 1968.

What is presented in this work is **NOT** the portrait of George Dyer, what is presented are two *studies*, and we can only take the seated Figure and the image in the black rectangle as these two studies. The fact that the previous work was a portrait and this work is *'Studies for a Portrait'* has to be taken seriously, for it implies that "Portrait of George Dyer in a Mirror" has captured a fundamental dimension of Dyer, whereas "Two Studies for a Portrait of George Dyer" is an exploration that could possibly lead to further additions to this fundamental dimension, but has not quite reached that point. Normally we would assume, since the two images in "Two Studies for a Portrait of George Dyer" are juxtaposed in the same picture-space, that the Figure in the black rectangle is a rendering of the seated Figure; this seems reasonable. This realisation creates a conundrum for the seated Figure is obviously not how George Dyer appeared in 'real life' as a living human being, due to its distortion, but is itself a rendering by Bacon of the actual George Dyer. But we cannot assume the simple fact, because of Bacon's working methods, that George Dyer was ever present at any moment in the whole process. So we have a rendering, Figure in the black rectangle of the seated Figure, which is itself a rendering created by Bacon of the real George Dyer, but since the black rectangle could be a canvass itself upon which Bacon was working to create an image of Dyer we are also given in this work a view of the images in Bacon's mind as he laboured to create a Portrait, or *study*, of an individual, who may or may not have been in his studio. This implies that Bacon was both there and not there, that is he is both in and not in the work we see, but that he is on some level inside the picture-space so as to able to perform the action of making a rendering of a rendering, implying that there is no fundamental break between the space of the picture and the space of his 'lived' life. That is the whole conception of this work took place in a continuum of space and time that is radically different from that of ordinary consciousness, the import of this being that Bacon demonstrated with this work, just how different his mode of perception was from what we regard as normal in everyday life when he was involved in the process of creating his images.

The complexity of this work can only be understood in the context of the peculiarities of time-modes that weave in and out of themselves referred to previously, where it was stated that earlier developmental stages are able to exist alongside later ones within a plant. This is one effect of the meeting of Counter-Space and the Cartesian Space-Time continuum of ordinary consciousness at the cross-over point of lemniscatory space. What I find fascinating is that, in a sense, Bacon was painting his own consciousness, for these peculiarities with regard to inside/ outside/ presence/ absence are his experiences upon entering/ perceiving the invisible realms referred to. It is a well-documented fact that the first impressions of these realms are extremely confusing as one tries to orientate oneself within very different experiences of what was formerly taken for granted. The fact that time works in this manner is observable in everyday life through the memories we carry of people we know, which can in some cases attain an almost tangible presence, but as stated our capacity to visualise in most cases is weak and does not do justice to this ability in comparison to someone who has honed and trained this ability, such as Bacon, or for that matter Steiner and Goethe. So is Bacon with this series of portraits attempting to produce that which is normally considered impossible: an overall *'time'* portrait of Dyer that expresses the progression of that which contributed to his demise. The fact that we are aware through our capacity for memory and observation of plant growth that time, considered as an entity, is comprised of differing modes of which we normally only have the faintest inkling because we are fixated upon the linearity of the inorganic world, implies that with our ordinary consciousness we have become divorced from the time-modes pertinent to the living. The analysis of the above work indicates that Bacon reactivated his awareness of these time-modes through a rediscovery of the 'forgotten' self of childhood, when such time-modes are a vital if unconscious reality for the human being. Given this analysis of "Two Studies for a Portrait of George Dyer", the conclusion is that Bacon also investigated, with these images, his own abilities and capacities, which naturally have an import for our own abilities and capacities.

If "Portrait of George Dyer in a Mirror" recorded an essential aspect of Dyer's character that included a dimension of time, then a definite developmental process has been exposed, for "Two Studies for a Portrait of George Dyer" depicts the progression of that condition to its state at the time when this work was painted. Such reasoning means that it is in fact the Figure in the black rectangle that has empirical veracity, as a portrait, as this image represents the 'real' essence of George Dyer's condition, and without which it is impossible to understand why Dyer was the way in which he was in the *'here and now'*. There is some evidence for drawing this conclusion for in "Two Studies for a Portrait of George Dyer" the Figure in the rectangle has been pinned, or nailed down, by a number of tacks/pins or nails. But if Bacon in this work made a rendering of a rendering, then this rendering is in itself odd for although it demonstrates aspects of a mirror-image, for instance the position of crossed leg, it could never fulfil such a function due to its being unclothed and its distortions from the seated Figure in the work. The nailing down, or pinning, of this Figure in the black rectangle implies that it is evanescent/ transitory and that a great deal of effort is required to grasp it, which is consistent with accounts of perception within the spiritual worlds. Thus we have a strange image that has correspondences to a rendering of an actual living being, inhabiting an equally strange space that borders, or juts against, the space that the seated Figure occupies. Through the device of placing himself both within and without the picture Bacon is taking account of his own feelings, as a friend and lover, with respect to Dyer who is clearly in a perilous state and at a crisis-point. What are the clues for this assertion? To begin with the pinned down version has it attention focussed upon the seated Figure and has assumed an accusatory and exhortative manner, as if it has become exasperated in either its attempt to communicate something of vital importance to the seated Figure, or to take complete possession of Dyer, but is being held back on both counts. Dyer however looks in the opposite direction as if determined to take no notice of whatever advice, or actions, an aspect of his being is proffering. Dyer's refusal has two unsavoury consequences, firstly the pinned down Figure becomes more inhuman and demonic whilst, secondly, Dyer becomes increasingly unnerved, unsettled and agitated as shown by his posture and the ashtray strewn with the cigarette-butts. Dyer has reached the point-of-no-return.

So as to make us realise that this is no allegorical or casual remark that is being made concerning Dyer in this work Bacon has so constructed this work so as to leave no doubt of his involvement with Dyer. Bacon has achieved this by the dual status of the seated Figure, which on one level is a rendition of Dyer but can also function to mean that Bacon is in the room with the flesh-and-blood Dyer, who is literally coming apart at the seams - bone coming out of the leg of the seated Figure - and produced the pinned down version that is a rendition of how he perceived the psychic state of George Dyer to be. Thus Bacon is both in the room and outside the room as the painter and observer, thereby taking account of both the time sequences inherent to producing a portrait and to the subject, and that, furthermore through this methodology, he took account of what it meant for him to know Dyer as his lover and what it meant to him to portray Dyer as an individual in a state of mental collapse. Through this highly intricate, but deceptively simple, construction the events of the work almost become 'actual' and 'real', in the sense that time has become an object to be observed and analysed in the same manner as any other object in the material world, and so the spectator is not merely nonchalantly and dispassionately observing a work of art but is drawn into this intense drama as co-protagonists.

A Hunted Man.

It is a simple fact that some individuals undergoing mental trauma will go to any lengths to hide the fact that this is indeed the case, such as 'putting on a brave face' and developing all sorts of mannerisms to disguise how they inwardly feel. Russell describes how Dyer first came across as

"A compact and chunky force of nature, with a vivid and highly unparsonical turn of phrase, he embodied a pent-up energy. As a spirit of mischief, touched by times of melancholia…"

However there was a deeper side to this melancholia that Russell discerned

"When seen in profile he seemed to wrench his head away as if to deny a private despair he had trouble keeping at bay." (Russell, 1997: 160 & 165).

Peppiatt presents this aspect of Dyer in far bleaker terms

"…Dyer was of medium height with a compact, athletic build and (belying a docile, inwardly tormented nature) the air of a man who could land a decisive punch … Even when drunk, George took obsessive care with his appearance, flicking the slightest fragment of ash or dust off his well-pressed clothes. Most of the time, he was withdrawn and pale, with an anxious strained expression … 'When I met him, George had spent more time in prison than out', Bacon used to say…" (Peppiatt, 1996: 211-212).

Dyer was it seems a minor figure loosely associated with the criminal fraternity of the East End of London who failed despite any ambitions he may have had to be any more than that, and the portrait provided by the above authors is that of an individual who neurotically strove to hide his inner feelings through a smart, 'bravado' image. Dyer was clearly a troubled man who, it seems, was temperamentally disinclined to confront either his own behaviour or face the nature of his own soul, and who, as Russell saw, had the demeanour of a hunted man.

Bacon, however, knew Dyer as a lover and not an acquaintance and would have had a far deeper and intense understanding of that which troubled Dyer. Speaking of the aftermath to Dyer's death Peppiatt states

"Bacon suffered intensely for several years thereafter, and a feeling of loss and guilt remained with him until his death." (Peppiatt, 1996: 242).

The pinned-down figure in the black panel of "Two Studies for a Portrait of George Dyer" therefore represents a destructive soul condition that harangued and pursued Dyer throughout his life, and which over the years had become more virulent and destructive due to its being ignored and unacknowledged by Dyer. The effect of which was to further accelerate Dyer's worsening condition. Thus Bacon in this work has led us to understand that in composing a portrait that represents the essence of the individual being portrayed one has to start from the inner state of that person, but that, in turn, this inner state has to be distilled from an everyday perception of that person. It is now possible to consider that the works referenced in this chapter have to be taken in conjunction with each other, and so mutually influence each other, and where they, in total, constitute the 'Portrait' of George Dyer.

But this can be taken further by considering the first four as being precursors for "Two Studies for a Portrait of George Dyer". Although the dates of the works execution indicate this, this alone is not conclusive that they are precursors for that which is expressed in "Two Studies for a Portrait of George Dyer", or that there is necessarily a logical line running through the works. The proof for this is to be found in the soul-states of the four works. Why should anyone paint someone staring at a blind-chord as in "Portrait of George Dyer Staring a Blind Cord" unless it was of vital importance; the very notion appears absurd when considered by itself. However someone staring at a blind-chord would be in a trance-like almost catatonic state of consciousness where his or her ego has become immobilised and transfixed. Through what is known of Dyer's habits we can hazard a guess that Dyer was in a stupor brought on by a mixture of 'booze and pills' and whatever other substances he had taken, and that Bacon expressed his consternation in this work of Dyer's self-induced vegetative state. "Portrait of George Dyer Crouching" expands upon such a theme, except with this work, from the physical distortions of the head, Bacon is indicating that Dyer is in some manner, possibly through his habits, given the close dates of the two works, becoming sub-human.

If this is the case then Bacon records Dyer's continuing decline in "Two Studies of George Dyer with Dog". In this work the seated Dyer has the mien of a zombie due to the darkened eye-sockets, and where the more-life-like but drained and exhausted portrait of Dyer appears in the dog in the foreground. As though a part of Dyer's essence, his human-ness, has slipped out of his human form into a lower more animal configuration. The consequence of such a process is the appearance of another alien being in the form of what is presumed to be the shadow of the seated Dyer. The shadow issuing from the seated Dyer is depicted as something of a cross between an animal and a human being that only bears the slightest trace of resemblance to what would be a shadow of Dyer in those circumstances. From one direction sense can be made of Bacon's animal and shadow renditions of Dyer from Steiner's statement, previously referenced, that a person's passions, habits and so on appear in the astral worlds as animal forms of varying animosity. Therefore when we look at "Portrait of George Dyer in a Mirror", which bridges 1967 and 1968, we find Dyer in a state of shock and anxiety at his disassociation from his own self and the loss that has resulted from this disassociation, and where "Portrait of George Dyer Staring a Blind Cord", "Portrait of George Dyer Crouching", and "Two Studies of George Dyer with Dog" depict the stages leading to this condition.

"Two Studies for a Portrait of George Dyer" painted in 1968 records the fact that Dyer's condition has considerably worsened to the position where there are now *two* George Dyer's and that whereas in "Two Studies of George Dyer with Dog" and "Portrait of George Dyer in a Mirror" there still exists a connection between aspects of his being, this connection has now been broken to the point of conflict. But these are only studies and the import of this with respect to the Figure in the black panel – a black void - that lacks any parameters to define specifically what it is, and that has the ambiguous status of being a portrait, mirror-image or something else - is that the 'truth' he wishes to represent concerning Dyer is almost too unbearable to represent because it is so far removed from normal expectations. I say this because Bacon was well aware of what he was trying to depict when he states in conversation with Sylvester that

"I see the image all the time in a shifting way…one can take it from…what is called ordinary to a very, very far point."

That is underlined by Bacon stating in reply to Sylvester's statement

'You attempt a picture of reality that is conditioned as little as possible by general agreement as to what appearance is' with

"That is very well put. But there is yet another step: generally questioning what appearance is."

Thus Bacon made it abundantly clear that in order to depict the essence of his perception, in this case concerning Dyer, he had to radically revise what is meant as a 'general agreement as to what appearance is'.

It is unimaginable that there are any normal circumstances where this Figure in the black panel could be referred to as anything other than a ghastly apparition that confronts a distraught Dyer who recoils in horror. It was painted by Bacon in such a way that it has a volition, and is as 'real' for Bacon in its effect upon Dyer as Dyer himself. Although one could speculate on the further deeper aspects of Dyer's character, this is not my main interest, rather my interest is with the implication that Dyer is haunted by a malevolent spectral form that is his responsibility and mainly his creation, and which he refuses to acknowledge but which Bacon was able to perceive and record its genesis and evolution to the life-threatening state in "Two Studies for a Portrait of George Dyer".

Psychodrama.

The principal reason that Projective Geometry has been placed at the foreground of this *critique* is that mathematics is a powerful, objective persuasive tool for any attempts to cognise the invisible forces mentioned here, and to do this is especially important with respect to the materialistic, and in some cases hidebound, approach of Anglo-Saxon Empiricism to the nature of the Cosmos. Through reading the texts by Adams, Whicher and others, and then familiarising oneself with how the principles of Projective Geometry are descriptive of the growth and metamorphosis of the organic world one starts to realise the possibility of the existence of the realms described, even if one does not at this stage have direct perception of them. Nevertheless, to state that there are entities within the Emotional World of the Soul that exert a negative influence upon an individual, some of which are of our own making, and which have their own volition and being will be totally unacceptable to the majority of people. Notwithstanding this that is exactly what Bacon perceived to be the situation with Dyer as indicated above. This theme will be further developed below. To make such a statement begs the question as to why mental illnesses etc develop and become more virulent as time goes by, what is it that causes them to deepen their effects and why do individuals find themselves unable to cope with their effects?

From an ordinary point-of-view we can say that it is well-known that certain psychic configurations are detrimental to an individual's health both mentally and physically, and that these configurations have to be struggled with as if they were real and alive if a person wishes to recover their health. It has also been stated that these conditions have the capacity to evolve and become more insidious in their effect upon the individual if left to their own devices. Bacon was undoubtedly a keen and astute observer of the psychic state of those within his immediate circle of associates, however Bacon was able to translate this fascination with the psychic factors intrinsic to those close to him into an analysis of the mental state of humanity in general. Bacon's *oeuvre* displays, right from the early days in the 'Pope' paintings, a continuing interest with the theme of an individual terrorised by some unknown force that is never disclosed. However there is a gradual change from the 'Pope' paintings, where we are presented with just that - a terrified person, to an indication that this terror has its origins in the person's own psyche. This is demonstrated by the 'Head' series, which, as can be seen from the collars, evolved from the 'Pope' paintings, as in for example "Head VI", 1949, (ill. 93) and "Head II", 1949, (ill. 30). These two works show the Pope in the latter stages of his ordeal where it appears that the Head is being devoured by itself. Earlier it was indicated how the mere fact of being conscious 'uses up' the corporeal body, however with these head works we are given the impression that there is something that is inherent to human nature which is at the same time hostile to the individual. Almost as if some entity within it is inducing the Figure to indulge in an act of extremely gruesome self-destruction. In addition, due to the self-enclosed nature of these Head works, the import is that this state of affairs is largely self-induced. At this stage of his work there are no indications as to what could be the cause of this inner turmoil, or what its relationship is to the individual concerned. However, through the analysis above of the works "Portrait of George Dyer in a Mirror" and "Two Studies for a Portrait of George Dyer" it is argued that by the 1960's Bacon found, and then developed a technique, that was capable of depicting the inner cause of an individual's psychic disintegration and its relationship to that individual, in contrast to the more generalised earlier approach of the 'Pope' and 'Head' works.

The question is whether or not Bacon perceived psychic configurations as phenomenological facts that had a life of their own, and whether or not there are other individuals who had the same ability as Bacon, whose accounts match up to Bacon's images? Clearly this a rhetorical question for such an individual has been quoted many times already, and the following are some of Steiner's statements concerning the soul-state of modern humanity:

"We also pointed out that sensations, given through our senses, emerge and fill the soul life like waves that continually rise and fall on the sea…..We experience these sensations when we have contact with the outer world; they then transform themselves in such a way that they live on in us." (Steiner, 1999: 93).

"Essentially, human soul life is anything but unified. It is more like a dramatic battlefield, where opposites struggle continually. Anyone who listens with sensitivity and feeling to this soul life will certainly notice its dramatic character. When confronted by these opposing forces in the human soul, people in fact feel a lack of control, a passivity." (Steiner, 1999: 94).

"The soul cannot be a homogeneous entity; it would be unable to progress further. It is vital that we begin by gaining a feeling for this polarity, or contradiction, in the soul life." (Steiner, 1999: 95-96).

"As we progress inwardly, we must look at the dramatic contradictions of our soul life. We need to recognise that we are subject to a master there, just as we are in the external world – a master who makes sure we have a different soul life at the age of seven, for example, than at twenty, thirty, or later…..it is important to note that mental images really do have an existence of their own in the soul life; they have their own life. Please understand the full significance of that statement. Visualisations are like parasites, like living beings in the soul that lead their own existence there." (Steiner, 1999: 97).

It will be understood that emotions, passions, drives and satisfactions do not merely exist as abstract thoughts, or conditions, within our soul-life but are accompanied by endless visualisations. Whenever we decide to do something there is always a visualisation of the act to be performed, regardless, as to how conscious of it we are, and even if it flashes past our consciousness instantaneously. Bacon in "Two Studies for a Portrait of George Dyer" has made a representation of something that he clearly perceived was a threat to Dyer, the precise ontological status of which is unclear. Even if it was not of the same nature as everyday objects, nevertheless Bacon perceived that it had enough power to threaten Dyer's very existence. Particular paintings by Bacon after Dyer's death make it clear that he perceived this entity to be something that was unearthly and other-worldly, and that it gradually faded into those realms from which it had emerged after Dyer's death.

Dyer's Death.

The triptych "Triptych May-June", 1973, (ill. 23), painted after George Dyer's death depicts Dyer, in its three panels, in various states of distress, and specifically illustrates Dyer's death in the bathroom in Paris during Bacon's absence. In this work it is only the central panel in which there is a light-bulb that is switched off, but which nevertheless appears to be casting a shadow, so is this a rendering of Dyer at the point of death. But is it possible to state that the black shape advancing to the foreground of the panel is a shadow for it conforms to none of the expectations of a shadow cast by a light-bulb, even if it was switched on, from the painted Figure. This 'impossible' shadow is of the same nature as the 'impossible' shadow in "Two Studies of George Dyer with Dog", that was described as combining animal and human features. In both these examples the shadows appear

196

to have a mien that hints at some primitive life-force, but in the above triptych this shadow has now assumed a more sinister appearance. When the panel is turned upside-down this shadow has the shape of an unearthly, supernatural, inhuman entity that does not in the slightest conform to Dyer's bodily shape. Bacon, though, has with this triptych made clear its connection to Dyer, due to its close proximity to, or attachment to, Dyer. The shape of this shadow has a satanic dimension, if looked at upside-down, for it has a head with two horns protruding between two rounded forms that have attributes of bat-like wings. Given that this is a depiction of Dyer's death scene, then this could be an Angel of Death, and this shape has to be thought of alongside Dyer's accusatory self-made entity depicted in the black panel of "Two Studies for a Portrait of George Dyer", except that in this panel it has revealed its true malevolent nature. The effect of this entity upon Dyer is that he was driven, either deliberately or accidentally, to the desperate measure of precipitating his own demise. But there is also the implication that with "Triptych May-June" there is a fading away, meaning that whatever it was that plagued Dyer has now lost its power to torment Dyer and is disappearing into some other dimension. From this perspective the Figure in the black panel is, therefore, a spirit of retribution, a representation of a conscience that torments, which has become a fury, a demon, a force of destruction because Dyer failed to heed its warnings and remonstrations.

It may seem that this depiction of a satanic shadow in "Triptych May-June", 1973 is some sort of lapse, on Bacon's behalf, into arcane symbolism and artistic naivety but such a judgement would miss a vital point that has already been stressed. The shadow appears 'impossible' for the same reason that the entity in the black panel of "Two Studies for a Portrait of George Dyer" appears to be impossible with regard to its reflection of the seated Figure, and it is emphasised that this apparition, in both works, issues from a dimension that abuts onto the world of our ordinary senses but is not fully part of it. A further point to be discerned is that the shadow in "Triptych May-June 1973" appears to underline the true nature, and potency, of the entity in the black panel of "Two Studies for a Portrait of George Dyer".

There is nothing fanciful in viewing the 'shadows' Bacon painted in his works in such a manner, and other examples are readily available that show that Bacon viewed the 'shadow' as if not precisely containing a portion of the person's humanity, then having some primitive life-force. In "Triptych, August", 1972", (ill. 94), there is a pink 'blob' that emanates from each of the Figures in the three panels. These pink 'blobs' have an ambiguous status, for although they could be read as 'shadows' they also have the appearance of puddles made up of a turgid slow-moving liquid. It is also not without significance that the subject of this panel is George Dyer, and was painted the year after Dyer's demise in 1971. "Triptych – In Memory of George Dyer", 1971, (ill. 95), is a work that also includes a peculiar 'blob' attached to the figure of Dyer in the l. h. panel. The fact that these 'blobs' are pink gives the impression that they are of a fleshy, or sentient, nature. This is emphasised by the Figures in each of the panels being unclothed and similar in colour, this creates the impression that something of the subject's humanity has been 'sucked out' into, or has dissolved into, these 'blobs' leaving the Figures incomplete. The 'shadows' in "Three Portraits: Posthumous Portrait of George Dyer, Self-portrait, Portrait of Lucien Freud",1973, (ill. 55) have the appearance of voids from which the Figures have emerged, an impression that is re-inforced by their having been painted with edges. Additionally each of these 'shadows', or spaces, has a mobile quality to it resembling the movements of a liquid, a factor that is echoed in the circular patterns of the carpet. These shadows work to underline the simultaneity of this triptych by giving a commonality to the genesis of the three Figures depicted. The lively, quasi-living quality of these 'shadows', or 'blobs', resonates with how the shadow plays an important psychological role in the constitution of the self, particularly when viewed in the context of the 'Double'. The effect of the 'Double', since we are normally utterly unaware of its presence, is that it can have an extremely destructive influence upon our behavioural patterns. (V. Stoichita in his book "A Short History of the Shadow" puts forward the thesis that the shadow can be seen as pre-dating Lacan's 'mirror stage' of development in an infant, and as such forms a cornerstone in the infant's growing awareness of the world that surrounds it).

Earlier I claimed that "Portrait of George Dyer Staring at a Blind Cord", 1966, (ill. 90), "Portrait of George Dyer Crouching", 1966, (ill. 91), "Two Studies of George Dyer with Dog", 1968, (ill. 80) "Portrait of George Dyer in a Mirror", 1967-8, (ill. 92) and "Two Studies for a Portrait of George Dyer", 1968, (ill. 19) when taken together constituted Bacon's 'Portrait' of George Dyer. The reason for making such an assertion is that each of the Figures of these works is a stage in the progression of the deterioration of Dyer's mental health. Each Figure is thus a *compression of the time-period* related to that particular stage. "Portrait of George Dyer Staring at a Blind Cord" is thus a *compression of the time-period* that Bacon perceived as the first stage of Dyer's Soul disintegration, which concluded with Dyer displaying the characteristics of imbecility, that is Dyer's behaviour exhibited a mental paralysis with regarded to his habits and addictions. "Portrait of George Dyer Crouching" is a *compression of the time-period* from this mental paralysis to the state where Dyer has now started to assume a sort of bestial condition with regard to his 'inner' state of being. These works record the genesis of that which assumes such a demonic and inhuman appearance in "Two Studies for a Portrait of George Dyer". "Two Studies of George Dyer with Dog" is a *compression of the time-period* from this genesis to the state where Dyer's habits and addictions have created in the Astral world an entity that is starting to lead an independent existence in Dyer's Soul-life. "Portrait of George Dyer in a Mirror" is a *compression of the time-period* from the creation of that which is starting to lead an independent existence in Dyer's Soul to the moment of an actual schism. "Two Studies for a Portrait of George Dyer" depicts the dire consequences of this schism within Dyer's Soul, and as such is a *compression of the time-period* relating to the on-going effects of Dyer's state of Soul upon Dyer himself. As far as I am concerned this series of images is of far more value that the mountain of tomes upon Psychoanalysis, that in the main, have failed to uncover the mysteries of the Human Spirit and Soul. There are a number of reasons for making such a seemingly outrageous statement, and of prime importance is that 'the mountain of tomes upon Psychoanalysis' have only produced abstract, intellectual speculations about that which is not abstract and intellectual but *vital and living*. More of this in chapter 6. Of equal importance is that Bacon arrived at his understanding of Dyer's soul-state through a consciousness that was founded upon an enhanced inter-action of his Intellect and Imagination, and as such points to the Epistemological value of Artistic Cognition. Of supreme noteworthiness is that in conducting his investigation of Dyer's state he did this with a humanity and compassion that stands in sharp contrast to the moral bankruptcy that characterises present attitudes to scientific research.

In this chapter attention has been primarily drawn to how Bacon charted the effects upon Dyer's mental balance of Dyer's habits, desires and personal inclinations that eventually became an actual baleful, antagonistic force in his soul-life. Dyer in this respect was no different from thousands of other people, the difference is that he was associated with an artist who had the ability to literally see what it was that caused Dyer to succumb in such a tragic manner to forces he was unable to control, or stand against. That is not the end of the story for it is possible that the propensity for Dyer's own personality to cause his own downfall was greatly strengthened by other factors, if this was the case, and there is no way of knowing if it was, then our own judgement of Dyer should be tempered, for then he would have been facing a truly devastating conjunction of circumstances that even the most stoical and strong would find hard to stomach.

Chapter 6. The Other.

The course of human development from the Fall onwards, from one aspect, revolves around our ability to think for oneself, something that has been made possible through the absorption of the Ego into ourselves, even though this is only at a primitive stage of growth. Before this occurred individuals were simply unable to think for themselves, and as such were not free. The consciousness we now have of an interior, inner life, even though I have hinted that this is illusory, has gifted us with a freedom, for we are now able, under ideal conditions, to come to our own conclusions regarding any subject we wish to consider. The development of an interior life goes hand-in-hand with the first developments of Intellectuality. For ancient peoples there was no definitive borderline between themselves and what they perceived, something that is highlighted by comparing the differences of our waking-life with that of the ancients. For ourselves there is a distinct and undeniable difference between sleeping and waking, however this was not so for ancient peoples whereby one merged into the other. This means we have an awareness of inner soul-conditions that we regard as distinct from an outer world, whereas ancient peoples regarded that which we regard as inner soul-conditions as part and parcel of their overall sensory understanding of the reality within which they were situated. As stated above the World creates perception within us and there is nothing we can do about this unless we cease to sense, and this simple fact raises questions as to what we internalise as sensory impressions. In the past what was transmitted by the senses was worked over by the Imagination, hence the vibrant world of pictures handed down to us through myths and legends, now, however, what is transmitted by the senses is worked over by the Intellect resulting in the arid world of dead concepts and pictures we now possess. This process of movement away from the Imagination to the Intellect is readily observable in the development of the human being from infancy to adulthood. Ancient peoples simply did not consider what we would describe as an interior life as fantasy, or make belief, the consciousness of ancient peoples was one that was unified and unbroken. The over-riding characteristic of the Intellect is that it separates and makes into objects the components of a unified reality, and the peculiar bias of our present consciousness is that it valorises the phenomena of a waking consciousness projected outwards over the phenomena known when we direct our waking consciousness inwardly. It is from this state of affairs that all discourses regarding **The Other** devolve. So because we now have a consciousness largely based upon abstraction and intellectualism, that also includes an awareness of the presence of the Ego, we have objectivised the world and turned it into **The Other**, purely because we have no awareness of the manner of the inter-relationships between phenomena as did the ancients. Nothing will change until the Imagination is integrated into our consciousness as an equal partner to the Intellect for the purposes of cognition.

All that is **The Other** is all that is not **I**, and this covers everything conceivable, and it follows that the **I** cannot be **The Other** to itself. Fundamentally an individual's awareness of their existence is founded upon an indivisible union of self-consciousness (I am me) with the fact that I know I am alive (I am here) underpinned by a particular (to that individual) emotional state. All else flows from this - I have a body, I am happy or sad, I am ill or well and so on. This is normal, and this normality has at the foreground the fact that all that is living has a body, or more precisely, a form, and unless an individual is suffering from some sort of illness an individual unconsciously accepts that their consciousness and body are a reflection of each other. However there is no precise understanding as to why our consciousness gives rise to our particular form and no other, and why the various consciousness of other life forms give rise to their specific forms. Of course there exists explanations regarding this state of affairs, but the factor they all have in common is that they answer it through a process of displacement, which merely defers meaning to another area, for instance if one states that the way in which the human corporeal body appears is because of its genetic make-up this only raises more questions as to why the genes should act in this manner etc. The situation is much like when a child asks why is it raining (or some such other question) and is given the answer because it is cloudy, the child then asks why is it cloudy, a process that continues interminably until the adult either loses patience or the child grows bored with the unsatisfactory answers it is given - anyone who has been involved with children will be well aware of this process. A child would be more satisfied, especially if this was done imaginatively, if it was explained how rain is a particular form of water, and that it follows a cyclical pattern of expansion and condensation which is linked to the sun and conditions upon the earth, supplemented by explaining to the child how water supports life and growth, thus showing the child that despite appearances there is an inherent unity to the world.

I have been arguing that our adult abstract, intellectually based consciousness divorces us from *'life'* and, further, that this is not the case with a child, because this dimension of their being has not yet developed. The child lives within *life* and only gradually, as it matures, feels the force of separateness from the world as its intellectuality expands, this has been discussed, above, from a number of angles. Despite the rise and fall of various paradigms concerning the functionality of our body it still remains a mystery. Let me put this another way, in essence our consciousness divorces us from ourselves, that is through our adult abstract, intellectually based consciousness we have become strangers to ourselves. At present the paradigm of our corporeal body that is virtually universally accepted within the medical profession is that of the Chemical-Genetic model, but it is impossible to discover within this model reasons for the structure of a human being. At the very fundamental level of our own corporeality we are estranged by the absolute **'Otherness'** of our own being, and as a consequence of this primary sense of the **'Otherness'** of our own being we are prone to experience an alienation from the cosmos and society, which may be exacerbated by many other factors.

Even if one is disinclined to accept the existence of invisible, hidden realms of existence it is undeniable that we are under the influence of powerful emotions and compulsive habits. These can only be conceived as illusory if one accepts the postulations of Epiphenomenalism, otherwise we have to admit that there are forces we experience that we cannot say are synonymous with our I consciousness, they are **Other** than us. This argument can be extended to cover such aspects of our being in that it is undeniable that we have a heat body, the most basic elements of which can be detected by instruments sensitive to infra-red radiations, similarly, although less obvious, we have an air body, and none of these can we say are us. When it comes to our corporeal body we are only too aware that we have a material (earth) body and a water body, although again we cannot say that they are us. Bacon was certainly aware of our water body as is shown by the image "Water from a Running Tap", 1982, (ill. 96), contemplation of which reveals a quasi-animal shape in the outflow from the tap. This is an image that attempts to convey the teeming, never-ceasing, life-filled flow of water that is imbued with aspects of the sound/ chemical ether, something no other artist I know of has tried to do, even if this image has a somewhat naïve directness to it. Nevertheless I regard this as a brilliant painting because it encapsulates the sheer force and abundance of life with Bacon's usual rawness and panache. Water is the principal carrier of Etheric body, which has four principle modes - the warmth ether, the light/ air ether, the sound/ chemical ether and the life ether From this perspective our understanding of the Chemical-Genetic model of the human being facilitates an intellectual, rational exploration of the activity of the sound/ chemical ether aspect of the ether body and the life ether as they operate within our water body.

Much more could be said concerning the *otherness* of all that constitutes our corporeal body with regard to our sense of being, but this is not my main concern with this *critique*. Rather it is the *otherness* of what constitutes our Soul to our sense of being that is of concern here. To someone who has reached this level of understanding it becomes a fascinating mystery as to why one has particular modes of thought, opinions, desires and passions, to name a few aspects of the Soul. These are for the majority of people unconsciously constructed elements that have developed over the course of the journey from childhood to adulthood. Leaving aside for the moment the 'positive' life-enhancing power of such passions as love and awe, we are also aware of a whole range of 'negative' passions, such as anger, greed, lust and so on, where the major distinction is that the 'positive' passions are directed away from the self whereas the 'negative' passions are directed towards the self. Upon reaching this understanding an individual surveys the whole shambolic and jumbled condition of that which is referred to as the Self, and it is the purification and ordering of the Self that eventually leads to a transformation of the Soul.

The profound 'otherness' of the state of our Soul and Self is only ameliorated when an individual consciously begins to 'pick apart' the various strands of this conglomeration. This can start to occur naturally in our congress with others if we are open-minded enough, however it is only when such an activity is consciously undertaken that it becomes a redemptive soul-force that leads to higher powers of the Soul. The very first stage is to make a distinction between that which has an exterior origin, that is from the society we have been born within, and that which is inherent to our own individuality. Equally important in defusing the emotional impact caused by the realisation of the absolute 'otherness' of *everything* to our innermost sense of being, a condition that , if unchecked, leads to a devastating alienation and loneliness, is healing the imbalance within the Soul that results from the passage from childhood to adulthood. I have characterised this healing as the re-integration of the 'forgotten self' of infancy into our intellectually based ordinary consciousness of maturity. This loss of the Imaginative Intelligence of infancy induces an 'emptiness' at the base of our comprehension of the world that normally is *'glossed over'* by the whole gamut of pleasures, indulgences, passions and intellectual constructs that characterise human being's lived lives. This unthinking automatic indulgence only serves to heighten our sense of alienation because through this indulgence one creates within the Soul structures that are inimical to our 'true' selves, and as such this brings us to the dialogue concerning the 'higher self' and the 'lower self', an understanding of which is instrumental for an understanding of Bacon's images. For the most part we are hardly aware of the ramifications of possessing a 'self' let alone a 'higher self' and a 'lower self', mostly life is conducted within a maze of dead abstractions drained of any vitality, ill-cognised will impulses and incessant desires and passions. It is simply the case that our adult, intellectual consciousness not only divorces us from perceiving our living connection with the cosmos, but with the deadly consequence that it divorces us from ourselves. Because we are not conscious of this severance, this division, this split, except, as a much commented upon, existential and ontological unease. This was not the case with Bacon he was vitally aware of the crucial role a 'self', of any delineation, plays in the organization of our psychological disposition. He was, I have argued, aware of other subtle aspects of our being, as I have pointed out above with the image "Water from a Running Tap", 1982, (ill. 96). With his self-portraits Bacon made plain the absolute otherness of the 'self' that is the understanding of someone with his abilities, something that unfortunately cannot be further explored at present,

The text so far suggests that we all have an invisible potent 'other' that is multi-dimensional, and although the implications of this statement cannot be rigorously examined here the above indicates that the starting-place for healing relations with 'otherness', in general, is with ourselves. Primarily this means regaining the lost kingdom of childhood, which I have designated as the 'forgotten self'. By refreshing ideas on this topic an introduction is created for further exploration of the 'Other', in broad terms, which in turn leads to an investigation of the implications of such an exploration for an understanding of Bacon's work. It is worth mentioning at this point that our inability to resurrect the 'forgotten self' of infancy leads to an intensification of the power of the Double, meaning that one aspect of *not knowing ourselves* precipitates detrimental psychic conditions that everyone has to 'face up' to sooner or later. However, I will not be examining in any detail, here, how the genesis of the Double is related to our inability as adults to recover the consciousness we possessed as infants.

The Forgotten Self.

The analysis of Bacon's portraits of George Dyer in the previous chapter described how Bacon was able to actually perceive the entity which hounded and terrorised Dyer so much that he reached the point whereby he accidentally, or determinedly, committed suicide - how did Bacon find that he had the ability to do this, and just as pertinently from whence did this ability originate. Earlier it has been described how there is to be found in Bacon's work references to the early years of our existence before the acquisition of language and this has been named our 'forgotten self', and this is of such importance in understanding Bacon's images that it bears further examination. Intellectual observation of this period of life is largely unable to penetrate into the state of consciousness we have during this period with any degree of certainty, despite the fact that everyone has traversed it; for ordinary consciousness this period of development is a *terra incognito.* So far it has been suggested that the transformation of ordinary consciousness can lead to not only the acquisition of enhanced perceptual abilities, but of an enhanced consciousness that is capable of consciously grasping the state of awareness during this first period of life, that is one is able to resurrect the lost consciousness of the 'forgotten self' of infancy.

Steiner explained the difference between consciousness in childhood and adults as revolving around the fact that although the child lives in intimate contact with the creative cosmos it is unaware of this because it has not developed abstract thinking, whereas an adult has lost contact with the creative cosmos because it has not developed and strengthened its abstract thinking. Such a description is echoed in the differences between Bacon's canvasses of "Man Carrying a Child" (ill. 62) and "Man and Child" (ill. 63). In the former the adult still maintains in contact with its childhood (early years of infancy) and is clearly un-dividedly dwelling in that time, whereas "Man and Child" depicts the estrangement from our childhood consciousness that results from the passive, intellectual thinking characteristic of adulthood, and where Sophia (as the girl) is a veritable stranger who is only tolerated in a strained atmosphere. Steiner's comments upon the condition of thinking as an adult also relates to the puddles of garbled letters that appear in "Triptych-Studies from the Human Body", and other works, for these puddles are interpretable as related to a thinking that has solidified and become lifeless in the manner of ordinary, abstract and intellectual thinking. Thus by transforming our thinking in a Goethean manner, and in other similar ways, the 'forgotten self' of early infancy can be regained, so that an individual is now able to cognise the world from the position of an undivided communion with the totality of existence rather than the partial picture given by the intellectually-based consciousness of adulthood.

If this is the case then what is the relationship between the two for a person who has reached such a point? This can be approached by examining ordinary consciousness, for there is with every human being an awareness within the individual self of an element that remains unchanged throughout life, and this is the 'I'. Without this unchanging element there could be no knowledge that one is a *self*. This is demonstrated by the fact that an individual can know themselves as a 10 year old child and as an adult, but the self known as a child has changed radically from the self known in adulthood, and from this understanding the inference is drawn that the *self* functions in, and is conditioned by, time whereas the 'I' is unaffected by time: *i.e. the self is a product of time but the 'I' stands beyond time.*

This is a repetition from above but its repetition has a different import here, for there have been a number of allegations concerning time in the above analysis of Bacon's images and these can be partly answered by further examination of the relationship between the 'I' and the plane of time. If the 'I' has a relationship to time that is different from a linear mode and is diametrically opposed to the plane of time, an assumption that seems reasonable in view of the fact that our ego remains unaffected by the passage of time unlike all the phenomena of the physical world including the corporeal body that houses the ego, then through its connection with the *self* there is the possibility of experiencing the **Eternal**. Meaning that if one has a broader view of what constitutes time, and how phenomena behave within this enhanced understanding, then through the ego rising up its pole towards the **Eternal** one automatically has an enhanced consciousness as to what constitutes the reality of the Cosmos. In order to understand the implications of this enhanced understanding of time requires a different understanding of the nature of time itself as Steiner indicates:

" … in the spiritual sense, what is 'past' has not really vanished, but is still there. In physical life men have this conception in regard to space only. If you stand in front of a tree, then go away and look back …. the tree has not disappeared … In the spiritual world the same is true in regard to *time*. If you experience something at one moment, it has passed away the next as far as physical consciousness is concerned; spiritually conceived, it has not passed away. You can look back on it just as you can look back at the tree. Richard Wagner showed he possessed knowledge of this with the remarkable words: 'Time has become space'".

This quote is taken from a lecture delivered by Steiner in 1918 entitled "The Dead are with Us", and relates to what was said earlier regarding time with regard to plant growth and movement, in general, through a deepening of one's cognition of the phenomenal world. It is contended that during infancy an individual is completing the journey down, let us say, the pole of the ego from the **Eternal** to the **Earthly**, and that journey is effectively completed upon the acquisition of a mother tongue, from which point onwards one's earthly incarnation effectively begins as a member of society. Thus if an individual is able to reactivate this period of their life they have succeeded, through their strivings, to gain a more comprehensive understanding of the Cosmos whilst retaining their rational faculties. As stated the important point is that this return is one that retains our rational faculties so that we are able to integrate, meaningfully, into our understanding of the world the experiences of our enhanced consciousness. This commentary sheds light upon the peculiarities of the images of Dyer in the mirrors/ canvasses depicted in "Portrait of George Dyer in a Mirror" (ill. 92) and "Two Studies for a Portrait of George Dyer" (ill. 19), for, as Steiner indicated, the events in time may be perused from the vantage-point described above, and so with these works, and others, Bacon combines into one work glimpses of the subject-matter from multiple time-modes and integrates these into the present, or the Now, through the force of his creative will. Thus when Bacon represented through the Figure a *compression of the time-span* of the progression of an emotional disposition, let us say the start of anger through to its dissipation, or the evolution of a psychic state, this can be compared to standing in a forest of trees (our ordinary consciousness of time), and then rising up above the trees and seeing the layout of the forest within the landscape (how time appears to an enhanced consciousness).

The peculiar time-mode of Bacon's figures that has been compared to the time-body of a plant, where there is a kind of 'stasis', (static dynamism), to ordinary senses, as time weaves in and out of itself, would then relate to how the **Eternal**, or the 'everlasting', interacts with the plane of time, upon which dwells the corruptible. The **Eternal** which is the totality of time naturally includes within itself the linear time of the physical world, which in itself is the **Eternal** stripped of its higher time modes, thus the time-body of any particular organism is the outcome of **The Eternal** reclaiming, or reabsorbing, its own being. When an individual develops to the position where they can 'sense themselves sensing' and subsequently renew contact with their 'forgotten self' then the present becomes the **NOW,** and this is because the **Eternal** (during the first three years of life we live to all intents and purposes in the **Eternal**) within one's self is now cognised as an existential fact.

*

Although there is nothing intrinsically unusual about Dyer's lifestyle and habits – ever since the Fall there has been the tendency for the misuse of substances as individuals attempt to heal their fractured souls by material means, however, from the 1960's up until the present day the combination of alcohol and 'substance' abuse (whether 'pills', cocaine, heroin or any other chemical products) has been culturally prevalent and in may cases leads to 'premature' death – what is unusual is the presence of an artist of Bacon's calibre and abilities to record , for want of a better word, scientifically, the demise of the subject through prolonged indulgence. There can be little doubt from what is known of Dyer's psychological state that it was exacerbated by his habits and predilections. An individual's soul disposition is primarily an interweaving of impulses that originate from an 'higher' self and those issuing from a 'lower' self. One way to understand this is by returning to the previous depiction of the 'I' standing at right-angles to the plane of time and reaching upwards to the **Eternal**. The closer the 'I' approaches the **Eternal** the more it embraces the purest, highest imaginable impulses and by the process of integrating these impulses into ourselves so is the *lower self* gradually transformed into the *higher self*. Because the 'I' meets the plane of time, and self-consciousness ensues at a particular point, so the 'I' meets with all that constitutes the plane of time, regardless as to whether this is 'good' or 'bad', and depending upon an individual's disposition they will to a greater or lesser extent have an affinity with those aspects of the plane of time that strengthen or weaken the higher 'self' and the lower 'self'. Right from the moment of birth the make-up of our soul, whether from a higher or lower aspect, is dependant upon the desires , passions and instincts of the individual concerned, heredity and the social conditions into which the individual has incarnated.

As stated the 'soul' is far from homogeneous and a tension exists within every human being between its higher and lower aspects that is mediated by the I. Thus the Self is largely conditioned by the distinctiveness of an individual's likes and dislikes, and if there was no 'I' then the individual would respond automatically to these impulses issuing from their lower aspects in a manner redolent of the Law of Cause and Effect. However because we have an 'I' we have self-consciousness and so are able to freely chose to change if we can summon up enough strength of will. Through the intervention of the 'I' the Self now has two facets: a 'higher' and a 'lower' self and the composition of these has a direct impact upon the ability of 'I' to initiate change. The 'higher' self is created through the capacity of an individual to allow the 'I' to influence the Self through what may be loosely called moral impulses that flow from the **Eternal**, where the aptitude for altruism and the ability to 'become the Other' may be classed as moral impulses. Bacon was fascinated by this tension between a higher and lower dimension of an individual's soul, and how this tension affected the course of their lives, and this theme finds expression in a remarkable picture that Bacon produced in his seventies upon the subject of the Sphinx, a subject that had remained a fascination for him since the 1950's.

The Double.

Before considering issues concerned with the Sphinx I will return to the identification of the Double at the end of the last chapter as a significant interpretative factor for understanding the meaning of Bacon's iconography. The 'Double' as far as I am concerned is a combination of positive and negative factors, and is in essence a self-made mirror-image of our soul and spirit that serves to inform, and act as a guide for future development. For the purposes of this text the Double acts as a Guardian, which restrains an individual until they reach a point when they have sufficient spiritual strength to confront that which they have created for good or bad. It is perhaps unfortunate that in this day and age the higher aspects of the Double are occluded by a morbid fascination with the darker side of human nature. This darker side undoubtedly exists but through this biased focus the beneficial aspects of the Double are missed.

There are many reasons for this and some will be discussed below, however for now I will focus on the 'lower' self, which in many ways resists the transformation of the self, as whole, into the 'higher' self, and circumstances are such that differing forces can affect the power of the 'Double', in both its aspects, to a greater or lesser degree. There are those forces that are inherited through the blood, and there are those forces within our own soul that arise from our own actions and inclinations, and much depends upon how far an individual can resist the allure of the latter. The determining factor in this is the strength of an individual's 'I', if the 'I' is not strong enough to resist the desires and drives inherent to the lower self, then the outcome is a reification, or hardening of the current state of the totality of the self. The strength of the 'I' is dependant upon the personality traits an individual has developed over the course of time. Therefore when we are born we have not only to contend with that which is inherited, but also with that aspect of ourselves which in itself may resist the injunctions issuing from the 'I' to change. Through every single thought and act we perform, we affect the 'higher' and 'lower' dimensions of the 'self' to a greater or lesser extent. In considering the 'lower' self of adulthood an account must be taken of how our primeval self of infancy has been distorted by a host of factors, ranging from familial to societal conditions, all of which have to be accounted for by the adult. Thus those actions we perform that are ego-centric, malicious and thoughtless mark and transform our soul. To be perfectly clear, by performing negative actions, we create configurations within our astral body that can act in no other way than the manner of their creation, and consequently live a life of their own within our souls, and this then effectively becomes a sub-world of its own within our soul. They are many artists in the history of Western art who were able to perceive such entities and Hieronymous Bosch is a prominent example. The effect of such entities is to tie the ego, in all its aspects, to them, and to induce individuals to maintain their existence by continuing to act in the manner that created them in the first place, and they do this by reflecting pictures into our soul life of the satisfactions and pleasures that brought them into being, thereby tempting individuals to perform further actions so as to perpetuate their existence.

Credible evidence that the theme of the 'Double' plays a role in deciphering Bacon's images is provided by Van Alphen. Firstly he argues that the experience of looking at Bacon's images causes in him 'a momentary *loss of self*', which is not an uncommon experience when viewing Bacon's images. What Van Alphen appears to mean is that what he considered to be his 'self' was momentarily erased, or dissolved/ paralysed, in the face of that which was evoked within himself by Bacon's images. The effect of this, for Van Alphen, is that it caused 'a paralysis in my intercourse with the works', (Van Alphen, 1992: 9). In general it is argued that upon encountering Bacon's paintings there is precipitated a dislodging of our 'self' from its usual familiar parameters, a 'self' that has evolved, along with our personality, to produce a sense of identity that permits us to negotiate the physical and social worlds as perceived from our individual, limited point-of-view. The effect of this dislodgement, during the time of viewing Bacon's images and afterwards, is to activate an unconscious, or half-conscious, awareness of our own 'lower self' as related to the 'Double', which usually lies dormant and outside our normal consciousness. Secondly Van Alphen sees issues surrounding the Doppelgänger (Double) as being relevant in the r. h. panel of "Crucifixion",

"The two bodies are so similar that one could claim that they each constitutes the other's double: they are *doppelgänger*… In fact doppelgänger were already present in the triptych…" (Van Alphen, 1992: 74-75).

Van Alphen in the above statement considers the Double, and the Doppelgänger, to be identical, and for present purposes I will follow this lead. Bacon's analysis of Dyer's personality and character is a recording of the conjunction of factors relating to inherited forces and factors related to Dyer's own self with the emphasis upon the 'lower self'. From the evidence of Bacon's images of Dyer we have a recording of how the malicious aspect of Dyer's Double intensified over a period of time due to Dyer ignoring its presence, and it is clear that this was not a metaphorical investigation by Bacon, but that he was able to perceive the actions of this entity upon the spiritual planes.

The Ego has as its base the Blood within the corporeal body. This understanding illuminates an aspect of Bacon's character, for it is a well-known fact that Bacon had a fascination with blood and meat, as referred to above. In conversation with Sylvester Bacon made the following remark

"When you go into a butcher's shop and see how beautiful meat can be and then you think about it, you can think of the whole horror of life…". (Sylvester, 1987: 48).

Peppiatt provides the evidence that this interest in meat and blood was not a morbid, facile obsession by highlighting Bacon's interest in the "Oresteia" by Aeschylus and its blood-soaked imagery. Bacon also produced a work, "Blood on the Floor", 1976, (ill. 97), and Peppiatt quotes Bacon's comments on this image

"Things are not shocking unless they have been put into memorable form. Otherwise, it's just blood splattered against a wall. In the end, if you see that two or three times, it's no longer shocking. It must be a form that has more than the implication of blood splashed against a wall. It's when it has much wider implications. It's something that reverberates within your psyche, it disturbs the whole life cycle within a person. It affects the atmosphere in which you live."

The profounder aspects of Aeschylus's plays will be examined further below, but it is enough at present to state that Aeschylus in his Tragedies dramatised drastic changes that were occurring to the relationship between the Ego, Soul and Etheric body. In effect Aeschylus stood at a turning-point in human evolution whereby the human being evolved from an ancient configuration of body, soul and spirit to one that eventually led to our present state. Thus Bacon's interest in blood and flesh is more thoughtful that the common ghoulish and macabre reactions to this subject, and the above work, through its conjunction of blood and a switched-on light-bulb (commentary of the lamp as a metaphor for the ego), demonstrates that Bacon understood the relationship between the Ego and the Blood. There is, however, a simple observation to be made about blood that connects with all that has been stated of the occurrence of flesh and bones in Bacon's work and, especially, invagination, and that is that it forms a bridge between the inside and the outside. This is observable through the fact that our blood makes contact with the outside world through our lungs, but we also have blood that flows through the arteries and blood that flows through the veins – and that these two separate systems are brought into conjunction through the heart – the seat of our passions.

That which Casts a Shadow: the Higher Self and the Lower Self.

Georg Kuhlewind in his book "The Life of the Soul" presents an exposition that enables us to understand why the 'lower self' assumes the form that it has, and why it is so difficult to transform. The sub-title of this book is 'Between Subconsciousness and Supraconsciousness' and this indicates that our ordinary consciousness is open to impulses from two directions; the lower realms governed by gravity and the higher spiritual realms governed by levity. Because the higher aspects of our 'I', which are at an embryonic stage of development, are able to shine into our self, we are able, through the development of a 'higher' self, to bring into the earthly realm inspirations that have their origin in the **Eternal** – the Supraconscious. In contrast, because our 'I' has also been drawn down into lower realms through our attachment to particular desires and patterns of mechanical thinking we have created within ourselves a 'lower' self that is more related to the gravity pole of the Universe, and is related to our subconscious. There is thus an inherent conflict within ourselves between that which wishes to facilitate our development to stages of higher being and that which works to impede this progress.

"The life of the soul usually consists of a conglomeration of non-cognitive feelings and will-impulses of non-conscious or half-conscious origin, of psychological and mental habit-formations and thought-forms that weave through the whole of it. Mixed into this conglomeration is the occasional lightning-flash of new thinking. This partly serves the self-sentient mentality, the ego, but it is partly the still-untouched universal, autonomous element." (Kuhlewind, 1990: 10).

All that is created in the soul that is only related to egotistic desires and selfishness dwells mainly in a subconscious region that has, in some ways, sealed itself off from ordinary consciousness. The reason why it has 'sealed itself off' is that our egotism leads to a complacency that paralyses the ego and this can only be redressed by a desire or intention, combined with an act of will, to do something about our circumstances. It can now be stated that one aspect of the Supraconscious is an autonomous, in the sense of self sufficient, and formless realm (sometimes referred to as chaos when this word is understood in it true meaning) that is capable of new creation, in contrast to the subconscious that consists only of the formed and the determined, and is capable of no new creativity only repetition and enlargement of that which is *inherent* to itself. The Supraconscious, as stated relates to levity whereas the subconscious relates to gravity, so that in our everyday lives we are open to impulses from the Supraconscious that are normally inadequately integrated into our consciousness because we simply lack the cognitive abilities to do so, and to impulses from the subconscious that, because they have strongly contoured, magnetic forms, are difficult to resist due to our egotistic attachment to them. The result of this is that because the Supraconscious is so fluid and mobile it, except in unusual circumstances, such as intuitive feelings and inspired thinking passes us by, whereas we are tied to that which under the influence of gravity has coagulated into set and difficult to dissolve forms. Consequently through our thinking and actions we effect changes in our consciousness that either draw us to 'higher' or 'lower' realms.

Our normal condition of soul-life is characterised by Kuhlewind as a ferment of semi-cognised formations that have differing origins. Some issue from impulses that have not been fully examined and integrated into ourselves (from the supraconscious), whereas others relate to barely conscious will-impulses and habitual thinking (from the subconscious) that has not been thoroughly permeated by our 'I', the totality of which is occasionally illuminated by the flash of new thinking.. This description of the normal condition of soul-life is one that is apt for those works by Bacon that appear to be non-specific thematically, but which concentrate instead on general states of being. One work that falls into this category is "Triptych", 1976, (ill. 98), which has a portrait in each side panel and multiple symbols in all panels that are interpretable as representing various aspects of the soul, such as the news-print that represents habitual thinking that is old, formed, finished and calcified. A thoroughgoing analysis of this fascinating work will not be undertaken, however given that the work has a portrait in each side panel we are permitted to assume that these symbols relate to the consciousness of the individual portrayed. Leaving aside the fact that there may be a specific meaning for the symbols with regard to the individual portrayed, this work depicts the complexity of any individual's soul-life where there will be a bewildering array of influences and attributes that are the individual's responsibility to cognise and comprehend. From this perspective it can be said that if this act of comprehension is piecemeal and slipshod then the 'lower' self is not transformed but becomes more entrenched at the expense of the 'higher' self. In this work, and others of this type, Bacon depicts the normal state of soul-life from which a pathological condition may arise, such as happened with George Dyer. Given that this work occurs after Dyer's death this indicates that Bacon had further refined his understanding of his life-long investigation into humanity's soul condition and those intangible forces that pursue humanity and cause the agonising, psychic distress that had been the case for George Dyer.

In the r. h. panel of this work we see in front of the portrait a grotesque, malformed human shape resting on newsprint with a puddle of pink liquid. I have already presented a meaning for these pink puddles as being symbolic of a 'loss of being' and the newsprint is perceivable as being symbolic of the 'psychological and mental habit-formations' as outlined by Kuhlewind above. In this context then the grotesque form becomes an image of how the soul is distorted into the 'lower' self. Also the strange monkey-like creature on the rail in the central panel that has a strong sexual overtone, leads us to an understanding of how instincts themselves are capable of being distorted into something 'animalistic', in the pejorative sense, and as such are a caricature of our higher self. When examined it is surprising to realise just how much of our desiring life is based upon simple instincts, and that these desires then create a configuration that is largely outside the orbit of our conscious control. Given that our ability to deal with this configuration depends upon the I, our self-sentient mentality, then further attention has to paid in its meeting with the Emotional body.

"What is autocratic and arbitrary in the soul, and frequently works against the I's autonomy, begins as self-sentient emotional life. It has sealed itself off from the feeling that lives beyond form, to become closed patterns of feeling. As these relatively visible feeling-forms have cut themselves off, the further development of the emotions proceeds *downwards*, to where the gaze of everyday consciousness cannot follow." (Kuhlewind, 1990: 46-47).

Because our egos are only at an early stage of development, we are unable to fully cognise and integrate into ourselves, through our thinking, those experiences we have of the universal, Supraconscious, Eternal dimensions of existence, with the result that we contain within our consciousness formations that are incomplete and partial with respect to their universal, original state. These formations behave in a manner similar to those resulting from our egotism and desires. Kuhlewind describes this other aspect of our consciousness as being the effect of the fact that with our abstract, intellectual thinking we atrophy the process of cosmic creativity.

"The cause of all this is to be found in the fact that universal processes come to a standstill in man; he interrupts them. A part of these processes becomes conscious for man; the remainder cannot be consciously grasped because his consciousness is not adequate to the task. The remainder becomes 'effect'. It is not a physical, mechanical effect; rather, man is confronted by psycho-spiritual forces that he cannot *consciously* receive. By the very fact that part of the universal Word becomes conscious, these forces are sealed off from the universal wisdom and make independent 'forms'. Today, as subconscious impulses in human behaviour, they erupt into consciousness. Self-sentient emotional formations arise out of the cognitive forces of feeling that speak from the world, forces that were originally cognitive, but have not been consciously assimilated. This process can clearly be followed with regard to the will." (Kuhlewind, 1990: 47-48).

Our 'normal' consciousness is thus composed of a number of factors over which we do not have full control, and which have not been thoroughly permeated with a 'higher' thinking, and the net effect of this is to create a force that sweeps us along so that we come to resemble, in many of our actions and behaviour-patterns, automated puppets - and Kuhlewind makes it plain just how debilitating this can be.

"From the uncomprehended feeling and willing elements, non-cognising formations of emotion and will are built under the aegis of egotism. These dream-like formations that man experiences as if they were a wave that sweeps him along, determine his life to a great extent…they flow into one another; they are conceptually incomprehensible in their essence, because they are alive…Out of these psychological formations, unless they are adequately cognised, there arise life-forms, life-habits, functional diseases and finally physical symptoms. If these go on undissolved- unilluminated by cognition …they can then be called forces of destiny." (Kuhlewind, 1990: 540.

The Double is not a poetic fantasy but a *living* psychic formation pertinent to everyone that we personalise through our soul-state and which *speaks from the world,* and which because we fail to cognise its constitution as issuing from our own base passions and supraconscious impulses goes ignored as a force for good, and subsequently assumes a menacing, threatening countenance. Thus it is our failure to cognise adequately impulses from the Supraconscious, the 'higher' dimensions of the cosmos, that results in the creation of formations in ourselves that are subconsciousness-like, that is they have become frozen at a particular point beyond conscious cognition. With this we have another possible level of meaning for Bacon's use of garbled pools of newsprint in his images. For if we consider a newspaper as informing and giving information, then the newsprint now stands not just for mechanical patterns of thinking and past thinking, but also for the lack of a mode of thinking that is capable of understanding the 'New'. Consequently it may be posited that one interpretation of the confusion shown by Figures in "Triptych – Studies from the Human Body", 1970, (ill. 16), results from an inability to escape the past combined with an incapacity to accept the 'New' that is streaming towards us from the Supraconscious. There is the feeling that these lumps of newsprint and 'odd' shadows in Bacon's work represent portions of our thinking and being that have become detached from our ability to cognise and control them, and if we accept this view this then leads to other comments by Steiner on our soul-life in "Secrets of the Threshold":

"All human beings have elements in their souls beyond their full control, elements to
which they are emotionally attached….The soul contains portions that can be prised loose from its entirety, and because we do not fully control these components….a tendency arises for those parts of man's etheric and astral being that are inclined to separate from the rest of the soul's life and become independent

to be formed…and even given human shape. As a matter of fact, there are all sorts of thoughts sitting in us that are capable of taking on human form…they confront us in the elemental world as our…" (Steiner, 1987: 110).

These descriptions of an ordinary human soul given by Kuhlewind and Steiner in this chapter, and the previous one, are very significant for a 'reading' of Bacon's images, and as such the above statement by Steiner is most instructive for comprehending why "Triptych, May-June", 1973, (ill. 23), appears the way it does. It has already been stated that the shadow of the central panel of this triptych has a demonic demeanour, but when we observe the outer panels the Figures have no shadows. This implies that anyone attempting to 'read' this work has to ask themselves why Bacon gave a shadow to the Figure in the central panel, even though the light-bulb is incapable of casting a shadow given that it is not switched on, and not to the other Figures? This 'shadow' has grown out of, or emerged from, the darkness within which the Figures are situated in each of the three panels, and if this darkness is taken to represent Dyer's unconscious then the 'shadow' of the central panel can be taken as emanation from Dyer's unconscious. This means then that this 'shadow' that harangued Dyer in "Two Studies for a Portrait of George Dyer", 1970, (ill. 19), represents all the thoughts and feelings that Dyer lost control of that have metamorphosed into a 'human' form, which has volition, and which then confronts Dyer as his 'Doppelgänger', or 'double'.

This is how things stand from the position that humanity has reached and Bacon's images are instructive in this respect, but this text has laid considerable emphasis upon enhanced perceptual abilities, and has attempted to speak of this in plain, everyday terms for there is, at the end of the day, nothing mysterious or out of the ordinary to it. The path to achieving such abilities is through the strengthening, development and purification of our thinking and feeling life **we already possess**, not of adding anything new or exotic, and when this done then the Double, 'Shadow' or Doppelgänger is transformed into what is known as 'The Lesser Guardian of the Threshold'. This being, which issues from our self, has to be 'faced' before entry into and full cognition of the 'higher' worlds that have been spoken of is possible. Steiner in his book "Knowledge of the Higher Worlds how is it Achieved?" speaks of this entity in the form of a dialogue between it and the would-be initiate who has to face this entity in full consciousness, and which assumes a terrible spectral form. This Being then informs the candidate that all their deeds, and the consequences resulting from those deeds, that had lived unknown to the candidate have now taken an independent existence that the candidate has now to confront and face.

"A truly terrible, spectral Being confronts the pupil 'Hitherto, Powers invisible to yourself had charge of you. They saw to it that each of your good deeds had its reward and that each of your bad deeds had its woeful consequences…In your character there are many fine sides and many ugly flaws. You yourself has caused both through previous experiences and thoughts. These were, until now, unknown to you; their effects alone were made manifest to you….Now all the good and the bad aspects of your bygone lives are to be revealed to you. Until now they were woven into your being; they were within you and you could not see them…But now these aspects release themselves; they emerge from your personality. They assume an independent form which you can see, just as you see the stones and plants of the outer world. And I …. am that very Being who has formed a body out of your noble and ignoble deeds.." (Steiner, 1993: 191-193).

Is "Painting, 1946" a depiction of this terrifying figure, and is this Bacon confronting his own Lesser Guardian of the Threshold'? I would make a strong case that this is so especially when we consider the spiritual journey he undertook as outlined in Chapter 1 "The Prodigal Son".

These subconscious formations that formerly constituted the candidate's 'lower self'/ Double, together with that which has escaped conscious control, have now become manifest as 'The Lesser Guardian of the Threshold'. Furthermore 'The Lesser Guardian of the Threshold' is shown not to have existed in isolation but to exist within a family, a people and a race, and that standing above the candidate's own self stand the destinies of those families, peoples and races into which it has been born.

"Now the Guardian of the Threshold is connected with another matter. The individual concerned belongs to a family, to a people, to a race; his activity in the physical world depends upon his relationship to this kind of community. His particular character is also connected with it. The conscious activity of single individuals by no means exhausts everything to be reckoned with in a family, a people, or a race. As well as their characters, families, peoples and races also have their destinies." (Steiner, 1993: 197-198).

This is a crucial point to be considered in relation to Bacon's portraits for at present we do not possess anything like the fullness of our ego's potential - the ego can be pictured as constituting a sort of hollow within our spiritual organisation – we only know our self as belonging to our 'I' initially through the fact that we are born into a family which in turn is part of a people and a race. Thus whatever psychic struggle an individual may be experiencing takes place within a specific 'family, peoples and races' and whatever appertains to that nexus of conditions, but, nevertheless, it is ultimately the responsibility of the individual to either triumph over, or succumb to, that which they are, which devolves from a combination of what they have made of themselves and what lives within the blood they have inherited. This nexus of conditions upon the plane of time cannot be ignored but has to be acknowledged, and so the 'The Lesser Guardian of the Threshold' is not purely 'evil', or negative, in itself, rather it is a vital aid to our continued spiritual evolution.

If "Painting, 1946", (ill. 33), has the implications alleged, this implies that Bacon was possibly a conscious 'unconscious initiate', in that it seems he was not fully aware of the significance of his own abilities. This is a tricky subject for there is no factual evidence pointing to an interest in esoteric, or occult, matters, on Bacon's behalf. However, much of Bacon's life is simply unknown to us because, as stated he was remarkably tight-lipped, over his innermost thoughts. The knowledge we have is only the information he chose to divulge in public interviews, in which he answered mainly technical questions, and during which he rarely ventured to profess his own opinions. On the other hand we have those accounts from individuals who were eye-witnesses to events in his Soho public social life, which have subsequently been melded into the popular figure of legend Bacon has become. This is an anglo-centric interpretation of Bacon that does not do justice to the totality of his life. I suspect that Bacon encouraged this as it camouflaged his actual intentions and deflected enquiry into areas he had no intention of answering questions upon. For instance, he continued throughout his life to spend extended periods in France - what was he doing there and who was he speaking to? I have found very little reference to this aspect of his life, with the main interest being focussed upon, as stated, Soho shenanigans.

This one-sided focus of critiques of Bacon's work have imbued his images with a particular 'aura' without his images necessarily being concerned with the attributes of that 'aura'. Nevertheless, Bacon's images do have a sexual frisson to them, so it is partially understandable why such attention to Soho is displayed, and this sexual frisson is so strong that it is quite capable of producing a 'loss of self', in the wider sense, through its reverberating with the 'lower' self of the viewer. Little needs to be said of the power of the sexual instinct and how it sometimes acts as an irresistible force that completely eludes conscious control, also little needs to be said of how reticent individuals are to be reminded of their own sexual proclivities in public, even indirectly, or of how even in the most consensual of circumstances the sexual act if vigourously pursued involves a substantial degree of pain and pleasure that is subsequently 'forgotten' upon completion of the act, but nevertheless remains in the unconscious.

The difference with an individual of Steiner's abilities and Bacon is that Steiner was scrupulous in preventing his own personal likes and dislikes from influencing his observations of the 'invisible' worlds discussed. In effect this means that there is the elimination of all of that which related to him personally, but this does not imply that the 'self' or feelings are not present. Steiner describes perception of the supersensible realms spoken of here in the following terms,

"..then their spiritual eyes and ears actually open and new realms unfold around them. I have also shown you that those who enter this realm are confused by all the impressions that work upon them. Whereas in the physical world there are objects with sharp outlines from which we take our bearings, in the spiritual world we have a confused feeling of interweaving, hovering form – just as Goethe desribes it in the second part of *Faust*." (Steiner, 2003: 91).

This and other statements by Steiner, especially those related to the schooling of logical thinking, make it clear why it is necessary to eliminate the 'personal' when cognising supersensible realms, for if this dimension of our being was not controlled then we would never get beyond our own prejudices, feelings and opinions when coming to conclusions concerning our perceptions. So although Bacon did not completely separate out and definitively categorise all of his perceptions, and did not completely eliminate all his personal reactions to what he perceived, nevertheless his achievement is impressive, for through the strength of his will, imaginative faculties and discipline Bacon was able to sufficiently combat his own Double to give an account of the supersensible dimensions of the human being that is consonant with statements by Steiner and others.

The commentaries by Steiner and Kuhlewind provide the means for understanding how Bacon in his work explored issues relating to both the 'Double'/ 'lower self' and the tension that ensues in relation to the 'higher' self, whilst placing this within the context of 'external' factors, such as 'families, peoples and races', an exploration which reached a high-point with his portraits and studies of George Dyer. The fundamental note to Bacon's exploration of the psychic condition of humanity demonstrates how human beings are, in general, largely trapped within a mental landscape of feelings and thoughts that are of their own making, irrespective as to whether these compromise an individual's sanity or well-being. Thus the works referenced above: "Portrait of George Dyer Staring at a Blind Cord", 1966, (ill. 90), "Portrait of George Dyer Crouching", 1966, (ill. 91), "Two Studies of George Dyer with Dog", 1968, (ill. 80) "Portrait of George Dyer in a Mirror", 1967-8, (ill. 92) and "Two Studies for a Portrait of George Dyer", 1968, (ill. 19) present an almost Hogarthian vision of the specific stages of Dyer's struggle with his own 'self'. In "Portrait of George Dyer in a Mirror", Bacon portrays the meeting of Dyer with his 'lower self' that is in the process of separating from Dyer, and how Dyer reacted to this meeting (I have already drawn attention to the fascinating resemblance to the same understanding Wilde displayed with his book "A Picture Of Dorian Grey"). The fact that Bacon portrays Dyer in such a fractured state means that Dyer had reached a state where he was at his wits end and unable to cope, and that although he may have been able to perceive the effect of his habits and life-style upon himself he was either unwilling to do, or incapable of doing, anything to mitigate his circumstances. If this is so then "Two Studies of George Dyer with Dog" is a representation of the initial stages that develop into Dyer's psychic condition in "Portrait of George Dyer in a Mirror", perhaps "Two Studies of George Dyer with Dog" indicates the paralysis, or degradation, of Dyer's 'higher self' resulting in the formation of that which utterly slips out of his conscious control. "Two Studies for a Portrait of George Dyer" illustrates the final act in this drama for now Bacon depicts a Dyer who, although fully appraised of what he has become with respect to his blood-line and the ramifications of his own nature, turns away in fear and disgust at its form, rather than facing it and acting. This is a truly tragic image and one cannot but help having the sympathy for Dyer that Bacon surely felt, and which is a condition that is the daily lot for large numbers of individuals in this day and age, but the grandeur of these images is that Bacon presents us with the 'facts' of our soul-life rather than lapsing into sentimentality or dwelling upon his own particular feelings for Dyer.

The Sphinx.

Bacon's interest in Ancient Greece was by no means limited to an understanding of Greek Tragedies of that period as is indicted by his work "Oedipus and the Sphinx after Ingres", 1983, (ill. 99). This is a work that leaves no doubt as to what the subject-matter of the image is, and like his "Study after Velasquez's Portrait of Pope Innocent X", 1953, Bacon uses as a template for his own image the work of a renowned artist from the past, in this case Ingres' "Oedipus and the Sphinx", 1808, (ill. 100). Ingres produced three versions based upon this subject, however they all have the same compositional structure of the profile of Oedipus conversing with the Sphinx (one of which is reversed), with in the background one of Oedipus's companions fleeing in terror. Bacon first produced images of the Sphinx during the 1950's with "Sphinx I", 1953, (ill. 101) being a prominent example. The difference with the 1983 image is that Bacon goes to the very heart of the mystery that was played out in Ancient Greece. The fact that there is a monument to the Sphinx in Ancient Egypt indicates that the events of Oedipal legend were a common concern to both the Greeks and the Egyptians, which is a very important point to be considered in what follows with respect to the evolution of European Culture; a point that is underlined by the commentary upon the Bull above. Avigdor W. G. Poseq in his article for the periodical "Source: Notes in the History of Art, vol 21, no 1, 2001" makes the interesting comment, (which will be explored below), that the Ingres work is 'usually seen as allegories of the intellect's struggles with the mysteries of human destiny', Poseq further informs us that Ingres had a troubled relationship with his father, the pertinence of these remarks will be explored below.

If we compare Bacon's work with the original by Ingres then we observe a number of striking similarities and differences. In Bacon's painting the format of a Figure confronting the Sphinx is maintained, with a Figure in the background, this basic format which is the crux of the Oedipus legend is consonant with the placement of the two protagonists in the Ingres painting. The three fundamental changes are that the Figure in the background is no longer a recognisable human form, the setting is not outside with the rocks of a cave-like space enclosing the Sphinx, rather the setting in Bacon's work is that of a room with a door-like opening giving a view of the 'form' in the background. That being said it is however to be noted that the walls of the room in Bacon's image echo the vertical structure of the rocks in the Ingres work, nevertheless the greatest difference is that the Figure, as Oedipus, to the right in the Bacon work has a wounded and heavily bandaged foot that the Figure appears to be exhibiting to the Sphinx, something that is entirely lacking in the Ingres piece, the significance of which will be investigated below. Thus the Bacon Figure seems to be attempting to draw the Sphinx's attention to its wound in contradistinction to the Ingres work which creates the impression that Oedipus is engaged in a dialogue with the Sphinx. The Oedipus legend has a multi-faceted significance, and to begin with, although traditionally there has been a focus upon Oedipus's answer to the Sphinx's riddle, it cannot be ignored that the confrontation of the two emerges from Oedipus's disastrous relationship with his father. Much has been made of this within the various schools of psychology and psychoanalysis, however, is Bacon by producing this work referencing his own relationship with his father? If this is so then the exaggerated proffering of the wounded foot is drawing a parallel between Bacon's fathers treatment of Bacon himself and Laius's treatment of Oedipus, whereby Laius ordered Oedipus's feet to be pierced, and then had him abandoned in the wilderness to perish. The relationship between the Father and the Son lies at the heart of the changed spiritual conditions of our modern age, and the consequent consciousness we now possess. In this respect this work by Bacon places his own spiritual journey with respect to the Father, already outlined, in a wider cultural context. The whole edifice of Western civilisation has its roots, and foundation, in the experiences of the Ancient Greeks, especially with the development of our intellectual abilities during the Classical Greek period.

In modern times, with respect to the Oedipus legend, we are mostly familiar with the psychological theories of Sigmund Freud that, in part, reduce the Oedipus story to the issue of infantile sexuality. Freud's theorisations of the Oedipus Complex propose that the infant male child has a subconscious desire to have intercourse with it's Mother and usurp the position of the Father. This is a literal, and intellectual, reading of the Oedipus legend that has a number of flaws. It is well-known fact that Oedipus was unaware that it was his mother that he had intercourse with, after answering the Sphinx's question and becoming King Of Thebes, nevertheless Freud's theory makes the assumption that what was an unknown must have been a subconscious desire, in the first place, in the light of subsequent events. By making this assumption the Freudian postulation is given a universality, regardless of the manifestly different consciousness of Ancient Greece to our own, in that intellectuality had not yet developed for the human race at that time. Whilst there is a place for Retrocausality, as discussed above, it has to based upon perceptible phenomenal circumstances, which the Freudian theory is not. Through a sort of mental, slight-of-hand it is implied that Oedipus must have had this subconscious urge before having intercourse with his Mother, making the actual intercourse a manifestation of that which lies below the surface of consciousness. This is a turning of logic upon its head, for it is only an assumption that Oedipus had such an urge buried in his psyche. By concentrating upon sexuality alone a distorted image is created for the psychic construction of a human being, that deflects attention away from such issues as the recovery of the 'forgotten' self of childhood by the adult, referred to here. By placing sexual desire at the centre of childhood consciousness Freud not only trivialises the profundity of the Oedipus story, but also reduces the world of the child to the level of 'fallen' adult sexuality, which in the process shrinks our spirituality through a process of abstract, intellectualising to that of an exclusive consideration of our corporeality. The ability to be able to conceptualise through an abstract, intellectual reasoning is a stage of consciousness that humanity is presently passing through, and which, as will be shown below, was inaugurated by Oedipus, however Freud's use of this power in his theorisations 'materialises' our understanding of our psychology by making it exclusively object-based (bodily organs, erogenous zones etc). In effect the whole gamut of human motivation is reduced to the operation of one instinct - our sexual drive - the upshot of this is that it 'animalises' the human being, thereby creating a model that is ripe for a 'materialistic' interpretation. In a nutshell abstract, intellectual thinking has been deployed to project the characteristics of our adult mentality upon an infant when there is no evidence that this is appropriate. In addition such a theory as Freud's can only have some sort of justification if the individual is capable of recovering the 'forgotten self' of childhood themselves, and there is no evidence that this was the case with Freud, or any of the later supporters of this theory.

Steiner was certainly aware of this movement towards psychoanalysis by Freud and others and had much to say upon the subject of which the quotation below is an example

"Where psychoanalysis is correct in a certain sense is in its demonstration that there is something in the depths of human nature which, in whatever form it exists there, can be raised into consciousness; that there is something present in the body which, when it is raised to consciousness, appears as something spiritual. It is, of course, an extremely primitive action for a psychoanalyst to raise what remains of past experience from the depths of the human psyche in this way; past experience which has not been assimilated intensively enough to satisfy the emotional needs of a person, so that it sinks to the bottom, as it were, and settles there as sediment, creating an unstable rather than a stable equilibrium. But once brought into consciousness it is possible to come to terms with such experiences, thus liberating the human being from their unhealthy presence.

Jung is particularly interesting. It occurred to him that somewhere in the depths — of course there is some difficulty in defining where — there are all the experiences with which the human being has failed to come to terms since birth; that embedded in the individual psyche there are all kinds of ancestral and cultural experiences stretching far back. And today some poor soul goes to his therapist who psychoanalyses him and discovers something so deep-seated in the psyche that it did not originate in his present life, but came through his father, grandfather, great-grandfather and so on, until we arrive at the ancient Greeks who experienced the Oedipus problem. It passed down through the blood and today, when these Oedipal feelings make their presence felt in the human psyche, they can be psychoanalysed away. Furthermore, people believe that they have discovered some very interesting connections through their ability to psychoanalyse away what lies in the far distant past of ones civilization.

The only problem is that these are thoroughly unscientific research methods. You need only have a basic knowledge of anthroposophy to know that all kinds of things can be extracted from the depths of the human psyche. First there is our life before birth, the things which the human being has experienced before he descended into the physical world, and then there are those things which he has experienced in earlier lives on earth. That takes you from a dilettantish approach to reality! But one also learns to recognize how the human psyche contains in condensed form, as it were, the secrets of the cosmos. Indeed, that was the view of past ages. That is why the human being was described as a microcosm"(Steiner: The Anthroposophic Movement, Lecture Three, The Opposition to Spiritual Revelations, Dornach, 12 June 1923).

Steiner in this quotation makes it abundantly clear just how complex our psychological constitution is and by implication, with respect to my statements above, just how threadbare Freud's postulations are. But to consider that Steiner did not recognise the importance of the role played by our corporeality, psychologically, would not be correct for he presents, in the quote below, a deeper appreciation of the role of our corporeality than a piece-meal object-based, psychoanalytical approach.

"What we encounter as psychoanalysis today really is dilettantish in the extreme. On the one hand it is psychologically amateurish because it does not recognize that at certain levels physical and spiritual life become one. It considers the superficial life of the soul in abstract terms, and does not advance to the level where this soul life weaves creatively in the blood and in the breathing — in other words, where it is united with our so-called material functions. But the physical life is also amateurishly conceived, because it is observed purely in its outer physical aspects and there is no understanding that the spiritual is present everywhere in physical life, and above all in the human organism. When these two amateurish views are brought together in such a way that the one is supposed to illuminate the other, as in psychoanalysis, then we are simply left with dilettantism". (Steiner: The Anthroposophic Movement, Lecture Three, The Opposition to Spiritual Revelations, Dornach, 12 June 1923).

It almost goes without saying that if it is not accepted that there is a specific, spiritual dimension to life, and that the idea as to what is 'living' is expanded to that which, although it cannot be ordinarily be precisely perceived, exhibits attributes of volition and transformation, then Steiner's statements will appear as unsubstantiated fantasy. Given that we live in age where materialistic thinking is propagated through the media, which is used as a tool of mass-indoctrination, and that there is no systematic *thinking* within the general world of esotericism that appeals to a modern rational approach, then it comes as no surprise that such concepts as the Etheric and Re-incarnation are treated as manifestations of the lunatic fringe, and this is reinforced by the frivolous presentation of such subjects within the entertainment industry. However, Steiner certainly did not dismiss that which lies in the unconscious nor did he dismiss the therapeutic value of conversation, what he was at pains to point out was that the Freudian and Jungian approach was not sufficiently thorough to achieve the hoped for results. As an aside it is well-known and documented within the Anthroposophical movement that there is a therapeutic and healing value to conversation and this takes the form of Goethean conversation. This cannot be taken further here. But it is apposite to note that although the story of Oedipus is in many ways considered, culturally and academically, to be a myth or fairy tale, meaning that it is supposed to be a fantasy that was conjured up at some unknown point in the past, it is nevertheless taken as having a *real* import for the structure of our consciousness. Such a viewpoint ignores the fact that the reality of myths and fairy tales derives from a mode of consciousness that the intellect is utterly unable to appreciate, and on this point Steiner states the following;

"The secret of all legends and fairy-tales is that their content was originally actual experience, arising either from man's relation to the Sphinx or from his relation to Mephistopheles." (Steiner, The Balance in the World and Man, Lucifer and Ahriman: 8).

Perhaps the most important implication of these statements by Steiner upon the story of Oedipus and psychoanalysis is that there has to be a re-evaluation of how it is that we have evolved an abstract, intellectual consciousness based upon a logical manipulation of concepts, and which primarily focuses upon sensory derived objects in an exclusively materialistic manner. Such a re-evaluation would not be satisfied by merely assuming that the Ancient Greeks perceived the world, and had a consciousness similar to our own, albeit in a more primitive form. At the time of Oedipus individuals (even if they did not consider themselves to be individuals in the modern sense) would not have been able to carry in their minds in abstract form the concepts of infancy, adulthood and old-age and then apply this to an abstract understanding of a human being so as to reply to the Sphinx - this is something which came much later with Plato and Aristotle, in particular with the latter who is rightly famous for his making explicit the functioning of logical thinking. We now use our thinking with ease, but it cannot be ignored that the Intellectualism, founded upon abstraction, which characterises our present consciousness petrifies all that it comes into contact with, and in doing so leaches life out of all it touches, making the Universe a dead realm of blind, interacting material forces. This is one reason why deploying a humanitarian, abstract, intellectualism for an understanding of Ancient writings of any form cannot recover the original meaning of those texts, for, in effect, one is using a methodology which is contrary to the one used in the original composition of those documents. This leads to perplexing conclusions such as Freud's deductions concerning the Oedipus legend, where events that appertain to events after Oedipus's meeting with the Sphinx are applied retrospectively. The condition of infancy has a correlation with Oedipus before he meets the Sphinx in that intellectuality has not yet developed, in developing intellectuality the child is undergoing processes upon the mental level that are not synonymous with a material counter-part, and this will be further discussed below. Unravelling all the strands pertinent to such a re-evaluation of the legend of Oedipus is not an easy matter, however, Bacon's "Oedipus and the Sphinx after Ingres" offers some clues as to what direction to take.

The story of Oedipus is sufficiently well-known that it is not necessary to examine in-depth all the connected aspects, fascinating though these are, what is necessary, however, is to draw attention to Bacon's enthralment with the Ancient Greek Tragedies in general. This will be examined further in greater detail below. Pertinent to these Ancient Greek Tragedies is the role played by 'The Furies' as grisly, spectral, astral beings that resulted as a consequence of the immoral acts performed by human beings, and which subsequently harangued and plagued the perpetrators of such acts. Bacon stated to Preppiatt that he was able to actually perceive these Furies - Preppiatt assumed Bacon was speaking allegorically - but Bacon denied this was the case. If it is accepted that Bacon was able to perceive these beings, are there other beings associated with the story of Oedipus that Bacon was able to perceive. On this point Steiner stated the following

"When persons who have remained standing at a certain stage of evolution, among the peasants perhaps, rest in the fields at midday in the hot glow of the summer sun, and fall asleep, they may have what could be called a latent sun-stroke. Through such an impact on the physical body, the astral and etheric are loosened from a part of the physical. Then such persons are translated to the astral plane and they see this last decadent offspring of the Sphinx. This apparition is called by different names. In certain regions it is called the midday woman. Many people in the country will recount that they have met the midday woman. She appears in many regions under many different names. She is a descendent of the ancient Sphinx, and as the ancient Sphinx put questions to the men who experienced her, so this midday woman also asks questions. You may hear it told how the midday woman asks endless questions of the men whom she meets. This torment by questions is a relic of the old Sphinx. The midday woman has grown out of the ancient Sphinx. This indicates how evolution proceeds beyond the physical world, how whole tribes of spiritual beings decline until at last they are mere shadows of what they were originally. Here we see another characteristic of the way in which things are connected in evolution. We have mentioned this so it may be seen how manifold evolution is." (Steiner: The Ancient Egyptian Doctrine of Evolution. The Cosmic View of the Organs and their Coarsening in Modern Times. September 13, 1908).

Granted that the 'Furies' are not the same as this declining figure of the Sphinx, nevertheless it shows the great range of supersensible entities that impinge upon our consciousness even if we cannot, in general, at present perceive them, and this raises questions as to the significance of the spectral Figures that populate Bacon's images. The import of the above statement by Steiner is that unless one is able to explore the conditions of human consciousness at the actual time of such an event as Oedipus's confrontation of the Sphinx, then one is only dealing with that which has degenerated and is fading away. In particular it implies that all this intellectualising upon ancient myths etc completely misses the point, for the only outcome is that vapid and insubstantial mental constructs are proposed for actual and vital spiritual processes taking place in the human being, this has already been alluded to. With respect to Bacon's image we see that Oedipus's terrified companion in the Ingres piece has been transformed into a ghastly, spectral apparition that is convulsed and distorted in appearance. What did Bacon wish to communicate through this? On one level this Figure, and this could be applied to the Ingres work, is a metaphor for the abject terror that lurks in the depths of everyone's psyche in the face of the sheer sublimity of existence, which in this case would refer to an old testament characterisation of the Father (God) as a figure of relentless and remorseless judgement of those who contravened his Laws. Perhaps this Figure is displaying horror as it realises that Oedipus is about to answer the Sphinx and that henceforth the world will be utterly changed. The fact that Bacon has placed an arrow upon this Figure, thereby marking its importance, indicates that Bacon had a clear understanding of the historical significance of this figure as expressing the change from a picture-based consciousness to one based upon the intellect, and abstraction.

As an aside it is a fact that, from the perspective of this document, the physical body is undergoing profound evolutionary changes, there are organs that are gradually atrophying and wasting away, whilst others are only at the start of their evolutionary path, and this knowledge furnishes another possible explanation as to why Bacon's grisly, spectral Figures are so anatomically distorted. However, the task now is to outline how it can be ascertained that the Ancient Greek era pertinent to Oedipus is the time when the Intellectual dimension of our being made its first nascent development, that is the ability to think conceptually and logically in an abstract manner. Before this momentous change in humanity's consciousness people simply could not think and evaluate in the manner that we do to-day, and it is due to the efforts of individuals such as Socrates, Plato and Aristotle, as indicated above, that we are able to think in such a manner. As stated it is a well-known fact that Bacon was intensely absorbed in the literature of the Ancient Greek Tragedians and their psychological insights into humanities psychic constitution, and that Bacon found echoes of their insights in what he perceived as the psychic condition of those around him. However it is Steiner who illuminates the importance that the story of Oedipus has for the evolution of our consciousness to its present condition, and crucial to this evolution is the 'maiming' of Oedipus's feet. I find it extraordinary that Bacon focuses upon this aspect in his "Oedipus and the Sphinx after Ingres" thereby charging his image with an emotional intensity that is entirely lacking in Ingres somewhat insipid work. Steiner states of this 'maiming', which he refers to as 'club-feet', that

"Oedipus is the son of Laios. Laios had been warned against having a child because it was said that this would bring misfortune to his whole race. He therefore cast out the boy who was born to him. He pierced his feet, and the child was therefore called "Oedipus," i.e., "club foot." That is the reason why, in the drama, Oedipus has deformed feet.

I have said already that when etheric forces are impoverished, the feet cannot develop normally, but will wither. In the case of Oedipus this condition was induced artificially. The legend tells us that he was found and reared by shepherds after an attempt had been made to get rid of him. He goes through life with clubbed feet. Oedipus is Mephistopheles — but in this case Mephistopheles is working in his rightful place, in connection with the task devolving upon the Fourth Post-Atlantean epoch.

The harmony between ether-body and physical body so wonderfully expressed in the creations of Greek Art, everything that constituted the typical greatness of the Greek — of all this, Oedipus is deprived in order that he may become a personality in the real sense. The Ego that has now passed into the head becomes strong, and the feet wither.

The man of the Fifth Post-Atlantean epoch has quite a different task. In order to confront and conquer the Sphinx, Oedipus was obliged to receive Ahriman into himself. The man of the Fifth Post-Atlantean epoch, who confronts Ahriman-Mephistopheles, must take Lucifer into himself. The process is the reverse of that enacted by Oedipus. Everything that the Ego accumulates in the head must be pressed down into the rest of man's nature. The Ego, living in the nerve-process, has accumulated "Philosophy, Law, Medicine, and, alas, Theology too" — all nerve-processes. And now there is the urge to get rid of it all from the head — just as Oedipus deprived the feet of their normal forces — and to penetrate through the veils of material existence".(Steiner, The Balance in the World and Man, Lucifer and Ahriman, Lecture I).

I will comment upon such spiritual beings as Ahriman and Lucifer and their stranglehold upon our thinking and emotional abilities a little later, at this juncture, however, I will draw attention to their incipient pertinence with respect to the commentary already given upon Bacon's portrayal of the demonic beings that assailed G. Dyer. In the above quotation Steiner indicates how the 'spiritual', how "this soul life weaves creatively in the blood and in the breathing — in other words, where it is united with our so-called material functions", interacts with the physical. It is also indicated how Oedipus inaugurated the age of intellectual thinking by drawing the Ego and etheric forces into the head, i.e. the brain which is the centre of all our nerve processes, and it is further indicated that in the present day and age we are too firmly embedded in the head region and need to counterbalance this one-sidedness.

"Man no longer believes that direct intercourse with Nature brings him near to the Divine Wisdom of the world, but he sets out to study, to approach it via the nerve-process, not via the breathing and the blood. The search for wisdom has become a nerve-process; modern theology is a nerve-process.

Oedipus must prove himself master of the forces contained in the processes of the breathing and the blood. He personifies the nerve-process with its impoverished ether-forces, in contrast to those human beings who are altogether under the sway of the breathing and blood processes. Oedipus takes into his own nature those forces which are connected with the nerve-process" (Steiner, The Balance in the World and Man, Lucifer and Ahriman, Lecture I)

It is clear from this quotation from Steiner that Laios represents the state of humanities consciousness prior to the development of our consciousness to its present condition as initiated by Oedipus. As is natural to the human condition Laios abhorred change, preferring to remain within what we would term his 'comfort zone'. The crucial importance of the 'maiming' of Oedipus's feet is that the re-arrangement of the etheric body was such, that after the act, a portion of the etheric body became available for humanities new powers of intellectual thinking, and for this to be achieved the feet had to 'wither'. This meant that in order for this change to take place there had to be a radical re-arrangement of the functioning of the various aspects of a human being. This has been alluded to above in how the Ego moves from a focus in the astral body to the brain as the centre of nerve processes. Bacon by focusing on the wounded feet goes straight to the decisive moment during the Ancient Greek Era when humanity received the impulse to develop abstract, intellectual thinking. In addition this story of how the son kills the father no doubt had significance for Bacon with respect to his own spiritual journey, as discussed in the above section on the Prodigal Son. Steiner in the following quotation comments upon the relationship between the blood, breathing and ego forces as they are expressed through the asking of questions:

"It is to be presumed that science will be led some day to study how the breathing process is connected with the urge to question, or with the feeling of being assailed by doubt; but whether this happens or not, everything that is associated with questioning and doubt, with feelings of dissatisfaction caused when something in the world demands an answer and we are thrown back entirely upon our own resources .... In its normal state, the ether-body moulds and shapes the physical form of man. But as soon as the ether-body expands, as soon as it tries to create for itself greater space and an arena transcending the boundaries of the human skin, it tends to produce other forms. The human form cannot here be retained; the ether-body strives to grow out of and beyond the human form. In olden days men found the solution for this problem. When an extended ether-body — which is not suited to the nature of man but to the Luciferic nature — makes itself felt and takes shape before the eye of soul, what kind of form emerges? The Sphinx!........The Sphinx is the being who brings doubts, who torments the soul with questions. And so there is a definite connection between the Sphinx and the breathing process. But we also know that the breathing process is connected in a very special way with the blood.

226

Therefore the Luciferic forces also operate in the blood, permeating and surging through it. By way of the breathing, the Luciferic forces can everywhere make their way into the blood of the human being and when excessive energy is promoted in the blood, the Luciferic nature — the Sphinx — becomes very strong. Because man is open to the Cosmos in his breathing, he is confronted by the Sphinx. It was paramountly during the Greco-Latin epoch of civilization that, in their breathing, men felt themselves confronting the Sphinx in the Cosmos. The legend of Oedipus describes how the human being faces the Sphinx, how the Sphinx torments him with questions. The picture of the human being and the Sphinx, or of the human being and the Luciferic powers in the Cosmos, gives expression to a deeply-rooted experience of men as they were during the Fourth Post-Atlantean epoch, and indicates that when, in however small a degree, a man breaks through the boundaries of his normal life on the physical plane, he comes into contact with the Sphinx-nature" (Steiner, The Balance in the World and Man, Lucifer and Ahriman, Lecture I).

Before progressing further I will now make some preliminary remarks about Lucifer and Ahriman, who are generally known as the Devil and Satan respectively. Steiner made it perfectly clear that these are not one and the same being but quite different beings with differing Cosmic aims, although it is the case that at present they do work in conjunction in specific areas to achieve their own particular goals. There is no doubt that mention of these two beings will evoke all sorts of images of witchcraft, superstition etc, which the humanitarian, rational consciousness of our time prides itself for having eradicated from modern epistemology. Part of the dialogue above was to indicate how the ego has its own internal self-sufficiency that has become compromised through its identification with particular thoughts and feelings. It is simply not logical to state that I *am* a particular thought or a particular feeling, because they are in constant flux and there would be no centre to my consciousness if it was true that I was either of them, it can only be stated, in normal consciousness, that I *have* particular thoughts and feelings, and that having such I am none the wiser as to the nature of their being. Steiner's approach was to define the characteristics of Luciferic and Ahrimanic activity and demonstrate how it influenced thinking and feeling in our everyday lives. *At this juncture I would like to refer to an important distinction that Steiner delineated, one that has been extremely helpful to me and which I believe Bacon understood. This distinction consists of the fact that we do not live in a polarity but that of a **Trinity** of spiritual forces represented by Christ, Ahriman and Lucifer.*

Continuing with my discourse I would argue that it is the concept of 'Otherness' that provides an opportunity for open-minded thinkers to approach this controversial subject, and in harmony with this I have pointed out that there is nothing so strange, and Other, than ourselves. It is only when one starts to experience the Otherness of one's own thinking and feeling, to develop the attitude that these are like strangers we have become attached to that one begins to appreciate the spiritual conditions we live in and our psychic structure. In some respects Ahriman and Lucifer represent a polarity and the nature of their activity can be discerned by looking at the polarities to be ordinarily noted within our civilisation. Two of the most obvious and fundamental polarities are those between the individual and the community, and those between the genders, within both of which there is an ever evolving tension. I can only provide brief indications here, thus one of Lucifer's aims is to convince an individual that it is his own individuality which is paramount even to the cost of the community, whereas one of Ahriman's aims is to suppress any individuality within the community, thereby creating a mass of people which he can manipulate to his will, consequently creating a machine-like, materialistic civilisation, both of these deny the existence of anything other than itself. The situation is complicated by, as stated, the working 'together' of Lucifer and Ahriman, so that a Luciferic endeavour may display Ahrimanic overtones and vice-versa. They thus represent a polarity within our psychic life the machinations of which if we are not fully conscious of them determine our character and personality in a way that is not under our control. It goes without saying that the Christ aspect of the Trinity outlined above is, if not utterly ignored, completely undervalued by modern epistemology.

To continue with the legend of Oedipus, there is a deeper esoteric meaning to the 'death' of the Father and 'intercourse' with the Mother that reflects into social conditions, which as a by-product gives an insight in Freud's theorisations concerning the Oedipus Complex. This also provides some reasons as to why disaster pursued Oedipus and those under his dominion after his confrontation with the Sphinx. If Laios remained within a consciousness that was 'fading away' then it is also apparent that Oedipus did not fully extricate himself from that consciousness.

"Without knowing it he had slain his father and wedded his mother. He now reigned as king. But because he had attained his power in such a way, and because this terrible fate clung to him, he brought unspeakable misery upon his country, so that he is presented to us in Sophocles' drama as blinded, as one who had himself destroyed his eyesight!

This is a story the imagery of which went forth from the ancient sanctuaries of wisdom. Its meaning is that Oedipus was still, to a certain extent, in touch with the spiritual world in the old way. His father had enquired of the oracle. These oracles were the last heritage of ancient seership. But the inherited remnants were inadequate to establish peace in the outer world. They could not give humanity the desired harmony between the maternal and paternal elements. The circumstance that Oedipus solved the riddle of the Sphinx clearly indicates that he is intended to represent one who has inherited a certain seership in the old style, and who possessed a knowledge of human nature in keeping with the remnants of ancient wisdom. This was powerless to avert that war of human passions typified by the parricide and the union with the mother. In spite of his connection with the ancient wisdom, he is unable to see through the complex of circumstances. The old wisdom no longer confers seership. Had it sufficed to open the eyes, as formerly, through the blood tie, the blood would have spoken when Oedipus met his father and again when he met his mother. The blood was silent! This represents to us in graphic manner the decay of ancient wisdom". (Steiner:The Gospel of St. John Lecture XI)

Steiner also describes how initiation was achieved through the ancient methods that were becoming redundant for the new age that was dawning at the time of Oedipus:

"In an initiation of this nature the etheric and astral bodies were withdrawn from the complex of physical, etheric, astral bodies and Ego. The Ego remained behind. It was for this reason that the candidate was without self-consciousness during the three and a half days of the initiation. His self-consciousness was extinguished, and another consciousness was infused into him from the higher spiritual worlds by the Priest-initiator, who placed his own Ego at the disposal of the candidate and acted as his guide in every sense. What actually happened then was expressed in a formula which will sound strange to you. They said: When a candidate was initiated in the old way, the maternal element went forth and the paternal element remained behind; that is to say, he killed the paternal element in him and united himself with the maternal element; in other words, he killed his father and wedded his mother. When therefore the initiate of old lay in the lethargic condition for three and a half days, he had 'united himself with his mother and killed his father.' He became fatherless. This was necessary, for he had to renounce his individuality and live in a higher spiritual world." (Steiner: The Gospel of St. John, Lecture XI)

In this instance the ego and physical body are the masculine (father) aspect of our being in distinction to the astral and etheric body which is the feminine (mother), so Oedipus stood at the crossroads of history but was unable to fully distinguish that which was spiritual, in the sense of a psychic event, and that which related to the plane of time. Because he was unable to fully comprehend his own circumstances he enacted out that which he encountered on a supersensible level in his actual life thereby causing disaster. However, we also still live in the shadow of Oedipus's error which humanity at present has not fully resolved. By latching on to this Freud seeks to perpetuate a shadowy fallen aspect of being that can only lead to disaster, that is Freud reiterates Oedipus's mistake by emphasising the dynamics of that mistake within the realm of the family rather than recognising it as a supersensible, psychic event for the individual to resolve.

"…the suffering awaiting the human being of our modern time is rather that of being in the grip of preconceptions and prejudices, of having as an incubus at his side a second "body" consisting of all these preconceived judgments and opinions. What is it that is leading to this state of things?

Let us be quite candid about the trend of evolution. During the course of the Fifth Post-Atlantean epoch, so many problems have lost all inner, vital warmth. The countless questions which confront us when we study Spiritual Science with any depth, simply do not exist for the modern man with his materialistic outlook. The riddle of the Sphinx means nothing to him, whereas the man of ancient Greece was vitally aware of it. A different form of experience will come to the man of modern times. In his own opinion he knows everything so well; he observes the material world, uses his intellect to establish the interconnections between its phenomena and believes that all its riddles are solved in this way, never realizing that he is simply groping in a phantasmagoria. But this way of working coarsens and dries up his ether-body, with the ultimate result that the Mephistophelean powers, like a second nature, will attach themselves to him now and in times to come.

The Mephistophelean nature is strengthened by all the prejudices and limitations of materialism, and a future can already be perceived when everyone will be born with a second being by his side, a being who whispers to him of the foolishness of those who speak of the reality of the spiritual world. Man will, of course, disavow the riddle of Mephistopheles, just as he disavows that of the Sphinx; nevertheless he will chain a second being to his heels. Accompanied by this second being, he will feel the urge to think materialistic thoughts, to think, not through his own being, but through the second being who is his companion." (Steiner: The Balance in the World and Man, Lucifer and Ahriman, Lecture I).

The thrust of the above statements by Steiner concerning the Sphinx draw attention to the necessity of harmonising the relationship between the masculine and the feminine, both on the physical and the mental levels, and this, as will be appreciated, is a thread that runs through this text. It has also been alluded to how this theme plays an important role in Bacon's iconography, and this will be analysed in greater depth in the next chapter. As an introduction to that chapter I will quote some of Steiner's comments upon the psychic relationship between the masculine and the feminine in the context of our corporeal division into man and woman, and the consequences for our civilisation of a failure to integrate these two aspects of our psyche harmoniously,

"Let us look into our own inner selves. We have seen that the maternal element dominates where the etheric and astral bodies interpenetrate, while the paternal element comes to expression where the Ego is present in the physical body. That is to say: the mother, the female element, reigns in all that we have in common with our species, in everything which pertains to our life of thought and knowledge; while the father, the male element, predominates in all that arises from the union of the Ego with the physical body, in the inwardly differentiated form, in that which makes man an Ego. What then must the ancient sages, who viewed life in this way, have expected above all things of human beings? They required that man should come to a clear understanding of the relation of the physical body and Ego to the etheric and astral bodies — of the paternal to the maternal element. Inasmuch as man has an etheric and an astral body, the maternal element is in him; beside the external mother, so to speak, on the physical plane, he bears within him the maternal element, the mother; and beside the father on the physical plane, he has within him the paternal element, the father. To bring into harmonious relationship the father and mother in him was a great ideal. If this were not achieved, the disharmony between the paternal and maternal elements would be reproduced outside, on the physical plane, with disastrous results. The old sage therefore taught: 'It is the duty of man to establish harmony within himself between the paternal and maternal elements. The failure to do so cannot but show itself in the outer world as the most appalling crimes.' (Steiner: The Gospel of St. John, Lecture XI)

In the following quotation Steiner further expands upon the connection of the maternal and paternal to the various dimensions of our being

"Man says to himself: Within me there lives an etheric body and in this etheric body an astral body. The astral body is the bearer of ideas, thoughts, sensations, and feelings; it lives in the etheric body. Now we have seen that the etheric body is the principle which acts immediately and in the fullest measure upon the physical body; it contains the forces which lend form to the physical body. We see therefore that the etheric body, being permeated by the astral body, contains everything that fashions man to be 'man', imprinting upon him a definite form from within, that is, from his spiritual parts. The element which produces resemblance among men comes from the forces at work within man; it is not merely external and therefore does not depend on the physical but on the etheric and astral bodies. For these are the inner principles. A man gifted with insight into such matters will therefore feel that the force permeating his etheric and astral bodies comes to him from the maternal element; while the force which gives his physical body the definite form imprinted upon it by the Ego (by the Ego in the physical body) must be regarded as a paternal inheritance.

'From my father I have my stature and life's most earnest conduct;
From my mother a happy nature and delight in telling fables,'

says Goethe. You see, this is an interpretation of what I have said. 'From my father I have stature', that is, what is worked out by the Ego; from the mother, ideas and the gift of telling fables; these are inherent in the etheric and astral bodies." (Steiner:The Gospel of St. John Lecture XI)

By quoting Goethe Steiner indicates how an understanding of how the maternal and paternal were integrated into the totality of a human being was once tacitly known culturally. The tension between masculine and feminine modes of consciousness, and how this is heightened or resolved, is an integral aspect of Bacon's work. I have no wish in this document to comment upon Bacon's own sexuality, but there is plenty of evidence that the polarity of masculine and feminine, and how this polarity functioned, captivated Bacon's attention. I will give one example before examining this theme, in greater depth, in the next chapter, and that is "Man and Child", 1963, (ill.   ). It is quite clear that the child is female in this work, however what strikes one, as has already been noted, is the almost excruciating and agonised tension that exists between the adult and child, which comments not only upon the tension between masculine and feminine but the gulf between the worlds of the adult and that of the child.

The Bull.

Ostensibly, "Study for a Bullfight No. 1", 1969, (ill. 52), appears to be nothing more than a contemporary study of a matador performing the age-old ritual of a bull-fight, except for two factors. Firstly the above work was preceded by "Portrait of Elizabeth Rawsthorne Standing in a Street in Soho", 1967, (ill. 51), which features a bull in the background mirror-like device. This work has already been critiqued, above, with regard as to how a human being has to overcome the onslaught of primal urges in order to make manifest their humanity. A statement that could equally be applied to "Study for a Bullfight No. 1", 1969. The second factor is that examination of this work reveals another mirror-like device in the background, which links it to "Portrait of Elizabeth Rawsthorne Standing in a Street in Soho", where this mirror-like device has overtones of a mirrored cabinet of some sort. Pertinent to both these works is the fact that the ritual of the bull-fight has historical links to the story of Theseus and the Minotaur. The course of Theseus's life is long and complex, but the first point to note is that Theseus dealt with bull-like creatures on two occasions: the Marathonian Bull and the Minotaur. The part of Theseus's life that has wide-spread familiarity is how he reached the centre of the Labyrinth with the help of Ariadne's thread, and this forms a link to the story of Oedipus. Oedipus stood at a turning-point in time where the Intellect started to emerge from an ancient clairvoyant, consciousness based upon the sympathetic nervous system - that is the autonomous nervous system related to the metabolic aspect of our corporeality this has been commented upon above. The consciousness, as stated, of the ancients was instinctive and not at all clear, even if it was wisdom-filled. With Theseus we have the inauguration of how the Intellect and the Imagination can work in harmony to give an individual a crystal-clear understanding of the world. The stories of Oedipus and Theseus are closely interconnected through humanities development of the ability to think intellectually and critically by logically manipulating concepts in the search for truth and meaning. This was not the case before Oedipus and Theseus, for then humanities consciousness, as indicated, was then structured upon imaginative revelation. With Oedipus's confrontation with the Sphinx humanity acquired the ability to actually think intellectually, whereas with Theseus's escape from the Labyrinth (symbolic of the brain) humanity was able to link this new ability with the organ of the brain, and hence the two hemispheres of the Intellect and the Imagination. Bacon's interest in the ability to think is demonstrated by the work "Figure Writing Reflected in a Mirror",1976, (ill. 10), where the salient feature of this work is how Bacon has investigated how thinking is externalised from the sanctum of the **I** and given a transient permanency through the written word. However although there has been established a link between Oedipus and Theseus with respect to thinking

232

the symbolism of the Bull has a much longer history

"Then the sun entered Taurus. Here we have the third post-Atlantean period with its veneration of the Bull in the Egyptian Apis cult, the Babylonian cult of the Bull and its sacrifice, and the Mithraic cult of ancient Persia. Man brought the sacrifice of the Bull down to earth from the heavens where it was inscribed.

The fourth post-Atlantean period, in which Christianity arose, began with the entrance of the sun into Aries. This important turning point in history is indicated by the story of the Greek hero, Jason, who captured the Golden Fleece. A further important turning point is indicated by the sacrifice of the Mystical Lamb upon the Cross.

Let us understand this whole course of evolution correctly. After the duality of good and evil had been comprehended in human consciousness, the concept of the trinity arose and appeared in various religions. We recognize it in the Mithraic Mysteries that existed in many Mediterranean countries. Let us look at one of these Mystery temples. Only a symbolic action was performed for those who participated in the lesser Mysteries, but for those who were permitted to participate in the greater Mysteries, the same events also took place as an event in the astral world. I can only describe the lesser Mysteries of the Mithraic cult now. The symbolic Bull became visible and the Mediator, the God, rode upon his back. He covered the Bull's nostrils, plunged a sword into his side and a snake and a scorpion appeared. Above the head of the God Mithras was a bird and over the whole group, on one side a being soared with a lowered torch, on the other a being with a raised torch, symbolizing the course of the sun across the heavens.

This description represents human life as it lived in the consciousness of the men of that time. Man had reached the point of looking within himself for redemption, for the third divine principle that could lead him beyond evil, reconciling evil with good. Evil here consisted of the passions that drag man down to earth, symbolized by the Bull. The Mediator who killed the lower nature by thrusting the sword into the side of the bull appeared as the immortal in man that can raise him to his higher self. Thus, during the time of the third post-Atlantean period a divine trinity appeared as mediator between good and evil, and mankind came to comprehend what is called in theosophy, atman, buddhi and manas. At the moment the mediator appeared, the mystical secret was accomplished; the trinity had been awakened in man's consciousness." (Steiner: The Birth of the Light, Berlin, December 19, 1904).

The stories of Oedipus and Theseus are concerned with the transition from the third post Atlantean epoch to the fourth and this essentially focuses upon the movement from the sentient soul to the intellectual soul. For the present purposes this means that the human being has evolved from working with the main focus of their ego in their emotions to mainly working with their ego within their brain-based thinking.

233

It is necessary for a human being to have some mastery over their feelings, otherwise it becomes quite impossible to maintain a strand of thought whilst under the sway of strong emotions, and, furthermore to have clear, logical thinking whilst maintaining this focus of thinking.

"Let us go back to the first half of the Atlantean period. Man consisted already of physical, etheric, and astral bodies, plus the ego, but the physical body still looked quite different. We might compare it with the bodies of certain sea-animals, transparent, hardly to be seen, although laced with luminous threads in certain directions. It was much softer than today, having as yet no bones. It is true that there was already cartilage in some parts, but in these ancient times the physical body was definitely not of its present form." (Steiner: The Old Initiation Centers. The Human Form as the Subject of Meditation. September 4, 1908).

This description by Steiner of the human form in ancient times is one that is applicable to some of Bacon's Figures after 1957/58 as can be seen, for instance, by contemplating "Study of Red Pope (Study from Innocent X)", 1962, (ill.   ). The above statement by Steiner indicates that we have progressed through a number of animal-like forms throughout our history, but what is important here is how these forms evolved and their relationship to each other. I have no intention at this juncture of arguing the pro's and con's of Darwin's theory of evolution, but would point out that for those who have developed their sensory capabilities to be able to perceive the etheric body, then this is a real phenomenon in the real world, whereas the theory of 'survival of the fittest' (developed from Darwin) is a metaphysical principle which is purported to effect evolution from a realm other than the real world, one can only ask what directs this principle, for an idea can only have an effect if there are beings endowed with sufficient will-power to put it into effect.

"The etheric body was a much more important member. The physical body was then more or less the same size as now, but the etheric body was extraordinarily large. This etheric body varied among individuals, but one could perceive four different types. One part of mankind would resemble one type, another part another. These four types may be designated by the names of the apocalyptic beasts: bull, lion, eagle, man. It would not be correct to imagine that these beasts were exactly similar to the present animals, but the impression that they made reminds us of these. The impressions that the etheric bodies made can be understood through the picture of a lion, bull, eagle, or man. We can compare with the bull the portion of mankind that gave the impression of having powerful reproductive forces or an unusual appetite. Another portion lived more in the spiritual; these were the eagle men, who felt less at home in the physical world. Then there were men in whom the etheric body was already similar to the present-day physical body; it was not quite identical, but it was like the human form. However, we must not imagine that each man represented only one type; all four types would show some traces in each person, but one or another would predominate". (Steiner: The Old Initiation Centers. The Human Form as the Subject of Meditation. September 4, 1908).

Certainly on an ordinary level the characterisation of the Bull by Steiner applies to the two works by Bacon referred to above that depict Bulls, but Steiner's description of the spiritual import of the Bull in conjunction with the Lion, Eagle and Man has further implications for our evolution.

"He also saw what happened to man between death and a new birth. The Sphinx appeared to him as a real form; he experienced it. He could say, "Oh, I have seen the Sphinx, man as he was when he still had an animal-like form, and his etheric body — similar to the human — only projected out of this animal-like form!" The Sphinx was a real experience for the initiate. He even heard the question of the Sphinx with its enigmatic content. He saw how the human body prepared itself out of the animality, at a time when the head was only an etheric form, the ether-head of the Sphinx. This was truth for the initiate, as were also the older forms of the gods, who had, so to speak, taken a different course of evolution.

This is indicated in the legend of Theseus who took the Thread of Ariadne with him into the labyrinth. Now what is the Thread of Ariadne today? The concepts and mental pictures of the supersensible world we form in the soul! It is the spiritual knowledge that is made available to us in order that we may penetrate safely into the Macrocosm. And so Spiritual Science which, to begin with, speaks purely to the intellect, can be a Thread of Ariadne, helping us to overcome the bewilderment that might come if we were to enter unprepared into the spiritual world of the Macrocosm." (Steiner: Egyptian Myths and Mysteries, Lecture 11, The Ancient Egyptian Doctrine of Evolution. The Cosmic View of the Organs and their Coarsening in Modern Times. September 13, 1908).

These statements give us some inkling as to the nature of what it was that Bacon perceived through his meditations, and why he depicted human beings with animal heads. The point of congruence between the evolutionary process espoused here and that of Darwin is that the animal kingdom is central to both, however Darwin's theory was developed intellectually upon the plane of time without an insight into the super-sensible foundations of that which is observed. There is no such recourse needed here to principles such as the 'survival of the fittest' for it is through the strength of the human spirit to transform itself, according to changing world circumstances, that evolution proceeds. So the animal kingdom perceived today devolved from evolutionary processes that the human being has initiated in response to changed planetary conditions, so as to have the form we have now, in part, largely unsullied by animal characteristics, although to a keen observation of human beings echoes of these animal prototypes can be discerned, bringing us back to Bacon's images:

"In the way in which the four Evangelists are depicted in old paintings with symbolic beasts, we see a final understanding for the different natures of men the writers of the gospels were. St. John was symbolised by the eagle, which raises itself as wisdom above everything human; the power of St. Luke, the healer, is symbolised by the bull, the beast of sacrifice; the strength of St. Mark by the lion; and St. Matthew by the man or angel — that man who had harmonised the forces of all three in himself."(Steiner: A Guide to the Spiritual Science of Rudolf Steiner. Lecture 11).

Returning to the manner by which Bacon depicts the human head, which is in many cases indeterminate as in "Study for a Portrait", 1966, (ill.   ), and, as in other instances, an imprecise mixture of human and animal characteristics, we find that this manner of execution has a resonance with a statement Steiner made in his collection of lectures "The Effects of Spiritual Development",

"We must become familiar with the idea that when the Self and the astral body are outside the human being they can scarcely see the head; it appears to be quite nebulous; it is not completely effaced, but appears to be quite vague and indefinite. On the other hand the rest of the organism seems more distinct. It is also nebulous, but gives the impression that the human being is not a being of flesh and blood, but is endowed with a more powerful organisation." (Steiner: The Effects of Spiritual Development, 1978: 131).

The Griffin and The Lion.

The symbolism of the griffin and the lion represents the struggle that a human being has with that which has come under the dominion of the ego and that which has not. Thus the griffin symbolises all those aspects of ourselves that are wild and ungoverned and which lead to chaotic conditions within the soul, whilst the lion symbolises the power of the heart that has overcome these rampaging forces thereby transforming the soul into something infinitely more sublime, filled with goodness, beauty and truth. From a more modern, if not common, point-of-view it could be said that the lion is associated with the strength of the higher self to prevail, whilst the griffin is associated with those forces working through the lower self whose only objective is chaos, destruction of any order, and the consummation of the most vile and depraved satisfactions. An understanding of the dire struggle between these two aspects of the self only comes to someone who has reached a certain point of development, and Bacon was one of these individuals. Anyone with the inclination can look into their own soul and perceive aspects of the above statement.

Between the higher self and the lower self lies our everyday consciousness – what one might call our 'self' where the higher and lower intersect, and where the lower end of the ego abides. The condition of our ordinary consciousness has been described with reference to Kuhlewind above. Through the corporeal body that supports our consciousness the self makes itself manifest through three distinct

236

modes, that of feeling, thinking and willing, and each of these is immediately responsive to the influence of either the higher or lower self. I have no intention in even trying to list and examine the malfunctions that can arise within any of these spheres but will instead look at a few examples. With regard to thinking I will examine the conditions of rigid thinking and obsessive thinking, with rigid thinking there is a situation where thinking seems to have lost its elasticity and become frozen within a particular pattern. Both obsessive and rigid thinking exhibit a tendency of being overly attached to specific thought-patterns, for various reasons, such as those associated with the lower self and either through habit or the influence of social factors, which in extreme cases 'solidifies' the plasticity of the brain, thereby restricting the influence of impulses from the higher self and the spiritual worlds where the higher self dwells. In one sense thinking has become sclerotic and has lost its open-ness, and by becoming trapped within the corporeality that supports the ability to think has thus left itself prey to the lower self and other unwholesome influences. Is Bacon's image "Figure at a Washbasin", 1976, (ill. 9), a portrayal of George Dyer under the influence of such an obsessive thinking underpinning his habits that eventually lead to his death? Evidence of such an assertion is displayed by "Figure Writing Reflected in a Mirror", 1976, (ill. 10), and "Seated Figure", 1977, (ill. 102), both of which, from one angle, show the Figure under the influence of compulsive and fixated thinking, as indicated by the disorganised writing on the floor of these works.

The lower self is composed of all those thoughts, feelings and actions that are in essence the antithesis of all that is good, beautiful and true (in the sense of being in harmony with all that enhances our humanity rather than degrading it). There is a great range of these configurations with respect to their virulence and definition. It goes without saying that we all perform actions we regret, have thoughts we are ashamed of and express feelings that are unworthy of us, that is what it is to be human, but it has to be understood that by exhibiting any of the above we endow the above with some part of our being thereby giving them an intimation of volition. To begin with this is not a serious problem for our ego in ordinary consciousness is strong enough to cope with them, but if they are reinforced by a constant repetition that involves enjoyment and justification then the ego, which is at present only at the beginning of its development, is overwhelmed. If these actions, thoughts and feelings are repeated for long enough with no struggle against them then eventually they assume a demonic form that becomes the home for adversarial forces.

In obsessive and compulsive disorders an individual's thinking has become fixated upon a series of actions that involve barely conscious impulses of will and emotional reactions to specific situations. In the majority of cases the circumstances that underlie these conditions are illusory, but the individual is as if possessed by a compulsion that is not within their control and are stimulated, in the manner of a machine, to perform their compulsive actions as soon as the stimulus enters their consciousness. It is significant that any malfunctioning of our thinking, feeling and willing involves all three areas to a lesser or greater degree. For instance if an individual decides to steal something then this is clearly an act of will but the individual involved will first have thoughts and images as to why the action is justifiable, from his point-of-view, even if this is in the background of consciousness for an habitual criminal, and the whole process will be accompanied by various emotions as the resolution to steal is made manifest. Individuals are capable of intense emotional reactions to particular circumstances which never change because either they are incapable of objectifying their emotional responses, or that the thoughts which accompany the emotional response are rigid and set. When considering the ego we find that it can become fixated upon itself through such conditions as megalomania and extreme forms of narcissism. An image by Bacon that hints at such narcissism is "Studies from the Human Body", 1975, (ill 68).

Earlier commentary has described how any of these patterns of distorted thinking, violent, negative feelings and passions and addictions become degenerate facsimiles of our 'self' that have a primitive volition to perform that which has been 'programmed' into them simply because we have transferred aspects of our own being into them. That Bacon understood this process of development in the lower self is demonstrated by his series of portraits and images of George Dyer. "Portrait of George Dyer in a Mirror", 1968, (ill 13), depicts the beginning of the process of Dyer's mental disintegration by depicting the split in Dyer's psyche as reflected in a mirror, by this device Bacon demonstrates that he was able to perceive beyond the immediate appearance of Dyer those conditions that were responsible for his present state of mental health. "Two Studies of George Dyer with Dog", 1968, (ill 80), where Dyer's shadow is a metaphor for the Doppelgänger/ lower self, depicts the further deterioration of Dyer's psychic condition, for now a part of his being is detaching itself and assuming a sub-human, animal form. This worsening situation is illustrated by "Two Studies for a Portrait of George Dyer", 1968, (ill 19), for now this detaching dimension of Dyer's self (depicted in the black mirror/ canvas/ doorway) has now completely separated from Dyer as a bestial, inhuman caricature of himself that constantly harangues and plagues a distracted Dyer who is at his wit's end. "Triptych May-June", 1973, (ill 23), depicts in the central panel (when it is turned upside-down) the demonic being that had effectively destroyed Dyer's life in the process of departing from the now dead Dyer. This assumption is plausible because examination of this central panel reveals that Dyer's eyes are closed and that the light-bulb in the room is turned off, which, as stated above, Bacon used as a symbol for representing the ego.

Steiner made many comments concerning the Doppelgänger and the following ones from a lecture by Steiner ("The Mystery of the Double. Geographic Medicine", St. Gallen, 16 Nov. 1917) are relevant at this juncture,

"So, we arrive in this world with the garment of our organism without being able to reach down into it with our soul to any great extent. Instead, shortly before we are born, not very long before we are born, there is also an opportunity for another spiritual being, apart from our soul, to take possession of our body, namely, of the subconscious part of our body. This is a fact. Shortly before we are born another being indwells us; in the terminology we use today we would call this an ahrimanic being. It is just as much in us as is our own soul." (Steiner, Secret Brotherhoods, 2004, 56).

However, the characteristic of this ahrimanic being is that it cannot accompany us into the spiritual worlds we inhabit after death and this is extremely frustrating to this being

"But there is one aspect of human life which they cannot stand, and that is death. So they always have to depart from the human body they have invaded before it is afflicted by death. This is again and again a bitter disappointment for them, for what they so much want to succeed in is to remain in the human body after death. In their own kingdom this would be a high achievement for these beings; but so far they have failed in this." (Steiner, Secret Brotherhoods, 2004, 56).

From the above definition of an ahrimanic being, which enters at birth and has to leave before death, there is a distinct correlation with the central panel of the above triptych by Bacon. Before proceeding further I will add to the brief description of those beings which are our adversaries and give some indications of their origin. The spiritual evolution of the human being has commenced from times immemorial to the present day, and what I shall now provide is an extremely brief synopsis of the evolution of the adversarial powers. At certain specific points in the course of our evolution there have been marked and fundamental transformations of our being that have engendered our present day form. As the reader will appreciate, during the progress of my critique of Bacon's painting, I have presented a picture of the human being as built-up of four intertwining parts – the physical/ corporeal body, the etheric body, the astral body and the ego – and that our consciousness operates through the three modes of thinking, feeling and willing. The adversarial beings, of which there are three principal classes, the Asuric, the Ahrimanic and the Luciferic, came into existence at each point where we acquired a new dimension to our being. These are beings who did not achieve their full potential when they were evolving as a class whilst we were involved in one of the tremendous steps forward in our own evolution. Thus the Asuras are those beings of the Archai who did not achieve there full potential whilst we were in the process of acquiring our physical/ corporeal body, the Ahrimanic are those beings of the Archangels who did not achieve there full potential whilst we were in the process of acquiring our etheric body and finally the Luciferic are those beings of the Angels who did not achieve there full potential whilst we were in the process of acquiring our astral body. All of these are known as 'backward' spirits, certainly not in terms of their abilities which are far superior to our own, but merely because they have not achieved their full potential and have to 'catch up' at later stages of evolution, however, and this sacrifice should be noted, some of these beings have foregone their own personal evolution so as to stimulate our own progress. In one sense these 'backward' spirits are part and parcel of our evolution and our responsibility because of the gifts they have given us, however this does not mean that they are a benign presence – far from it – they constantly wish to stir up trouble and deflected our evolution in the direction of evolutionary goals appropriate to their own 'fallen-ness', and are in many ways antagonistic to each other. Without the influence of the Luciferic beings we would have no sense of freedom and without the influence of the Ahrimanic beings we would be bereft of our intellectual abilities.

The point is that we have the opportunity to evolve into a higher state of being by transforming the astral body, the etheric body and our physical/ corporeal body to more purified states by deploying our ego forces for this purpose. This cannot be done whilst our consciousness is under the sway of the lower self where the adversarial forces operate and become manifest. Instead impulses have to enter our consciousness through the higher self and the higher dimension of the ego, which are in constant contact with the **Eternal**, so that we have the strength to keep the adversarial forces in their rightful place. The above is a crude and simplistic picture of particular aspects of our spiritual condition and it is inappropriate here, which is a critique of Bacon's *oeuvre*, to go into greater detail, instead the reader, if they so wish, can consult in the first instance, Steiner's book "Occult Science".

If we return now to Steiner's description of some of the negative influences of these beings then we find that the significance of Bacon's work is further illuminated,

"…whose nature is luciferic rather than ahrimanic, is the originator of all neuro-psychological and neurotic diseases, all diseases which are really not diseases at all but merely, as one says, nervous diseases, hysterical diseases and so on." (Steiner, Secret Brotherhoods, 2004, 60).

There can be little doubt that even the most perfunctory examination of Bacon's Figures reveals the human being under the stress of mental torment etc, this has been emphasised with respect to the Pope and the Businessmen series, but what has not been considered so far is to why this should have become such a continuing concern from the mid to late 19th Century until the present day. In fact Bacon is the only artist I know of who has taken this modern-day phenomenon of mental dysfunction as the, almost, exclusive focus for his work.

"I have also spoken of the profoundly significant battle which took place in the spiritual regions of the world between the early 1840s and the autumn of 1879. This was one of the battles which occur repeatedly in world and human evolution and are customarily represented by the image of Michael or St George fighting the dragon. Michael won one such victory over the dragon on behalf of the spiritual worlds in 1879. At that time the spirits of darkness who worked against the

Michaelic impulses were cast down from the spiritual realm into the human realms. As I said, from that time onwards they have been active in the feeling, will and mind impulses of human beings. Present-day events can therefore only be understood if one turns the inner eye to the spiritual powers which are now moving among us." (Steiner: Fall of the Spirits of Darkness, Lecture 13, The Fallen Spirits' Influence in the World
Dornach, 27 October 1917).

The 'spirits of darkness' is a collective name for the adversarial forces, or powers, and so from 1879 onwards we have the influence of Luciferic and Ahrimanic beings upon both the individual and the wider social and cultural context. As stated it is the Luciferic beings that we must consider if we are to understand the rapid increase in hysterical, neurotic and other psychological disorders from the 19th Century onwards, the physical effects of whom upon the human being Bacon made the focus of his work. However, Bacon depicted other monstrous deformations of the human being and for the present I will consider "Fragment of a Crucifixion", 1950, (ill. 103), because it relates to the actual presence of the adversarial forces within human affairs.

I shall not at this stage comment upon the fact that this image is related to a crucifixion, but merely state that it is not only Christ who was crucified but that at the time of His Crucifixion a powerful black magician was crucified on the opposite side of the world. Nevertheless, this work was produced at the time of "Painting", 1946, (ill. 33) and "Figure in a Landscape", 1945, (ill. 36) and these two works, already commented upon, relate to the 'breaking into' of the social world of murderous, monstrous impulses, and it can be seen that there is a clear reference to the modern world in the background of "Fragment of a Crucifixion". "Fragment of a Crucifixion" is perceivable as marking an end to Bacon making specific social comments for during the 1950's we have the series of 'pope' and 'businessman' images that demonstrate an exclusive concern with the psychological conditions of a humanity under stress, in the context of a spiritual point-of-view, from the perspective of individuals.

In "Fragment of a Crucifixion" we see not Christ but instead a bestial monstrosity of a creature crawling over the top of the crucifix above a deformed chimera that is hovering in the place where one would expect the Christ to be positioned. Both these abhorrent creatures have not only human characteristics, mouth and frontal limbs, but the lower one also possesses wings that appear to be both feathered and diaphanous (appearance of the left-hand side of the creature through the wing on the left-hand side). Given the fact that Bacon has situated these abhorrences within a framework that has already been interpreted as representing a cross-over point between different types of space, it is possible to state that here this frame-work represents a sort of portal through which this beast is manifesting from some other dimension. As to whether this is the past or future is not indicated and neither is it made clear as to whether this is something which is intrinsic to the present, i.e. is it a symbolic representation of aspects of the state of the soul of modern humanity? This latter point is important because it can only be viewed in the *present* by an individual regardless as to whether this is 1950 or 2012. I hope I have made it clear just how great the depth of Bacon's abilities as a painter were and the subtlety of his images, and that being the case, as with all great painters, no mark or ambiguity would be there by chance.

If this is accepted then it has to be also accepted that this work is a kind of augury as to what could transpire if certain trends in society were to predominate, if this is the case this would indicate that Bacon thought that our future development depended upon the individual, that we have the choice to pursue unimaginable evil or sublime goodness, and that the choice will determine the future. From this perspective there are a number of writers who have communicated the consequences for society, and the individual, that are the possible results of not recognising that we are spiritual beings. It is not appropriate to initiate a discussion as to what is 'evil' in this context, but let us take the fact that we do not, in general, recognise ourselves as spiritual beings, and that the planet Earth is also a spiritual being to whom we are inseparably connected. A recognition of this fact was urged by Steiner as long ago as 1917.

"For example one must know that our earth is not the dead object described by mineralogy or geology, but a living being. Mineralogy or geology know as much of the earth as we would know of a person if we were familiar with solely the skeleton.....The earth which is known only as a skeleton is, in reality, a living organism; and as a living organism it influences the beings who move upon, namely, human beings themselves. Just as a human being is differentiated in the way his organs are distributed around his body, so is the earth differentiated in what develops within it, which in turn influences the human beings moving about upon it." (Steiner, Secret Brotherhoods, 2004, 60-61).

From this, because of the absolute intertwining of ourselves within the being of the earth, it follows that our actions affect the health and well-being of the earth and ultimately the environment we have to live in. So let us take one example of our actions, collectively, and ask whether or not this is 'evil'. At present because of the unregulated industrial expansion during the last 150 years we have effectively poisoned the seas and the earth itself, and through the modes of transport reliant upon oil we are in the process of destroying the atmosphere – the very air we breathe. This is a recognised fact now and needs very little expansion, as to what the final outcome is that is effectively anyone's guess. However it is obvious that we have affected the organic life of the earth drastically and further actions in this direction, (especially genetic manipulation and experimentation), can only lead to more dire conditions. K. Martin-Kuri in her book "A Message for Humanity" states the following as one consequence of an unthinking feeling for nature and lack of reverence for the living world,

"Huge, hostile insects will overwhelm the earth." (K. Martin-Kuri: 212)

Is the bestial abomination hovering in "Fragment of a Crucifixion" an imaginative representation of the consequence of our actions with regard to future developments of the earth. When considering questions of evil if we consider the cycle of the year from spring to winter it is obvious that there is from the fertility of the earth the production of that which is necessary for human survival, and this does not alter from year to year, that is strawberries are not delicious to eat one year and poisonous the next, there is within nature a moral goodness and respect towards us. But this is not a one-way street, and because we are now self-conscious creatures endowed with the possibilities of freewill and intellectual capabilities, we are now behoven to take responsibility for our actions. Principally this means honouring nature as nature honours us. Naturally there are poisonous plants and these do not proliferate at present to the detriment of life-giving food, but if we continue to disrespect how this balance between nature and ourselves has come into being with such disastrous policies as mass monoculture, drenching the earth in poisonous chemicals and altering the structure of organic life through genetic engineering, then it will come as no great surprise if equilibrium is restored in a manner that is not as favourable to us as was the previous state of affairs. All life is one, even if it manifests as different orders, which means if we alter the constitution of plants then as a natural consequence insect life will respond with scarcely imaginable outcomes.

Such ruminations are commonplace today even if there are very few intelligent responses as to how to proceed, but what fascinates me is that by carefully considering Bacon's work it is possible to discern a far greater depth of spiritual understanding of the Human Condition than has hitherto been credited to him. For instance I regard as a significant theme pertinent to Bacon's intentions, as expressed through his works, the question as to how 'goodness' is transformed into 'evil'. The right and left-hand panels of "Crucifixion", 1965, (ill. 14) evince such a response. In one sense it is possible to state that 'evil' does not exist, however it is certainly true that people can act immorally or morally, and that this affects both our evolution and that of the earth in a positive or negative way with respect to our well-being.

Such thoughts regarding the moral effects of our actions upon both our and nature's evolutionary course is pertinent to interpreting Bacon's work, for throughout his career he interspersed his images with ghastly chimera that display human characteristics similar to the one in "Fragment of a Crucifixion". "Seated Figure", 1974, (ill. 79) the left-hand panel of "Triptych Inspired by the Oresteia of Aeschylus", 1981, (ill. 34) and in the background of "Oedipus and the Sphinx after Ingres", 1983, (ill. 99) are a few examples of these abominations. Nevertheless fundamental to Bacon's *oeuvre* is the never ending struggle to be undergone by human beings, precipitated either by their physical handicaps, their mental state or their social context. In this spirit I would draw attention to Rene Magritte's painting

"Gigantic Days/ Les jours gigantesques", 1928, (ill. 104) where we see depicted a being that is composed of an intermingling of masculine and feminine characteristics that are involved in an internal wrestling-match. This is an image that has an ancient lineage, especially within alchemy, where it is usually depicted as a light and dark figure grappling within one figure. Bacon has condensed this symbol of the struggle between the higher and lower self, that marks the human being, into the intensity of his Figures, so as to demonstrate its relevance to the present-day, and to divest it of any pictorial dimensions that would only serve to distance the viewer from its meaning, so that the full impact of this ancient understanding of the spiritual condition of humanity can be felt by the viewer. The following quote from Steiner ties together a number of themes discussed above,

"The upper man, as man sees him when he turns back to look upon himself, is different in different people. The picture that presents itself here is also more or less transient. It gives nevertheless an approximate idea of the impression man experiences. There is no longer a human countenance; the countenance is suggestive of a bull, or else of a lion. Experiences in the supersensible world have often a quite grotesque appearance; and it transpires that, although not always, yet generally speaking, a woman who looks back in this way perceives herself more like a lion, a man more like a bull. There is no getting away from it, it is really so! And connected with these two pictures — which are intermingled, for the man is not entirely devoid of lion, nor the woman entirely devoid of bull, the two merge into one another — blended in at the same time with these is the picture of a bird, which has always been called the eagle and which belongs in the whole picture.

Nor has the worst yet been told! Many a man might be ready to make up his mind to be a bull, a lion or an eagle as a price for immortality. That is, however, only the upper man. The continuation down below is a wild, savage dragon. Here you have the source of all the numerous sagas and stories of the dragon. Traditional religious symbolism has always given man the four pictures, — Man, Lion, Bull, Eagle; but it has given no more than indications, as, e.g., in the account of the Fall, that a wild Dragon also belongs to man. The dragon, however, has its place in the totality of man, it is to be found there; and man has to say to himself: Lucifer is indeed able to promise you immortality — it is a sure and well-founded promise — but only at the cost of your form and figure, so that you go on living in the form you have become under the influence of Lucifer. And now we can see how it has come about that we have received such an inner form; it is because of the influence of Lucifer in Earth evolution. We perceive also that this Earth evolution under the influence of Lucifer has given to man supersensible gifts one after another. Wisdom and everything connected with wisdom comes to man by many and manifold paths from Lucifer. Lucifer can show man, when he meets him, how much man really owes to him. But what I described just now has also to be reckoned among the things man owes to Lucifer". (Steiner: Man in the Light of Occultism, Theosophy and Philosophy, Lecture VIII, Christiania, 10th June, 1912).

The hovering Figure of "Fragment of a Crucifixion", 1950, (ill. 103) may not be everyone's idea of a dragon and I am not definitively implying that it is, however there are a number of points to be considered. Firstly the creature does have prototype wings and secondly there can be little doubt that it is a 'wild, savage' entity. Also it has to be taken very seriously that Bacon was adamant in his determination to eschew the pictorial, and it appears that he simply had very little interest in symbolic representations, per se. This being so it has to be concluded that Bacon actually perceived the presence of, within the total ambit of our spirituality, distorted and ghastly chimera that are a caricature of ourselves. It also has to considered that it is not only the luciferic spirits that distort, deform and warp our originary being but the ahrimanic and asuric spirits as well.

An Other.

So far it has been intimated that our 'higher' selves have a close affinity with the **Eternal** where the not-yet-formed exists and which is ruled by the force of levity, whereas our 'lower' selves have a closer connection with the gravity-ruled, subconscious on the plane of time where the formed and set presides. Consequently, because gravity primarily exerts an accretive, cohesive force, there is in the subconscious regions a strong propensity to create strongly contoured forms which are resilient to change. However it must not be imagined that these subconscious formations in the soul are in any way similar to the objects perceived in the natural world; they are not. Instead they have a dream-like substantiality and behave in a manner similar to dream images, and are able to come and go, and in a very limited way to dissolve into and interpenetrate other formations. These formations are semi-visible and turbid in appearance and are related to the antipathy pole of the soul. This semi-visibilty escapes our attention in the flow of everyday life, but is occasionally noticeable in times of distress or momentaily heightened consciousness, and so these formations are accessible to everyday perception in a hapzard and unpredictable manner. In contrast the formations related to the sympathy pole are light-filled and absolutely transparent to ordinary perception, because we have not developed and controlled our perceptive faculties so as to distinguish the various subtle manifestations of light in which they live. This why there is a rich and vivid store, culturally, of accounts and descriptions of the formations related to the 'lower' self, whereas accounts and references to those related to our 'higher' selves and higher worlds are much vaguer and more insubstantial.

The argument presented concerning the existence, or otherwise, of various phenomena and 'invisible' worlds has always taken its starting-point from simple observations that can easily be made in everyday life, and the case is no different when considering those entities created through our desires and passions. In performing the following experiment, or exercise, presented by Steiner for the examination of our life histories, we initially focus upon the gap that exists between what we desire and that which we subsequently achieve together with those inexplicable instances of success and failure.

"Let us look around a little at our lives. Here is a useful experiment for everyone. We could gather together all the things we cannot see the causes of, that is, successes that led us to say 'Even a fool can be right sometimes'- in short successes we cannot attribute to ourselves. We can do the same for failures and for those seemingly accidental outer events for which we know no of no motivating influence. And now we can make the following experiment. We construct in our mind an artificial human being, so to speak, who through his own abilities brought about all of those of our successes we cannot explain....or in the case of an outer event, we proceed in this way: let us say a brick falls on our head. We can see no reason for this, but we imagine someone who brought it about by running up on the roof and loosening the brick, so that it could only be a short time before it must fall down. Then this person runs down quickly and the brick hits him. We can do this with events that with our ordinary consciousness we know that we have not brought about, events that sometimes happen very much against our will." (Steiner, 2003: 87).

Here Steiner has provided us with very simple but specific instructions for approaching the enigmatic nature of our lives. The applicability of this exercise is infinite. If this exercise is performed with due diligence it soon becomes apparent that our consciousness consists largely of associated emotional reactions and predetermined thought patterns over which we have little control or sway, as described above. That is, although, in everyday life we feel we are freely living our lives there is in actual fact a second, 'hidden' self, or Double. This has already been commented upon with respect to the 'lower' self, and it has been indicated how what may loosely be called the negative and destructive patterns of thinking, feeling and willing give rise to a dark super-sensible entity that has volition simply because we have given a part of our soul-life to it, and, due to it's nature, it attracts to it those beings who have been described, above, as the adversarial forces. The cultivation of postive thinking, feeling and willing similarly gives rise to a light-filled entity that attracts to it those light-filled beings struggling to ensure that our evolution takes a propitious course. The super-sensible dimension of our being is extremely complex, and until an individual takes some measure of control over the forces that comprise one's soul the individual will be unable to discern any order to the pattern of their life. The shocking realisation is that we largely conduct our lives at the behest of that which is 'invisible', and that consequently, to begin with, the space for free, truly inspired, thinking is relatively small. Whereas the majority of people happily carry on with their lives despite this state of affairs, it is not difficult to find individuals who are instinctively aware of this condition and who attempt to do something about it.

Although this exercise at first appears an incongruous act to undertake Steiner does illuminate it through an analogy. Steiner stated that one can grasp the existence of this Other by imagining all the events, good or bad, of one's life fulfilling the role of the habits and actions of an 'invisible' animal, that to continue the above would be related to either the positive or negative aspects of our being. To take the analogy further, let us say we imagined that a cat, or any other creature, was invisible to us in the natural world we inhabit, we would, nevertheless, be aware of its existence through all the changes that occurred in the environment due to this invisible animal living out its life. However this is not all that Steiner had to say on this subject and he also indicated the essential connection that our actions have to our environment, to the social context especially, and that performing this exercise brings one into a better relationship with one's destiny. Steiner also indicated that this 'artificial human being' develops and changes over time:

"At first it seems to us merely grotesque to do this, perhaps even without understanding the reason for it. However, everyone who tries this will make a strange discovery, namely, the astonishing discovery that he or she no longer wants to get rid of this being but rather begins to find it interesting. If you try it, you will see for yourself: you cannot get away from this artificial human being; it lives within you. And strangely enough, it not only lives within us, but it also transforms itself radically to such an extent that at last it becomes something completely different from what it had been. It turns into something we must admit indeed exists within us..Now this is just what has, so to speak, brought about the things in our life that have apparently no causes…In other words, what I have described to you is not only the way to look into your own soul life and find something, but also the way from the soul life into the environment. For our failures do not remain with us, but belong to our environment. We have taken something out of our environment that does not agree with the facts of our consciousness, but presents itself as if it were within us. Then we get the feeling that we really have something to do with events that seem to have no cause in real life. In this way we get a sense of our connection with our destiny…When our soul follows such paths, it becomes used not only to living within itself, in its own wishes and desires, but to seeing its relationship to outer events and to considering them…Then we can face our destiny in such a way that we can calmly take it upon us." Steiner, 2003: 88-89.

In trying to understand these differing dimensions of ourselves it is not a struggle against the 'lower self' that is required, but rather an approach that integrates, and transforms, this aspect of our being into the totality of our personality. This is achieved by re-establishing the link between the inner and the outer, or if you will between the subject and the object, by treating oneself as an Other to be known and understood, as one would treat another person. A reconciliation with, or understanding of, the 'lower self' therefore can only be achieved, to start with, by coming to terms with the 'otherness' of our own 'self'. The above statements by Steiner, together with the accompanying thoughts, fill out the previous commentary regarding, when it is considered, the absolute 'otherness' of our own self, the starting-point for which is the realisation that I am not either my thoughts or my feelings - I merely have them.

"Only when you have made good all your past misdeeds and have so purified yourself that all further evil is impossible for you, only then will my being be transformed into radiant beauty. Then, too, I shall again be able to unite with you for the blessing of your future activity." (Steiner,1993: 194).

From such remarks it is arguable that the 'forgotten' self that is our state of consciousness when born is intimately related to the 'lower' self in that dimensions of the 'lower self' are a distorted caricature of the 'forgotten' self, and that it is through an unmitigated, slavish adherence to our habits and inclinations, that have been little purified that entraps the 'forgotten' self within the configuration of the 'lower' self. Consequently the 'forgotten' self can only be released by the development of our 'higher' self so as to transform the 'lower' self thereby blunting the capacity of the 'lower self' to captivate and enrapture the ego. It has been demonstrated, above, how Bacon's portraits of George Dyer depict the progression of that which is 'invisible' into a deleterious condition through Dyer's persistence in his habits and refusal to change. But it was argued that this depiction by Bacon was in no way metaphorical, but based upon the facts as he perceived them, namely that Dyer through his life-style created a virulent transformation of his 'lower' self into an entity that had no other aim than to utterly destroy and ruin Dyer. Bacon also indicated how Dyer's habits fed and maintained the growth of this entity until Dyer's demise. This 'entity' the potential of which dwells within all of us, can only come to fruition, that is grow and develop, through our actions both mental and physical. Steiner's exercise outlined above has the effect of focussing attention upon this invisible 'other self', which for the purposes here is multi-dimensional, and which is for the majority of people a fairly innocuous mixture of positive and negative aspects/ propensities, even if it has potentially lethal consequences for those not mindful of their individual responsibilities. This commentary has drawn attention to a more subtle dimension of movement/ dynamism inherent to Bacon's imagery, for Bacon had a particular awareness of the movement and dynamism of *invisible* phenomena that dwell upon the mental planes of our existence, something that we are barely, if at all, aware of in our ordinary consciousness.

Bacon's Demons.

From the early 1950's onward Bacon's awareness of the presence of the psychic configurations spoken of gradually evolved. His early attempts to depict these entities, or conditions, had its genesis with 'strange spaces' that contain distorted Figures undergoing various distressing emotional states that cause their psychic disintegration. Thus when the 'Pope' series is viewed, and it is stated that Bacon is through the Pope depicting humanities struggle against inexorable forces largely of its own making, this point is emphasised by Bacon's use of the crucifixion, a universal symbol of suffering. "Fragment of a Crucifixion", 1950, (ill. 103) shows demonic beings crawling over a crucifixion that abuts, or joins onto, an everyday scene of a busy high-street. The figure of Christ is completely absent being replaced by grotesque shapes, beings or things. This image has already been

248

commented upon extensively above, nevertheless it is the case that an image can be examined from varied aspects without ever exhausting its meaning, and with this image Bacon created an image of immense ramifications. Due to the fact that Bacon's declared intent was to expunge any 'storytelling' we do not know whether Christ has been crucified or is about to be crucified, and so we do not know whether these demonic beings relate to events before or after the crucifixion. This creates a stasis, a sort of interruption, in the way we usually view, for the attempt to 'read' the image in terms of the dialogue with which a crucifixion is traditionally considered is stymied—a 'fragment of a crucifixion'.

"Fragment of a Crucifixion" has overtones of that genre of works that take the 'Descent from the Cross' as their subject-matter. The bestial figures of this work descend into a tubular frame that traverses the foreground of the picture. We cannot make sense of the spatial relationships in the picture as being that of one homogenous space for it can be read as a cross on a hill against the background of an everyday high-street with people and traffic passing apparently oblivious to the suffering being undergone on the cross, or it can be read as a series of events taking place in a room where everyday life is hypothetically depicted and referenced in the two picture-panels either side of the cross, and where the cross then becomes the wall of the room. This ambiguity between background and foreground serves to heighten the hallucinatory atmosphere of this work. The former interpretation would imply the lack of concern that humanity, as a whole, expresses for the suffering of its fellow beings having only an interest in its own limited perspective, whereas the latter reading would imply that the suffering undergone by an individual, through the wall of the room functioning as a crucifixion, is something that is an internal and private affair.

The monstrosities depicted in this work have a similarity with the three Figures depicted in the three panels of the triptych "Three Studies for Figures at the Base of a Crucifixion", 1944, (ill. 105). However, the three Figures depicted in this latter work have an emotional distance from us the viewers; we are able to separate them from our emotional world. Partly this is due to their depiction hinting at them being exhibits, but is largely due to the fact that they can interpreted, in relation to the title of the work, as relating to the theme of the three monkeys that 'Speak no evil, Hear no evil, See no evil', thus giving them a literary quality that blunts their emotional impact upon us. There is here the first appearance of our insensitivity and disregard to the suffering of others. "Painting 1946", (ill. 33) is very close to "Three Studies for Figures at the Base of a Crucifixion" not only chronologically but thematically as well, and this work indicates that the origin for this mass insensitivity lies in dark, malevolent recesses of the human psyche. The Figure in this work exudes a powerful, malignant atmosphere that mocks the very notion of Christian virtues, and if it could speak would surely say "This is what you are deep down, why struggle to be any different". In the work "Fragment of a Crucifixion", 1950, (ill. 103) an external and an internal approach to the problem of 'evil' are brought into conjunction in the same space in such a manner that we can discern indications for the future direction of Bacon's treatment of individual suffering.

Furthermore there is in "Fragment of a Crucifixion" an animated and persecutory character to the central bestial creature that projects the impression that if it were able to it would fly out of the picture and attack whoever happened to be in the vicinity. This impression is emphasised by the fact that it is possible, as stated, to detect wing-like structures on its shoulders that give it the appearance of an infernal half-animal, half-insect abomination hovering in the air as it scrutinises its surroundings for a suitable target. As a result this work has a gripping fascination that engages the viewer's attention in a more direct and visceral way than "Three Studies for Figures at the Base of a Crucifixion". This persecutory element to Bacon's imagery that also occurs with the Dyer works is not of my invention, but issues from Bacon's interest in Greek tragedy and the phenomenon of the Furies, which as stated above he claimed to be able to perceive; and these Furies are grotesque, elemental beings full of vindictiveness and malice brought into being through acts of 'evil', and which then proceed to harass and hound those who perpetrated these acts. The bestial creature on the cross in "Fragment of a Crucifixion", from this interpretation, is thus a universal symbolic depiction of a 'fury' that issues from humanities crimes against itself and insensitivity to the suffering of *others*. George Peppiatt makes reference to this theme in his book "Francis Bacon" with the following words

"...and he read William Bedell Stanford's *Aeschylus in his Style*...this fascinating, highly specialized study ....made a deep impression on the artist. Clearly, the theme of obsessive guilt....had great resonance for him. Time and again, the sense of guilt and suffering...runs almost tangibly through his painting, as if it were embodied in the thick swirls of paint...The Furies were a personal reality for Bacon...he felt himself pursued by them. In one interview, filmed in 1964 in his studio, he admitted in a jocular but unequivocal aside that the Furies 'visited' him." (Peppiatt, 1996: 90-91).

Given the trajectory of this *critique* there is no reason to doubt that Bacon had an actual perception of these beings, which can also be related to that which is inherited through the blood and to the deformed emotional entities of our 'lower' self, for Steiner stated that with the evolution of our intellectually-based, modern awareness the Furies metamorphosed into our conscience; a sense of right and wrong. To be more precise Steiner in the series of lectures "Metamorphosis of the Soul" stated that consciousness in Ancient Greece was such that there was no conscience as we know it, as an inner voice, instead there was a perception of the consequences of an action.

"...what does the seer tell us concerning the human conscience of those times when a man had, for example, committed an evil deed? His deed did not present itself to him as something he could inwardly assess. He beheld it with all its harmfulness and shamefulness as a ghostly vision confronting his soul. And when a feeling concerning his evil deed arose within his soul, the shamefulness of it came before him as a spiritual reality, so that he was as though surrounded by a vision of the evil he had wrought." (Steiner, 1983: 109).

This change of consciousness from that of Ancient Greece to the intellectual ego-based consciousness of our time meant that an individual was no longer able to perceive the effects of their actions in the Emotional world, but had instead a nagging 'inner voice'.

."Then, in the course of time, this dreamlike clairvoyance faded and man's ego increasingly came to the fore. In so far as man found this central point of his being within himself, the old clairvoyance was extinguished and self-consciousness established itself more and more clearly. The vision he previously had of his good and bad deeds was transposed into his inner life, and deeds once clairvoyantly beheld were mirrored in his soul." (Steiner, 1983: 109).

This is the situation we now have, where if one commits an 'evil' act we do not perceive the consequences of this act but rather we cognise what we have done within an intellectual framework of moral concepts. Some individuals lead tormented inner lives because of the thoughts and feelings associated with what they have perpetrated and how they conduct themselves, and these thoughts and feelings, for them, lead a life of their own that is in essence accusatory. However it is possible to perceive, when one has developed one's powers, the entities that stand behind these inner voices, and Peppiatt indicates that Bacon had this capacity through Bacon's own admissions.

"Bacon explained his fascination with the *Oresteia* by saying that the play 'bred' images in him – that a particular phrase or figure of speech might trigger off a sequence of visual associations in his imagination which in turn fed into his paintings. The fragment which he quoted most frequently – 'The reek of human blood smiles out at me' – is uttered by the leader of the Furies as they close in around the hunted Orestes in Athena's shrine." (Peppiatt, 1996: 91).

It is very easy to overlook the significance of Bacon's statement that the *Oresteia* 'bred' images in him - what could Bacon have meant? I have already highlighted Bacon's highly developed powers of concentration above, and clearly the text of the *Oresteia* acted as a meditative focus for those powers. Consequently the instrumental significance of Bacon's fascination with Aeschylus' 'Oresteia' is that Bacon focussed upon the very historical point when there was a change in functioning of human conscience. I will not develop this point further, however it is perfectly possible that Bacon was able to perceive the plane of time from a higher viewpoint, as described above, so as to become cognisant of these events in the spiritual world. Steiner in his analysis of this period shows how through the works of Aeschylus and Sophocles we can witness the struggle to express this change through dramatic works.

251

"It is not very long since the time when the birth of conscience can be seen to occur. If we look back to the fifth and sixth centuries BC, we encounter in ancient Greece the great dramatic poet Aeschylus...Aeschylus shows how the burden of matricide calls forth in Orestes a mode of seeing which was no longer normal in those times...Orestes sees before him, in dreamlike clairvoyance, the effect of his matricide in its external form...Aeschylus wished to indicate that a still higher cosmic ordinance obtains, and this he could only do by making Orestes clairvoyant at that moment. For he had not yet gone far enough to dramatise what today we call an inner voice. If we study his work, we feel that he was at the stage when something like conscience ought to emerge from the content of the human soul, but he never quite reached that point."
(Steiner, 1983: 110-111).

"Now we will pass over Sophocles and come to Euripides who described the same situation only a generation later...Here we have palpable evidence of the stages whereby the idea of conscience was taken hold of by the art of poetry. We see how Aeschylus, great poet though he was, cannot speak of conscience itself, while his successor, Euripides, does speak of it...The force now active in conscience was also active in ancient times; the pictures showing the effects of man's deeds arose before his clairvoyant sight. The only difference is that this force became internalised..."
(Steiner, 1983: 111).

Aeschylus thus attempted to dramatise the transformation from the old clairvoyant consciousness, where the consequences of one's 'evil' acts were perceived as malicious Emotional entities that hounded the perpetrator of the acts, to the emerging ego-consciousness, where these forces become internalised as 'inner voices' that will not leave an individual alone, but was unable to fully grasp, dramatically, the import of this change, and so is an individual who records a turning-point in human consciousness, whereas it is with Euripides that we find the first hints of what we now understand as 'conscience'.

These quotes graphically illustrate the fact that Blood was not merely a material fluid to Bacon, but that he perceived it as relating to the very depths of our psyche. Steiner's statements concerning the development of the higher nervous system and the relation of this to the Blood now have a specificity that also relates to Bacon's imagery. It is not without foundation to state that Blood is a gateway to the perception of supersensible entities because of its intimate connection to the Emotional realms and the Ego. Bacon's own statements and his images – "Two Studies for a Portrait of George Dyer" – provide the evidence that it is highly likely that Bacon was indeed able to perceive the spiritual entities that we create through the nature of our actions. This is reinforced by the images that he created concerning the sympathetic nervous system and the higher nervous system, and the relationship of this, as the above quotes by Steiner demonstrate, to Aeschylus, whose "Oresteia" Bacon found so fascinating - as expressed with his work

252

"Triptych Inspired by the Oresteia of Aeschylus", (ill. 34). After "Fragment of a Crucifixion" Bacon turns away from such depictions, perhaps because, they have an illustrational quality, of that which hounds and pursues an individual in favour of an examination of the effect of these entities upon the outer appearance of an individual's physiognomy. Hence the 'Pope' series and the 'Businessman' series that Bacon produced during the 1950's, and he did not return to the depiction of those entities productive of states of severe mental distress, and ungoverned appetites, until the 1960's with the images he created of George Dyer.

That which cannot be Named.

There is no disagreement in this text with the facts of scientific enquiry, only with the interpretation of those facts, for which there is always scope to reinterpret if knowledge is to advance. This has always been the case with any theory, be it that of a flat earth or the genesis of the human being. During the course of this critique I have referenced the Body Schema, a well-known invisible phenomenon related to our corporeal body, and proffered a review of this from the perspective of alternative evidence. This has been necessary for there is a reluctance to accept that everyday phenomena when examined from differing angles display extraordinary features that are simply ignored in the course of events, such as the fact that a plant demonstrates differing time-modes during its process of its growth.

Such a case has arisen with the 'invisible' dimensions of the human being discussed here. So far the argument has presented evidence that there is with emotional configurations, of any composition, the appearance that they are in possession of some sort of volition, or 'unknown' life-force. If the hypothesis presented here has any validity then instead of calling such negative entities that afflicted Dyer as 'evil', which only serves to evoke outmoded visions of past representations and mechanical thinking, there has to be a re-evaluation of the concept 'evil'. Although such a re-evaluation is implicit in Bacon's imagery it will not be pursued at this point, rather it will be shown how it is possible to familiarise oneself with 'invisible' aspects of our being by refining our sensitivity of how they impinge upon ordinary consciousness. This fundamentally requires that an individual initiates a radical re-evaluation of the course of their life by paying particular attention to the role played by successes and failures in determining the course that their life has taken, as discussed above. To fulfil such a purpose Steiner's simple exercise, highlighted above, utilised a methodology that is no different than that deployed by Bacon, Goethe and any competent scientist, and that is by making precise, exact and unprejudiced observations, with particular emphasis upon abandoning any preconceptions regarding the nature of that which is observed. In this case it is through an examination of the nature of our soul as it unfolds through the events that constitute the course of our lives.

As human beings we have the opportunity of following either of two paths, one path leads to the purification and transformation of our state of being into that which is worthy of unimaginable, higher states of consciousness, the other path leads to states of being that would be of an equally unimaginable blackness and 'evil' from a human perspective. As human beings we hover between the two paths and have the freedom to choose which one to follow. The significance of this terrifying, darker aspect of ourselves becomes apparent if we make a general, preliminary examination of the Western psyche, where a defining characteristic of the Western psyche is that of anxiety and fear. This has been much commented upon throughout the 20th Century, from one direction through the chronicling of the effect of Modernism on our state of well-being, and so requires no further explanation, but this fact was also perfectly plain to Steiner as he made clear in the cycle of lectures entitled "Cosmosophy", vol. 1, Lecture I. So far our ordinary consciousness has been described as primarily making use of our intellectual capacities for the ordering and manipulation of abstract concepts derived from sense impressions that have been worked over by our feelings and will, that is through our feelings and will we psychically 'digest' sense impressions. The effect of our abstract, intellectual consciousness is to produce what may be called an 'objective self-consciousness', in that an individual is able to perceive themselves, objectively, as an empirical object amongst the array of empirical objects available to sense-perception, and this ability, from the perspective of this text, is known as the 'consciousness soul', which has still a long way to go before even approaching anything which may be termed maturity. Our corporeal body together with the body of Formative Forces, as discussed above, behaves in the manner of a 'mirror' so that our consciousness is able to cognise sense-impressions, consequently we are only aware of reflections of the outer world because our ordinary consciousness cannot penetrate into the inner reality of the phenomena we perceive. The overall implication of this is that we are aware of the contents of our consciousness only as abstract intellectual concepts derived from an assessment of only the surface of the phenomena that comprise the 'outer' world.

"The ordinary human being of today is aware of the world around him by means of his outer, physical sense impressions. What he sees, he orders and arranges with his intellect. Then he looks also into his inner being. Basically this is the world that man surveys and out of which he acts. The sense impressions received from the outside, the mental images developed from these sense impressions, these mental images as they penetrate within, become transformed by impulses of feeling and will, together with everything that is reflected back into consciousness as memories – here we have what forms the content of the soul, the content of life in which man weaves and out of which he acts" (Steiner, 1985: 6).

"This ordinary consciousness, however, only emerges from what actually originated in outer sense impressions and has been transformed by feeling and will. One finds only the reflections, the mirror-images, of outer life when looking into one's inner being with ordinary consciousness; and although the outer impressions are transformed by feeling and will, man still does not know how feeling and will actually work. For this reason he often fails to recognise what he sees in his inner

being as a transformed mirror-image of the outer world and takes it, perhaps, as a special message from the divine, eternal world. This is not the case, however. What appears to the ordinary consciousness of modern man as self-knowledge is only the transformed outer world, which is reflected out of man's inner being into his consciousness."
(Steiner, 1985: 7).

The picture that arises is that our consciousness acts like a skin that has been stretched over the surface of the world, and so we resemble those water-spiders that run across the surface of a lake unaware of the depths below and the heights above, where the surface-tension that keeps the insect afloat metaphorically reflects the manner by which we are attached to our immediate desires, passions and intellectualisations. The commentary so far has endeavoured to show how even though everyday consciousness can be considered an illusory construction (analysis of perspective, how thinking is wedded to the intellectual and earthly) it is at the same time entirely necessary for our present state of evolution and development. However, the desire for self-knowledge is one that echoes down the ages, and is no less insistent today than in ancient times, but Steiner made it clear that no amount of intellectual ponderings on the content of one's soul will achieve this end. Instead Steiner pointed out that it is necessary to get 'behind' this content of ordinary consciousness, or as he puts it to 'break the mirror' that reflects the mirror-images derived from sensory impressions.

Deleuze comes close to this understanding "Hence the fascination: nothing is behind the mirror, everything is inside it" (Deleuze, 2004: 18). Deleuze comes close because a 'mirror' is only an analogy for how we perceive the reflections spoken of, and when we penetrate this surface that has 'everything inside it' we reach the spiritual realities and not the back of a mirror. This astute insight by Deleuze also relates to the above commentary concerning the 'great outpouring' with respect to a mirror, and, as it has been emphasised, the Gothean, scientific methodology is the healthiest means presently available for humanity of achieving knowledge of the essential nature of the Cosmos and its phenomena.

The re-absorption of the consciousness of the early years of infancy, the 'forgotten self', into adult consciousness has been likened to an ascent up the pole of the ego that stands at a right-angle to the plane of time, and to understand Steiner's statements it is necessary to take this analogy further. If an individual has reached the stage of integrating their 'forgotten self' into their adult consciousness this is not the end of the process and further ascent upon the pole of the Ego is possible. This process does not leave the corporeal body behind, and as one rises upon the pole of the Ego not only is there a deepening of cognition of the structure of the Cosmos but of the absolute integration of our being into the Cosmos. There is, for instance, a more intimate understanding of the consciousness associated with the sympathetic nervous system, which reflects the working of the Cosmos, except now it is in clear consciousness and not in the dull dream-like manner of the atavistic clairvoyance of ancient peoples. Once the reflecting 'mirror' of our corporeality has been 'broken' or 'penetrated', so to speak, one becomes aware that the human metabolism is a sphere of intense destruction. (The sympathetic nervous system regulates all the functions that appertain to the corporeal body, and is also the seat for the will). When Steiner speaks of 'breaking the mirror' he is in one sense referring to the fact that we have to let go of the fascinating picture world that arises through the integration of the 'forgotten self' so as to allow other dimensions of perception to develop. At its most simple level this sphere of destruction functions to provide, by breaking down the *forms of the food* we eat, the conditions whereby we may have a physical body and so be able to have ego-consciousness and thinking.

"… what is harmful to plants is natural for men and animals: when taking in nourishment the latter are able to bring about quickly and purposefully a transformation of matter into the purely dynamic state. Their metabolic system is designed to take alien material from outer nature and to transform it through the forces of various enzymes; in the course of this process the material passes through a condition of complete 'chaos', in order to emerge from this state in a form typical of the species." (Lehrs, 1985: 272-273).

Steiner thus describes our metabolic system as a 'fury of destruction', and he states that if we are to ascend, to develop, we have to become conscious of this fact, if we do not then it will break out and penetrate our *instincts*.

"Thereupon a complete transformation arises of the material existence that is within the physical body of man …. Within the human being, matter is completely dissolved into nothingness. The very essence of matter is fully destroyed. It is precisely upon this fact that our human nature is based: upon being able to throw back matter into chaos, to destroy matter utterly, within that sphere that lies deeper than memory." (Steiner, 1985: 8-9).

"Within Western civilisation man is the sheath for a source of destruction, and actually the forces of decline can be transformed into the forces of ascent only if man becomes conscious of this, that he is the sheath for a source of destruction." (Steiner, 1985: 10).

" If, therefore, a person ventures into this inner being of man with the same attitude with which he penetrates as far as memory, he enters a realm of being where man wants to destroy, to extinguish, what is there. For the purpose of developing the human, thought-filled 'I' or ego, we all bear within us, below the memory-mirror, a fury of destruction, a fury of dissolution, in relation to matter." (Steiner, 1985: 9).

This is connected with the implications of the fact that humanity, in general, is 'crossing the threshold'. Rather than this being merely theoretical and abstract Steiner was at pains to indicate where such states of affairs were observable at the time of the lectures in 1921.

"What would happen if man were not to be led by spiritual science out of this consciousness? Already in the evolution of our time we can see what would happen. What is isolated, separated, as it were, in the human being, and should work only *within* him, at the single spot where matter is thrown back into chaos, now breaks out and penetrates human instincts. That is what will happen to Western civilisation, yes, and to the civilisation of the whole earth. This is shown by all the destructive forces appearing today – in Eastern Europe, for instance. It is a fury of destruction thrust out of the inner being of man into the outer world... ". (Steiner, 1985: 10).

The overall conclusion by Steiner is that unless this 'fury of destruction' that is necessary for our ego-consciousness, which is our metabolic system, is not consciously grappled with then the 'destruction' that it represents will spread over the whole world with disastrous consequences.

"Here is the source of destruction, here the human sheath. If what is inside were to spread out over the whole world, what would then live in the world through man? Evil! Evil is nothing but the chaos thrust outside, the chaos that is necessary in man's inner being. In this chaos which must be within man, this necessary source of evil in man, the human I, the human egoity, must be forged." (Steiner, 1985: 14).

So it is that these matters are not merely abstract and intellectually based but of the utmost importance, and this is emphasised by the fact that humanity is 'crossing the threshold' thereby becoming instinctively aware of dimensions of our being hidden from everyday consciousness. Virtually everyone is aware of the events that occurred in Germany throughout the decadent Weimar republic (see Dix and Beckmann) and the subsequent rise of the Nazi party, and the monstrous acts committed in its name after 1921 when Steiner delivered these lectures.

Various commentators have attempted to relate Bacon's work to the events of W.W. II, and the subsequent horror felt at the abominable acts perpetrated by the Nazi's; actions which, sadly, we are all to familiar with in this day and age. However, it is arguable when considering the effect of social conditions upon Bacon's state of mind that W.W.I is more crucial. The fact that Bacon lived in Berlin in the late 1920's as a young man before living in Paris, and then settling in London, would have exposed him to the then current awareness of the chronic aftermath of W.W.I and its subsequent effect upon European consciousness. These are well-documented facts and it is inconceivable that an intelligent and sensitive young man, as Bacon was, could have been left unmoved by such events. "Painting 1946", (ill. 33) and "Figure in a Landscape", 1941, (ill. 36) are now interpretable in the light of the above commentary as a touchstone depictions of the malevolent forces that dwell within the human being, for we see a dark, brutal Figures that with their blackness and grimness are the very antithesis of all that is human; (the

Lesser Guardian of the Threshold) harbingers of doom. From this perspective "Three Studies for Figures at the Base of a Crucifixion", 1941, (ill. 105) displays Figures that embody how a 'fury of destruction' is engendered through a perversion of our instincts. Bacon has placed the Figure of "Painting 1946" within a framework that acts as a metaphor for the Counter-Space of Formative Forces, as has been delineated above, so as to indicate that if one presses into the inner being of man, below the memory-mirror of 'normal' consciousness, one encounters within oneself this terrifying spectre of the Lesser Guardian of the Threshold. The evidence for Bacon's awareness of these facts comes from his own work. Illustration 41 is a reproduction of the central section of "Painting 1946" and in it we are able to perceive a ghostly visage, this is particularly noticeable when one concentrates on the upper, left hand side where there is a quite distinct eye, with the curve of the head, complemented by a less distinct eye to the right, and where if one looks closely there are hints of a nose and mouth below. There are unmistakeable cat-like and reptilian overtones to these features. "Figure in a Landscape", 1945, echoes this interpretation for what image better expresses a 'fury of destruction' than a headless figure, functioning from the metabolic (the seat of the will) alone, that is indiscriminately firing a machine-gun. I will now repeat an earlier passage in the section on Digestion so as to emphasise the depth of Bacon's understanding

"When the infant receives nothing he cries, and when the stomach is not fed, it begins to 'growl', because its desires have not been fulfilled. Imagine a hungry living creature such as a cat, a dog, or even a baby, and picture it as a stomach – only then do you have the right idea of what the stomach is." (Buhler: 1979, 79).

If it is accepted that the ghostly creature present in the Bacon work, (ill. 83) is not a figment of my imagination, which it clearly is not, and that Bacon did not create it by chance – an absurd notion at the best of times – then we have a remarkable agreement concerning our metabolic-limb system between two entirely unrelated individuals, one a doctor the other an artist. There are many images that demonstrate that Bacon was aware of how our metabolic-limb system operates autonomously despite the fact that it is inseparably intertwined with the thinking and feeling systems in a living human being. Clearly "Painting", 1946, is one such image and another is "Painting", 1978, (ill. 54) which depicts a Figure in the act of opening a door with its foot. The metabolic-limb system is emphasised by the reduction of the Figure's functioning to its legs, whilst the will is stressed by the focus upon the keyhole of the Figure's gaze. The thinking dimension of the Figure is rendered explicit through the depiction of the discarded newsprint upon the floor, the subtlety of this metaphor for thinking is that once a newspaper is read it is laid aside, and similarly once we have finished thinking upon a subject it is laid aside except that in this case it is laid aside within the memory. Our feeling dimension is referenced in this work through the rhythms of the work which are integrated more complexly within the overall composition of this work than "Painting", 1946, and particularly by the overall ambience of the work which combines a mood of forlornness with excited anticipation.

It is to Bacon's credit that after these images, and ones closely associated to them, he went on to depict images that reflect the struggles of the higher aspects of our being. Rather than focussing upon this terrifying dimension of our being he chose to represent how we tussle to overcome and deal with these forces within ourselves so as to maintain a civilised existence.

Chapter 7. The Chymical Wedding of Christian Rosenkreutz.

When we view Bacon's images of the female nude it is a mistake to take these as depictions of a naked woman. Western figurative art has, since Michelangelo until the mid to late 19th century, focussed upon the physicality of the human form. There has been a degeneration of the magnificence of Michelangelo's vision of the human form (female as well as male) to that of a coarse sensualism and sexuality that demeans our dignity. Not that the beauty and sensuality of the female is to be ignored, denigrated, or, for that matter, not to be celebrated, it is just that the common focus upon the female form as a *desirable object,* together with a focus upon the prowess and muscularity of the male, has precipitated a vulgarity and crudity of vision in popular culture that is mercilessly pursued for economic reasons . Bacon's depiction of the female Figure is one that severely abuses such expectations to such an extent that one at first wonders if there was a misogynistic element to his creativity. Certainly this was one of my first reactions and it was only when I realised the error of taking Bacon's female Figures as individual works rather components of a *whole*, that I realised that Bacon's female nudes are an examination of the *crisis of the feminine dimension of the human being*, not only for the individual but our entire culture. As far as I am concerned the debate appertaining to the functioning of the masculine and feminine aspects of our being within the individual is obfuscated and distorted by the insistence of exclusively identifying them to our gendered existence. This in itself betrays the gross materialism of those who espouse a spiritual approach to these matters. Nevertheless it is the case that Bacon's female Figures are, in the main, literally of *fallen women*, I do not believe that Bacon by doing this was particularly interested in the subject of prostitution, still a subject that engenders wide-spread opprobrium and condemnation, rather I believe he was referring to the treatment of those supposedly feminine qualities, traditionally associated with the Muses, within a brutal and antihuman, materialistic culture. One can speculate endlessly on this topic and bring all sorts of ideological theories to bear upon Bacon's images of women, but what does this have to do with Bacon's work? In many cases it just serves to promote the agendas and careers of those proposing such conjectures.

I do not at this stage wish to explore the fact that Bacon chose females who were literally so-called *fallen women* within the context of his images of the Crucifixion, but rather to open up further dimensions of elements I deem to be pertinent to an understanding Bacon's *oeuvre,* in particular the 'forgotten self' of infancy within the context of the harmonisation of the two pillars of our Spirit and Soul in relation to our mind, and consciousness. As I have already indicated these are the Masculine and the Feminine that make themselves materially manifest through the two hemispheres of the brain. Fortunately modern science is ceasing to view these qualities as exclusively tied to either hemisphere of the brain. The manner by which the 'invisible' aspects of our being integrate with the 'visible', for instance the brain, dimensions of our being is through a correlative mode and not a one-to-one linear mode. Bacon is with these images of a *crisis of femininity* drawing attention to the bias, and subsequent impoverishment of consciousness, that has ensued for Epistemology through the dominance of a rampant, all-consuming Intellectualism. Through the example of Goethe it was demonstrated that human consciousness only finds its true meaning by bringing the Masculine and the Feminine into an harmonious resonance; a state that we unconsciously possess during infancy. The pertinence of this, interpretatively, for Bacon's images was demonstrated by indicating the relevance of concepts relating to the 'forgotten self' of infancy. Thus a viewer who mistakes the depiction of a female nude in Bacon's work as referring to the naked female form of their experience is very wide of the mark. The consequences of equating the Feminine purely with the corporeal, and this applies to the Masculine, is graphically illustrated by the Chymical Wedding of Christian Rosenkreutz'. Before going further, however, it is important to note, and this has already been referred to through the analysis of "Two Studies of George Dyer and Isabel Rawsthorne", 1970, (ill. 87), that neither a Man nor a Woman makes apparent the totality of the Masculine and the Feminine respectively, the ability to make explicit these at, present, ideal qualities lies in the future. In this respect the Chymical Wedding of Christian Rosenkreutz' is very instructive, for Christian Rosenkreutz's whole mission fails when he illicitly views the naked Venus in her bed after being warned not to do this. This medieval tale has a direct connection to the story of Dianae and Acteon, whereby the hunter Acteon espies the naked Dianae in a pool and is subsequently transformed into a stag, that is he loses an aspect of his humanity through his self-centred desires. The implication of this is that there is a loss of our spiritual status when the focus is upon the physicality of the Female alone. From one point-of-view 'The Chymical Wedding of Christian Rosenkreutz' is an account of the mysteries of the miraculous constitution of the human form from a cosmic perspective, and anyone who has read this tale cannot help but be struck by the rhythmic interweaving of the Masculine and the Feminine in a number of guises, indicating how the human form is brought into being through an interaction of the Cosmic Masculine and Feminine energies, and this is especially noticeable, for me, with respect to the fluidic element of our corporeality.

It has already been alluded to that one of the basic facets of our understanding of the Cosmos is that it functions through polarities that intensify and resonate with each other, and it appears that Bacon was fully aware of this fact. The fundamental polarity of society is that of the Self and the Other and how these integrate and resound through their interaction with each other, and the above has demonstrated how Bacon, through his work, explored such an interaction from many directions both private and public, as with "Three Portraits: Posthumous Portrait of G. Dyer, Self-Portrait and Portrait of L. Freud", 1973, (ill. 55), and "Portrait of Isabel Rawsthorne Standing in a Street in Soho", 1967, (ill. 51). If our social relations operate through the interfacing of Self and Other, then this is conditioned through the manner by which our individual consciousness has as its bedrock the relationship between the Masculine and the Feminine, and the means by which Bacon approached this fact, and made it explicit through his Figure, has already been referred to above.

Further Aspects of The Chymical Wedding of Christian Rosencruetz.

"The Chymical Wedding of Christian Rosencruetz", an esoteric and controversial document, as stated is in part concerned with how the Masculine and the Feminine dimensions of the human spirit mutually interact with each other so as to create the human body. Through modern research we now know that our consciousness, which is focussed upon the brain, operates through Masculine and Feminine qualities, which in turn have varying relationships with the two hemispheres of the brain. What this means is that the human spirit has two operative modes, each with its specific virtues, that enable it to act, through the auspices of the corporeal body, within the World. The tremendous importance of this fundamental fact is obscured and complicated by the fact of our gendered condition for the purpose of the propagation of the species. The volatility of the sexual instinct creates further confusion, for due to the pleasurable sensations associated with the release of sexual tension there ensues what may be described as a 'roaming across our the totality of our corporeality' of the sexual drive in search of a suitable object for the consummation of such desires, in the past such 'roaming' was subject to social sanctions. Consequently human sexuality is both divorced and attached to our corporeality in that an individual does not have to be governed, and determined, by the instinct to propagate the species, Rosencruetz's error was that he failed to cognise this fact and mistook the gendered woman as the Eternal Feminine. Given modern-day epistemological assumptions there is probably little point in drawing attention to the fact that, by and large, we alternate between masculine and female bodies in successive incarnations, nevertheless such knowledge illustrates one of the main proposals of this *critique* of Bacon's *oeuvre*, namely that a comprehension of the roles played by the Masculine and Feminine components of our psychology facilitates an unravelling of the mysteries of Bacon's Figures. Thus neither a man nor a woman possesses the fullness of either, and it is easily observable than a woman may display excessive masculinity and vice-versa. The modern-day fascination with brain chemistry, and the like, misses the point which is that no matter how much it can be shown that by altering the chemical balance of the brain etc., so that an individual subsequently displays transformed behaviour this does not mean that consciousness is an effect of its material base. I have already made the point that to think in such a manner is akin to believing that the ability to drive arises from the materiality of a car. However, this analogy also highlights that it is in conjunction with the materiality of the world that the human spirit acts in order to make its will manifest, an important point to bear in mind with respect to all artists.

One could state that Christian Rosencruetz on the threshold of further spiritual enlightenment lapsed into an abstract, intellectual thinking based upon his own desires and passions, that is, in effect he could not maintain the purity of his own development that had brought him to his present state of understanding, which

262

anyone who peruses this so-called fantasy will realise was based upon a fructification of his own imaginative and intellectual abilities. The fact we live in the shadow of Christian Rosencrantz 's error is demonstrated by the manner by which modern, everyday consciousness is predicated upon abstract, intellectual thinking, despite the wealth of published texts that focus upon modern research into the overall functioning of the brain from the perspective of the mental and physiological benefits to be gained from an harmonious and unbiased activation of all aspects of the materiality of the brain. In effect this means an educative programme that stimulates all the aspects of a child's spiritual constitution , something that then allows the brain to develop into an healthy organism rather than one that has an unhealthy imbalance. This in essence is the gist of Betty Edwards' book quoted in the introduction, the substance of which I will repeat here,

"But the emphasis of our culture is so strongly slanted toward rewarding left-brain skills that we are surely losing a very large proportion of the potential ability of the other halves of our children's brains. Scientist Jerre Levy has said … That American scientific training through graduate school may entirely *destroy* the right hemisphere. We certainly are aware of the effects of inadequate training in verbal, computational skills. The verbal left hemisphere never seems to recover fully, and the effects may handicap students for life. What happens, then, to the right hemisphere which is hardly trained at all?" (Edwards, 1979: 37).

And quoting from myself: 'A good question, which this text addresses, but the validity of Edward's analysis becomes more apparent if we continue with Bortoft's analysis of discoveries made in the field of child development. Bortoft's commentary revealed that the receptive mode specifically relates to the approximately first three years of life before we acquire the ability to speak, a period when we do not cognise the world through the auspices of our *brains*. The conclusion is drawn, following Edwards' statements, that the action mode relates to the left hemisphere, whereas the receptive mode relates to the right hemisphere, and that the right hemisphere is developed through play and exploration of the world up until the time of learning to speak when the action mode gradually begins to emerge and take over. The action mode becomes dominant with ego-consciousness, after which time as we know, the focus is exclusively, and this has become more so in the last few years, upon the left hemisphere skills and not right hemisphere skills'.

By those following the trajectory of my argument concerning the contrast between adult consciousness and that of infancy there will be the realisation that the fact that in infancy we do not think, or cognise, with our 'brains', simply because the use of the brain for intellectual, abstract thinking has not developed yet, is a vital component of the 'forgotten' self that has been discerned, above, as an important interpretative theme for an understanding of Bacon's iconography. In this respect it is also the case that the hand plays a vitally important role in the development of the brain, and an investigation of the role of the hand in the context of brain development has been provided by Frank Wilson in his book "The Hand". The fundamental conclusion arrived at by Wilson is that the hand when engaged in skilful activity causes neurological development, which in turn creates the opportunity for further creative thinking and language capacities:

"We are left with a rather startling but inescapable conclusion: it was the biomechanics of the modern hand that set the stage for the creation of neurological machinery needed to support a host of behaviours centred on skilled use of the hand. If the hand did not quite literally build the brain, it almost certainly provided the structural template around which an ancient brain built both a new system for hand control and a new bodily domain of experience, cognition and imaginative life … If the hand and brain learn to speak to each other intimately and harmoniously, something that humans seem to prize greatly which we call autonomy, begins to take shape." (Wilson, 1998).

Wilson's statement makes it clear that our evolution from so-called primitive states, both corporeally and mentally, to a modern condition is not something that happened through pure chance, but is a development that has been brought about, amongst other factors, through our willed activity. The link between our creative actions and our neurological development is not one that we have any consciousness of but nevertheless is taking place through every creative act we perform. This process, however, is not linear and finished, for as we create we are then able to contemplate our production, and through this contemplation initiate further creativity that eventually effects more changes in our neurological state, and so is a process that is 'correlative' and lemniscatory in nature. The human being is not a finished product and the difference now, in contrast to the past, is that we are gradually becoming conscious of the absolute interrelatedness of body, soul and spirit; and that this interrelatedness is now powered through a thinking, of which we are barely aware of the possibilities, that is the engine of our consciousness. The present stage of human development displays a struggle from being dependant upon the **Spirit** for its further evolution to a state that is dependant upon its own auspices. This is inevitable for nothing stays the same and we either rise to the challenge or fall behind, this can be summed up by stating that we free ourselves of the **Spirit**, as a guiding-principle in our evolution, so as to make manifest the glory of the **Spirit**. The fact of the absolute necessity of *play* for infants and children with its *free-form fantasy* (hand and senses) in effecting our development from child to adult is simply missed by the abstract and intellectual. In becoming ego-conscious beings we are all heirs to that which was achieved in the past, and it makes a great deal of difference of how we think and create to the outcome of our future development, in effect, henceforth, we have to take responsibility in full consciousness for how we evolve, no matter how tempting it is to dreamily blunder forward influenced by unbridled passions and dead thinking in the same old ways - a *new vision* is needed. This clearly relates to the statements at the end of the previous section upon the Lion and the Griffin.

264

Renewing the Past.

Deleuze was astute enough to recognise that Bacon reconstituted modes of representation related to the consciousness belonging to past cultures, in this instance the Haptic vision of ancient Egypt and, as already referenced, the Gothic line. Deleuze's analysis of Bacon's paintings centres upon how the two sides of the brain function in relation to the eye and the hand, not only in knowing the world but in subsequent artistic creation, and his account makes a distinction between four ways in which the hand may be deployed: the digital, the tactile, the manual proper and the Haptic. Deleuze's argument is that the digital represents the maximum subordination of the hand to the eye:

"...vision is internalised, and the hand is reduced to the finger; it intervenes only in order to choose the units that correspond to pure visual forms. The more the hand is subordinated in this way, the more sight develops an 'ideal' optical space, and tends to grasp its forms through an optical code." 10.

This would be the situation where one produces a *ruled* drawing purely based upon the rules and principles of perspective. Such a drawing displays no individual characteristics and its purpose could be to appraise someone of the lay-out of a particular locale, but it is possible for this type of drawing to include visual referents, such as depth and relief, in which case Deleuze says it would display the tactile aspect of the hand. This also applies to those styles of painting that are mimetic in their production, something that I am sure Bacon equated with 'story-telling'. The reverse, where the hand has complete control, thereby subordinating the eye is where the hand works to demolish all optical codes, and this is what Deleuze calls the 'manual proper'. The 'digital hand' (left hemisphere), as described by Deleuze would, therefore, be a tyrannical, unqualified submission of the hand to the abstraction of the intellect that defines the 'active mode of consciousness' as defined by Bortoft, and which predominates in our overall modern consciousness, whereas the 'manual proper' (right hemisphere) would be an anarchical display of the hand allied to the imagination, as per, Bortoft's childhood receptive phase of consciousness, but lacking any guidelines. Deleuze argues that a balance occurred, in the past, with the haptic, where the hand displays properties of 'seeing' and the eye displays properties of 'touching', the secret of which has been lost according to Deleuze. (Deleuze, 2003: 155).

Deleuze contends that the digital - the blueprint-like - is ever present in the thinking of an artist, and this I would maintain is true of everyone because of our evolution to an intellectually-based, ego-consciousness, which, as I have argued above, found expression through the means of Perspective to reflect this fact. The 'digital hand' (left hemisphere), therefore, would be a tyrannical, unqualified submission of the hand to the abstraction of the intellect that defines the *active mode of consciousness*, whereas the 'manual proper' (right hemisphere) would be an anarchical display of the hand allied to the imagination of the *receptive phase* of infancy, but lacking any guidelines. These two aspects of the hand can be summed-up as 'I am knowledge but I lack being' for 'digital hand', with 'I am imagination but I lack truth' for the 'manual proper'. The phrase 'I am knowledge but I lack being' has to be considered against the contrast between meaning and information. At the present time through the virtually exclusive deployment of our intellectuality for epistemological purposes there has been garnered an incalculable store of information about the world, this is readily understood as being the current state of affairs. This process continues unabated, and this accumulation of information may be compared to the amassing of a huge store of flour, which awaits the yeast to convert it into bread. In this analogy, the yeast stands for any 'meaning' that is intrinsic to the accumulated information. In the first instance, leaving aside the relationship between meaning and wisdom, the 'meaning' extracted from information is knowledge, and if this knowledge remains at this preliminary stage of only an abstract, intellectual knowledge then it has not reached its full potential as 'meaning'. This knowledge is empty and lacks any 'real' connection to reality unless a functional, utilitarian purpose is found for it, and this only serves to cloak its emptiness by creating an illusion of authenticity.

Deleuze goes on to claim that Bacon uses these two modes of the hand to create what he calls a 'catastrophe' that is not *catastrophic* by bringing about a collision between the 'digital hand' (figurative, mimetic form) and the 'manual proper';

"..one starts with a figurative form, a diagram intervenes and scrambles it, and a form of a completely different nature arises from the diagram, which is called the Figure". 11.

Through this technique Bacon has brought, through his Figures, 'being' to the lifeless, moribund abstractions of the 'digital hand' whilst giving order to the lawlessness of the imaginations of the 'manual proper'. This achievement also included the rhythmic, systolic and diastolic movements that are characteristic of the cross-over point of lemniscatory space and where points-at-infinity can be identified in his work as the tips of umbrellas and the plug-holes of sinks. So Bacon, in clear self-consciousness, has rehabilitated a Haptic mode of painting through clear, logical, wide-awake thinking that appeals to a modern consciousness. An Haptic mode of painting, with its intimate conjunction of hand and eye, is expressive of the consciousness of humanity during the time of Ancient Egypt, just as the 'digital' had is expressive of our own abstract, intellectualised consciousness. The manner by which our consciousness is associated with our corporeality changes with the varying stages of our evolution, and in contrast to ancient times when consciousness focussed upon the sympathetic nervous and metabolic systems, with their murky pictures and imaginative revelations of which we were only dimly conscious, our consciousness now focuses upon the brain and higher nervous system which facilitates a crystal-clear, highly defined and contoured vision of the world. This does not mean that the former manner of apprehending the world has been lost, this is not so, and it makes itself felt through an indirect route to the imaginative capacities of he right-hand hemisphere of the brain, whereas our wide-awake crystal-clear vision of the world, that is intellectually-based, is directly and immediately focused upon the left-hand side of the brain. Thus what Deleuze defines as the 'catastrophe that is not *catastrophic*' with regards to Bacon's Figures is in essence an harmonious integration of two heterogeneous visual codes: the Haptic vision of Ancient Egypt with the 'digital hand' of modern times. And this is clarified further by returning to how Bacon handled the 'point-at-infinity' in his work. The consciousness of Ancient times, based upon the sympathetic nervous and metabolic systems, meant that they lived in an intimate relationship with the plane-at-infinity, and as such had no real awareness of infinity, for they lived within a rhythmic and 'time-less' world with no rigid , or highly defined boundary, between themselves and the spiritual realities of the phenomena that surrounded them, it is only with the slowly evolving intellect that such a boundary became apparent. Historically this is demonstrated through the fact that during the time of Classical Greece, together with later Roman times, there was an embryonic understanding of Perspective that reflected their growing intellectual understanding of the world. The fact that this knowledge was lost until the Renaissance illustrates the prescience of Classical Greek and Roman cultures. It has been referred to how Bacon disrupted the rules of perspective so as to make evident what he perceived, and through Bacon's technique we can now recognise these points-at-infinity as being palpable presences, as 'organs of perception', that inform us of the interrelatedness, and not separateness, of humanity with each other and the organic world. Deleuzes's perceptive remarks, in conjunction with my *critique*, make us aware that one of Bacon's intentions was to make plain just how dissociated humanity has become through its unrestrained reliance upon an abstract intellect, and the subsequent crisis this has caused.

It might be argued that Bacon's work is mere representation and has no further value than that, and no doubt this is true of someone who only looks upon their surfaces and tries to find comparison with other works. However, to someone who is deeply affected by Bacon's images they are symbolic in the true sense of the word. Van James gives us an idea of this word's true sense and its derivation:

"The Greek word *symbolon* means to 'join what is separated, to join together'. The symbol, though often meaningless to the uninitiated, unites a sensory phenomenon to its supersensible reality by means of a picture."

He also states of the symbol that

"They appear before the use of letter signs and written words, as they precede abstract concepts and formal ideas. It is likely that in earlier times the meaning of a symbol was not grasped through the intellect, but through instinctual cognition and direct spiritual perception." 12..

One of Bacon's most persistent claims was that he wanted to affect the viewer's nervous system, in effect to shock and wake-up. But this was not arbitrary and self-indulgent but meant to stimulate that side of ourselves (the 'forgotten' self of the receptive phase of development) that has been overshadowed and side-lined in terms of importance by our obsession to cognise the world through the lifeless, abstract concepts of the intellect alone. The effect of Bacon's images is thus to give a jolt to the right hemisphere that in turn destabilises assumptions as to how reality is constituted, thus through the 'catastrophe' of his Figures Bacon evokes an awareness of the crisis he perceived as inherent to humanity in the viewer. Bacon's images act like a link, or a yoke, from our evermore sterile intellectual thinking to the vibrant imaginative world of the 'forgotten' self, so that, potentially, our intellect is enriched and an inherently unruly imagination is ordered with the result that the 'out of phase', or misaligned, nature of our consciousness has the potential to be healed.

Division of the Sexes.

These can be no doubt that the two hemispheres of the brain have a complex but definite relationship to the division of the sexes that is not linear or in any way a mirror-like reflection, by absolutely identifying the left hemisphere with the male and the right hemisphere relates to the female. That would be a mistake for the intellectual mode of the left hemisphere that is based upon linear, logical, abstract has only achieved an absolute epistemological dominance, as materialism, within the last 150 yrs. Before the mid 19th Century the right hemisphere that is related to non-linear, imaginative thinking played a far greater role in a human understanding of the Cosmos, hence one of the aims of my critique of Bacon's work is the rehabilitation of artistic (right hemisphere) thinking, epistemologically, by demonstrating how Bacon accessed knowledge of the constitution of the human being by means not available to a left hemisphere mode of thought alone. It may well be asked why there was such an explosion of materialistic thinking from the mid-nineteenth century onwards? This question is, in part, answered by continuing a theme from the previous section through the following quote from Steiner

"The first is that the purely physical intellect and a culture based on this showed a tremendous upsurge in the 1840s, 50s, 60s and 70s, much more so than people imagine today — future observers will see this more clearly. It is reasonable to say that anyone who studies the evolution of humanity and has an eye for more subtle elements in human life will note that there has never been such an upsurge in subtlety of conception, acumen and critical faculties for the adherents of materialism as during those decades. All the thinking I have characterized, thinking that leads to technical inventions, to criticism and to brilliant definitions, is physical thinking and is bound to the brain. A materialist who wanted to describe human evolution would have reason to say: 'Humanity has never been as clever as during those decades.' It really was clever. If you study the literature — here I mean not only fine literature — you will find that at no other time were ideas so well defined and critical thinking so well developed as in those years, and this was in all kinds of areas". (Steiner: Fall of the Spirits of Darkness, Lecture 9, The Battle between Michael and 'The Dragon', Dornach, 14 October 1917).

This increase in intellectuality that found expression in a materialistic comprehension of the Universe is attributed by Steiner to the influence of ahrimanic spirits that had been driven onto the earthly plane

"But what does it signify that the powers of the dragon, this crowd of ahrimanic spirits, are driven down into the human realms, banished from heaven to earth, as it were? Losing the battle means they are no longer to be found in the heavens, to use the biblical term. Instead they are to be found in the human realms, which means that the late 1870s were a particular time when human souls became subject to ahrimanic powers with regard to certain powers of perception. Before this, these powers were active in the spiritual realms and therefore left human beings more in peace; when they were driven out of the spiritual realms they came upon human beings. And if we enquire into the nature of the ahrimanic powers which entered into human beings when they had to leave the realms of the spirit, the answer is, the ahrimanic materialistic view with its personal — mark this well — its personal bias.

Materialism had, of course, reached its peak in the 1840s, but in those days its impulses were more instinctive in humans, for the crowd of ahrimanic spirits still sent their impulses from the spiritual world into human instincts. From the autumn of 1879 onwards, these ahrimanic impulses — powers of perception and of will — became the personal property of human beings. Before this they were more of a general property, now they were transplanted to become personal property. We are thus able to say that due to the presence of these ahrimanic powers from 1879 onwards, personal ambitions and inclinations to interpret the world in materialistic terms came to exist in the human realm. You only have to trace some of the events which have arisen because of personal inclinations since then, to understand that they resulted when the Archangel Michael drove the dragon, that is the crowd of ahrimanic spirits, from the realms of the spirit, from the heavens, down to earth". (Steiner: Fall of the Spirits of Darkness, Lecture 9, The Battle between Michael and 'The Dragon', Dornach, 14 October 1917).

From the 1840's onwards such individuals as Goethe who employed a thinking based upon a synthesis of the possibilities of both hemispheres of the brain for comprehending the cosmos were over-shadowed by a materialism that was no longer merely a theoretical mode of thought, but an ingrained, individualised, impassioned personal belief. This relates to the comments above that an ahrimanic being enters us at birth and is expelled at death, for now this being can influence an individual's thinking from within rather than influencing human beings from spiritual worlds 'exterior' to the human race. The effect of this is that the feeling realm is distorted so that one is no longer merely thinking ideas and propositions, but that ideas, especially materialism, have a strong, entrenched emotional charge associated with them, consequently transforming materialistic propositions from intellectual conjectures to questions of belief thereby invoking religious sentiments. I am not advocating some emotionless response to Ideas and the Cosmos, as that in itself would be an ahrimanic influence, but simply pointing out the emotional grip that materialistic paradigms have on particular individuals despite rational arguments that demonstrate the limitations of such materialistic assumptions. The argument here does not at this stage appertain to the existence or not of atoms, as scientifically conceived at present, rather this argument concerning materialism revolves around such questions as to whether there are spiritual dimensions to our existence or not. Materialists deny the existence of any form of the spirit believing that all arises from materiality despite the fact that the so-called material world has vanished as an absolute ponderable substance for present scientific theories – it is now understood that all is energy that adopts specific configurations, which is not very far from my arguments, all that is needed now is a refined understanding of *energy*.

Two keystone paintings by Bacon that relate to these conjectures are "Man Carrying a Child", 1956, (ill. 62) and "Man and Child", 1963, (ill. 63) where in the latter we observe the juxtaposition of an adult male and young girl, both of whose posture suggests tension and anxiety. The mood of this work is one that evokes an unbearable expectation of an event that will induce an act of reconciliation between the two parties depicted. These works have already been examined with respect to a 'forgotten' self, that is our unified spiritual condition at birth until the age of approx. 3yrs., or until we learn to speak. I would therefore argue that these two works relate to how the two hemispheres of the brain interact with each other, however before proceeding I will investigate just how it is that we have come to possess a brain in the first place and how it has evolved into the two modes delineated above. Rudolf Steiner describes in the chapter of his book "Cosmic Memory", entitled "The Division of the Sexes", how in the distant past we had bodies that were neither masculine nor feminine but both at the same time;

"Much as the human form in those ancient times described in the preceding chapters differed from the form of present-day man, one comes to conditions still more dissimilar if one goes even further back in the history of mankind. For only in the course of time did the forms of man and woman develop from an older, basic form in which human beings were neither the one nor the other, but rather were both at once. He who wants to form an idea of these enormously distant periods of the past must however liberate himself completely from the habitual conceptions taken from what man sees around him.

The times into which we now look back lie somewhat before the middle of the epoch which in the preceding passages was designated as the Lemurian. At that time the human body still consisted of soft and malleable materials. The other forms of earth also were still soft and malleable. As opposed to its later hardened condition, earth was still in a welling, more fluid condition. As the human soul at

270

that time embodied itself in matter, it could adapt this matter to itself in a much greater degree than later. That the soul takes on a male or a female body is due to the fact that the development of external terrestrial nature forces the one or the other upon it.

While the material substances had not yet become rigid, the soul could force these substances to obey its own laws. It made of the body an impression of its own nature. But when they became denser the soul had to submit to the laws impressed upon this matter by external terrestrial nature. As long as the soul could still control matter, it formed its body as neither male nor female, but, instead gave it qualities which embraced both at the same time. For the soul is simultaneously male and female. It carries these two natures in itself, its male element — is related to what is called will, its female element to what is called imagination.

The external formation of earth resulted in that the body assumed a one-sided form. The male body has taken a form which is conditioned by the element of will; the female body on the other hand, bears the stamp of imagination. Thus it comes about that the two-sexed, male-female soul inhabits a single sexed, male or female body. In the course of development the body had taken a form determined by the external terrestrial forces, so that it was no longer possible for the soul to pour its whole inner energy into this body. The soul had to retain something of this energy within itself and could let only a part of it flow into the body". (Steiner: Cosmic Memory, 39).

What has been depicted, above, as 'The Fall', as a relevant interpretive aspect of Bacon's iconography, is as an imaginative description of radical geographical changes that occurred to the constitution of the world, the result of which was that the world no longer had its prior fluid condition but a more dense condition, much as with the condensation of rain from the overall moisture of the planet due to changing meteorological conditions. The consequence for human beings was that humanity, and this why it is imaginatively described as a 'Fall, descended from a fluidic corporeality to a more dense and coarser corporeality. Thus "Man Carrying a Child", 1956, and "Man and Child", 1963 may be interpreted as relating to the transformation of our being effected by 'The Fall'. Steiner also describes in the same book how the human brain developed through this division of the human body into two sexes,

"The division into sexes takes place when the earth enters a certain stage of its densification. The density of matter inhibits a portion of the force of reproduction. That portion of this force which is still active needs an external complementation through the opposite force of another human being. The soul however must retain a portion of its earlier energy within itself, in man as well as in woman. It cannot use this portion in the physical external world. This portion of energy is now directed toward the interior of man. It cannot emerge toward the exterior; therefore it is freed for inner organs.

Here an important point in the development of mankind appears. Previously that which has been referred to here as the Spirit, the faculty of thought, could not find a place in man. For this faculty would have found no organs for exercising its functions. The soul had employed all its energy toward the exterior, in order to build up the body. But now, due to the division of the sexes, the energy of the soul, which finds no external employment, can become associated with the spiritual energy, and through this association those organs are developed in the body which later make it possible for us to become a thinking being. Thus the human being could make use of a portion of the energy which previously been employed for the production of beings like ourselves, so as to perfect our own nature.

The force by which mankind forms a thinking brain for itself is the same by which man impregnated himself in ancient times. The price of thought is single-sexedness. By no longer impregnating themselves, but rather by impregnating each other, human beings can turn a part of their productive energy within, and so become thinking creatures. Thus the male and the female body each represent an imperfect external embodiment of the soul, but thereby they become more perfect inwardly". (Steiner: Cosmic Memory, 40).

Certainly Steiner's statement that "the male and the female body each represent an imperfect external embodiment of the soul, but thereby they become more perfect inwardly", may seem a little cryptic, however, it is made clear that one reason for the dissolution of one 'perfection' is to facilitate a perfection at an higher level, that is the human being is able to personally encompass aspects of the mystery of existence as its own achievement. This relates to the principle of **Renunciation** that has already been referred to, whereby a developing organism 'gives up' the perfection of one developmental stage so as to initiate a further developmental stage, a process that has been illustrated by a reference to a plant's developmental path The implication is not that our gendered bodies are somehow inferior, or lesser, for they are in themselves miraculous, but what it does mean is that it is now up to the individual to be an active component within their own evolution, that is by a process of **Renunciation** we spur our own higher spiritual growth. This is a general principle for since the mid- nineteenth century when the spiritual beings described above became associated with humanity it became possible for an individual to activate potentialities that had long been prepared within the entelechy of the human being but which had lain dormant, in general, until the present. Much has been said of the ferocious battle between the 'higher' and the 'lower' self that is a defining characteristic of the soul-life of modern humanity, and one implication of this is that, in order to truly find oneself, one has to transcend not only one's particularity of family, race, gender and social conditions but also the particularity of one's own state of soul, rather than being defined by the particularity one has been born into

For the present it is possible to state that masculinity and femininity are polarities which when brought together - or intensified - initiate a process of transformation, the final results of which lie in the far future. The immediate effects of such an intensification is the modification of consciousness to a higher state, not necessarily Initiation to begin with, but an awareness of the epistemological ramifications of what it means to be a *self-conscious* human being. Through the development of the two sexes, which facilitated the physical organ of the brain, it is now possible for the spiritual component of thinking to become a personal possession of any individual, thereby enabling each person to become a self-conscious participator in their own evolution. However, the adversaries to this development - the Luciferic and Ahrimanic who at the present work in conjunction-strive to prevent this from taking place so as to further there own ambitions. For present purposes they strive to keep individuals tied to past conditions and to direct thinking along false interpretations of the nature of the Cosmos. Once one starts to appreciate the 'otherness' of one's own thinking, which can take place in any manner of ways, one begins to question why one should have a particular thought in the first place - where has it come from etc. Such a process of becoming aware of one's thinking is similar to a fish becoming aware of the fact that it is swimming in water. Through long and hard effort, once this understanding has come about, one begins to realise that particular strands of thinking have a common base, or have a particular slant, to them. There is also the realisation that one inhabits, with thinking, a world not of one's own making, and that one is not the only spiritual being that is doing the thinking. So although such terms as Ahriman and Lucifer may appear absurd and ridiculous to the modern rational, intellectual thinker they are in fact only names, and as such it is not the name that is important but, rather, the activity associated with the name.

In conjunction with the above, it is the case that as we evolve particular organs are in decline whilst others are in ascendancy, the meaning of which is that as these new organs develop so do new abilities become available for the human being. As a matter of fact we are surrounded in the outer world with that which is coming-into-being and that which is passing away - was Bacon hinting at such processes of transformation within the human body with the apparently jumble of forms in his Figures that have a passing resemblance to organs? Upon this subject Steiner states

"You will remember I explained how if the soul enters upon these moods or conditions, man's faculty of knowledge can gradually rise to a perception of two converse processes that are everywhere around him. Man learns to distinguish in his environment between what is becoming and what is dying away. He says to himself at every turn: Here I have to do with a process of becoming, something that will reach perfection only in the future, and here again, on the other hand, I encounter a gradual dying away, a gradual disappearing. We perceive the things of the world as existing in a region where everything is either coming into being or passing away." (Steiner, World of the Senses and the World of the Spirit: Lecture VI).

In this context it is the larynx which is on an upward path whilst the ear is on a downward path:

"And I pointed out in particular how the human larynx is really an organ of the future, how it is called to be in the future something entirely different from what it is to-day. To-day it merely communicates to the outer world by means of the spoken word our inner moods and conditions, whereas in the future it will communicate what we ourselves are in our entirety; that is to say, it will serve for the procreation of the whole human being. It will be the reproductive organ of the future. A time will come when the larynx will not merely help man to express by means of the word what is in his heart and mind, but man will use the larynx to place his own self before the world; that is to say, the propagation of man will be intimately connected with the organ of the larynx….And the corresponding organ for the larynx is the organ of hearing. In proportion as the hearing apparatus little by little disappears, in proportion as it grows ever less and less, will the larynx grow more and more perfect and become more and more important." (Steiner, World of the Senses and the World of the Spirit: Lecture VI).

Even if one is an adherent of the more extreme, modern interpretations of Darwin one has a belief in evolution, and if we are evolving then it stands to reason, even if we are unable to perceive the process, that organs are in a state of transition. Whilst by itself the above is not conclusive proof for a positive 'reading' of the jumbled forms in Bacon's images, it does, nevertheless, add to a growing picture provided by Steiner of the complexity of the human body when seen from the perspective of an enhanced perception, and this in total does provide an insight into the jumbled forms in Bacon's work, if it is accepted, and I have provided evidence, that Bacon had unusual abilities of perception. This can be allied to further statements by Steiner concerning our sexual passions, given that our *drives* constitute a significant portion of our soul, and as such is a theme that has been demonstrated as being an important, interpretatively, for an understanding of Bacon's images. One way the adversarial forces work is that they attempt to achieve their aims through the astral body by influencing individuals to place an undue importance, not only upon particular ideas, as discussed, but also upon sexual pleasure and sexual activity. However, the wild ungoverned sexuality at present to be perceived virtually everywhere on the planet, although prompted by the adversaries mentioned above, is further entrenched, and propagated by those adversaries named the Asuras.

"Asuras are starting to work in the post-Atlantean epoch. They're the words of the three and they mainly work into sexual life in the physical body. The many sexual aberrations today are to be ascribed to this strong influx. All forces of hindrances try to hold onto currently existing things that are still imperfect, carry them out and intensify them." (Steiner, Esoteric Lesson: Muenchen, 11-1-1906).

As depicted above the Ahrimanic spirits have poured into human evolution since the middle of the nineteenth century and they have influenced thinking in the direction of a materialistic interpretation of the nature of the Cosmos, and this suits their purpose of mechanising humanity and removing any concept of free-will and individual development, for if people believe there are no spiritual beings and no spiritual worlds then they have a clear field within which to operate. The influence of the Asuras embeds such a mind-set by influencing human beings in the direction of an over-emphasis upon the value of the physical pleasure that is biologically part of propagation. More than this over-emphasis upon physical pleasure human beings are influenced to consider the sexual act exclusively from the perspective of its physicality. This is readily apparent in the deluge of pornographic images, films, videos etc, and sex paraphernalia that at present swamps the world. Human beings in this genre are reduced to their genitalia alone, with no place in this genre for the higher dimensions of human love and affection. There has always been carnality and lust, and as such are perfectly natural for they are in essence the most basic expression of Love. What is different about this deluge of pornography that has occurred since the 19th century is its technical aspect, for now individuals are able to view this material either individually, or in groups, in private and public situations where there is virtually no human interaction and the stress is placed upon a 'disembodied eye'. Given the commentary upon Ahrimanic spirits above it is not difficult to see how human beings are becoming mechanised not only over their livelihood but with regard to how we interact and reproduce. Many commentators have commented upon the deleterious effects upon the health of society of these trends, however for me in the context of this *critique*, it is the fact that pornography etches into the mind and imagination the exclusivity of the sexes rather than their mutability. That is with this genre evolution is depicted as having come to a standstill - this is what you are and no more, just copulating animals - and this suit's the Luciferic spirits for they desire that human beings perceive themselves exclusively within the terms of the 'Fall'. In effect all of this serves to deflect Humanity from the absolutely crucial tasks at hand that face the future evolution of Humanity.

It is very rare to find explicit references to genitalia in Bacon's Figuration, in general there is no bias towards either the masculine or the feminine form. I would argue that his Figuration hints at an interaction of the masculine and feminine principles on a mental, or spiritual level, whilst bearing in mind it is impossible to depict a female nude without some sort of reference to physical characteristics, but this is not done in a titillating or provocative manner. In my opinion Bacon, thereby, avoided the two pitfalls that the masculine and the feminine gendered bodies have evoked in the past - that of predominately depicting the masculine as a repository of power and dynamism whilst the feminine is depicted as being allied to the sensual and emotional. It is true that the male incarnates more deeply into the material world, ideally, than does the female and as such the masculine is firmly associated with the Will. On the other hand the feminine holds back from fully entering the material realm (body tissue has to remain more pliable for the purpose of child birth), meaning that the feminine is able to make manifest all that which is linked to the Imagination. But both of these are *ideal qualities*, in the sense of never coming to an absolute physical manifestation, and are therefore the common possession of humanity and not the exclusive property of either gender. As indicated above it is how the masculine and the feminine aspects of ourselves are integrated within an individual that is of importance for the future - how instead of being perceived as mutually exclusive their polarity is intensified within an individual so as to unlock the potentialities inherent to the human form, as demonstrated by Goethe. Bacon's work "Studies of George Dyer and Isabel Rawsthorne", 1970, (ill. 62) is specifically concerned with the intensification of the polarity of the masculine and the feminine at the higher level of the spiritual, rather than focussing upon their conjoining at the corporeal level of the gendered human being for the purposes of procreation. Bacon highlights the fact that the ever-changing corporeal foundation of the human being is the outcome of spiritual forces and not gross mechanical forces, and cannot be understood by reference to animal kingdom alone. In contrast the series of works upon George Dyer indicate that the masculine by itself, and I mean this in the sense of not only individual existence but also the egotism of believing that the human being is the only spiritual being inhabiting the Cosmos, becomes prey to those spiritual beings already referred to that occupy the sub-realms of nature, in particular the Ahrimanic. The work "Man Carrying a Child", 1956, (ill. 14), which has been much commented upon, is a depiction of the human being where the Masculine and Feminine are in harmony within the context of their spiritual origins.

In general one can make the comment that Bacon's individual masculine and feminine Figures impress upon one not only the devastating loneliness that an individual can feel as a result of the division of our corporeality into the sexes, but also the desperation that ensues in the search for the consummation of our wholeness through the Other purely upon a corporeal level. There are many layers of significance to this comment upon Bacon's Figures that it is simply not possible to explore at present, but from my brief commentary it is clear that Bacon had decisive insights into the nature of our sexuality and how it is gendered within the corporeal body, even to the extent of considering how a 'healthy' intensification of the Intellect and the Imagination has propitious consequences for our spiritual development and psychic well-being. As stated a consideration of 'The Fall' is vital to an understanding Bacon's iconography, and commentaries relevant to 'The Fall' only acquire their full significance in the context of Bacon's Crucifixion works. The thematic link between 'The Fall' and the Crucifixion is that of the relationship between the Masculine and the Feminine, and the triptych "Crucifixion", 1965, (ill 32), makes this abundantly clear. The Fall was not purely a case of the gendered female being tempted by Luciferic spirits, what occurred with 'The Fall' was that the corporeal constitution of the human being was no longer synchronised with the rest of nature, it had to a certain extent *fallen out* of the integral unity of the Cosmos. However, as indicated above, this gendering of the human being not only provided the opportunity for us to develop as *thinking* beings, but also had the effect of initiating the ability to love, for sexual attraction is the first stage of the ability to love, and the ability to love is capable of enhancement to a stage that is scarcely credible in this day and age, aspects of which were made manifest through Christ's supreme sacrifice. It cannot be ignored that Bacon chose to create a number of triptych's concerned with Christ's Crucifixion, and "Crucifixion", 1965, makes explicit a number of points already raised. For instance we perceive in the left-hand panel a female Figure looking at a highly distorted Figure (in comparison to the female) that we assume to be masculine. This masculine Figure displays all the 'angst' of the masculine gender that has fallen too deeply into matter and who then looks to the female for redemption. Perhaps Bacon wished with his Crucifixion scenes to make the point that we have all been 'crucified' collectively, and from an esoteric point-of-view this is 'not far off the mark'. Objectively whether one believes in the existence of the Spiritual beings highlighted here or not, matters not one jot to them - for if they exist their existence is totally unaffected by our beliefs, we merely give them more mental space to act - but it matters to us for if their existence is unacknowledged for then we are completely unaware of how they affect us in manifold ways, and it is in this sense that we are 'crucified' collectively. These considerations cannot be ignored when considering the meaning of Bacon's work for Bacon's 'Pope' images of the 1950's make explicit the agonising consequences ensuing when individuals try to come to self-knowledge through the auspices of their particular gender by itself, and Bacon underlines his point by utilising the image of the Pope as an individual who is the figure-head of an institution that propagates the illusion of gendered transcendence. However, as has been stated many times, it is the beneficial effect of the harmonisation of our Masculine and Feminine dimensions upon the well-being of an individual that interested Bacon, as well as the consequences for mental health and psychic stability when this does not occur.

Conclusion.

In this *critique* I have presented what many will regard as a fictional, hypothetical model of the human being. Anyone who dismisses the text on those grounds has failed to understand the role played by fictional, hypothetical models in modern epistemology. Margaret Morrison in her article "Fictional Models in Science" (Physicsworld: volume 27, no 2, February 2014) asks the following

"Attempts to differentiate fiction from theoretical speculation give rise to an important question: how should we interpret scientific models that incorporate idealised, abstract descriptions that bear little resemblance to the physical and social world we inhabit?"

Although Morrison does not answer this question directly she does by taking various examples demonstrate how ideal and imaginary models play a crucial role in our thinking. One example is the hypothesis of the 'rational, economic man' that lies at the heart of many economic models, whereby the 'rational, economic man' is a conjectured individual who has perfect information concerning the economic system and consequently makes wholly rational decisions - clearly no one individual can ever fulfil such criteria. Nevertheless, as with gas models, adjustments can be made as problematic circumstances occur in an attempt to make the model more realistic thereby leading to empirically testable predictions that have greater veracity. This is an attempt to construct a *unity out of multiplicity* and not an attempt to discover the *multiplicity in unity*, and as such are abstract, intellectual speculations that only have a feeble imaginative content. However, Morrison's concern is with James Clerk Maxwell's model of electromagnetism that proposed an aether filled with elastic vortices surrounded by electrical particles. In contrast to the those theories that related an electromagnetic field to its electric current source, and consequently was object based, Maxwell hoped to build upon Michael Faraday's discovery, through the use of iron filings, of *invisible* lines of electromagnetic force which Faraday proposed constituted a 'field', by theorising how such a field could operate. There was thus a shift from objects, which Maxwell referred to as 'centres of force', to the invisible as the locus of electromagnetic forces and power. Although the full implications of Maxwell's understanding have not been fully grasped, partially due to his own inclusion of particles conceived basically as objects into his theorisations rather than themselves as centres of force, nevertheless his thinking represents a tremendous step forward in the manner by which we attempt to cognise the modus operandi of the Cosmos we inhabit.

There is no need to reference the importance of Maxwell with respect to electromagnetism this is well-known enough, but what is not generally well-known is that he demonstrated how the velocity of electromagnetic waves matched that of light thereby showing how these waves could travel in 'free' space. The inter-relatedness of light and electromagnetism cannot be investigated here, but the weight of the example of Maxwell for this critique is that established how a theoretical model can have a practical outcome. I have referred to several fields of force above that are instrumental to our existence, and from this perspective the human being is the most complex 'centre of force/ forces' we know of, an understanding bedevilled by our personal subjectivity and entrancement with the surface of phenomena as objects. I have in the above provided an insight, derived from a theoretical model based upon 'multiplicity within unity', into the significance of Bacon's work that radically re-evaluates common assumptions not only of Bacon's images but in the process common assumptions of the epistemological value of artistic cognisance. Bacon's profound understanding of humanities spiritual and soul condition is clearly delineated by his focus upon key events associated with our evolution. "Man Carrying a Child", 1956, (ill. 62) and "Man and Child", 1963, (ill. 62) are images which depict humanities spiritual and soul condition before 'The Fall' and after 'The Fall', with the latter depicting humanities gendered division that is one consequence of that incisive event. Bacon's works investigating the Oedipal legend and the Ancient Greek Tragedies focus upon a further two equally important milestones in the evolution of humanity, namely the acquisition Intelligence and Rationality, and a Conscience as a personal possession rather than witnessing the effects of one's deeds as the Furies, this is one notable consequence of the change in our consciousness from an ancient clairvoyance to modern rationality. Bacon's images that contain discarded newsprint, such as "Figure Writing Reflected in a Mirror", 1967, (ill. 10), examine the detrimental and agonising effects upon an individual's psyche of an abstract, intellectual thinking divorced from the imagination, that has the propensity to endlessly travel in circles without ever reaching a conclusion, forever trapped within its own abstractions. Bacon also recognised the vital importance of the Crucifixion as a turning-point in humanities spiritual evolution. "Three Studies for a Crucifixion", 1962, (ill. 35) depicts a transition from an Old Testament mentality to a New Testament mentality and consciousness that at present is still at an embryonic stage. In effect this means a transition from an ancient consciousness based upon the sympathetic nervous system which was murky and, because humanity had not yet developed to the stage of self-consciousness, was one where humanity was primarily a receiver of inspiration from the spiritual worlds rather than an initiator. Central to this, as Bacon was fully aware, is the relationship between the Masculine and Feminine dimensions of our being, and in this respect the Crucifixion enacts a re-unification of the Masculine and Feminine in a manner that is scarcely understood today. "Crucifixion", 1965, (ill. 14) is a work where Bacon examines the implications of this potential, for we know have to initiate it ourselves as per Goethe, and we conduct this re-unification within the context of 'The Fall' and notions of 'Good and Evil'. The chapter upon "the Prodigal Son" delineated the course of Bacon's own spiritual journey whereby he achieved his own unification with the Spirit, that is he brought about a re-unification of his own Intellectual and Imaginative abilities that are rent asunder for all of us in the development from infancy to adulthood, as a conscious act. That this was the case is further elucidated by the implications of his meditative technique, which has been examined above.

So as to elicit some credence, and render more acceptable, what are, for most people, the outrageous and fantastic proposals of this critique of Bacon's oeuvre I have deployed the mathematics of Projective Geometry, and demonstrated how its tenets and principles, which of themselves are a mathematical and intellectual abstract cognisance of *invisible* forces, have an incisive interpretative value with regard to deciphering Bacon's enigmatic work. As the verse by William Blake at the opening of the Introduction shows the substance of such a deployment revolves around ontological questions regarding the role, allied to questions as to what exactly its exact nature is, that Infinity plays in our ordinary lived existence. This factor, mainly cognised abstractly and intellectually, that invisibly and unconsciously orders our perception of the world, is demonstrated by Bacon to have a palpable and 'real' effect upon our everyday lives. "Figure at a Washbasin", 1976, (ill. 9) clearly depicts a distressed Figure crouching over a washbasin that is turning on the taps in a desperate attempt to cleanse itself of that which is causing it pain. Although the Figure appears to be vomiting the discarded newsprint leads us to believe that the anguish of this Figure was not merely physical but also psychological. There are strong indications that the Figure is a representation of George Dyer, who was found dead in a bathroom in Paris, and if this is so then Dyer would have not only being trying to rid himself of the drugs he had presumably over-dosed upon, either accidentally or deliberately, but given his condition would have been in a tortured state of mind. By making the plug-hole of the sink so prominent in relation to the Figure Bacon presents an image of Dyer's final moments when his life literally ebbed out of his body. Bacon in this work metaphorically refers to Infinity, or the 'vanishing point', through this depiction of the plug-hole, and from my perspective this is apposite for it is through Infinity that individuals incarnate and excarnate in the manner of a vortex.. The relationship of Projective Geometry to the invisible force fields referred to here is not one that is just ideal, in the sense of a proposal, and Lawrence Edwards in his book "Fields of Form", together with other work, has demonstrated how Projective Geometry is quantitatively descriptive of the force of growth (Formative Forces) by mathematically tabulating the developmental course of differing plants.

Projective Geometry is thus a tool that is a utilizable and valid methodology for an abstract, intellectual and rational investigation of *invisible* forces, such as those of Growth, that has an exploitable, inherent Imaginative dimension for the purpose of a 'higher' cognition of those forces than the mere intellect alone. It may come as a surprise to some readers that *all forces are invisible* and are only made manifest through the will of a being, or as things now stand some form of machinery, which are in themselves subsidiary to the will of the creative human being, that redirects and focuses those forces in some manner. There are no forces, mechanical or otherwise, that are visible to our present abstract, intellectual consciousness, and the same applies to natural phenomena. One does not perceive the tremendous terrestrial forces of a volcano erupting, nor the violence of a tornado merely their manifestation in their effect upon the environment. Thus logically, unless there is conjured up some parallel universe to our own from which unknowable forces issue through an unknown manner - an unacceptable Kantian metaphysical proposition - then we have to accept that all forces issue from the will of, at present *unknown and invisible*, beings. In coming to this understanding I had to re-evaluate, and in many ways jettison, a whole raft of past assumptions which I had not examined merely intellectually consumed. Furthermore, and this is a spiritual journey that is the same for everyone, I had to confront my *prejudices against the Spirit*, something that is exceedingly difficult to achieve, so as to come to an objective, as possible, understanding of the Cosmos. The reason why this is exceedingly difficult to achieve is because we do not, individually or collectively, understand the nature of thinking. We do not understand the implications of this sublime achievement of humanity, one of which is that, under normal conditions, humanity has taken the first step towards Freedom through the ability to manipulate abstract concepts without restraint, so as to reach, ideally, logical conclusions bereft of error. I have in the introduction indicated the mysterious nature of thinking in that it is both an object and subject to itself, in that thinking makes an object of that which is thought as an idea, concept etc. It can only become subjective through a being utilising this invisible force of the Cosmos if it has the means to do so, but then in turn this being becomes objective to the very force it is utilising due to its essential nature. . It is this Moebius- like nature of thinking that is so confusing, because it is difficult to see beyond one's own deployment of this force and comprehend it in its universality, especially as our own thinking is in the main hobbled by the imperfect nature of our emotional disposition and current preconceptions. At present it is only a cloudy, but subconsciously tacitly accepted, assumption that other people think, naturally we become aware of this when individuals make their thinking explicit through, in the first place, speaking, but in everyday life the hub of our consciousness is upon our ability to think. This simple fact relates to the, at present, barely cognised sense of idea and sense of ego referred to in the Introduction, and their further reference to the sense of language. From this it is easily comprehended that there is a subtle inter-relationship between the ego, thinking and speech that lies at the heart of our consciousness, even if there is, in the main, only an instinctive activation of these senses at present. The fact that I can make an object of another person's thinking through my ability to think implies that I can become an object to the thinking of any other being. What does this mean? Does a bird, or any other creature, make an object of us through their ability to be aware through their own capacity to be conscious, they clearly do through their approaches to us as pets, for instance, in their demands for attention etc but they only perform this instinctively not as self-conscious thinking beings. This straightforward piece of evidence has far-reaching implications, and in addition to this it is a given fact the manifold ways in which a human being can affect the thinking of another human being, even down to the very thoughts they think and the emotions they feel. So long as human beings fail to cognise the true nature of thinking as an independent realm of the Spirit, where the brain acts in a similar manner to the eye in perceiving light, for the perception of ideas and concepts they will remain unaware as to why they have thoughts in the first place, and why their consciousness has its particular form. The analogy presented by

Steiner in chapter 6 for the purpose of understanding how that which is invisible affects our everyday lives, whereby he pointed out that if a particular creature was invisible then one would know of its presence by its effect upon the environment is particularly apposite with regard to our thinking.

The question of active beings that do not come to physical manifestation within the world that we know through our ordinary consciousness cannot be adequately addressed here, and the only reason for broaching this subject is that in my *critique* of Bacon's work I have presented evidence that Bacon honed, and developed, a natural ability to perceive the realms that such beings occupy. When discussing the realm of Formative Forces (the Etheric) Steiner commented that it would not be long before this realm would be cognised, mathematically, in an abstract and intellectual structure. This has now taken place over the past 75yrs as Quantum Mechanics. There are numerous points of correspondence between Quantum Mechanics and what is known of Formative Forces, and a reasonably well-known one, which is also relevant to Projective Geometry, is what Einstein named as *Spukhafte Fernwirkung*, which may loosely be translated as 'mysterious action at a distance'. It has been discovered that when two objects interact at a quantum level for a period of time they retain their interconnectedness even when separated over vast distances, with the remarkable consequence that they are still able to affect each other in any number of ways. It has already been explained how upon the plane-at-infinity everything conceivable is interconnected and related, there is no separation only integration. A further example is the comparison between the nomenclature of the Spiritual worlds and the nomenclature of the Atomic world. The Spiritual worlds are described in terms of hierarchies each one of which is comprised of three beings, with that of the Angels, Archangels and Archai being the closest to us in terms of access, whilst the Atomic world is described as having a nucleus of protons and neutrons surrounded by shells or zones containing electrons, whereby these fundamental particles can be teased apart to reveal the existence of quarks, neutrinos, bosons etc. The interesting point to this is that investigation of the Atomic world terminates in what is defined as *vibrating strings of energy*, in other words one has reached what may be termed as the unknowable, and the same is true of investigation of the investigation of the Spiritual worlds where that which lies beyond the realm of Thrones, Cherubim and Seraphim is simply unknowable to even the highest Initiates. Whilst the spiritual beings described here are not analogous to 'vibrating strings of energy' as described by the scientific community, they certainly have a form and relationship to the forces and energies within which they dwell, and which have been partially described here as 'centres of force'. The simplistic delineation of mechanical, electrical and terrestrial forces etc in relation to what is postulated as the Atomic world fails to cognise that the energies spoken of are transformed states of original spiritual energies and forces that have come under the influence of present earth conditions. Meaning that as various 'spiritual' energies, and forces, pass through the cross-over point of lemniscatory space, or issue forth from infinity, into earthly conditions they exhibit differing properties, and modes of action, than they do in 'heavenly' conditions Such as can be seen in everyday lives with the conversion of the various states of energy commonly known to us into each other. The implication of this is that what is designated as the energy signature of an atom is only a partial view, that is, so to speak, only the tip of the ice-berg, and, as per Einstein's *Spukhafte Fernwirkung*, because the energy signature of an atom still retains a connection with its original state holds forth the prospect of fabulous discoveries. Whilst I have no wish to belittle and denigrate the tremendous scientific advances that have been made there is basically no recognition that the attempt to cognise the Cosmos in terms of Intellectual and Abstract propositions, upon which have been pasted what one can only call immature imaginative pictures, so as to make these Intellectual and Abstract propositions somehow intelligible to the general public, for obvious reasons, can only lead to a misrepresentation of the Cosmos. That is the Cosmos is itself founded upon the harmonious integration of what at our level of understanding we define as the masculine and feminine qualities of the Intellect and the Imagination respectively, and a 'false' monism based upon the Intellect alone can never hope to comprehend a 'true' monism that is based upon the mutual interpenetration and harmonisation of the Intellect and the Imagination. This has been one of the fundamental arguments of this text, and it is an argument made clear by highlighting how the Imaginative aspect of our being has been denigrated over the last 200yrs. The implications for Art Historical methodologies are obvious for that which issues from a varied utilisation of our Intellectual and Imaginative propensities can never be adequately cognised by just one of those alone.

One of the main driving-forces of this *critique* is focussed upon my unwillingness to ignore, what I consider to be, the clear implications of Bacon's portrayal of the human being, and the subsequent implications of this portrayal for Bacon's own perceptual abilities. The fact that he admitted his own ability to perceive spiritual beings and his depiction of them in his work left me with no choice but to pursue this line of investigation. Bacon never doubted that making public such an ability would be akin to committing 'career-suicide', and he strove on every level to camouflage his true intentions and tone-down what he perceived so as to make it acceptable to a wider public. A prominent example is with regard to "Painting", 1946, (ill. 33) where in a conversation with David Sylvester he stated that his first intention was to place a rendition of a bird over the Figure but he later changed it to an umbrella. Whatever it was that Bacon originally perceived as the foundation to this works production his statement has a clear connection to Steiner's statement (chapter 6) that upon a super sensible level it is possible to discern an eagle-like bird associated with the human being. I will take this no further, however it is the case that Bacon had a greater depth of esoteric knowledge than is commonly assumed, and he playfully hinted at this by drawing attention to his presumed descent from the renowned Occulist and Alchemist of Elizabethan times: Francis Bacon.

Illustrations.

1. "Self-portrait", 1973.
2. "Study for Portrait 1 (after the Life-mask of William Blake)", 1955.
3. "Study for Portrait 11 (after the Life-mask of William Blake)", 1955.
4. "Study for Portrait 111 (after the Life-mask of William Blake)", 1955.
5. "Study for Portrait V (after the Life-mask of William Blake), 1956.
6. "Three Studies of the Human Head", 1953
7. "Three Studies of Lucien Freud", 1968-69.
8. "Three Studies of Figures on Beds", 1972.
9. "Figure at a Washbasin", 1976.
10. "Figure Writing Reflected in a Mirror", 1967.
11. "Study of Nude with Figure in a Mirror", 1969.
12. "Triptych", 1970.
13. "Portrait of George Dyer in a Mirror", 1968.
14. "Crucifixion", 1965.
15. "Two Studies of George Dyer and Isabel Rawsthorne ", 1970.
16. "Triptych - Studies of the Human Body", 1970.
17. "Seated Figure", 1961.
18. "Study for a Portrait", 1977.
19. "Two Studies for a Portrait of George Dyer", 1968.
20. "Triptych - Studies from the Human Body", 1970.
21. "Man eating a Leg of Chicken", 1952.
22. "Man Drinking", 1955.
23. "Triptych May-June", 1973.
24. " Nude Descending the Staircase, No. 2", 1912.
25. "Figure Turning", 1962.
26. "Figure Turning", 1962.
27. "Turning Figure", 1962.
28. "Turning Figure" , 1963.
29. "Head I", 1948.
30. "Head II", 1949.
31. "Portrait of George Dyer Riding a Bicycle", 1966.
32. "Three Studies from the Human Body", 1967.
33. "Painting", 1946.
34 "Triptych Inspired by the Oresteia of Aeschylus", 1981.
35. "Three Studies for a Crucifixion", 1962.
36. "Figure in a Landscape", 1945.
37. "The Painter on the Road to Tarascon (the Painter on his Way to Work)", 1888.
38. "Landscape", 1978.
39. "Elephant Fording a River", 1952.
40. "Landscape", 1978.
41. "Study for a Portrait of van Gogh II", 1957.
42. "Landscape after van Gogh", 1957.
43. "Landscape after van Gogh", 1957.

44. "Van Gogh dans un passage", (1957).
45. "Study for a Portrait of van Gogh III", 1957.
46. "Study for a Portrait of van Gogh IV", 1957.
47. "Study for a Portrait of van Gogh V", 1957.
48. "Study for a Portrait of van Gogh VI", 1957.
49. "Study after Velazquez's Portrait of Pope Innocent X", 1953.
50. "The Prodigal Son", 1487-1516.
51. "Portrait of Isabel Rawsthorne Standing in a Street in Soho", 1967.
52. "Study for a Bullfight No. 1", 1969.
53. "Three Studies of the Human Head", 1953.
54. "Painting 1978", 1978.
55. "Three Portraits: Posthumous Portrait of G. Dyer, Self-Portrait and Portrait of L. Freud", 1973.
56. "Lying Figure", 1958.
57. Lemniscate.
58. "Three Studies for Portrait of Lucien Freud", 1966.
59. "Study of a Baboon", 1953.
60. "Man Drinking", 1955.
61. "Henrietta Moraes", 1966.
62. "Man Carrying a Child", 1956.
63. "Man and Child", 1963.
64. "Study from the Human Body", 1981.
65. "Study for a Human Body (Man Turning on the Light), 1973-74.
66. "Study for a Pope, VI", 1961.
67. "Study of Red Pope", 1962.
68. "Studies from the Human Body", 1975.
69. "Three Studies of Isabel Rawsthorne", 1967.
70. "Three Studies of the Male Back", 1970.
71. "Sand Dune", 1981.
72. "Sand Dune", 1983.
73. "Triptych (inspired by T.S. Eliot's poem 'Sweeney Agonistes')", 1967.
74. "Head VI", 1949.
75. "Moebius Leaf".
76. "Portrait of Michael Leiris", 1976.
77. "Figure in Movement", 1978.
78. "Portrait of George Dyer in a Mirror", 1967-68.
79. "Seated Figure", 1974.
80. "Two Studies of George Dyer with Dog", 1968.
81 "Autumnal Cannibalism", 1936.
82. "Soft Construction with Boiled Beans", 1936.
83. Section
84. "Three Figures and Portrait", 1975.
85. "Painting", 1986.
86. "Three Studies for Portraits (including Self-Portrait)", 1969.
87. "Two Studies of George Dyer and Isabel Rawsthorne", 1970.
88. "Three Studies for Portrait of Henrietta Moraes", 1963.

89.   "Three Studies for Portrait of Isabel Rawsthorne", 1965.
90.   "Portrait of George Dyer Staring at a Blind Cord", 1966
91.   "Portrait of George Dyer Crouching", 1966.
92.   "Portrait of George Dyer in a Mirror", 1967-8.
93   "Head VI", 1949.
94.   "Triptych, August",1972.
95.   "Triptych – In Memory of George Dyer", 1971.
96.   "Water from a Running Tap", 1982.
97.   "Blood on the Floor", 1976.
98.   "Triptych", 1976.
99.   "Oedipus and the Sphinx after Ingres", 1983.
100.   "Oedipus and the Sphinx", 1808.
101.   "Sphinx I", 1953.
102.   "Seated Figure", 1977.
103.   "Fragment of a Crucifixion", 1950.
104.   "Gigantic Days/ Les jours gigantesques", 1928.
105.   "Three Studies for Figures at the Base of a Crucifixion", 1944.

Bibliography.

Adams, G. and Whicher O. The Plant between Heaven and Earth. 1980, The Rudolf Steiner Press.
Alphens, Ernst van. Francis Bacon and the Loss of Self. 1992, Reaction Books Ltd. London.
Archimbaud, M. Francis Bacon. 1993, Phaidon Press Ltd. London.
Barthes, Roland. "The Death of the Author" in Image, Music, Text, ed. Stephen Heath. 1977,
Hill and Wang, New York.
Baudrillard, J. The Anti-Aesthetic, etd. Hal Foster. Bay Press, 1983. Seattle.
Berman, Marshall. All that is Solid Melts into Air. 1982, Verso, London.
Bochemuhl, J. ed. Toward a Phenomenology of the Etheric World. 1985, The Anthroposophic Press.
Bogue, Ronald. Deleuze and Guattari. 1989, Routledge, London.
Bornedal, P. The Interpretations of Art. 1996, University Press of America. London.
Bortoft, H. The Wholeness of Nature. Goethe's Way of Science. 2004, Floris Books.
Boundas, Constantin & Olkowski, Dorothea. Gilles Deleuze. 1994, Routledge, London.
Braidotti, Rosi. Nomadic Subjects. 1994, Columbia University Press, New York.
Braidotti, Rosi. Patterns of Dissonance. 1991, Polity Press, Cambridge UK
Brighton, Andrew. Francis Bacon. 2001, Tate Publishing.
Brunton, Paul. 1987, The Notebooks; Human Experience, the Arts in Culture. NY, Larson
Publications.
Butler, Christopher. Early Modernism. 1994, Oxford University Press, Oxford.
Butler, Judith. Bodies that Matter. 1993, Routledge, London.
Burgoyne, R.; Flitterman-Lewis S.; Stam R. New Vocabularies in Film Semiotics. 1992, Routledge.
London.
Caygill, H. Walter Benjamin. 1998, Icon Books. Cambridge.
Cahoone, L. From Modernism to Postmodernism. 1996, Blackwell Publishers Ltd. Oxford.
Davies, Hugh. Francis Bacon: 1928-1958, 1978, Garland Publishing Inc., New York.
Deleuze, Gilles. Francis Bacon: The Logic of Sensation. 2004, Continuum, London.
Deleuze and Guattari. Anti-Oedipus. 1984, The Athlone Press, London.
Docherty, Thomas. Alterities. 1996, Oxford University Press, Oxford.
M. Dumas and F. Bacon. Malmo Konsthall. 1995.
Eagleton, Terry. The Ideology of the Aesthetic. 1990, Blackwell Publishers, Oxford.
Edwards, Betty. Drawing on the Right Side of the Brain. 1979, Fontana/ Collins. London.
Farson, Daniel. Soho in the Fifties. Pimlico, London.
Featherstone, Mike, Hepworth, Mike and Turner, Bryan. The Body. 1996, Sage

Publications, London.

Fink, B. The Lacanian Subject. 1995,

Fitzgerald, A. 1996, An Artist's Book of Inspiration. Hudson, NY: Lindisfarne.

Flew, A. Western Philosophy. 1971, Thames and Hudson. London.

Flew, A. *Dictionary of Philosophy*. 1976, Pan Reference Books. London.

Foster H. The Return of the Real. 1996, The MIT Press. Massachusetts.

Foster H. Recodings. 1996, Bay Press. Seattle.

Foucault, Michael. "What is an Author?" in Language, Counter-Memory, Practice, ed.

Freedburg, D. and De Vries, J. Art in History: History in Art. 1987, University of Chicago Press.

Freud, S. On Sexuality. Penguin, 1977. London.

Freud, Sigmund. The Three Essays on Sexuality. Standard Edition, vol. 7.

Frosh, S. Identity Crisis. 1991, Macmillan Press Ltd. London.

Furedi, Frank. Therapy Culture. 2004, Roultledge, London.

Gallagher, C.; Lacqueur T. The Making of the Modern Body. 1987, University of California Press. London.

Goodchild, Philip. Deleuze and Guattari. 1996, Sage Publications, London.

Godfrey, T. Conceptual Art. 1998, Phaidon Press Ltd. London.

Grosz, Elizabeth. Volatile Bodies. 1994, Indiana University Press, Indianapolis.

Grunewald, Peter. Gold and the Philosopher's Stone. 2002, Temple Lodge.

Harris, Jonathan and Harrison, Charles and Frascina, Francis and Wood, Paul. Modernism in Dispute. 1993, The Open University, London.

Harrison C.; Gaiger, J.; Wood, P. Art in Theory, 1815- 1900. 1998, Blackwell Publishers Ltd. Oxford.

Harrison C.; Gaiger, J.; Wood, P. Art in Theory, 1900-1990. 1998, Blackwell Publishers Ltd. Oxford.

Held, D. Introduction to Critical Theory. 1980, Hutchinson. London.

Hewison, R. Future Tense. 1990, Methuen Paperback. London.

Heywood, I. Social Theories of Art. 1997, Macmillan Press Ltd. London.

Howard, A. Thinking about Thinking. St. George Publications. Spring Valley, New York 10977.

Husemann, Armin. The Harmony of the Human body. 2002, Floris Books.

Jay, M. The Dialectical Imagination. 1973, Heinemann Educational Books. London.

Jay, Martin. Downcast Eyes. 1993, California University Press, London.

Jefferson and Robey. Modern Literary Theory. 1997, B.T.Batsford Ltd. London.

Kohut, H. The Restoration of the Self. International Universities Press, 1977. N.Y.

Lacan, J. The Four Fundamentals of Psychoanalysis. Penguin, 1977. London.

Laplanche and Pontalis. Language of Psychoanalysis. Karnac Books, 1988.

Lechte, J. J. Kristeva. Routledge, 1991.

Lehrs E. Man or Matter. 1985, Rudolf Steiner Press.

Leslie, Richard. Surrealism. 1997, Tiger Books International PLC, Twickenham.

Lunn, E. Marxism and Modernism. 1985, Verso. London.

Karl, Frederick R. Modern and Modernism. 1985, Macmillan Publishing Company, N. Y.

Kutzli, R. Creative Form Drawing I. 1981, Hawthorn Press, Gloucester, UK.

McGee, P. Cinema, Theory, And Political Responsibility in Contemporary Culture. 1997, Cambridge University Press. Cambridge.

Mees, L.F.C. Secrets of the Skeleton. 1984, The Anthroposophic Poress.

Mirzhoeff, Nicholas. Bodyspace. 1995, Routledge, London.

Moi. T. The Kristeva Reader. Basil Blackwell, 1986.

Moore, B.; Fine, B. Psychoanalysis; The Major Concepts. 1995, Yale University Press Ltd. London.

Moxey, Keith The Practice of Theory. 1994, Cornell Paperbacks, New York.

Oliver, K. Reading Kristeva. Indiana University Press, 1993.

Peppiatt, M. Francis Bacon. 1996, Weidenfeld and Nicolson.

Popkin, R. & Stroll, A. Philosophy. 1986, Heinemann. London.

Powell, T.G.E. The Celts. 1987, Thames and London.

Prokofiev, Sergei O. Why become a Member of the School for Spiritual Science. 2012. Temple

Lodge Publishing.

Radin, Dean. The Conscious Universe. 1997. HarperCollins Publishers. N.Y.

Rothenstein, J and Alley, R. Francis Bacon. 1964. Thames and Hudson.

Russell, J. Francis Bacon. Thames and Hudson, 1997. London.

Sarup, M. Post-Structuralism and Post-Modernism. Harvester Wheatsheaf, 1993.

Schwenk, T. Sensitive Chaos. 1976, Rudolf Steiner Press.

Schmied, Wieland. 2006, Prestel Publishing Ltd. London.

Scruton, R. Modern Philosophy. 1994, Reed Consumer Books Ltd. London.

Stein, W.J. The Ninth Century and the Holy Grail. 2001, Temple Books. London.

Steiner, R. A Psychology of Body, Soul and Spirit. 1999, The Anthroposophic Press.

Steiner, R. A Road to Self Knowledge, The Threshold of the Spiritual World. 1975, The Rudolf Steiner Press.

Steiner, R. An Outline of Occult Science. 1997, Anthroposophic Press.

Steiner, R. Atlantis. 2001, Sophia Books (Rudolf Steiner Press).

Steiner, R. A Theory of Knowledge. 1978, The Anthroposophic Press. N.Y.

Steiner, R. Cosmosophy vol. 1. 1985, Anthroposophic Press.

Steiner, R. Egyptian Myths and Mysteries. 1971, Anthroposophic Press.

Steiner, R. Esoteric Development. 1982, The Anthroposophic Press.

Steiner, R. From Beetroot to Buddhism. 1999, Rudolf Steiner Press.

Steiner, R. Goethe's World View. 1985, Mercury Press. N.Y.

Steiner, R. Goethean Science. 1988, Mercury Press. N.Y.

Steiner, R. Isis Mary Sophia. 2003. Steinerbooks, Great Barrington MA 01230 USA.

Steiner, R. Knowledge of the Higher Worlds. 1993, The Rudolf Steiner Press.

Steiner, R. Metamorphoses of the Soul, vol. 2. 1983, The Rudolf Steiner Press.

Steiner, R. Philosophy, Cosmosophy and Religion. 1984, Anthroposophic Press.

Steiner, R. Riddles of Philosophy. 1973, Anthroposophic Press.

Steiner, R. Secrets of the Threshold. 1987, Rudolf Steiner Press.

Steiner, R. Study of Man. 1981, The Rudolf Steiner Press.

Steiner, R. The Evolution of Consciousness. 1991, The Rudolf Steiner Press.

Steiner, R. The Fourth Dimension. 2001, Anthroposophic Press.

Steiner, R. The Kingdom of Childhood. 1982, The Rudolf Steiner Press.

Steiner, R. The Occult Significance of the Blood. 1926, Anthroposophical Publishing Company, London.

Steiner, R. The Philosophy of Spiritual Activity. 1986, Anthroposophic Press.

Steiner, R. The Riddles of Philosophy. 1973, The Anthroposophic Press. N.Y.

Steiner, R. Theosophy. 1989, The Rudolf Steiner Press.

Steiner, R. Truth and Knowledge. 1981, Steinerbooks.

Steiner, R. Universe, Earth and Man. 1987, The Rudolf Steiner Press. London.

Stevens, R. Understanding the Self. 1996, Sage Publications Ltd. London.

Stoichita, V. A Short History of the Shadow. 1997, Reaktion Books Ltd. London.

Sylvester, D. The Brutality of Fact. 1987, Thames and Hudson. London.

Sylvester, D. Francis Bacon: The Human Body. 1998, University of California Press. London.

Sylvester, D. Interviews with Francis Bacon. 1993, Thames and Hudson.

Sylvester, D. Figurabile. Electra, 1993.

The Violence of Real" various authors. 2007 Thames and Hudson. London.

Tilley, Christopher. Reading Material Culture. 1991, Basil Blackwell Ltd., London.

Urieli, B. L. and Muller-Wiedemann, H. Learning to Experience the Etheric World. 2000. Temple Lodge.

Wayne, M. Theorising Video Practice. 1997, Lawrence and Wishart Ltd. London.

Wehr, G. Jung and Steiner. 2002, The Anthroposophic Press.

Welburn, A. Rudolf Steiner's Philosophy. 2004, Floris Press.

Weigel, Sigrid. Body- and Image- Space. 1996, Routledge, London.

Whicher, O. Projective Geometry. 1985, The Rudolf Steiner Press.

Whicher, O. Sunspace. 1989, Rudolf Steiner Press.

Wilson, F. The Hand. 1998.

Wright, E. Feminism and Psychoanalysis. Blakewell Reference, 1992.
Wolin, R. Walter Benjamin.